D030695E

1 6 JUN 2014

# RICHARD BREITMAN

# Official Secrets

## WHAT THE NAZIS PLANNED,
## WHAT THE BRITISH
## AND AMERICANS KNEW

ALLEN LANE
THE PENGUIN PRESS

ALLEN LANE
THE PENGUIN PRESS

Published by the Penguin Group
Penguin Books Ltd, 27 Wrights Lane, London W8 5TZ, England
Penguin Putnam Inc., 375 Hudson Street, New York, New York 10014, USA
Penguin Books Australia Ltd, Ringwood, Victoria, Australia
Penguin Books Canada Ltd, 10 Alcorn Avenue, Toronto, Ontario, Canada M4V 3B2
Penguin Books (NZ) Ltd, Private Bag 102902, NSMC, Auckland, New Zealand

Penguin Books Ltd, Registered Offices: Harmondsworth, Middlesex, England

First published in the USA by Hill and Wang 1998
First published in Great Britain by Allen Lane The Penguin Press 1999
1 3 5 7 9 10 8 6 4 2

Printed and bound in Great Britain by The Bath Press, Bath

A CIP catalogue record for this book is available from the British Library

ISBN 0–713–99292–1

To the victims
and the survivors

# ACKNOWLEDGMENTS

ALL SERIOUS HISTORICAL RESEARCH is difficult, but with this project I had to overcome unusual obstacles connected with Nazi efforts to disguise criminal policies as well as the reluctance of British and American intelligence organizations to make some of their records available for historical research. I discuss some of these problems in the epilogue. If I have managed to put together a treatment to some degree coherent, it is in large part because others helped greatly.

Konrad Kwiet encouraged me to undertake this project in the first place and suggested how I might obtain enough sources to do it. John P. Fox, acting on his own initiative, provided the crucial impetus for the release of some relevant British intelligence records in the United Kingdom. Both scholars were also kind enough to read part of this manuscript and to offer corrections and improvements. Both also shared with me documents from their own research. I am most grateful to them for their assistance and their friendship.

Himmler's copy of *Mein Kampf* added an important piece of evidence about early Nazi thought. I am grateful to the owner for making it available to me. Arthur Levinson, a member of the first group of Americans to work at Bletchley Park, was kind enough to talk to me about his experiences there.

Colleagues and friends took time from their busy schedules, read large portions of this work, and helped to reduce the number of deficiencies. They included Shlomo Aronson, Deborah Cohen, George Kent, Walter Laqueur, Richard S. Levy, Allan Lichtman, Jürgen Matthäus, Michael Neufeld, Beate Ruhm von Oppen, and Katrin Paehler.

Larry McDonald and John Taylor helped with sources at the U.S. National Archives. Dr. Louise Atherton supplied information about collections at the Public Record Office. David Bankier, Wendy Lower, David Marwell, Charles Sydnor, and Stephen Tyas also provided a number of useful references and documents to me.

My editor at Hill and Wang, Elisabeth Sifton, offered constant encouragement and astute advice on a subject she knows well.

I received financial support for my research from the College of Arts and Sciences at American University, Macquarie University (Sydney), and the Schechter Fellowship at the U.S. Holocaust Memorial Museum.

At times my research and writing became a family project, in part because I cluttered up most of our house with paper. My wife, Carol, helped me copy documents and advised me on keeping my style readable; my sons, David and Marc, helped me keep order among the piles of documents and chapters. They, above all, will appreciate the end of this work.

# CONTENTS

Introduction    3

1. Foreshadowings    13

2. Planning Race War    27

3. A Battalion Gets the Word    43

4. Reports of Ethnic Cleansing    54

5. Transitions and Transports    69

6. British Restraint    88

7 Auschwitz Partially Decoded    110

8. American Assessments    122

9. Breakthrough in the West    137

10. Reactions to Publicity    155

11. Competition and Collaboration    177

12. The Treasury Department's Offensive    192

13. The Mills of the Gods    212

Conclusion    225

Epilogue    235

Notes    247

Index    311

# OFFICIAL
# SECRETS

✳

# INTRODUCTION

A BARBARIC REGIME equipped with modern technology and organizational skills committed monstrous crimes in the course of a war
for world domination and a projected racial utopia. As defeat neared,
high officials and subordinates tried to destroy the mountain of physical
and documentary evidence of the murder of millions. They failed, but
they created large gaps in the historical record. Above all, they made it
difficult for historians to reconstruct how the Nazi leaders had planned
the Holocaust, with tens of thousands of Germans and non-Germans
serving as mass executioners.

The West already possessed some of the evidence, however. Britain
literally plucked some German information out of the air, for its intelligence services intercepted and decoded many German police messages
sent by wireless telegraphy (hereafter called radio) and, later, some from
the SS as well. This critical evidence about the Holocaust and Nazi
occupation policies, marked "Most Secret," "To Be Kept Under Lock
and Key," and "Never to Be Removed from This Office," was sealed
away. It has reappeared more than fifty years later, and it may now be
used to address several related historical controversies.

For nearly a quarter century, scholars have discussed whether Adolf
Hitler envisioned a Holocaust in advance and ordered it once he got
the opportunity, under the cover of war. Or did Nazi officials such as
Adolf Eichmann and government technocrats concerned with practical
issues improvise genocide in the middle of the war after other, lesser
forms of persecution of Jews failed to end their problems and when the
wartime climate heightened German animosities toward Jews? Else-

where, I have argued that Nazi antagonism toward Jews was long-standing and fundamental, that certain goals, including mass murder, were evident before the war broke out and sanctioned from above, but that the scope and methods of killing evolved substantially over time.[1] Nonetheless, controversies over when and how decisions on Jewish policy were made in Nazi Germany continue; they are difficult to resolve conclusively in part because of the inherent limitations on how much incriminating information Nazi officials initially put on paper.

The surviving documents have contributed to a picture of the Holocaust in which Reinhard Heydrich and his police and intelligence subordinates in the Reich Security Main Office (RSHA), including Eichmann, and their organizations were dominant. On occasion, Heydrich asserted that he was in charge of the Final Solution of the Jewish question.[2] He and his subordinates *were* central. Following just behind the German armies that invaded the Soviet Union in June 1941, four Einsatzgruppen—literally "operational groups," or battalions of policemen subordinate to Heydrich[3]—disposed of large numbers of Jews and other selected "enemies" of the Third Reich, such as Communist officials and Gypsies. The company-sized subdivisions called Einsatzkommandos lined up their victims at the edge of trenches (or occasionally ravines) and shot them into their graves, or they placed their victims in the trenches, shot them there, and lined up the next group on top of the corpses. The Einsatzgruppen were at work for more than five months before the first operational extermination camp (at Chelmno) began to liquidate Jews in gas chambers, and they carried out most of the killings in the first phase of the Holocaust in the Soviet territories.

But Heydrich did not have a free hand, and he did have important rivals, though they have been less noticed by historians. Among them was Kurt Daluege, head of the German Order Police, the large and diverse force known until 1936 as the Uniformed Police. Heydrich's superior, Heinrich Himmler, head of the Nazi SS and chief of the German police, liked to divide authority, and Daluege's men and allies, as well as Heydrich's, shared the work of carrying out the Holocaust, both in its first phase and later.

Militarized battalions of German Order Police, more numerous than the Einsatzgruppen, conducted mass executions during the first wave of the Holocaust in conquered areas of the Soviet Union. Previous studies have overlooked or underestimated this Order Police involvement in the early "cleansing actions" (one of the Nazis' euphemisms), in part because of a scarcity of original documentary evidence about

Order Police activities.[4] In this work I draw on substantial new evidence about the Order Police and the Higher SS and Police Leaders who directed them in the East. Much of that evidence comes from radio messages intercepted and decoded by British intelligence in 1939, 1940, 1941, and thereafter that was declassified only recently.

The preparations for using Order Policemen as mass executioners in the Nazi campaign against the Soviet Union present another dimension of Nazi Germany's planning and implementation of genocide. When taken in conjunction with sources already known, new evidence strengthens the case that the highest officials of the Nazi regime brought about the Holocaust out of antipathy toward Jews and for reasons of ideology, not as a last resort and not to solve practical problems.

The men in Order Police battalions and other Order Policemen deployed in the East were not carefully selected for their tasks and given years of special indoctrination for mass murder. They did not constitute an elite force of true believers. Some Order Police battalion commanders joined the Nazi Party after Hitler came to power, suggesting that they thought membership useful for career purposes. The rank and file was likely even less political. The evidence about Order Police participation in the Holocaust therefore bears on another set of controversial questions: were significant numbers of ordinary Germans involved in the Holocaust; and were those who carried out mass murders motivated by hatred and fear of Jews.

Debate over these questions revived and escalated in the 1990s in the wake of an academic duel between two American specialists on the Holocaust who chose the same case study. In a widely praised work titled *Ordinary Men* (1992), the historian Christopher Browning highlighted the activities of Reserve (Order) Police Battalion 101, which in 1942–43 carried out a gruesome series of mass executions of Jews in small towns in eastern Poland. Four years later, in his controversial *Hitler's Willing Executioners* (1996), the political scientist Daniel Jonah Goldhagen reexamined Reserve Police Battalion 101.[5] One extraordinary event heightened the element of moral responsibility for the policemen in this unit and apparently attracted both scholars. Before the first killing, the battalion commander offered his men the option of not taking part. No one would be punished for refraining from mass murder. Yet the overwhelming majority of middle-aged policemen from Hamburg participated and continued to kill, week after week.

Browning and Goldhagen offer radically different descriptions of and explanations for this behavior. Drawing heavily on the extensive West

German postwar interrogations of surviving policemen from this battalion, Browning concludes that peer pressure and the climate of war
led most of them to follow orders despite the availability of an escape
to other tasks. Browning argued: "Nothing helped the Nazis to wage
a race war so much as the war itself. In wartime, when it was all too
usual to exclude the enemy from the community of human obligation,
it was also all too easy to subsume the Jews into the 'image of the
enemy.' "[6] The German police came to view all Jewish civilians as
opponents, and in a war to the death one had to use the harshest measures against them.

Goldhagen agreed that the battalion was hardly a group of fanatical
Nazis and that the Nazi authorities did not brainwash it to carry out
the elimination of the Jewish people. Ideological, as well as logistical,
training for mass murder was absent.[7] But, discounting exculpatory testimony by policemen after the war and looking at the brutality of the
police beatings and executions, Goldhagen decided that virulent anti-
Semitism was at the root of police atrocities. The Nazis did not have
to implant this eliminationist anti-Semitism through indoctrination because, Goldhagen believed, it was entrenched in German culture dating
back to the early nineteenth century. For historians, Goldhagen's picture of early German anti-Semitism was clearly overdrawn, but his narrower argument about popular anti-Semitism during the Holocaust is
not easily dismissed.

Goldhagen studied other types of "unconstrained" German behavior:
cases of loosely supervised guards who carried out atrocities against Jews
in work camps and even during the "death marches" of Jews toward
the end of the war, when the guards must have known that the general
cause was hopeless. The evidence he presented supports the argument
that specific groups of Germans who were not SS or Nazi Party fanatics
eagerly sought to rid Germany and Europe of Jews. From these cases
and from his broad historical overview, he drew a picture of a German
public generally implicated by virtue of its hostility toward Jews and its
knowledge of major portions of the Final Solution.[8]

Goldhagen's work drew severe, sometimes scathing, criticism from
historians. Among the charges were that he had chosen cases and evidence that fit his preconceptions and excluded what did not.[9] And even
if Goldhagen's selection of examples and evidence was without fault,
can one extrapolate from limited information about some police and
guards to draw conclusions about the German people as a whole? His
work appealed to readers who wanted a relatively simple version of

German history even in 1933–45, uncomplicated by variations over time, differences among regions, and contradictions in attitudes and behavior among (and within) individuals. Still, Browning had also extrapolated, suggesting in his conclusion that if the men of Reserve Police Battalion 101 had chosen to obey orders, anyone anywhere might do so too.[10]

The new evidence I present and analyze in this book indicates that larger numbers of Order Policemen were involved in the first phase of the Holocaust, and this lends some support to the narrower argument that ordinary Germans approved of, and took part in, the Holocaust. But I also examine contrary evidence that suggests high Nazi authorities did not find these Order Police executioners quite so willing or easy to employ. Some of the new material we now have about the planning of genocide also reveals how these high Nazi authorities tried to manipulate, and later to replace, the Germans they designated to carry out the messiest tasks. In addition, as has long been known but is now even clearer, they tried to keep the Final Solution of the Jewish question secret not only from the outside world but also from the German public. In short, the evidence I present here suggests an interpretation of German attitudes that is in some ways different from earlier scholars' views.

Measuring German attitudes in the Third Reich was and is no easy matter. There was, of course, nothing remotely approaching Gallup Polls in a police state. But scholars have used various gauges to assess German sentiments toward Jews from 1933 on.[11] Different types of sources— including the SS Sicherheitsdienst's (SD's) secret reports on public attitudes—suggest that anti-Semitism was an important part of German political culture and social life in 1933 but that the Nazi regime had to push to radicalize it.

In chapter 1 I use a small sample of evidence from the early period of the Nazi regime to help reveal later changes in popular attitudes, as well as differences between Nazi insiders (such as Heinrich Himmler) and the German public regarding Jews. New evidence demonstrates that, even before the beginning of the Nazi regime, Himmler was preparing to translate Hitler's pronouncements in *Mein Kampf* into reality. Different evidence about the German public's attitude toward Jews comes from knowledgeable foreigners who spent time in Germany, such as perceptive Western diplomats. These observers had only impressions, not scientific data, about German public opinion, but they were nonetheless not subject to the kinds of bias one sees in the avail-

able Nazi and anti-Nazi (Social Democratic) sources. This contemporary evidence from foreign observers complements other sources and
helps to correct overly broad generalizations about the German public
made long after the events. During World War II, Britain and the
United States tried to measure, and to some extent influence, German
public opinion, and I examine the evidence from these efforts as well.

Contemporaneous information about what we call the Holocaust that
Britain and the United States received from a range of sources varied
greatly in quality and content. Many people in the West were disinclined to take the worst reports at face value. The example of World
War I seemed to warrant this skepticism and disbelief nearly three decades later, for during that war Western governments had manufactured
some "atrocity" stories about the German occupation of Belgium and
part of France to sway world opinion against Germany; the actual
German occupation, it later turned out, was less saturated with atrocities
than the Allied propaganda led people to believe. The revelations after
1918 about manufactured atrocity reports were still fresh in the minds
of many observers and government officials.

As the historian Walter Laqueur has stressed, the psychological issue
during World War II was that of the difference between information
available and belief in it. The press published considerable information
about Nazi mass killings, and government insiders had access to additional reports and conversations. But many people could not "know"
something that tested the limits of their comprehension. For some, it
did not register until the end of the war, when photographs and newsreels provided gripping images of the horror. Even a well-informed
person (and Jew) like Felix Frankfurter, a Supreme Court justice who
was among the best-connected people in Washington, D.C., could not
quite bring himself to believe what he heard directly from Jan Karski,
a Polish underground courier, in 1943.[12] If Western governments and
citizens did not really or fully "know" what was happening to the Jews,
they could not very well act or make future plans for action.

The terminology itself was symptomatic of the problem. Western
governments and journalists referred to reported mass executions of
thousands of civilians as either war crimes or atrocities (sometimes as
atrocity tales), traditional concepts drawn from past wars and past eras.
The term "Holocaust" had not commonly been applied to the killing
of Jews specifically, and this use of traditional concepts showed a failure
to recognize the unprecedented nature of Nazi policies.

Western governments and the mainstream press suspected that Jewish and Polish information channels in particular exaggerated Nazi crimes, because these representatives had an interest in enlisting Western aid for their peoples.[13] Victor Cavendish-Bentinck, chairman of the British Joint Intelligence Committee, wrote in August 1943 that the Poles and even more so the Jews exaggerated Nazi atrocities "in order to stoke us up."[14]

For a time, the flow of information about the Holocaust had no effect on Allied policy or official statements, which has stirred another set of controversies about what the Western democracies might or might not have done. The limitations on what official London and Washington knew or recognized of the Holocaust have been used to explain British and American government behavior at least partially. But newly declassified documents reveal that certain British officials, including Cavendish-Bentinck, had in their hands some incontrovertible evidence of portions of the Holocaust—directly from decodes of German police and SS messages. So we must reexamine what Western governments knew or logically should have known (and to a lesser extent what they might have done) at various stages of the Holocaust.

From the existing literature on British and American reactions to the Holocaust, I have drawn much information about what steps Britain or the United States considered or took. I have also revisited archives in both countries to extract additional sources bearing on the relationship between Britain and the United States during the war and the Holocaust. The more I studied government records, the more my own thinking evolved. There were some obvious similarities between British and American approaches to Jewish issues during the war, but I also came to appreciate some significant differences and tensions between the two allies that are not fully reflected in previous books, even those of high quality.

These three controversies—the degree of Nazi planning and improvisation, the attitudes and participation of ordinary Germans, and the Western Allies' knowledge of and reaction to the killings—merit a more thorough description and analysis than I can manage in one book. Relying in part on previous studies, I have nonetheless brought these three subjects together because the newly available documents, used in conjunction with already known documents, contain important evidence about all three. In some cases, a single newly declassified item simultaneously gives us information about what high Nazi officials wanted done, how Order Police ("ordinary Germans") took part, and what British intelligence knew of it within days of the events.

Highly specialized studies are important in historical work and crucial to the study of the Holocaust, but there is also a place for broader approaches, such as this effort to grasp the relationship among Nazi decisions, German behavior, and Western assessments and responses. I also try to show very briefly how some British information about the perpetrators of the Holocaust went unused in the search for justice and political reform in occupied Germany after May 1945.

Each of these facets casts light on the others in some obvious ways, but also in some unexpected ones. British and American officials could not know more about events in Nazi-dominated Europe than high Nazi authorities themselves; nor could the West anticipate future Nazi actions. So narrating and dating the unfolding of Nazi Germany's Final Solution of the Jewish question helps us to understand Western reactions and options at given moments. But the inverse is also true. The conclusions of Western intelligence officials about Nazi intentions and practices may add to the evidence we have from incomplete or fragmentary German sources about events in Nazi territories. For example, if British intelligence analysts could determine in late 1941 that Nazi Germany was systematically slaughtering Jews, is it not peculiar that five decades later some historians cannot manage to come to the same conclusion? The contemporary British analysis would strengthen the case that the Final Solution was planned and coordinated. Another example: Western failures to pursue some of Germany's mass murderers after the war cast light on Western reactions to Nazi killings during the war.

A work of history must recognize constraints imposed by reality before it can consider what else might have happened and what lessons apply today. A historian cannot start with a determination that the world ought to have been different and select only those events and evidence that suggest how. The unparalleled nature of the Holocaust and its devastating effects tempt us long after the fact to uncover ways in which the world might have averted catastrophe. We may also blame those who, at the time, did not identify or pursue escape routes from the sequence of increasing Nazi persecution. But to prevent the Holocaust or to stop it entirely through military action or political pressure during the war was beyond the power of Western governments.

It is legitimate, however, to question whether the Western Allies might have saved more Jews. Geographically, the Soviet Union was in a better position to do this, but the Stalinist regime closely resembled Nazi Germany in its contempt for humanitarian principles, if not in the intensity of its anti-Semitism. The clash between nominal values and actual behavior in the West raises more political, historical, and ethical questions. In any case, in this work I do not cover the Soviet Union's knowledge of the Holocaust (except, in passing, in the epilogue) or Soviet reactions to it.

Almost any study of the Holocaust carries moral implications, and some writers make explicit political and moral judgments. This moral element introduces conviction and passion to even highly technical scholarly analyses. It has transformed discussions and disagreements into debates and controversies, some of which have reached the mass media. I make a number of political and moral judgments in this work, yet I know that using a strict moral standard of behavior to judge governments and government officials risks leading students of history far from the real world into utopian ideals. I have done my best to ensure that my judgments emerge from the examination of real historical situations and realistic options. Humanitarian actions that were considered and even carried out in the West in 1943 or 1944 cannot be dismissed out of hand as utopian and impossible for 1941 or 1942—provided that we take account of the constraints imposed by different military situations and that we establish how much Western governments knew in the earlier years.

I must admit to occasional use of the term "Western governments" as a shorthand phrase for Britain and the United States. The reactions and policies of other Western democratic countries (for example, Canada) have already received some attention from historians and may well deserve more study, but I cannot manage that here. Vichy France was by no means without information about the Holocaust, but it was hardly democratic and stood in a very different relationship to Nazi Germany than Britain or the United States. The French government-in-exile might be a good subject of study if sufficient sources become available, but it was not in a position to act during 1941–44. Britain and the United States belong in a separate category because of both the information they obtained contemporaneously and the power they wielded at the time.

# 1

✳

# FORESHADOWINGS

ADOLF HITLER MIXED CANDOR and dissimulation in nearly equal parts. His writings and speeches, as well as records of his private monologues and other sources, gave important indications of his thinking, but he was also a very secretive man. He sometimes issued instructions as to what not to record, and he boasted of his refusal to confide in others, of his willingness to lie. In modern times, only Joseph Stalin could compete with Hitler on the standard of deceit.[1]

Hitler organized a secret effort to overthrow the Bavarian state government in November 1923, designed as the first step toward a general revolution in Germany. After botching the coup d'état in Munich, the thirty-four-year-old Hitler was convicted of treason and served a brief prison sentence. During his stay in Landsberg prison, he began work on a long and rambling memoir and political tract, which he called *Mein Kampf* (*My Struggle*). The book appeared in two volumes, the first in July 1925, the second in December 1926.[2] The sections about Hitler's youth in Linz and Vienna traced his early rise to political and racial consciousness, as well as his view of history and politics. But they distorted and concealed as much as they revealed. Hitler may well have picked up racist and anti-Semitic sentiments in his youth, but (though some writers disagree) he actually drifted until he found his political orientation and his calling in a chaotic postwar Munich in 1919.[3]

The general, ideological sections of *Mein Kampf*, however, held broader political significance—so much so that the book posed a problem later for Hitler the politician and head of government. In 1938, Hitler supposedly told his onetime lawyer Hans Frank that, if he had known in 1924 that he was going to become chancellor, he would never have written his book.[4] This comment applied particularly to what Hitler had stated about Germany's foreign-policy options and goals, which revealed his conviction that the German race needed much more land to survive and to thrive. He had shown not only his proclivity for war but also his hostility to France and the Soviet Union. After *Mein Kampf*, he wrote a second book specifically on foreign policy, but by 1929 he had come far enough politically to recognize the wisdom of not publishing it. The work remained secret for decades; the historian Gerhard Weinberg discovered it and published the text only in 1961.[5]

Hitler's worldview—a blend of intense and expansionist nationalism, racism, antiliberalism, anti-Marxism, and, not least, anti-Semitism—pervaded both volumes of *Mein Kampf* as well as the unpublished second book. Anti-Semitism cropped up even in strange contexts. In chapters 10, 13, 14, and 15 of the second volume of *Mein Kampf*, Hitler repeatedly "explained" how the Jews were behind all foreign opposition to Germany and all internal problems afflicting the German people and obstructing the advance of Nazism. Disputes between Roman Catholics and Protestants within the Nazi Party were leading it from its true mission and thereby, consciously or not, serving Jewish interests. Russian Bolshevism was nothing other than the attempt by Jews to seize world domination.[6] In other words, Hitler automatically associated any problem, any difficulty, any opponent with Jewish efforts or Jewish interests.[7] He believed there was no need for specific evidence, which might be lacking because of Jewish secrecy and cunning. This conspiratorial view of history and politics had practical implications: only a conspirator could succeed in a conspiratorial world. Moreover, it suggested that, if he came to power and held to his views, Hitler would seek to neutralize what he perceived as the Jewish threat to Germany.[8]

Scholars have described Hitler's early writings as everything from a "blueprint for power" to "the generalizations of a powerful, but uninstructed intellect: dogmas which echo the conversation of any Austrian café or German beer-house."[9] Virtually every expert has accepted the sincerity of Hitler's early worldview; in dispute is whether the early Hitler fixed a clear course for the future and subsequently held fast to it.

Most individuals learn, adapt, and evolve over time; some politicians switch parties and programs. Many a statesman has been known to reverse previous foreign-policy pronouncements and respond primarily to circumstances and opportunities. Some have used heated rhetoric to make names for themselves or mobilize support. But there was a very high correlation between what Hitler wrote in the 1920s about *Lebensraum* (living space) and German foreign policy and the future path of the Third Reich.[10] Did Hitler tenaciously hold to his original vision in other respects, or did the policies and programs of the Third Reich occur because of the actions of others or the pressure of circumstances? There is unfortunately no definitive way to trace the range and consistency of Hitler's thinking and state of mind from 1925 until his suicide on April 30, 1945. His writings, speeches, and decisions supply crucial evidence but also contain mendacious elements, gaps, and camouflage.

If key Nazi officials took *Mein Kampf*—or the ideology expressed in it—as a guide for their actions, then it becomes even harder for a historian to discount the continuity and impact of Hitler's early ideology. If sophisticated non-Nazi observers at the time looked to *Mein Kampf* to help them understand the impulses and direction of the Nazi regime, the case is stronger still. This chapter offers a small sample of both types of assessments of *Mein Kampf.*

One of the most assiduous readers of *Mein Kampf* was a young Bavarian political organizer named Heinrich Himmler. Mortified by Germany's defeat in World War I, which he blamed on the Marxist left, and fascinated by the principles and methods of breeding in agriculture, which he had studied at Munich's Technische Hochschule, Himmler was particularly susceptible to Hitler's line of racial thought. In fact, he may have taken it more literally than Hitler himself.[11] Later, as Reich Führer SS, he would try to make his own organization into a racial and political elite.[12] Himmler first met the Führer in 1926, when he was serving as deputy Gauleiter (regional party leader) under Gregor Strasser in Lower Bavaria. Within a year Himmler was also deputy leader of the small unit of Nazi guards known as the SS, outnumbered by the larger Nazi paramilitary force, the Sturmabteilung, or SA.[13]

A meticulous record keeper, Himmler kept a partial, dated list of his reading, along with brief comments about each book. He finished the first volume of *Mein Kampf* on June 19, 1927, writing: "It contains tremendously many truths. The first chapters about his own youth contain many weaknesses."[14] Not captivated by Hitler's personal story, Himmler nonetheless found the book a great inspiration.

Himmler's copy of volume 2 of *Mein Kampf*, which he read in December 1927, has now emerged from obscurity.[15] From markings on this volume, it is possible to examine his early reactions to Hitler's ideology in greater detail. In general, he looked for practical ways to apply the "truths" of his Führer. Next to the passage about the importance of instilling self-confidence and a sense of racial superiority into youths through education and training, Himmler wrote in the margin: "education of SS and SA."[16] Hitler had blamed the German revolution of 1918, which he said had been carried out by pimps, deserters, and rabble, partly on the failure of the intellectual elite, hobbled by its upper-class etiquette and lack of manliness: they should have learned boxing. Himmler endorsed the criticism and Hitler's remedy.[17]

Himmler approved of Hitler's comment that, just as races were different and unequal, some individuals within a race were more valuable than others.[18] Hitler had expounded in some detail on how those races that had remained pure throughout history had thrived; they began to decline when they intermarried with others: nature did not love "bastards." Racial intermingling created a new hybrid but also tension between the hybrid and the remaining pure element of the "higher" race. The danger for the hybrid race would end only when the last pure elements of the higher race had been corrupted. Himmler took Hitler's remarks very seriously, writing: "the possibility of de-miscegenation is at hand" (die Möglichkeit der Entmischung ist vorhanden).[19] Just how this would be accomplished remained unclear in 1927.

This criticism of racial intermingling was directed at Germans as well as Jews. The current German population was already racially suspect according to this view; only a segment remained pure. Hitler believed that Jews were seeking to defile and corrupt the "Aryan race" through intermarriage and seduction of German women.[20] Ending the threat to the higher race meant not only neutralizing the hybrid but also removing the threat of Jewish infiltration and destructiveness. Himmler later used underlining and a margin line to highlight many passages in Mein Kampf, among them Hitler's retroactive solution for Germany's defeat in World War I:

If at the beginning of the War and during the War twelve or fifteen thousand of these Hebrew corrupters of the people had been held under [subjected to] poison gas, as happened to hundreds of thousands of our very best German workers in the [battle]field, the sacrifice of millions at the front would not have been in vain. On the contrary, twelve thousand scoundrels eliminated in time might have saved the lives of a million real Germans, valuable for the future.[21]

The idea of using poison gas against some Jews was already planted in not only Hitler's mind but also Himmler's.

Plenty of others read *Mein Kampf*, even if few took it so literally. Despite the hefty price of twelve marks per volume, 23,000 copies of volume 1 and 13,000 copies of volume 2 were sold before 1930. Then a cheaper edition and the Nazi breakthrough in the September 1930 national elections caused sales to take off dramatically. (By the time Hitler became chancellor in 1933, sales totaled 287,000.)[22] If Hitler the ideologue was an unknown quantity to the German public during the incessant election campaigns from 1928 to 1933, it was not for lack of evidence.

Political campaigns often do not bring clarity to the issues. Nazi organizers, speakers, and writers frequently campaigned against the "Marxists" and the unwieldy democratic regime known as the Weimar Republic. Successes came in part because their targets were widely un-popular except with the German working class. The Nazis also learned how to appeal to specific needs and fears of social and occupational groups and to adjust basic Nazi principles to local preferences. The image the Nazi movement presented to the German public was more differentiated and in some ways more sophisticated than what Hitler had formulated in *Mein Kampf* but also blurrier. The Nazis attracted the most diverse constituency in German politics, held together primarily by shared emotions—desperation, common resentment, and fear. Nazi campaign propaganda called for a new start, a rebirth of Germany through the creation of a national community that transcended tradi-tional divisions—a theme partly shared by right-wing nationalist parties, but Nazi presentation was more vigorous and more effective.[23] Partly for this reason, Hitler and other key Nazi speakers exploited better than more experienced political rivals first a rising tide of nationalism in the late 1920s, and then growing public frustration with, and despair about, the political system and the great economic depression.

In other words, a vote for Hitler or other Nazi candidates was hardly a direct endorsement of Hitler's worldview. Still, none of Hitler's themes, which other Nazi officials and candidates endorsed and re-inforced, hurt the Nazis politically; most of them found increasing res-onance from 1928 on. Shared ideas and emotions gave Hitler and the Nazi Party a substantial base of enthusiasts and willing followers, whose activity and dynamism drew others. The rise in the number of Nazi Party members and their increasingly visible activities created a sense of movement and hope for change in others. A substantial minority of

German voters either accepted the Nazi program or had no objection to it, in part because it derived from a familiar late-nineteenth-century current of radical nationalist and racist thought.[24] Nazi electoral support in democratic elections peaked at just over 37 percent of the vote in July 1932, making the Party the largest in parliament by a considerable margin. But the level of popular support was insufficient to bring Hitler to power, and he refused to join any coalition government unless he was made head of it, an intransigent stance that seemed to contribute to a substantial Nazi decline in the November 1932 elections.

Then a political deadlock and convoluted backroom negotiations gave Hitler coalition partners who were willing to accept his leadership at a moment when the incumbent chancellor, General Kurt von Schleicher, reached an impasse. Schleicher had no prospect of surviving a vote of confidence in the newly elected parliament, and he could hardly gain a breathing spell from still another dissolution of parliament and new elections. His predecessor, Franz von Papen, had already tried that tactic twice without success; it was played out. Schleicher could not govern around the constitution any longer. Shunning a move toward abolition of the constitution and a potential military dictatorship, on January 30, 1933, the aged conservative President Paul von Hindenburg reluctantly appointed Hitler as chancellor (head of government).[25]

Germany had seen chancellors come and go; coalition governments in the Weimar Republic had lasted on the average only a little more than a year. Some expected the pattern to continue, because the new government, like its predecessors, lacked a parliamentary majority and needed the President's emergency authority to bypass the deadlock in the Reichstag. Hitler, however, had not concealed his intention of abolishing the democratic system. Some voters had undoubtedly backed Nazi candidates for precisely that reason, thinking almost any change would be for the better. They were quite wrong, but it took many of them a decade or more to realize it—those who survived that long.

In a series of stages, and making use of constitutional devices as well as force, intimidation, and massive propaganda, the Nazis quickly destroyed what was left of the Weimar Republic.[26] Perhaps the most important legal step came less than a month after Hitler's appointment. Following arson at the Reichstag building that was blamed on a Communist conspiracy, the government formulated, and the President issued, an emergency decree for the protection of the German people and state. Suspending civil liberties, the national government now had an array of cudgels to use against political opponents and others; the decree also allowed Berlin to take over the powers of state governments. During elections in March 1933, some Communist and Social Democratic opponents were already in jail, and the opposition press was widely shackled. Not surprisingly, the Nazi Party raised its share of the vote to 43.9 percent in national elections. Its coalition partner, the German National People's Party, received only 8 percent, but that was enough to give the coalition a majority in parliament. Hitler gained increased public support as he launched a Nazi revolution.

By mid-March, the Nazis had effectively brought the various state governments under control.[27] To free himself from further political, constitutional, and Presidential restraints, Hitler then pushed for passage of an Enabling Act that would allow the cabinet (which he dominated) to act without consulting the Reichstag. Passage of the bill required a two-thirds majority in the Reichstag.

On March 21, the newly elected Reichstag convened, following a ceremony at Potsdam to commemorate the opening of the Reichstag after Germany's unification in 1871. The occasion allowed Hitler to claim some continuity with part of Germany's traditions, and it seemed to show that conservative nationalists such as Hindenburg could bestow their good wishes on the Third Reich.[28] The Reichstag passed the Enabling Act two days later.

Although overshadowed by the Potsdam ceremony, the opening of the Reichstag, and the maneuvers regarding the Enabling Act, striking statements by the new police chief of Munich, Heinrich Himmler, on March 21 appeared in the main Nazi newspaper, the *Völkischer Beobachter*. Himmler announced that Communists were planning to assassinate Hitler and other leading government officials. No independent evidence has ever emerged to verify this assertion, though Himmler claimed his information came from Swiss sources. Perhaps it was merely Himmler's nightmare, or perhaps it was another public pretext to act against Communists and other enemies. But Himmler's response to this alleged plot was nonetheless illuminating. He foresaw that public outrage would take the form of mass murder:

[I believe that] when the first shot occurs, whether it reaches its target or not, Germany will experience the greatest mass murders and pogroms in world history, and no state power and no police will be able to halt this murder.[29]

This public statement reflected the prevailing Nazi identification of Communism with Jews, for the term "pogroms" indicated mass violence, particularly against Jews. Himmler simultaneously predicted and, in effect, gave his blessing to an attempt to murder a good portion of German Jewry if a suitable provocation occurred. Nowhere else had one heard such a thing from a government official.

Although Himmler's exact motives remain obscure, this statement expressed an impulse that he and other Nazi "true believers" shared, an intensification of the direction Hitler had taken, and Himmler had previously endorsed, in *Mein Kampf.* They expected a Jewish assault on Nazi Germany, and they wanted to neutralize what they believed was the internal Jewish threat. Whether the German public would act spontaneously or at the appropriate signal remained to be seen.

With Hitler, Himmler determined what the state let happen in the way of violence against Nazi enemies. As head of the SS, he controlled the growing number of concentration camps, where brutality and death were a part of the regimen. During 1933–36 Himmler obtained appointments as chief of police in the various state governments, and in June 1936 he received the title of chief of the German police.

Hitler had written in chapter 11 of volume 2 of *Mein Kampf*: "If propaganda has imbued a whole people with an idea, the organization can draw the consequences with a handful of men."[30] This passage was suited to a time when the Nazi Party was still relatively small and on the fringes of German politics. Once in power, Hitler and Himmler wanted many more than a handful of men to carry out their bidding absolutely, and they were in a position to get them.

There was no assassination attempt against Hitler in March 1933, but scattered, uncoordinated violent acts were carried out by some SS and SA men against Jews. To demonstrate to Nazi activists the will to punish the prime enemy, the Nazi Party announced a boycott of Jewish businesses throughout the country. American diplomats expressed concern to German authorities about this planned boycott and protested various physical assaults on American Jews in Germany. After sharp foreign criticism and internal pressures suggested that the boycott would damage Germany's interests, Hitler agreed to shorten it.[31]

On April 1, the American consul general in Berlin, George S. Messersmith, sent two vice-consuls on a tour of the commercial areas of the city to survey the public reaction to the boycott that day. They reported that many Germans treated the boycott as a joke and continued to shop at their favorite stores. In general, Messersmith believed that the boycott was not popular with the German public, because it damaged the economy and Germany's image abroad. At the same time, he reported, many Germans came to accept Nazi propaganda that the boycott was necessary to convince foreign countries to stop their own boycotts and propaganda against Germany.[32]

Messersmith had served in Berlin since 1930 and was fluent in German, having been raised in a middle-class Pennsylvania Dutch family where German was a second language.[33] From a number of private conversations with German businessmen, he concluded that members of the German elites would not oppose the regime on the Jewish question; either they would express enthusiasm or they would bottle up their concerns.[34] Perhaps they had little choice.

After the boycott Hermann Göring, then in charge of the Prussian state government as well as the air force, invited Messersmith to the Air Ministry and denounced American press coverage of events in Germany and of the boycott in particular. Messersmith responded that the U.S. government had no control over the press but that many Americans, including some who worked for the newspapers, were concerned about Nazi persecution of Jews.[35]

In a May 1933 analysis of anti-Semitism in Germany, Messersmith concluded that the Nazi movement had aroused mass prejudices against Jews to such an extent that, even if official persecution ceased, professional and private life for Jews would be difficult for years to come.[36] Those who benefited from the elimination of Jewish competitors, as well as a substantial segment of German youth, had joined the original anti-Semites. Moreover, those opposed to anti-Semitic measures because of the practical consequences for the economy were, on balance, afraid to raise their voices.[37]

Britain received a similar assessment from Ambassador Sir Horace Rumbold, who drew on other evidence. From a family of diplomats and with decades of diplomatic experience, Rumbold had served in Germany during the summer of 1914, when war broke out. He knew firsthand where German nationalism could lead. He returned to Germany in 1928 as ambassador and observed Weimar's collapse and the Nazi revolution. Once it became clear that President Hindenburg, whom Rumbold admired, would not or could not impose restraints, the ambassador began to express alarm in his despatches to London.[38]

Rumbold perceived a major increase in anti-Semitism during the Weimar Republic. Since the revolution of 1918, he wrote, Jews had been given fair play in every walk of life, with the result that Jewish "racial superiority . . . at any rate in German eyes" asserted itself alarmingly. Jewish achievements and advances were entirely out of proportion to the number of Jews in the population (which was only 1 percent), and this provoked bitter resentment in some German circles. In addition, Jews were closely associated with the political left—with democracy and pacifism. The involvement of some Jews in financial scandals during periods of economic upheaval only made matters worse: the best elements of the Jewish community would suffer for the sins of the worst. The Nazis exploited and intensified these resentments.[39]

Rumbold suggested that exaggerated reports of Nazi atrocities (largely directed at first against Communists and Social Democrats) in the foreign press had contributed to heightened anti-Semitism, for some Germans believed that Jews had inspired the foreign criticism, which led to added pressure for actions against Jews on racial grounds. The Nazis used the boycott not only to recognize the anti-Semitic pressure but also to control it—to prevent it from going to excessive lengths.[40]

Where would all this hostility lead? In analyzing a dictatorship, a sensible observer scrutinized the dictator. Rumbold, who regarded Hitler and Göring as responsible for the campaign against the Jews,[41] was among those who looked to *Mein Kampf* for guidance. On April 13, 1933, in the course of a lengthy despatch to London about German and Nazi anti-Semitism, Rumbold accepted Hitler's account that his youthful experiences in Vienna—with both Jews and anti-Semites—made him a "Wagnerite" and convinced him to help save the Aryan race. Rumbold summarized Hitler:

> . . . Marxism and Judaism were responsible for every villainy. The Jews were the insidious foes of the blue-eyed Nordic race. Germany's defeat in 1918 was clearly encompassed by them. The November [1918] revolution and the Weimar system were achieved by international Jewish conspiracy, and the war-guilt lie was propagated by German Jews in order that Germany might be disarmed and delivered over to Marxism for all time . . .
>
> The soil became much more receptive for anti-Jewish propaganda in 1930 and subsequent years. It was easy to persuade workmen, and still easier to persuade students, that they had been deprived of a living by alien parasites . . .
>
> Foreign opinion does not appear to have fully grasped the fact that the National Socialist Party programme is intensely anti-Jewish . . .
>
> Hitler, in his book and in his speeches, advocates much more drastic

methods than the Nazi party programme. He would deprive the Jews of the franchise, of the right to own land or to lend money on mortgage. In addition, he would impose special taxation on them and exclude them from a great number of callings. Marriage between Jews and Christians would be vetoed, and every effort would be made to restore the German race to its pristine purity. The imposition of further disabilities on the Jews must therefore be anticipated, for it is certainly Hitler's intention to degrade and, if possible, expel the Jewish community from Germany ultimately . . .

Hitler himself has stated clearly in his book and in his speeches that his objection to the Jews is racial [not religious] . . . The Jews, he asserts, are parasites of alien race . . . and the German blood must be purified from this contamination.[42]

This diagnosis suggested that the situation of Jews in Germany would deteriorate over time and that Britain and other countries might have to confront a flood of desperate Jewish refugees. In fact, the growing refugee problem was the main reason why Britain and other countries could not simply deplore Germany's abuses of what later became known as human rights. Nazi persecution forced Western governments to make immediate policy decisions.

Messersmith and Rumbold brought different perspectives to the analysis of anti-Semitism in Germany. A former high school teacher and principal, Messersmith showed little sign of the genteel anti-Semitism that afflicted some in the American Foreign Service at the time. Joseph Hyman of the American Jewish Joint Distribution Committee said that Messersmith did monumental work in defending Jews during the early months of the Nazi regime, and Rabbi Stephen Wise of the American Jewish Congress praised him in equally high terms.[43] The aristocratic Rumbold at times seemed to share the German nationalist impulse to try to reduce the disproportionate presence of German Jews in some areas of German business, the professions, and education.[44] Messersmith regarded anti-Semitism as primarily a product of the Nazi movement, seeing Nazi leaders as having instilled hatred into their young followers over a number of years and then having to satisfy the masses they had aroused. Rumbold traced it back to the 1880s but emphasized the increase during the aftermath of World War I. Both observers discerned an escalation in popular anti-Semitism under the Nazi regime, and both forecast even greater problems in the future, given Hitler's view of Jews.[45]

Shortly before his departure from Berlin, Rumbold acknowledged that Hitler had gained absolute control and tried to assess the likely direction of the next four years. Hitler was said to have unlimited faith in propaganda; he believed he could mold German public opinion to an unprecedented extent. That meant in part that the regime would prepare the public for war. Hitler had explained in *Mein Kampf* that a country must fight for its existence or it was doomed. The fighting capacity of a race depended on its purity—hence the need to rid it of impurities. The repercussions of this ideology carried over into foreign policy: "To wage war with Russia against the West would be criminal, especially as the aim of the Soviets is the triumph of international Judaism." Hitler had to lull his adversaries into a coma in order to be able to engage them one by one. Emphasizing how obstinate Hitler was and how revealing *Mein Kampf* was, Rumbold commented that Hitler would probably be glad if he could now suppress all copies.[46]

Hitler could hardly have suppressed *Mein Kampf* without destroying the image of consistency that he had worked so hard to build up and that he regarded as essential in politics. Besides, he wanted more Germans to become familiar with its basic ideas. Foreign distribution was another matter. Unlike most authors, Hitler was none too eager to see his work translated.

In 1928, Hitler's publisher, Eher Verlag, had issued translation rights in English to a British literary firm, Curtis Brown Ltd. Until 1931, however, no British or American publishers expressed interest in Hitler's turgid prose. After the Nazi electoral breakthrough, it began to dawn on people that Hitler might be around for a while. At that point, an enterprising writer-translator named Edgar Dugdale showed up with an abridged translation that a British publisher, Hurst and Blackett, was willing to issue, paying a modest advance to Eher. But the London correspondent of the *Völkischer Beobachter* insisted that the German government had to approve the specific text, and Curtis Brown's contract with Eher gave Berlin the necessary leverage.

What started out as an abridgment for editorial reasons became more abridged for political reasons. Hurst and Blackett published a 297-page toned-down version of *Mein Kampf* in Britain, while Houghton Mifflin brought out the identical text in the United States. (The American edition identified Dugdale as translator; the British one did not.) Until 1939, it was the only version publicly available in English. And it was impossible to determine, except by laborious side-by-side reading with the original German, just what had been condensed or omitted. There were no ellipses or annotations to indicate deletions.[47]

The abridged version left out some of Hitler's choicest comments about foreign-policy expansion and the Jewish menace. It largely omitted Hitler's theme that Jews sought to pollute Aryan women. It left out the statement that Germany should have gassed twelve or fifteen thousand Jews during World War I. The overall impression of the translation was to make Hitler seem less a fanatic and more a clever politician.[48]

Some Westerners recognized the deficiencies of the English-language version. Rumbold's detailed reports analyzing *Mein Kampf* were circulated among members of the British cabinet. In a letter to the editor of *The Times* of London, which had printed four extracts from Dugdale's translation, the Jewish leader Chaim Weizmann protested use of Dugdale's abridgment and enclosed a translation of twenty-eight pages of missing material. The Foreign Office kept these extracts on file. In 1936, the British embassy in Berlin did its own translation of important passages from the German original.[49] Across the Atlantic, Houghton Mifflin gave Franklin Delano Roosevelt a copy of its edition of *Mein Kampf* in 1933. The President wrote inside: "This translation is so expurgated as to give a wholly false view of what Hitler is and says—the German original would make a different story."[50]

Here and there some government officials recognized that studying *Mein Kampf* provided a basic intelligence about Hitler's future course. Britain also undertook professional intelligence assessments of Nazi Germany during the 1930s; American intelligence was conspicuous largely by its absence. But none of the Western intelligence assessments influenced foreign policy or defense policy at the time.[51] Britain and the United States were far more concerned with Germany's foreign policy and economic policies than with its persecution of German Jews. And Western refugee policies were determined more by domestic political considerations than by what was taking place within Germany—let alone what might ultimately happen there. That story has been told elsewhere.[52]

The publishing history of *Mein Kampf* serves as a metaphor for later developments in three respects. First, Hitler made some threats openly and gave away much by his language and tone, even if he withheld, or had not yet formulated, the details of what he would like to do. Second, perceptive Westerners could figure out a great deal from the right evidence. Third, Western experts and diplomats learned more about Hitler's course and learned it earlier than the public did, an information gap that was of some consequence in Western democracies.

What stands out about Messersmith and Rumbold is that they cared about what was happening to German Jews. They undoubtedly had mixed motives: Nazi persecution of Jews created foreign-policy problems and potential immigration problems for their countries, and their opposition to this persecution did not translate into support for the open immigration of refugees into the United States or Britain. Still, both men had enough moral sensibility to know and to react to what was fundamentally wrong and to call others' attention to it. They also had enough historical consciousness to realize that events in Nazi Germany were in some ways unprecedented and that they might ultimately become far more catastrophic. In 1933, they could not know whether or not circumstances would permit that.

Even Hitler and Himmler could not know then how far or how soon they would be able to pursue their emotional impulses and ideological goals. But they knew that they needed manpower—officers and rank-and-file troops—for what they considered a political-racial war.

# 2

\*

# PLANNING RACE WAR

KURT DALUEGE was an able but dull man who constructed an important career in Nazi Germany out of a series of unglamorous jobs. His career track and style turned out to be advantages for his historical reputation. In 1990, a German historian who had written a book on the Nazi regime's policies toward Jews claimed that Daluege had had no interest in Nazi ideology or Jewish issues. He simply had executed the orders of others with regard to Jews, whereas Daluege's rival and contemporary Reinhard Heydrich had handled Jewish affairs for the police. Daluege's papers contained very little evidence to the contrary.[1] If nothing else, Daluege was a very good bureaucrat, and Nazi bureaucrats (like some others) knew how to tailor the documentary record.

Born in 1897 in Upper Silesia, Kurt Daluege served as an officer candidate in World War I and was decorated with the Iron Cross. After the war he joined one of the right-wing paramilitary formations known as the Free Corps that created difficulties for the new and increasingly unpopular republican government in Germany. He studied construction engineering at Berlin's Technical University and obtained his degree. Then he became head of construction for Berlin's municipal garbage disposal service, but in 1926 he joined the Nazi Party and quickly made politics his real career. At first a member of the Brownshirt SA force of Nazi roughnecks, he switched in 1928 to the smaller but more disciplined SS, soon to be led by Heinrich Himmler. Daluege played a small, but important, role in helping Hitler overcome a mutiny within the Berlin SA in September 1930. He used SS forces to help shore up Hitler's authority against malcontents led by Walter Stennes, and he seems to have earned Hitler's lasting gratitude.[2] He was presentable enough to be put forward as a Nazi candidate for parliament in Prussia, the largest German state, and just before the Nazi takeover of power he was also elected to the Reichstag.[3] He and his allies solicited funds for the SS and its intelligence branch (known as the SD) from German corporations after the Nazi dictatorship was established, sometimes using a little pressure.[4]

In the early jockeying for power and offices under the Nazi regime, at a time when the various German states had separate police forces, Daluege entered the Prussian political police (Gestapo), at first under the control of Hermann Göring. He built up the Prussian Landespolizei into a militarized police force with a nucleus of trained soldiers that could protect Germany's borders and assist the regular army. Members of the Landespolizei knew how to deal with riots and other threats to the state: the Bavarian Landespolizei had crushed Hitler's Beer Hall Putsch in November 1923. In 1935, this Prussian body was largely merged into the expanding armed services,[5] but some of the older policemen probably stayed in police ranks. Daluege was not done turning police units into combat forces. He would later repeat the pattern but retain control of the militarized police battalions.

Daluege's SS chief was Himmler, and Himmler and Göring were to some extent rivals. That put Daluege in an awkward position in 1933–34 but also enabled him to play one side off the other. In April 1934, however, Göring reached an understanding with Himmler, whose right-hand man, Heydrich, took over the Gestapo. By then the best course for Daluege had become clear, and by 1936 whatever tensions there had been between Daluege and Himmler were muted.[6]

A good bureaucrat himself, Himmler recognized Daluege's assets, among them an image of respectability, a storehouse of energy, and good organizational skills. He also knew that Daluege, who lacked Heydrich's acute political skills, was unlikely ever to become a serious threat to him. Upon his own appointment in 1936 as chief of the German police, now a unified national force, Himmler carried through a major reorganization, bringing the Gestapo and the Criminal Police together into the Security Police under Heydrich, who also controlled the SD. (Since Nazi ideologues tied most deviant behavior to genetics, they had some ideological justification for giving charge of the criminal detectives and other specialists to someone willing to take the most ruthless measures against enemies.) Daluege gained control of the uniformed police, which was renamed the Order Police (Ordnungspolizei).[7]

According to an internal history of the Order Police written by or for Daluege, long before Hitler came to power Himmler had explained to his colleagues that the future German police force would be constructed so that the policemen met the standards of the SS and became SS members. The tight connection established between an elite Nazi defense organization and the police was no accidental or improvised arrangement but, rather, the product of advance planning and organic development, he wrote (*es war schon vor der Machtübernahme festgelegt und entwickelte sich organisch*).[8]

This "organic development" was, however, a lengthy and sometimes complicated process. According to one internal report, before 1933 only seven hundred uniformed police (0.7 percent) throughout Germany had joined the Nazi Party. The number did not include criminal detectives; it may have omitted those who joined subsidiary Nazi organizations; and it reflected legal barriers to police membership in some states before 1933.[9] Nonetheless, Himmler and other Nazi officials had quite a task to turn the various state police forces into a suitable weapon for the SS.

Nazi officials did not find it necessary to conduct a massive purge of the police on political grounds. Less than 2 percent of the rank and file and 7 percent of the officers were ousted. Heydrich, whose first police role was as head of the Bavarian Political Police, preferred to keep on existing policemen in Bavaria, even if they had worked against right-wing political movements. One professional Bavarian policeman, Heinrich Müller, an expert on Communism but no Nazi, became a key recruit and later ended up in charge of the Gestapo.[10]

To the existing police, Nazi officials could emphasize that they, too, wished to restore law and order, free the police from encumbrances, and even give them much stronger powers to do their jobs. Many policemen also apparently responded to the Nazi call for a stronger Germany and to early measures designed to bring it about. Gradually, those who preferred harsh enforcement of the law came into contact with Nazi and SS culture and became even more radical.[11]

Still, there was a considerable difference between policemen accustomed to cracking down on illegal political activity and uniformed policemen whose normal tasks and daily horizons were completely apolitical. In general, the Order Police had a longer distance to go to reach the SS culture than the Security Police. The Nazi regime created a police state, but it did not yet know how far and how well the policemen themselves would enforce political and ideological measures.

All branches of the police had plenty of policemen who needed "education." Gradually, more and more of them joined the SS—those who seemed suitable were encouraged to do so. Those who aspired to become SS officers went through a formal course in which they learned about the Nazi state and the Nazi worldview, acquired military knowledge, and practiced athletic skills. They had to pass an examination at the end.[12] In early 1941, Heydrich also prepared a lengthy teaching plan for the academic-ideological instruction of the higher officers of the Security Police, and Himmler gave his blessing to it.[13]

Daluege's empire was far less glamorous and less focused. The Order Police included the municipal police, county police, gendarmerie, firemen, and technical auxiliary police—together more numerous than the Gestapo and criminal police. They were primarily responsible for keeping order, enforcing laws and protecting loyal citizens, and dealing with emergencies.

The Order Police also contained a substantial number of militarized battalions. These policemen had received military training and were housed in barracks but were exempt from the military draft and remained under Daluege's authority. Order Police battalions were a legacy of the strife-filled years after World War I, when the Treaty of Versailles limited Germany's army to a mere hundred thousand men. Police battalions had helped to maintain order in an era when political extremists frequently resorted to violence. They also served as an unofficial reserve for the military.[14] In the Nazi state in time of war, they served as another means for implementing political and racial policy.

Daluege worked hard to keep his police, many of them career police from the pre-Nazi period, content with their role and their salaries under the Nazi regime. He and his personnel specialists did not require instant conversion to the Nazi faith. Good policemen who carried out their jobs correctly received promotions and raises.[15] Some of them found Nazism attractive as the regime benefited from the economic upturn and as Germany regained its status as a military power.

Daluege also did his occasional part to advance Nazi anti-Semitic propaganda. In a September 1935 press conference in Berlin, he repudiated foreign criticism of the persecution of Jews in Germany with the argument that Jews promoted certain crimes—swindling, securities violations, fraud, selling narcotics, and gambling among them. Serving up an array of statistics allegedly showing disproportionate Jewish involvement in these activities, Daluege described Nazi efforts "in the direction of a general purge [of Jews]" as beneficial.[16]

Daluege and Heydrich presided over their respective parts of the police with jealous interdependency. Younger, intensely ambitious, and energetic, the flamboyant Heydrich sometimes acted as if Daluege would have or should have little interest in political and racial police matters. In February 1940, for example, Heydrich invited Daluege to attend a conference for police officials who were also members of the SD. The conference covered a range of current problems then facing the Reich Security Main Office (RSHA), the wartime conglomeration of the political and criminal police and the SD, including a presentation by Adolf Eichmann on "resettlement" and Jewish emigration. Still, Heydrich's letter of invitation was discouraging—the themes would be of no interest to Daluege, and the level of the presentation, adapted to the audience, would have some limitations, he said. (No secrets would be revealed.) Perhaps Daluege would wish to attend just the luncheon.[17] Despite Heydrich's condescension, Himmler kept promoting Daluege one rank ahead of Heydrich.[18]

Daluege's Order Police, however, had already become involved in anti-Jewish policies during the previous fall's campaign in Poland through the participation of its militarized battalions. According to Daluege, twelve such Order Police battalions, with approximately five hundred men in each, had followed the regular German army into Poland in September 1939.[19] The Einsatzgruppen (operational groups under the Security Police and SD), Order Police battalions, and Waffen-SS burned synagogues and carried out summary executions of thousands of Polish Jews and various other categories of Poles.[20]

Beneath Hitler and Himmler, three men had charge of the initial campaign against Germany's political and racial enemies in Poland—Heydrich, Theodor Eicke, and Daluege. (Heydrich and Eicke have shared the limelight in historians' accounts; Daluege has been invisible.) Heydrich had reached agreement with the army in August 1939 that his Einsatzgruppen would combat all elements hostile to Germany in the areas behind the front lines. On another occasion, Heydrich declared that his units would carry out (in conquered territory) essentially the same tasks as the police offices in the Reich.[21]

Brutal and pathologically anti-Semitic, Eicke was already the commander of three Death's Head regiments formed out of concentration-camp guards he had trained. In August 1939, he gained the title of Higher SS and Police Leader for the regions of Poland to be conquered by the Eighth and Tenth Armies. As a mortal enemy of Heydrich,[22] he had something in common with Daluege. Eicke's concentration-camp

guards were already accustomed to brutal and sometimes lethal treatment of Germany's internal enemies. Organized into Death's Head
forces, they knew to use the most extreme measures against the Polish
elite and against Jews generally.

On August 25, 1939, Himmler's chief of staff, Karl Wolff, following
Himmler's instructions, wrote to Daluege, Heydrich, and Eicke to have
them pass sealed envelopes along to the commanders of various police
and Waffen-SS units to be used in Poland; these envelopes contained
what Wolff described only as an SS order. The commanders were to
open the envelopes and alert their men to the contents just before
operations began. Daluege received eleven copies, ten of which were
distributed to Order Police battalion commanders sent into Poland.
One copy remained in the files, but it was not among Daluege's papers
at the end of the war—although Wolff's letter of instructions was
there.[23] What did Himmler order?

On September 1, 1939, the day Germany invaded Poland, Eicke gave
a lengthy speech to the three Death's Head regiments and others gathered at Oranienburg, north of Berlin, which was their jumping-off
point for the thrust into Poland. The speech made a considerable impression on one of his key subordinates, an enterprising man named
Rudolf Höss, later to be named commandant of Auschwitz. In his
memoirs, written just before he was hanged, Höss summarized Eicke's
speech.[24]

The severe laws of war, Eicke said, made every order sacrosanct.
Even the harshest and most severe order had to be carried out without
hesitation. Himmler required every SS man to fulfill his duty to the
utmost and devote himself to the German people and fatherland unto
death. The task of the SS was to protect Adolf Hitler's state and to
destroy anyone identifiable as an enemy or anyone who sabotaged the
war effort.[25]

Orders were absolute, the enemy would have to be destroyed, but
there was no spelling out in advance what this meant in terms of the
functions of each unit. During the course of the campaign in Poland,
Hitler and Himmler also issued special orders directly from the Führer's
train, which served as his mobile headquarters, such as the order to
shoot all Polish insurgents without courts-martial, which went to all
the Einsatzkommandos and Order Police battalion commanders.[26]

At least two of the Order Police battalions, the Eleventh and Twelfth,
were required to report the number of executions they had carried out.
Afterward, their superiors informed the executioners that they must

refrain from telling anyone about what was called their "special duties."[27] It is not clear how many of the other police battalions sent into
Poland participated in mass killings of Poles and Jews, but this secret
killing and the use of euphemisms to disguise it were omens of future,
even more widespread, practices.

In late September 1939, Daluege apparently suggested that Heydrich
make use of suitable Poles in anti-Jewish actions. (Daluege's letter does
not survive, but Heydrich's response alludes to this possibility.) The
problem, Heydrich explained, was foreign press reaction—especially
in the United States—to Germany, even if actions were carried out
by Poles. The most pressing task was to neutralize Poland politically
(through destruction of its political elite); as Heydrich explained elsewhere, resolution of the Jewish question had to take place incremen-
tally, but the Nazi regime could get to the final goal by stages.[28] It took
almost two more years to formulate and begin to implement what the
SS called the Final Solution.

The use of Order Police to carry out murderous SS policies in Poland
raised some potential problems, because many Order Policemen and at
least one commander were not SS members. For example, Lieutenant
Colonel Hermann Franz, a career policeman, commanded a police battalion that covered part of the territory conquered by the Eighth Army.
Franz had been a member of the Nazi Party since 1931 but applied to
the SS only in 1938. His application failed, and Himmler's Personnel
Main Office had to push it through in 1940, after Franz had demonstrated his worth in Poland and had advanced to head an Order Police
training school.[29] Apparently, he was able to convince his men to follow
even the harshest orders.

By the end of September 1939, when the Polish campaign ended,
the number of Order Police battalions had risen to twenty-one, with
two additional cavalry units. A month later Himmler decided to expand
further, adding training battalions and raising the total Order Police
battalion strength to twenty-six thousand men. Except for a newly
formed SS and Police Division, a division with full military equipment
that fought the French in the Argonne, the police battalions were not
prominent forces in the Nazi military offensives in the West in the
spring of 1940. But when the fighting ended, they were deployed to
carry out police tasks and maintain security in conquered Norway, Holland, France, and Alsace-Lorraine, as well as in Poland, where at least
eighteen battalions were serving in early 1941. A location list of German
police battalions, compiled then by British intelligence, showed a total

of 158 battalions, not all of which were confirmed. At just over five hundred men per battalion, that total meant about eighty thousand men.[30]

Nazi Germany's focus shifted farther to the East, when, on December 18, 1940, Adolf Hitler gave the German army the formal order to prepare an attack against the Soviet Union—code-named Operation Barbarossa. The military planners recognized that security behind the front lines would be a formidable problem. The country was huge, and innumerable forests and swamps would provide hiding places for enemies. The army could not afford to deploy very many troops in the rear areas. Even a German military force of three million men would find itself hard-pressed to accomplish all of what Hitler assigned—the destruction of the Soviet Union in a lightning campaign within ten weeks or less.

Among the forces the army hoped to use for security functions were Daluege's Order Police battalions. To be sure, the matter was sensitive, because the army had no authority over the police, the plans for the attack were top secret, and the police units themselves could not be told that they would be shifted from the West to the East. The commander in chief of the army, General Walther von Brauchitsch, had to approve any contact with the police before it was made.[31] Another problem beneath the surface was that some generals had bitterly criticized the SS in 1939–40 over atrocities in Poland and other matters, and Himmler and Brauchitsch had been forced to intervene to dampen the controversies. In July 1940, Brauchitsch had instructed army authorities not to try to interfere with the way political authorities carried out the racial struggle (Jewish problem) in the East.[32] Relations between the army and the SS and police were still far from good.

Himmler and Heydrich had their own reasons for opening negotiations with the army over Operation Barbarossa. They recognized that the military campaign in the East would provide the perfect opportunity for Nazi Germany to liquidate its racial and political enemies under cover of war. Like Hitler, they had a radical conception of what would be necessary to ensure security in the conquered territories of the East. Only the reduction or elimination of enemy populations and resettlement of conquered territories by Germans would suffice. Whereas the army might plan for a "normal" war, the SS and police had to destroy "Jewish Bolshevism" forever. They could take a big step toward achieving that aim by destroying the enemy's leadership as quickly as possible, but they had to move virtually alongside the army.

The "pacification" measures planned in connection with Operation Barbarossa were also linked to broader Nazi objectives. By early 1941, Heydrich had worked out at least a general conception of liquidating Jews throughout Europe after first concentrating them in the East.[33] By May 1941, one of Heydrich's very well informed subordinates was able to allude to what he called the "surely coming Final Solution" of the Jewish question.[34] Gradually, a few high officials outside the SS came into the circle of those initiated into the project.

At the end of March 1941, Heydrich met with Hermann Göring, the best-known Nazi leader after Hitler. A famous World War I ace, Göring had accumulated a wide range of functions and responsibilities, including the Office of the Four Year Plan. He had become a kind of economic boss and in that connection still exercised a certain nominal jurisdiction over Jewish policy. As head of the German Air Force, Göring also was involved in planning the military campaign in the East. Heydrich reported briefly about "the solution of the Jewish question" and gave Göring a copy of his draft plan (which does not survive). According to Heydrich's memorandum of the meeting, after requiring a minor change with regard to Alfred Rosenberg's jurisdiction—Rosenberg was to become Reich Minister for the Occupied Eastern Territories—Göring gave his approval. The reference to Rosenberg suggested that at least part of European Jewry would be liquidated on Soviet soil.[35]

Göring also recommended a three- or four-page instruction for the troops about the danger posed by the Soviet police, political commissars, Jews, and so on so that the soldiers would know how to handle the situation when they encountered the enemy. Heydrich condensed the key part of this task admirably. After describing Bolshevism as the mortal enemy of the National Socialist German people, he wrote that the struggle required merciless and energetic intervention (*Durchgreifen*) against Bolshevist agitators, guerrillas, saboteurs, and Jews. The troops would need to eliminate completely all active and passive resistance.[36]

Himmler and Heydrich had already initiated discussions with high military officials regarding the forthcoming campaign. The two met very early with Field Marshal Wilhelm Keitel, head of the High Command of the Armed Services, and Himmler also met with Franz Halder, chief of the Army General Staff. Heydrich claimed to have met in early February with Army Commander in Chief Walther von Brauchitsch. Formal negotiations of an agreement with the army began on March 13, after Himmler and Heydrich had worked out their own standpoint three days earlier.[37] The SS held a strong hand for various reasons; Hitler's direct involvement was not the least of them.

On March 3, General Alfred Jodl of the Operations Staff of the High Command of the Armed Forces had passed along to subordinates Hitler's instructions for administration of the conquered areas of the Soviet Union. The forthcoming war was more than "a mere armed conflict"; it was a collision between two ideologies. Accordingly, the Bolshevist-Jewish intelligentsia had to be eliminated. Written guidelines specified that Himmler would have special tasks authorized by the Führer in the operational area that were necessary to prepare for political administration. Himmler would carry out these tasks independent of the regular armed forces, and he would take care not to disturb military operations. The army was to control as little territory as possible, its supreme authority limited to the immediate areas of military operations; civilian commissioners, accompanied by police authorities, would rule over the rest. Whether the nonmilitary police (here Hitler specifically referred to organs of the Reich Führer SS) would also be needed in the operational areas was a matter that the army would have to clear with Himmler, but "the necessity to neutralize Bolshevik leaders and commissars immediately is an argument in favor." Hitler reinforced the message with a similarly bloodcurdling speech to military officers in March 1941.[38]

In mid-March, Himmler and his chief of staff, Karl Wolff, Daluege, and Heydrich apparently began the process of working out whose police forces would perform which functions in what territories during the campaign against the Soviet Union.[39] Given how much there was to do, it was hardly possible not to use Daluege's forces. Himmler probably preferred not to leave everything to Heydrich anyway—there was such a thing as a subordinate who was too good and too powerful. Daluege would not easily abide Heydrich's control. Hitler had made the creation of overlapping authority and functions for subordinates into a basic principle of administration. In this case, Himmler made it into an art form.[40]

On April 16, the same four men plus Hans Jüttner (head of the SS Leadership Main Office) met with Quartermaster General Eduard Wagner to work out the remaining issues in an agreement between the SS and the army regarding the use of SS and police troops in the Soviet territories. Heydrich got virtual independence for his Einsatzgruppen. The army was reassured that there would not be large numbers of police

running around killing people near the front lines—only small detachments were to operate close to the armies (*im rückwärtigen Armeegebieten*).
Most of the Security Police forces would stay to the rear (*im rückwärtigen
Heeresgebieten*). At least one key army figure, Chief of the General Staff
Franz Halder, was apparently relieved that the army itself would not be
forced to do all of what Hitler wanted done—Himmler's people would
take care of it. But Heydrich's guidelines for the troops and Hitler's
harangues to the top officers indicated that the army would have some
direct involvement. Himmler also revealed SS settlement plans in the
East to General Hermann Reinecke, so some key generals had at least
selected glimpses of the future.[41]

The April 16 negotiations with the army (and the document regarding the Einsatzgruppen) did not specifically cover Daluege's Order Police battalions, but Daluege had ensured their involvement anyway. On
April 8, he once again discussed with Himmler use of the Order Police
in Operation Barbarossa.[42] On April 21, he indicated directly to Hitler
that Order Police battalions would take part in this campaign, and in a
thank-you note he wrote for his latest military decoration, he promised
the Führer that the Order Police and its auxiliary organizations would
meet the coming new tasks with strength and courage.[43] Other evidence
suggests that Hitler either initiated or ratified the idea of using the
Order Police battalions. In a speech given to high-ranking police officials in early 1942, Daluege stated that before military operations
against the U.S.S.R. had begun the Führer had ordered preparations
for the use of Order Police formations in the rear army areas. He would
hardly have exaggerated Hitler's involvement, because he sent a copy
of his speech to Himmler, who passed it on to the Führer.[44]

Following the April 16 meeting, and picking up on what was discussed there, Himmler's personal staff worked out the draft of another
top secret document governing security in the soon-to-be-conquered
areas of the U.S.S.R. Like the agreement with the army regarding the
Einsatzgruppen, this document revealed that Hitler had given Himmler
unspecified special orders; to carry them out, Himmler would install,
in areas of German political administration, Higher SS and Police Leaders, who would receive their instructions directly from him and who
would have at their disposal SS and police troops (Waffen-SS units and
Order Police battalions), as well as Einsatzgruppen. Each Higher SS and
Police Leader would inform the corresponding commander in the rear
army area about the tasks Himmler gave him, and the commander could

give directives necessary to avoid disturbing military operations. If a dangerous situation developed, the army commander could make military use of the police troops with the approval of the Higher SS and Police Leader, but otherwise the police battalions were subordinated to SS and police authorities, specifically to the Higher SS and Police Leaders for northern, central, and southern Russia.[45]

Himmler's recourse to Higher SS and Police Leaders in the East followed precedent. From 1938 on, Himmler had installed such leaders in each military district within Germany. Nominally, they were responsible for order and security at ceremonies and mass meetings, but they also received special instructions as Himmler saw fit.[46] His goal was not only to coordinate regional SS and police activities but also to help bring two different organizations closer into a Nazi protective corps for the Third Reich. This corps would fight Germany's internal enemies, protect the German race, and facilitate military expansion.[47]

Political sensitivities within Germany were such that the Higher SS and Police Leaders still had to consider German law (such as it was in the Third Reich) and bureaucratic regulations. But in the conquered areas of the Soviet Union, where German law did not apply, they would have a free hand to carry out the Führer's special orders. From the start, then, they were more powerful than their counterparts in Germany itself. Careful coordination on a territorial scale was all the more important where SS and police forces were engaged in the destruction of millions of Nazi enemies. Himmler was to consider the principle of territorial coordination so important that he would follow up by appointing regional SS and Police Leaders, as well as local ones in key districts, both subordinate to the territorial Higher SS and Police Leaders.

The Higher SS and Police Leaders reported directly to Himmler, not Heydrich, and provided him with information from the field. They also used both Heydrich's Einsatzgruppen and Daluege's Order Police units without subordinating one to the other, enabling Himmler to continue his balancing act with his two key police subordinates.

Himmler did not take long to find the right men to fill these posts in the East. Forty-year-old Hans-Adolf Prützmann had already served as Higher SS and Police Leader for northwest Germany. He had joined the Nazi Party (1929) and the SS (1930) suitably early and had served in the Free Corps and in an undercover Reichswehr regiment in

1923–24. He was on good terms with Daluege, exchanging birthday greetings and occasional gifts. Himmler trusted him so much that, when Germany's military situation looked bleak in late 1944, he chose Prützmann to arrange for partisan warfare against the Allied troops about to invade Germany. Prützmann's appointment as Higher SS and Police Leader for northern Russia took effect on June 22, 1941, the day the German invasion began, but there are indications that it was planned in April 1941.[48]

Erich von dem Bach-Zelewski (who used a second surname because his wife had children from a previous marriage) had served in the army for five years during the Weimar Republic. Like Prützmann, he had a long career in the SS and was well acquainted with Daluege, who in 1933 had judged him to be "loyal, honorable, and strongly impulsive."[49] After Bach-Zelewski had quarreled with another high Nazi official and come under some criticism, possibly for having had contacts with Jews, Himmler referred the matter to Hitler, who decided to let him keep his SS offices.[50] In March 1941, Bach-Zelewski requested front-line duty; he must have already known about Operation Barbarossa.[51] In April, Himmler appointed him Higher SS and Police Leader Southeast (Silesia). One month later Bach-Zelewski was removed from this office, given a little time off, and then ordered to contact Himmler directly on May 26.[52]

Friedrich Jeckeln, the oldest of the group at forty-six, fit the same mold. After studying engineering, he had served as a decorated lieutenant in the German Army during World War I, joined the SS in 1930, and taken a high position in the municipal police of Braunschweig in 1933. He, too, was friendly with Daluege, and he had experience as Higher SS and Police Leader (for central Germany, then for western Germany). In early 1941, Jeckeln lobbied for a new post in the East, and it came through. On April 23, he wrote to a friend: "I myself will, as I have learned secretly, be used in connection with great events, which are to be expected . . ."[53] On May 1, Himmler issued a set of orders: effective May 10 Jeckeln was to report to Himmler's personal staff and to be at his disposal, then Jeckeln would have exactly eight days' vacation, and during May 19–31 he would serve with Heydrich for informational purposes.[54] Jeckeln's formal appointment as Higher SS and Police Leader for the Ukraine came on the day of the invasion, June 22.

Prützmann, Bach-Zelewski, and Jeckeln were all SS-Gruppenführer, generals in Himmler's elite order, and all held the rank of lieutenant general in the police as well. It was a close circle: they all had military backgrounds, police experience, and many years in the SS together. They did not get that far without Himmler's confidence that they would do what Hitler and he wanted done. The pattern of orders for all three in the spring of 1941 indicates that Himmler was grooming and preparing them for their forthcoming tasks in the occupied Soviet Union.[55]

There may have been one collective briefing in mid-June. In 1946, Bach-Zelewski testified that some weeks before the invasion of the U.S.S.R. began he attended a meeting in Himmler's castle at Wewelsburg with Daluege, Heydrich, Jeckeln, Prützmann, Karl Wolff, and several others. Himmler announced that the forthcoming campaign would determine whether Germany would become a great power for all time or instead would be annihilated. A man as great as Hitler was born only every thousand years or so; therefore, this generation had to solve Germany's problem of insufficient living space. Once Germany conquered a large portion of European Russia, all the Jews of Europe would be in its hands. Germany would proceed to remove all Jews from Europe and would massively reduce the Slavic population of the region by twenty or thirty million as well.[56]

According to Bach-Zelewski's postwar testimony, Himmler intended to use all branches of his various forces—Security Police, Order Police, and Waffen-SS—to accomplish his racial goals. From the start of the campaign in the U.S.S.R., he allowed the Security Police (and the Einsatzgruppen drawn from it) to operate more or less independently (under Heydrich), whereas the Order Police forces came under the control of the Higher SS and Police Leaders.[57] The actual relationships were somewhat more ambiguous and complicated, but Bach-Zelewski nonetheless captured a good portion of the picture.

To provide liaison with the conglomeration of Waffen-SS units and Order Police battalions to be used in the rear areas, Himmler had set up a task-force staff in April 1941, which in early May became the Command Staff of the Reich Führer SS (Kommandostab Reichsführer SS), headed by fifty-six-year-old Kurt Knoblauch, a longtime army officer. Knoblauch was more a military professional than a political type—he had joined the Nazi Party only after Hitler came to power and had entered the SS only in 1935.[58]

Himmler had considered subordinating all the actions against "partisans" in the rear areas to the Command Staff RFSS, but he changed his mind. Once the Waffen-SS units and police units left Germany, they came under the direct authority of the Higher SS and Police Leaders.[59] Still, a reduced Command Staff RFSS coordinated the movement of troops and supplies into the field, transmitted Himmler's orders, and received reports from the units in the rear army areas.

In a late June listing of the units attached to the Command Staff RFSS, Prützmann, Higher SS Leader for northern Russia, would direct Police Regiment North (consisting of three battalions and other assorted units) as well as three other police battalions. The Higher SS Leader for central Russia, Bach-Zelewski, got Police Regiment Center and three additional battalions, and Jeckeln in the South had the same strength. It was by no means a final listing: four other police battalions, a number of cavalry squadrons, and the Waffen-SS brigades and infantry regiments were listed separately.[60] At any rate, at least eighteen battalions of Order Police, or about nine thousand policemen, were listed for quick deployment into the areas penetrated, conquered, and left by front-line army troops.

We still do not know exactly how all these troops were recruited or what their previous experiences were. The battalions contained some young recruits, some existing police shifted to new duties, and some older policemen concentrated in special reserve battalions. In spite of the gaps in the picture, it is clear that the Order Police battalions were a less politicized force than the Einsatzgruppen. They may not have represented the average German—policemen in a police state share some characteristics and behavior that set them apart from the mass of the population. Still, what we know of their numbers and their institution suggests that they were not part of a political-ideological elite.

How much were the police executioners told in advance about their orders and the nature of Nazi policies? Again, many policemen testified after the war that they did not know their exact functions until just before their first action. The historian needs to be cautious about the use of such evidence, because the various officials and policemen interrogated were themselves in legal jeopardy, and many resisted testifying against former colleagues. Another problem is that some accounts directly contradict others, and who knows which perpetrators to believe?[61] Solid contemporary evidence is generally lacking.

Still, we do know that withholding information until the last minute was typical of the Nazi leadership. Hitler's fundamental command was never to tell a person something earlier than was absolutely necessary, never tell more than what was necessary to carry out a task, never tell more people than was necessary.[62] This order was perhaps more widely publicized than the Nazi government intended. When it was repeated in mid-1943 in a radio message, British code breakers picked it up and gave it to British Prime Minister Winston Churchill,[63] who must have found it interesting reading.

# 3

✳

# A BATTALION
# GETS THE WORD

ON JUNE 22, 1941, the day the German invasion of the Soviet Union began, German army troops captured border towns in Lithuania and advanced into the interior, suffering some casualties in the initial assault and afterward from snipers. The German authorities alleged that Jews had resisted the German advance and had even mutilated German corpses, and these accusations provided a justification for Berlin to move ahead with actions already envisioned. The head of the Gestapo, Heinrich Müller, issued directives by telex on June 23 and 24 to the Gestapo office in the German border city of Tilsit to set up a mobile killing unit (called Einsatzkommando Tilsit) and remove Jews from the nearby border area in Lithuania. The police commander, an SS Major Hans Joachim Böhme, recruited local men in the Gestapo, the border police, and the regular municipal police. The marksmen for the first executions in Garsden (Gargzdai), Kretinga, and Palanga, where Jews were held accountable for resistance to German troops, came from the municipal police. Within three days, 526 Jews, all but two of them adult males, were shot into pits prepared for the occasion.[1] It was the beginning of the Holocaust in the Soviet territories.

Heydrich and Müller closely directed the activities of all the Einsatzgruppen and Einsatzkommandos. But Daluege held authority over the Order Police battalions, and these would become the mainstay of the Higher SS and Police Leaders, who were also very much involved in the "cleansing" of enemies from conquered territory. At the end of June, therefore, Daluege held a briefing in Berlin for Prützmann, Bach-Zelewski, Jeckeln, and Gerret Korsemann, soon to become the fourth

Higher SS and Police Leader.[2] This meeting in Berlin has come to light only because Heydrich was absent. Daluege had neglected to give him much advance notice, and as a result Heydrich could not be there (and dominate); on July 2, he sent out a top secret message to the four men, complaining about Daluege and setting out, in condensed form, the directives he had already given to the Einsatzgruppen regarding security in the newly conquered territories.[3] Or so he said.

Without the ongoing battle between Heydrich and Daluege for control of SS and police functions in the conquered territories of the Soviet Union, Heydrich would not have set down anything on paper.[4] In a separate dispute with the Reich commissar for the eastern lands (Estonia, Latvia, Lithuania, and part of Byelorussia) in early August, Franz Walter Stahlecker, head of Einsatzgruppe A, revealed that he had received fundamental orders connected with the impending complete purge of Jews from Europe that were not to be written down but transmitted only orally.[5] The writing of what was normally handled orally, as well as Heydrich's use of the phrase "in compressed form" to describe a fairly long document, suggests that his words require considerable scrutiny.

Heydrich declared that the short-term goal was to pacify the newly conquered areas politically; the final goal was economic pacification. Referring to the agreement on relations between the Einsatzgruppen and the army, he explained the channels for reporting information, and then got to the heart of the matter: the Einsatzkommandos would execute all Comintern functionaries and Communist officials, people's commissars, Jews in Party and state positions, and other radical elements (saboteurs, propagandists, and such). He also instructed German authorities to encourage the non-Germans to carry out pogroms against Jews in their areas.[6]

Some police units and Einsatzkommandos were already liquidating Jews outside these categories. However, surviving members of the Einsatzkommandos generally testified in West German investigations and trials from the 1950s on that they did not kill Jewish women and children until early August or later in some cases.[7] One reading of the events is that the Einsatzgruppen commanders already knew the final goal of Nazi Jewish policy and were given some discretion to accomplish as much as they could with limited manpower. Jewish males were considered a more immediate threat, and it was easier to find "reasons" (pretexts) to kill them.

It is certainly possible that some Einsatzgruppen officers took Heydrich's July 2 message at face value, but it requires considerable credulity to maintain that Himmler, Heydrich, and Daluege did not yet know what to do with the Jewish "race." They did not yet know how smoothly the killing process would work, which leaders and units would prove effective, and whether there would be significant resistance, including resistance from the policemen themselves.

The war diary (*Kriegstagebuch*) kept by Order Police Battalion 322 and related original documents uncovered and first described by the German-Australian historian Konrad Kwiet substantiate some of the evidence about higher Nazi authorities.[8] From the beginning, Jews were a target. Rationalizations and pretexts sometimes concealed this fact from the executioners, who undertook liquidations by stages. A microhistory of this battalion sustains the view that the Nazi campaign to destroy Germany's enemies in the East was carefully planned in advance, and the Order Police battalions were from the beginning an essential component of the process.

On April 15, about the time Himmler was selecting his Higher SS and Police Leaders for the East,[9] he ordered Battalion 322 (and most likely others) to prepare for an operation outside Greater Germany. The war diary indicates that the battalion was at Himmler's personal disposal. Although explicit evidence is lacking, other battalions mobilized around this time were also Himmler's tools.

Battalion 322, called a bicycle battalion because it originally lacked motorized transport, originated in Vienna. Commanded by Major of the Municipal Police Gottlieb Nagel, Battalion 322 had a staff, three companies (each consisting of four platoons), and a motorized support group. There were 13 officers, 1 senior medical officer, 5 administrators, 107 noncommissioned officers (*Unterführer*), 493 constables (*Wachtmeister*), and a command staff. Germans and Austrians were present in roughly equal proportions, but most of the officers were German. The majority of the constables ranged in age from twenty-nine to thirty-three.[10]

In addition to its military training, Battalion 322 received political and ideological instruction that focused on the Jewish-Bolshevist enemy. On May 17, 1941, its members rejoiced at the news that they would be sent to the East. At their departure from Vienna on June 9, the commander of the Order Police in Vienna reminded them to obey orders, to fulfill their duty at all times, and to "confront the Slavic peoples as members of the master race."[11]

In Warsaw, Police Battalions 307, 316, and 322 joined to become the principal parts of Police Regiment Center, commanded by Police Lieutenant Colonel Max Montua. The fifty-five-year-old Montua was a decorated veteran of World War I and a career police officer. He was not yet a member of the SS, but he would soon demonstrate that he met its standards.[12] As soon as they crossed into the Soviet Union (including the Polish territory the U.S.S.R. had annexed in 1939), Montua and his regiment came under the authority of Higher SS and Police Leader Bach-Zelewski; on June 28, Bach-Zelewski and Major General Max von Schenckendorf, commander of the Rear Army Area Center, personally inspected Battalion 322.[13]

Several days later Battalion 322 received its first instructions regarding the treatment of the population in conquered territory. Any civilian found with arms was to be shot, as were political commissars. Nazi authorities considered Byelorussians, Ruthenians, and Ukrainians potentially friendly, so it was permissible to form auxiliary police units from their ranks. On July 7, the battalion reached the city of Bialystok, in the former Soviet zone of Poland, where it underwent its first real action and began to transform itself.[14]

Police Battalion 309 had already gone through the city and burned some seven hundred Jews to death in a fire in the main synagogue on June 27. Einsatzkommando 9 had also arrived and was still carrying out executions of Jews.[15] The passage of different units through major transportation centers and bases of perceived enemies was common in the first weeks following the Nazi invasion. Bialystok saw Einsatzkommandos, police battalions, and other German forces, which shared the work that their superiors wanted done there.

Some Battalion 322 policemen were immediately deployed as guards, others patrolled the city, still others were ordered to capture suspicious persons, especially Jews or Russian soldiers in disguise and turn them over to the SD. Soviet prisoners of war, most of them of Jewish origin, were shot from the first day onward; reports listed them as having been shot trying to escape. The battalion planned a raid on the Jewish quarter in the early morning of July 8. Six officers and 220 constables sealed off the streets in one sector and dispensed troops to inspect apartments and shops. Not only did they take what they needed; they found among the Jews items such as food, leather goods, textiles, kitchenware, and a hunting rifle. They concluded that the Jews had looted non-Jewish property in the chaotic days after the German invasion. During this raid and shortly thereafter, they executed twenty-two people (among them one woman), mostly Jews, who refused to admit to plundering. Other

Jews were forced to pose for photographs in front of their alleged plunder.[16]

The war diary of the battalion indicated that, based on the results of the first raid, the police could conclude that all Jewish and Polish residences would contain stolen goods. A couple of months later, one company from the battalion searched Jewish houses in the town of Krasnopolje only to find relatively little "plunder," so it assumed that the Jews had buried it.[17] These assumptions could have come straight from the works of Nazi racial propaganda.

Himmler unexpectedly turned up in Bialystok on the afternoon of July 8, and Higher SS and Police Leader Bach-Zelewski was already there. They inspected the booty from the first raid of the Jewish quarter, and Himmler asked the battalion members about their tasks.[18] He quickly found a way to build on what the battalion had already done.

After the war Bach-Zelewski told a tall tale about Himmler and the early July events in Bialystok. He said that Daluege arrived and that together they deplored the executions of Jews going on there and elsewhere. Then Himmler showed up and insisted on the maximum punishment for plundering and sabotage, overcoming Daluege's resistance.[19] Arthur Nebe, head of Einsatzgruppe B, had allegedly carried out the executions in the city after Bach-Zelewski had been removed from his command. In 1946, Bach-Zelewski put all the blame on those who were already dead.

There is no sign that Nebe was present in Bialystok on July 8, however, and plenty of evidence that Bach-Zelewski retained his command. He actually hosted a private dinner that evening for Himmler, which regimental commander Montua attended. (There is no sign of Daluege until the next day.) Other postwar testimony indicates that Himmler spoke privately to Bach-Zelewski, Montua, and the officers of several battalions about police organization in the conquered territories in the East. Word filtered down that he asked the police to intervene more against the Jews. An officer of Police Battalion 316 came back, disturbed, from the meeting with Himmler and revealed to a fellow officer that his battalion would have to shoot Jews. That same evening about one thousand Jews were executed. A West German court later determined that at least the first company of Police Battalion 322 took part in this action directed by the Einsatzkommando. The battalion's war diary noted laconically that the battalion was in action day and night.[20]

In a speech the next day, Daluege told the police regiment that it should take pride in its part in the destruction of the world enemy,

Bolshevism. This campaign was unprecedented in its importance. It would exterminate Bolshevism and benefit not only Germany but also Europe and the entire world.[21] So much for Daluege's resistance to Himmler. He seemed rather to have urged more radical intervention.

On July 11, Montua passed on a confidential order from Bach-Zelewski to Battalions 307, 316, and 322 requiring the immediate execution of male Jews between the ages of seventeen and forty-five who were "convicted" of looting. The order stipulated that executions be carried out at inconspicuous sites and the graves be leveled (to prevent later pilgrimages to them). Montua also prohibited photographs of the killing and advised battalion commanders and company commanders to reduce the strain on their men by holding social gatherings for them in the evening (after the executions). Finally, the commanders had to explain to their men the necessity of these killings. Another execution occurred that day. After the war one policeman testified that Bach-Zelewski himself appeared at the execution site outside the city on July 11 and allegedly told the men that the murder of these Jews was necessary for Greater Germany.[22]

Montua warned the officers to report execution totals regularly and carefully—they were not to exaggerate. He issued another order (no. 8) on July 20, which contained instructions about executions, but apparently no copy survives. Later reports of killings of Jewish men and women referred back to the July 20 order, which may have broadened the range of targets.[23]

The execution of looters did not require personal visits by Himmler and Daluege or speeches and special instructions by Bach-Zelewski and Montua. They involved themselves because the connection between looting and the many Jews targeted for murder was so feeble. But the battalion itself began the process of automatically associating Jews with looting—and selectively executing them—even before Himmler arrived. It was a sign that not all anti-Semitism came from the top. Himmler and Bach-Zelewski built on that foundation.

Himmler was keenly aware that the execution of civilians might have damaging psychological effects on the police executioners—even in 1940 he said he had been warned about this. So Himmler believed that, in addition to orders, the police needed a reason to kill, and they needed social gatherings in the evening to reduce the strain. Once they had carried out mass murder in response to an alleged crime or provocation, it would be easier to get them to follow broader killing orders later. The use of euphemisms also created a false record in documents—

which would be convenient if outsiders gained access to the files. Himmler was convinced that many among the German people were too soft to recognize the historical necessity of Nazi Germany's racial policies.[24]

One indicator of Himmler's concern about motivating police battalion executioners came less than a week after he met with Bach-Zelewski and the regimental and battalion commanders in Bialystok. An inquiry went out by radio to authorities in Bialystok, Baranowicze, and Minsk, asking if they could lay their hands on movie projectors needed to help the troops prepare for the "special duties."[25] There was a precedent of sorts for showing films. In September 1940, Himmler had ordered all SS members to see the popular new film *Jud Süss* (The Jew Süss) during the winter of 1940–41. An alternative, even more virulently anti-Semitic, was *The Eternal Jew*, which had premiered in November.[26]

*Jud Süss* was supposedly based on the career of Joseph Süss Oppenheimer, financier at the court of the eighteenth-century duke of Württemberg. The film ended with the hanging of Süss and the authorities banning all Jews from Württemberg. The Propaganda Minister, Joseph Goebbels, regarded this film as an excellent example of the power of the cinema to persuade. *The Eternal Jew*, a supposed documentary prepared by the Propaganda Ministry, was an alleged exposé of the secret crimes and characteristics of the Jews from ancient times to the present. It repeated Hitler's threat, made to the German Reichstag on January 30, 1939, that if war broke out the result would be the destruction of the Jewish race in Europe. At least one historian who specializes in Nazi cinema has speculated that these films were designed to help prepare the German people for the Final Solution.[27] But they could not help the Order Police before they carried out their onerous tasks in mid-July 1941, for the movie equipment was not at hand.[28] The commanders had to invoke rationalizations for the orders to carry out mass killings.

The war diary of Police Battalion 322 reveals much through its inclusions—and its omissions. It is not surprising that the battalion's records are discreet about July 8 (when the battalion was in action day and night), because that action in Bialystock was psychologically the most difficult. Another psychological turning point came at the end of August, by which time most of the battalion had moved temporarily into Minsk, the capital of Byelorussia. Local German authorities had forced the Jews of Minsk and surrounding villages into a quarter of the city, which became a ghetto, and required all Jews to wear a Star of David on their clothing. On August 31, two companies of Police Battalion 322 seized seven hundred Jews from the Minsk ghetto and brought them to jail. According to the war diary, seventy-nine policeman (about 16 percent of the men) reported sick that day and did not take part in the action. But the situation did not improve the next day, when all of the imprisoned Jews and 214 more—including 64 Jewish women—were shot. The war diary justified the execution of these women with the argument that they had failed to wear the Jewish star,[29] which was a crime, though not a crime commensurate with the punishment.

The commander of the third company of the battalion (by then also called the ninth company of Police Regiment Center) kept a contemporary total and brief characterization of the event. His company executed 290 Jewish men and 40 Jewish women in Minsk on September 1 in an action he described as "without friction" and without resistance.[30] This wording hardly did justice to a very carefully prepared joint action by the SD and Police Battalion 322. The Jewish men, women, and children were jammed onto trucks, which the police drove some kilometers north of the city until they reached a field with three large trenches, ten to fifteen meters long, two meters wide, and more than two meters deep. There was a graded incline at one end, so that the Jews could walk down into the pit. Still clothed, they were ordered to lie down in the pits, face to the ground. On one side of each trench stood an execution command of twelve policemen. Their commanding officer gave them the order: "One, two, fire." None of these details appeared in the battalion's war diary; battalion members reconstructed them in West German criminal investigations long after the war.[31]

These executions in Bialystok and Minsk were the most visible and memorable ones for Police Battalion 322 during the first two months, but there were others as well in towns and villages of the Bialystok district and in what the Nazis then called White Ruthenia, the western portion of Byelorussia. Starting with the execution of Jewish "plunderers," the battalion moved gradually to the liquidation of adult Jewish men, then Jewish men and women, and eventually, men, women, and children. The killing came as a result of direct orders from above, including some from Bach-Zelewski and Montua.[32]

This was the common situation early in the Soviet campaign—a situation that many other police battalions also faced. Einsatzkommando

Tilsit, the unit that carried out the very first Nazi executions of Jews in Soviet territories, faced a similar situation and evolved in a similar manner. None of the police knew in advance that they would have to kill Jews, and some later testified that they had been shocked at the news, yet most followed orders, first to liquidate mostly Jewish men, then women, and from mid-August children as well. Ideological instruction reinforced anti-Semitic stereotypes, and linguistic devices and rationalizations helped to disguise the policy of genocide.[33]

Unlike the now famous (but exceptional) case of Police Battalion 101 (the Order Police battalion that operated in eastern Poland during 1942–43[34]), the battalion and company commanders in Police Battalion 322 did not offer their men the opportunity to find other work on the days of killing actions. The commanders gave orders and expected their men to follow them. It was not for nothing that Himmler and his key subordinates had stressed, particularly since September 1939, the sanctity of orders. They recognized that Nazi policies challenged traditional or conventional standards of morality. They wanted the weight of authority to override qualms of conscience or simple distaste for unpleasant tasks.

We may assume that many policemen in Police Battalion 322 followed killing orders without any serious questions. Except for the case of the August 31 roundup in Minsk, there was no significant contemporary evidence of dissent. There never seemed to be a problem getting enough people to carry out the liquidations. Still, some postwar testimony (other than self-exculpatory accounts) indicated that a very few policemen from Police Battalion 322 declined to participate in the killing; perhaps only one held out until the end. The laggards were subjected to some pressure to obey orders and to conform, but they were not punished for failing to do so.[35]

There is one sign of a psychological toll for a small number of policemen who followed the German army into the Soviet Union. At least four policemen committed suicide in the East during July and early August 1941. The evidence does not indicate whether these policemen had taken part in mass killings.[36]

The historian Gerhard Weinberg has recently analyzed the general situation of those Germans expected to take part in mass murder. The initiative came from above. Habits of obedience, peer pressure, and even hopes of career advancement may each (or in some combination) have affected the thinking of particular individuals, but each person still had to make a choice at the end, and that choice was affected by the presence or absence of ethical convictions. For those who did not see Jews as equals or even as human, the decision was relatively easy.[37]

Would unbiased policemen, at the start of a war initiated by Germany, agree that mass murder of large numbers of any other group was necessary to protect Germany in a strictly military sense? Many German policemen carried out orders because of the weight of authority, but they could rationalize the orders probably because they had already internalized basic prejudices from the atmosphere in the Third Reich and Weimar Germany. They perceived Jews and Bolsheviks as the fundamental enemies of the German people, and they accepted Nazi propaganda charges that Jews were behind Bolshevism. They simply excluded Jews from their realm of concern. It did not take much special ideological training to move these police to kill. It also did not take the specter of defeat on the battlefield.[38]

On one level, the presence of Austrians in Battalion 322 requires only minor adjustment to these conclusions. Pre–World War I Austria-Hungary had stronger currents of anti-Semitism than did imperial Germany, and the young Hitler had imbibed some of that atmosphere in Linz and Vienna. Nor did anti-Semitism substantially decline in a democratic Austria after 1918. Military defeat, the dissolution of a once great empire, and the crippling loss of territory to neighboring countries created some of the same frustration and search for scapegoats as in Germany.[39] Austrian policemen were susceptible to these attitudes. Still, the Austrian example reminds us that anti-Semitism, even virulent anti-Semitism, was hardly limited to Germany. It was known throughout Europe and the West, and it was particularly strong in Eastern Europe. Nazi leaders knew how to exploit this situation. About two months after Police Battalion 322 killed hundreds of Jews in Minsk, Latvian and Lithuanian auxiliary police recruited by Nazi authorities acted in similar capacities in the same city. That, too, was in conformity with orders and according to plan.

On July 25, Himmler had authorized the creation of auxiliary police forces from the reliable non-Communist elements among Ukrainians, Estonians, Latvians, Lithuanians, and Byelorussians.[40] While the Einsatzgruppen created special non-German killing squads under a variety of names, the more numerous Order Police gained control over the non-German auxiliary police battalions called Schutzmannschaften (defense forces), which included battalions and stationary auxiliary police in towns and villages. Daluege and his subordinates had more men in the East than Heydrich, and perhaps Daluege was in a better position to deal with practical issues such as getting uniforms and weapons and training these auxiliary battalions, whose numbers expanded rapidly. Also, he had begun to use older policemen in battalions, the Reserve Police Battalions, and some of these older units were better suited for work with the non-German formations than for independent action.

The non-German battalions offered a way to extend German control, given limited manpower, in the conquered territories. With more manpower, the Nazis could reach and destroy more of their designated enemies in the East. In the beginning, Himmler intended many of the non-German auxiliary police forces to be sent outside their homelands, where they would be more dependent on German authorities, less likely to become a rallying point for nationalist leaders, and perhaps more inclined to obey any order.[41]

The creation of Schutzmannschaften and their future use as executioners reflected more than just a shortage of German policemen. Whereas Himmler, Daluege, Bach-Zelewski, and some other high officials had some concern for the morale of German police, they did not much care what happened psychologically to the non-Germans as long as there were enough of them to carry out their appointed tasks.

# 4

✳

# REPORTS OF
# ETHNIC CLEANSING

HIMMLER, HEYDRICH, AND DALUEGE apparently encouraged the Einsatzgruppen chiefs and Higher SS and Police Leaders to develop good relations with the army commanders in their regions, because they knew that army opposition to racial policies could raise serious obstacles to their implementation.[1] The Germans quickly established a civil administration in the conquered Soviet territories to remove the potential constraints of military control and to free army troops for other tasks. There was, however, some friction with the civil administration in the East.

Himmler had already clashed with Alfred Rosenberg, Reich Minister for the Occupied Eastern Territories, over whether his SS and police forces could act independently of the German civil administration in the Soviet territories. Martin Bormann, head of the Nazi Party bureaucracy, quickly prevented Rosenberg from delaying or interfering with Himmler during the first weeks.[2] Then, at a meeting at Hitler's East Prussian headquarters on July 16, 1941, over some apparent opposition from Rosenberg, Hitler and Göring insisted that Himmler have the same powers in the East that he enjoyed in Germany itself, that his powers were absolutely necessary.[3]

Hitler also revealed that Germany would undertake all measures necessary to settle disposition of the conquered areas, such as shooting and deportation. He rejoiced that the Soviets had issued a call for partisan warfare behind the lines. Germans could now exterminate anyone who represented opposition. By that, Hitler meant not just those who took up arms against German rule or who had been part of the Soviet apparatus but also racial enemies. In Hitler's eyes, a person's race would always determine his attitude and behavior.

This meeting told other high Nazi officials what Himmler had been saying since April, if not earlier—the Führer had entrusted him with a special mission to dispose of Germany's enemies. His position with Hitler was so secure that Himmler did not even have to attend this meeting, which unveiled Hitler's guidelines for carving up and administering the vast areas of the Soviet Union. Himmler spent time at his own headquarters nearby, appointing officials and doing other work without interference. Bormann later sent him a copy of the summary.[4]

The next day Hitler formalized Himmler's authority in the East with a decree stipulating that, even after the introduction of a civil administration in the East, Himmler would have the right to issue directives regarding security to civil authorities. The Higher SS and Police Leaders would be only nominally subordinate to Rosenberg's territorial commissioners; functionally they were subordinate only to Himmler.[5] This meeting and this decree did not end Himmler's difficulties with Rosenberg, but they gave him and his Higher SS and Police Leaders a major advantage.

By then the Higher SS and Police Leaders were already moving rapidly to carry out their tasks in the East. On July 14, Daluege had instructed Gerret Korsemann to prepare a staff for his intended future office—that of Higher SS and Police Leader for the Caucasus region. Korsemann also had to contact the military offices to be deployed there. Such preparations were a sign of confidence in the military campaign, since German troops were at least a thousand miles from the Caucasus. Also on July 14, Bach-Zelewski arrived in Baranowicze, in what the Germans called White Ruthenia (a portion of what is today Belarus).[6]

Following Daluege's request for census data about each locality, Bach-Zelewski signaled Berlin that he had transferred his headquarters to Baranowicze, which had a population of roughly thirty-five thousand, almost half Jewish and a quarter Polish. With him, Police Battalions 307, 316, and 322 were carrying out pacification activities to the southeast. Following the same pretext used in Bialystok, they had liquidated 1,153 Jewish "plunderers" in Slonim, a town west of Baranowicze. Police Battalion 309 was back in Bialowies, near Bialystok, and Police Battalion 131 was divided among the cities of Wilna, Lida, and Grodno.[7]

When it was a matter of carrying out special orders from the Führer regarding basic tenets of Nazi ideology, Himmler, Heydrich, and Daluege all had to be involved. The three men flew frequently into the Soviet territories in the summer and fall of 1941 to inspect police operations.[8] But they also regularly needed information from, and means of communicating with, the field.

Heydrich's means are best known. The company-sized Einsatzkommandos reported their killings and other activities to the Einsatzgruppen,[9] whose heads sent reports from the field to the Reich Security Main Office (RSHA), and Heydrich, in Berlin. According to one of those involved in processing the information, during the first months of the Soviet campaign, the Einsatzgruppen reported in code via short-wave radio every day. At the very least, they passed on one or two short radio reports per week and a longer written report at least once a month. An office within the RSHA directly under Heinrich Müller compiled the reports periodically and distributed them to a very select list of officials.[10] These "operational situation reports" about the Soviet Union were essential—and not only for Heydrich and Himmler. On August 1, Müller wired the heads of the Einsatzgruppen that the RSHA was keeping Hitler constantly informed of their activities; they were asked to send visual materials to supplement their regular reports.[11]

The Higher SS and Police Leaders had to report back constantly as well. Occasionally, the Einsatzgruppen reports passed along to Berlin some of their major undertakings,[12] but officials who were directly subordinate to Himmler required separate channels of communication to reach him. Daluege also wanted regular reports from the Order Police regiments assigned to the Higher SS and Police Leaders.[13] Some means of communication were secure; others were not.

The German invasion did not do any good to the telephone and telegraph system of the Soviet Union—which was completely inadequate to start with. Telephone communication from the East to the Reich and vice versa was severely limited. Among the Order Police, for example, only Daluege, heads of the main offices within the Order Police, the Higher SS and Police Leaders, and the commanders (*Befehlshabern*) of the Order Police attached to the Higher SS and Police Leaders, and their chiefs of staff were authorized to make long-distance telephone calls to and from the East. Even they had to categorize their calls as exceptional, urgent, or ordinary, and the high-priority calls went onto a waiting list that included military requests as well. It was only slightly easier to get permission to telegraph.[14] This was the communications situation at the start of 1942. It must have been even worse earlier, except for Hans-Adolf Prützmann, who was frequently in Riga

(Latvia). Riga was relatively close to Hitler and Himmler in East Prussia, and telegraph connections apparently survived. Nevertheless, German forces built a five-hundred-watt transmitter in Riga.[15]

Bach-Zelewski, Jeckeln, and later Korsemann were much farther away and often on the move. For them, air-courier service and radio became essential means of communicating back to Germany. Courier service was limited and had start-up problems. The police had a small fleet of planes, but they were largely of the small Fieseler Storch model, which was not intended or suitable for long flights and had limited space. From August 1941 on, some courier service reached the Higher SS and Police Leaders, and a regular schedule began in September: Berlin to Lublin and Berditschev on Sundays and Wednesdays; Berditschev to Mogilev and Riga on Mondays and Thursdays; Riga to Königsberg and Berlin on Tuesdays and Fridays. But beginning in October, bad weather and mechanical problems impeded the flights. Not until mid-1942 did Higher SS and Police Leaders Jeckeln and Prützmann each get their own planes suitable for regular courier operations.[16] At best, the high authorities in the East could count on direct delivery twice a week.

From the beginning, Himmler and his subordinates recognized the importance of signals communication. Himmler was himself well equipped for shortwave and long-wave radio. He had a central office responsible for signals communication for all SS and police agencies under his control. This office communicated with Himmler's headquarters, high authorities in Berlin, and the heads of the SS main offices (such as the Security Police, the Order Police) via a rapid Teletype. Himmler also kept a signals section of approximately one hundred men at his East Prussian headquarters, and when he traveled on his special train "Heinrich," a generator, telephone, telegraph, and long-wave and shortwave radio facilities went with him.[17] The Command Staff RFSS also had its signals company and communications headquarters near Arys, in East Prussia. It, too, was directly connected by telegraph and telephone to Himmler's permanent headquarters, and the signals experts rigged up a telegraph connection through Königsberg to Himmler's train. The field units under the Command Staff RFSS received enough signals equipment, trained personnel, and transport vehicles to make daily communication possible without constant couriers or long-distance phone calls.[18]

Everything sent by radio from the field went up to Himmler, but it got there through different routes. The Einsatzgruppen used the equipment, frequencies, and codes of the RSHA, while the Waffen-SS brigades employed those of the Command Staff RFSS. Attached to each Higher SS and Police Leader was a communications specialist from the Order Police. Most messages sent by Prützmann, Bach-Zelewski, Jeckeln, and Korsemann went simultaneously to three sites—Himmler's headquarters, the Command Staff RFSS, and the chief of the Order Police (Daluege)—but they all went through the communications system of the Order Police.[19] The separate communications arrangements reflected the complicated, overlapping structures Himmler had created.

The Order Police signals officers tended to be older men, many of whom had started in signals work during World War I. Their chief, Robert Schlake, was also a veteran of that war who had joined the Nazi Party only in 1937 and was not even a member of the SS in 1941. The Order Police maintained a school for signals training in Berlin, but it relied on equipment and methods that its personnel was familiar with.[20] Perhaps that is one reason why it did not use the advanced coding machine known as Enigma, which was used by the RSHA (and the German military) for radio transmissions. They used instead a "hand" coding system adapted from one used by the British during World War I. It did not take complicated machinery to work, but it required a lot of effort and care.

From July through September 1941 the Order Police used a code system called Double Transposition. In mid-September they began to switch to Double Playfair, a modification of a British cipher called Playfair, and the shift was completed by November 1. As codes go, both were relatively simple. The basic principle of Playfair was to construct a square (or two squares) composed of twenty-five letters of the alphabet, with *j* omitted and encoded as *ii*. Each square began with a key word, and the remaining letters of the alphabet followed (either in alphabetical order or randomly). If the key word on a given day was "jockey," then *a* would be encoded as *j*, *b* as *o*, *c* as *c*, *d* as *k*, and so on.[21]

Couriers brought to units in the field sets of words to be used as key words. The key words also sometimes went from Berlin to Lublin, and then from Lublin to the Higher SS and Police Leader in the field, when telegraph facilities were nearby.[22] As long as the keys got through and the cipher clerks and recipients were careful, the system worked. It did not depend on highly trained personnel—one could learn and use the system quickly.[23] Of course, all the coding and transmission took a lot of time, so most messages sent by radio were kept short.

Himmler's signals communication chief was sixty-one-year-old Ernst Sachs. He had led a radio company in the German Army even before 1914 and served in a high signals position during World War I. After 1936 he carried out research on the history of wartime signals communication.[24] He should have known from his experience and research that Playfair was vulnerable, since the Germans had broken and read British World War I Playfair codes. Double Playfair was more difficult to decode but far from impossible.[25]

According to British intelligence analysts, the Germans showed no sign of appreciating the vulnerabilities of these codes.[26] Any large organization gets used to its procedures and finds it hard to break with them. One expert cryptographer noted that just changing telephone numbers in a large organization can cause chaos. To change coding systems dramatically and to retrain all the signals personnel in the midst of war were unappealing prospects. They would have caused paralysis for quite some time,[27] and they would have severely hindered the Order Police in their cooperation/competition with the Einsatzgruppen. Perhaps there was also an element of arrogance—simple underestimation of the enemy.

Himmler showed considerable restraint in what he sent out by radio. For the most sensitive matters, he relied on word of mouth, which was one reason why he traveled around so much.[28] At the end of July 1941, Himmler conferred with Higher SS and Police Leader Prützmann, also inspecting a company of Latvian auxiliary police in Riga. Just afterward, Prützmann mentioned to some subordinates that Himmler had instructed him to resettle "criminal elements." When someone asked where, Prützmann in effect responded that "resettlement" was a euphemism: they would be resettled into the next world.[29]

After meeting with Prutzmann, Himmler flew to meet Bach-Zelewski at his headquarters in Baranowicze, where two SS cavalry regiments were assembled for action. Again Himmler did not have to issue written orders, and there was no danger of enemy interception of this information. Exactly what Himmler told Bach-Zelewski is still unknown,[30] but it can be guessed at from subsequent conversations and actions.

Himmler then met Daluege in Rowno, and one or both of them conferred with Higher SS and Police Leader Jeckeln.[31] In any case, Jeckeln quickly received Himmler's order to shoot all Jews, except those required for labor, and he passed along the information orally to the head of Einsatzgruppe C in Zhitomir.[32] Himmler or Bach-Zelewski gave roughly the same message to the Second SS Cavalry Regiment, which was cleaning out anyone deemed suspicious from the Pripet Marshes between the Ukraine and Byelorussia. An SS cavalry detachment was then operating independently, so the regiment sent by radio the following: "Express order of the RFSS [Himmler]. All [male] Jews must be shot. Drive Jewish females into the swamps."[33] (The file copy of this message is among the incriminating original radio messages that survived.[34]) But when Jeckeln, on the same day, sent a written report on a "cleansing" action carried out on July 28–30, he was careful not to be so blunt. His forces had liquidated 73 guerrillas, 165 Communist functionaries, and 1,658 Jews who had (allegedly) served the Bolshevist system and delivered Ukrainians to Bolshevist authorities. Jeckeln used a rationale for executing these Jews partly because this report went to General Karl von Roques and General Alfred von Puttkamer, as well as Himmler and Daluege.[35] Himmler appreciated such discretion about SS policy.

On August 4, Himmler was back in his East Prussian headquarters, and Bach–Zelewski sent various progress reports to him, to the Command Staff RFSS communications headquarters, and to the Order Police. The SS Cavalry Brigade had just shot ninety Bolshevists and Jews in a cleansing action. Through the evening of August 3, this brigade had liquidated 3,274 partisans and "Jewish Bolsheviks" without suffering any losses of its own. (The absence of any German casualties indicated that the victims labeled as partisans were not really such.) Bach–Zelewski was using the police forces for smaller actions only, but Police Battalion 306 had shot 260 civilian insurgents. Some stray Russian cavalry got in a firefight with the army and SS. The 162nd Infantry Division was nearby but had no communication with the SS, so Bach–Zelewski had flown to the division's headquarters. Finally, Army Field Marshal Fedor von Bock had telephoned and congratulated Bach–Zelewski on his leadership and on the successes of his troops.[36]

On August 7, in another radio message, Bach–Zelewski announced that his forces, including a portion of one police battalion, had suffered some small losses in combat. Because the male inhabitants of the village of Jazyl had fired on one company of Police Battalion 316, Bach–Zelewski had ordered them all executed. The SS Cavalry Brigade had executed another thirty-six hundred (through noon that day). The total number of executions in the territory under his control now exceeded thirty thousand. On August 8 came a massive liquidation of eight thousand Jews in Pinsk, with a few thousand more several days later.[37]

Himmler wanted an even better sense of how things were going in the central sector. After Prützmann arrived to join his party, on August 14, Himmler flew with a group of ten subordinates to Baranowicze, where Bach-Zelewski and Standartenführer Hermann Fegelein, commander of the SS Cavalry Brigade, received them. The group then traveled by way of Slutsk to Minsk, by now partly in ruins.[38]

After the war Bach-Zelewski claimed that Himmler had summoned Arthur Nebe to meet him in Minsk. It is possible that Nebe was present, but Himmler's itinerary does not mention him, and Bach-Zelewski conveniently placed Nebe (and not himself) at the center of the action. The Reich Führer SS asked Nebe how many prisoners were scheduled for execution, and Nebe said about one hundred. Himmler asked for an execution the next morning, so he could gain his own impressions. Accompanied by Bach-Zelewski and (Himmler's) Chief of Staff Karl Wolff, Himmler watched a firing squad dispatch the prisoners, supposedly all partisans and their supporters. According to Bach-Zelewski, one-third to one half were Jews, and they included two women. Himmler blanched as Einsatzkommando 8 and part of Order Police Battalion 9 carried out the job, none too smoothly in the case of the women, who were only wounded at first. Bach-Zelewski took advantage of Himmler's discomfort to complain about the effect of such executions on the policemen, and Himmler gave a speech to them justifying the harshest measures against Jews and Slavs, the historical enemies of Germany; one did not have to hate them personally, but the need for self-preservation dictated the destruction of vermin. Besides, he was responsible to God and the Führer for what was done; their job was to follow orders unconditionally. This, at least, was Bach-Zelewski's 1946 version of what occurred, with some support from the much later court testimony of Otto Bradfisch, head of Einsatzkommando 8. Bradfisch also claimed that Himmler confirmed the policy of complete liquidation of Jews in the East.[39]

In separate testimony to American interrogators shortly after the war, Bach-Zelewski expounded on the difficulties of mass shootings. Stalin's minions could liquidate countless numbers by hand, but Central Europeans were more civilized—and incapable of that. Auschwitz, he said, was a German invention.[40] In testimony for another proceeding in 1958, he was even more specific. At that moment when Himmler recognized the difficulties of the executioners at Minsk, Bach-Zelewski stated, the gas chamber was born.[41]

He exaggerated somewhat. As early as December 1939 Himmler had planned to discuss the idea of producing a combined gas chamber–crematorium with the head of the SS economic operations.[42] The idea was around, but Himmler had not pushed forward with it. There were, after all, many ways to kill people in large numbers. The sequence of events suggests that Bach-Zelewski did provide an important impulse in mid-August 1941 for Himmler and the SS to shift toward the extermination camp equipped with gas chambers. (And he knew more about it than he revealed in 1946 or 1958.) In a letter to Karl Wolff, Bach-Zelewski stated that during his visit Himmler had authorized him to spend one hundred thousand marks for urgently needed provisions. Bach-Zelewski was eager to collect the money, and when it was not immediately paid, he and Wolff both cajoled the SS Economic-Administrative Office. One hundred thousand marks was a large sum; the request went to Oswald Pohl, head of the office.[43] Bach-Zelewski got the money, if with some delay. It remained to be seen how he would use it.

After the August 15 execution, Himmler's party inspected a prisoner-of-war camp and drove through the Minsk ghetto, which then contained more than eighty thousand Jews. Most would not survive the year. Himmler inspected an insane asylum, and Nebe allegedly received permission to try dynamite on its inhabitants as a test of another means of execution. The next day Himmler toured a museum in Minsk, flew over the Pripet Marsh region and Pinsk, then headed back to Hitler's East Prussian headquarters, where he had lunch with the Führer and presumably discussed what he had seen.[44]

For the next month Bach-Zelewski continued to send reports by radio of constant executions in the course of "pacification." Nazi pacification involved some real combat but also elimination of anyone who was actually a threat, or whom Nazi authorities considered a threat, to permanent German rule. The Waffen-SS brigades and the Einsatzkommandos carried out the largest portion of the early killing in White Ruthenia, but the Order Police battalions shot Jews, stranded Soviet soldiers, and guerrillas or civilians as well. Bach-Zelewski had by this time at least fifteen Order Police battalions (about seventy-five hundred men) at his disposal to complement the two SS brigades (about twelve thousand men).[45]

Higher SS and Police Leader Jeckeln was, if anything, even more active in pacifying the Ukraine, but his situation and strategy were somewhat different. With the largest geographical area to cover, he relied heavily on the nine full police battalions (and a portion of another one) at his disposal for mass executions, with the First SS Brigade used more for anti-partisan actions. Jeckeln claimed on August 23 that his forces had destroyed the better part of three partisan battalions and perhaps half of another nine partisan battalions. Some weapons were captured, including a few machine guns and a supply of grenades, but Jeckeln's forces suffered no casualties, which means that the partisans cannot have fought much, if they were actually partisans at all. Himmler's orders had targeted anyone suspected of being a partisan or of providing support to partisans.[46]

Jeckeln had a standard procedure for dealing with Jews that had little to do with military action against partisans. He gave oral orders to the commander of Police Regiment South to dispose of all Jews in a particular territory or locality; the regimental commander or his staff passed on the order orally to the battalion commanders, who in turn explained it personally to the company commanders. The troops got the information only the day or evening before the action, when different units received their assigned tasks. Some had to block off a village, others search houses, find and assemble Jews—often they got help from locals in identifying the Jews. Other police had to convey them to the execution sites, and still others serve as guards there. Then there were the executioners.[47]

Three Order Police battalions (45, 303, and 314) formed the major part of Police Regiment South. Police Battalion 45 liquidated 1,059 Jews at or near Slavuta on August 19–22. Police Battalion 314 participated in killing 367 Jews on August 23 and another 468 Jews the next day around Kowel. The German police suffered no losses.[48] The next day Police Regiment South shot 12 "bandits" and 70 Jews, while Battalions 45 and 314 within the regiment were separately credited with the murder of 61 and 294 Jews, respectively.[49]

August 25 was a very busy day for Police Regiment South, with 1,342 Jews killed in a "cleansing" action, while the First SS Brigade shot 85 prisoners and 283 Jews.[50] The regiment was hardly exhausted —another 549 Jews were killed on August 27, and the staff company attached to the Higher SS and Police Leader executed 546 Jews that day. Police Battalion 314 killed 69 Jews.[51] Later that day Police Regiment South shot another 914 Jews.[52]

An action against Hungarian Jews deported to the Ukraine dwarfed all previous killings in the South. Responding to initiatives from its

Central Alien Control Office, the Hungarian government, in late June, had decided to rid the country of many of the Jewish refugees who had flocked there since 1938. Alien Jews were rounded up, crammed into freight cars, transferred across the border into the Ukraine, and marched to Kamenets-Podolsk, along the Dnieper River. Unprepared German authorities feared that these Jews would threaten their lines of communication, but Hungarian authorities had no interest in taking them back. On August 25, various German civil and military officials met at Vinnitsa, in the Ukraine, to deal with issues surrounding the impending transfer of authority from the military to a civilian administration (scheduled for September 1). During that meeting, a representative of the civil administration announced that Jeckeln hoped to complete the liquidation of eleven thousand Hungarian Jews by September 1.[53]

Mass executions at Kamenets-Podolsk occurred over several days. The victims were forced to march into an area pocked with bomb craters and then to undress. A cross fire of machine guns brought them down; some were buried alive. Until recently, the best available information was that the executioners were units of the SS, Ukrainian auxiliaries, and a Hungarian sappers platoon.[54] At the beginning of the events, Jeckeln listed the participating units and described their tasks: his staff company did the shooting, and Police Battalion 320 cordoned off the area. A related transmission revealed that the same two forces shot another forty-two hundred Jews two days later. Then his staff company claimed eleven thousand Jews. Another transmission near the end of the action indicated that Police Battalion 320 itself killed another twenty-two hundred Jews at Minkowy, just northeast of Kamenets-Podolsk.[55]

After two days Jeckeln proudly reported that the grand total of Jews liquidated at Kamenets-Podolsk was about 20,000. The Einsatzgruppen report of September 11, couriered back to Berlin, contained updated information—the overall total of 23,600, the fact that Jeckeln was in charge, and that "his commando unit" carried out the action—but less detail about the participants.[56]

The victims included fourteen thousand to sixteen thousand Hungarian Jews; the remainder were Ukrainian Jews rounded up from nearby towns and villages. About two thousand of the deported Hungarian Jews escaped and survived.[57] After initially withdrawing to quarters in nearby Proskurov, Police Battalion 320 sent patrols back to Kamenets-Podolsk to look for those who escaped and to deal with plundering by Ukrainians.[58] Through the end of August 1941, Kamenets-Podolsk represented the largest single Nazi liquidation of Jews. (It was soon eclipsed by Babi Yar, outside Kiev, at the end of September.) It was not the work of the notorious Einsatzgruppen but the product of Jeckeln's leadership and the efforts of his staff company and Order Policemen.

On September 4, Daluege flew to visit Jeckeln at his headquarters in Berditschev. In the district of Zhitomir, Berditschev had thirty thousand Jews out of a total population of some sixty-six thousand. The Jewish community traced its origins back to the sixteenth century, and it was known as a center of Jewish scholarship. Just over a week earlier, the occupying force established a Jewish ghetto in the poor section of the city. On the day of Daluege's arrival and probably in his honor, Jeckeln ordered the execution of 1,303 young Jews, among them 875 girls over the age of twelve. His own staff company had the privilege of complying.[59] The mass killings occurred in the village of Khazhin, about five miles south of where prisoners of war had prepared two large pits alongside a rail line.[60]

Although Jeckeln's staff company carried out the largest portion of the September 4 killings in Berditschev, decades after the war one of the former members of Police Battalion 45 described its work on that occasion, and a contemporary source reveals that Police Battalion 45 was in fact in Berditschev.[61] The police led some hundreds of Jews one after another to an entrance to the pit, which was deep enough that they disappeared from the sight of the police guards perhaps twenty meters away. The executioners shot down directly into the pit. Afterward, others shoveled dirt atop the corpses.[62]

Police Battalion 45 was a composite battalion, containing some young policemen and some reserve (older) police remobilized during the war. It included Germans from different locations, with a large component of Sudeten-Germans, ethnic Germans who had lived in the former Czechoslovakia. It was apparently not a unit with a great deal of prior cohesiveness. Quite a number of its survivors after the war denied ever having been members of the Nazi Party.[63] No doubt, there were some Nazi true believers among them, but it would be hard to see this group as one of political fanatics.

Even the limited information available about Order Police battalion *commanders* suggests that career policemen were tardy in entering the elite SS. Robert Franz, commander of Police Battalion 303, joined in August 1939, just before the start of the war.[64] At the end of 1941, 70 percent of the active officers of the Order Police and 93 percent of its reserve officers were *not* members of the SS.[65] If a commander or an officer was not closely associated with key Nazi institutions, how much more true this must have been of ordinary policemen. Yet they managed to carry out mass murder repeatedly anyway.

At the same time, there were limits to the Order Police battalions. The Einsatzgruppen and Waffen-SS brigades did most of the early killing in the central region, and Jeckeln relied heavily on his own staff company in the South. The Order Police battalions carried out plenty of executions, but fewer than their share of the manpower would suggest. When Einsatzkommandos and Order Police units were both on the scene, the former usually dominated. At the infamous Babi Yar massacre at the end of September 1941, Sonderkommando 4a executed 33,871 Jews, while policemen from Order Police Battalion 45 cordoned off the restricted areas.[66]

Here and there a particular Order Police battalion or a particular company of a battalion proved eager and adept at mass murder. Police Lieutenant Gerhard Riebel, who commanded the third company of Police Battalion 322 (also called the ninth company, Police Regiment Center), later received an absolutely glowing performance evaluation that described him as an enthusiastic Nazi who knew how to communicate his ideas to his men. The evaluation did not go into detail about his unspecified activities during the period beginning October 1, 1941, for which he received the Iron Cross, Second Class.[67] But Riebel's report of one big action survives, as does the company's war diary.

On October 2, the ninth company, the staff of Higher SS and Police Leader Bach-Zelewski, and a force of twenty-three Ukrainian auxiliary policemen moved into the newly established ghetto in Mogilev and seized 2,208 Jews. Riebel wrote that some of the Jews were cowardly enough to try to hide, and the difficulties of dragging them out of their filthy places resulted in company nine's shooting sixty-five of them in the ghetto. The others were loaded onto trucks and driven to a holding site for prisoners. The roundup took about five hours. The next morning they were executed, with company nine itself accounting for 555 shootings. Company nine continued to be active thereafter, shooting alleged partisans, Communists, and Jews in villages around Mogilev.[68]

Not everyone was so eager. Contemporary sources also suggest some concerns about the police executions. Himmler's and Daluege's recurring visits to execution sites—a task Himmler in particular did not enjoy—indicate that *they* at least wondered about the ability of ordinary German police to serve repeatedly as killers. There were also problems of secrecy. On August 30, Heydrich had to warn the Einsatzgruppen not to allow spectators—even soldiers—at the execution sites.[69]

The extermination camps were to offer greater seclusion and less chance of flight by the victims. Nazi officials could prevent outsiders from penetrating anywhere near the gas chambers and could disguise the assembly-line killing process to deceive the victims until the last possible moment. Although mass shootings continued throughout the war, and although even the extermination camps could not preserve the terrible secret of the Holocaust, the new camps did offer enough advantages to become the preferred method of killing by 1942.

Nazi fixation with the secrecy of the early Final Solution emerged in discussions of record-keeping and communication policies. On August 15, 1941, Heydrich sent a coded radio message to the Einsatzgruppen warning them against letting unauthorized persons or the enemy see their operational orders and instructions. If there was any chance of lapses of security, they had to return written orders or burn them completely.[70] In September 1941, Himmler's communications chief Ernst Sachs worked out signals guidelines that Daluege, Heydrich, and other high SS officials ratified. Undoubtedly drawing on what Sachs had written, on September 13 Daluege warned the Higher SS and Police Leaders that field units could send by radio ordinary messages, confidential messages, and anything classified as secret. They could, however, not send anything top secret (*Geheime Reichssache*), such as the data on executions. That information had to go by courier only.[71]

This order on signals secrecy itself went out by radio and was passed along to the Order Police regiments and battalions, which generally followed it. In subsequent execution reports sent by courier, Bach-Zelewski even referred specifically to Daluege's instruction no. 31 of September 13, 1941.[72] After the war, he gave a misleading account of the secrecy order, saying that early in the Soviet campaign Himmler had issued a fundamental order not to use the word "Jew" in radio traffic at all.[73] Bach-Zelewski was more discreet in his radio messages than Jeckeln, but if Himmler gave such an order, it was not generally observed until mid-September and not completely followed even thereafter.

Heydrich's radio messages to the Einsatzgruppen and their radio reports back used the sophisticated Enigma codes and remained secret. With a looser organization, Daluege's people used the outmoded hand ciphers. As a result, by mid-September 1941, it was already too late to shield the fact of massive police executions of Jews—or to hide the order cutting off radio reports of execution totals—from British ears.

# 5

＊

# TRANSITIONS AND
# TRANSPORTS

ON SEPTEMBER 3, 1941, Reinhard Heydrich issued an order to his Security Police and SD to avoid measures that might damage the solidarity (*einheitliche Stimmung*) of the German people. The reason was that the Führer had repeatedly indicated that all enemies of the Reich would exploit every opportunity to sow dissension—just as they had during World War I.[1] Hitler was still concerned about German public opinion; it might affect Germany's ability to fight. These considerations had some bearing on the methods the Nazis were to use against German Jews.

Through increasingly stringent laws, massive propaganda, and intimidation, the Nazi regime had done everything—short of establishing ghettos in Germany—to separate Jews from what it considered true Germans. Still, in spite of the official line, some Jews retained spouses, friends, relatives, and acquaintances among the Germans. Liquidation of German Jews, therefore, posed some political problems. It was one thing for the SS and police to kill hundreds of thousands of East European Jews on site in the East—in inaccessible places, with police cordons preventing spectators from attending.[2] It was quite another thing to murder Jews in Germany or Western European countries, where the geographical possibilities of isolation were limited and the likelihood of information leaks—and potential damage from them—far greater.

The understanding that the German people might not stand behind outright murder in their midst gradually emerged from what the Nazi leaders called their "euthanasia" program secretly conducted in six major gassing centers in Germany between the end of 1939 and August

1941. The actual targets of euthanasia were not Germans who were incurably ill and suffering horribly but a wide range of children and adults deemed physically or mentally defective for genetic reasons. (Most of them today would be called physically or mentally disabled.) The officials in Hitler's personal chancellery who ran the program did their utmost to camouflage the killing operations, and the regime also engaged in a major propaganda campaign to promote the notion that subnormal individuals were an intolerable burden on society. Problems quickly developed, however. The false causes of death reported raised some suspicions, the residents in the vicinity of the gassing centers began to realize what was going on nearby, and other leaks occurred as well. Adverse public reaction and even signs of open protest induced Hitler to shut down the gassing centers in late August; the euthanasia killings continued in a more decentralized—and even less noticeable—fashion. Still, the experience did not generate confidence about the secrecy of killing on a large scale within Germany.[3] In fact, Heydrich's order of September 3 may have reflected concern about the political damage from euthanasia.

German Jews could not stay in place much longer, however. One of Hitler's ideés fixes since 1919 was that Jews represented a seat of infection, that their presence had caused Germany to lose the war.[4] Hitler and other leading Nazis believed that Jews were carriers of disease. When Heydrich took steps to set up the concentration camp at Theresienstadt, not far from Prague, he declared that Jews who died there would on no account be buried—they might contaminate a nearby river. Their bodies would go to a crematorium.[5]

In a letter to Gauleiter Arthur Greiser of the Wartheland (formerly Polish East Prussia, annexed by Germany in 1939), Himmler stipulated that the Führer wanted Germany proper (*das Altreich*) and the protectorate of Bohemia-Moravia (what had been the Czech portion of Czechoslovakia) cleared of Jews as quickly as possible. A few weeks later, when time was even shorter, Heydrich revealed that Hitler wanted the job done by the end of the year.[6] There was little concern that removing Jews from Germany would impair the German public's support for the regime or the war, but it would not have mattered. Hitler considered removal urgent.

Nazi Party Gauleiter of Berlin Joseph Goebbels had tried for some time to rid the capital of the Jewish "menace." There were practical reasons in addition to ideological ones: the supply of Jewish apartments and residences was widely coveted. Other Nazi officials too had weighed in with specific suggestions. Heydrich and his subordinates had insisted on a more or less uniform policy and on their own jurisdiction.[7] Berlin might or might not be the first German city to become *judenfrei*, but it would not become an isolated solution. Himmler and Heydrich would incorporate deportations of Jews from Berlin into their over-arching plans for German and European Jews.[8]

But where to deport them? From October 1939 on, the former Poland was divided into three parts: several areas in western Poland annexed directly by Germany; a large central portion, called the General Government of Poland, headed by Hitler's onetime lawyer Hans Frank and with its own administration; and the eastern portion occupied and ruled by the Soviet Union (according to the August 1939 treaty between Germany and the U.S.S.R.). None of these territories, it turned out, was immediately available to take Jews from the outside. German territory was out of bounds, the Soviets did not want German Jews, and Governor Frank had different plans for his realm.

In 1940, deportations of Jews from Stettin and Schneidemühl into Poland had set off a bitter fight with Frank and his civil administration. Frank was able to enlist Hermann Göring and to send out (by radio) a blunt warning from him:

> The General Governor has complained about the continuation of de-portations of Jews from the [annexed areas of the] Reich into the General Government despite the current lack of absorption capacity. I hereby forbid further such deportations without my approval and without the agreement of the General Governor. I will not accept excuses that sub-ordinate officials had undertaken such expulsions.[9]

This message was aimed directly at Himmler.

The Nazis had already established ghettos in numerous Polish cities, where disease and malnourishment—and occasional killings—took their toll on Polish Jews. They had begun to force Jews from the coun-tryside to join their urban brethren behind ghetto walls. From the spring of 1941 on, Frank was straining to get more than two million Jews removed from his territory, and not to take in more of them, and his civil administration had repeatedly contested the independent authority of the SS and police in Poland over Polish ghettos. The army was a factor in Poland as well. Himmler and Heydrich both complained to the Reich chancellery in September and October 1941 that the Führer had given various officials in the General Government independent authority that overlapped the functions of the police and interfered with them.[10]

In any case, on September 2, Himmler discussed deportations of Jews from Germany with Friedrich-Wilhelm Krüger, Higher SS and Police Leader for the General Government.[11] If Krüger and his very aggressive and ambitious subordinate in Lublin, SS and Police Leader Odilo Globocnik, could clear away the obstacles, perhaps some German Jews could be deported to the Lublin region or the Warsaw ghetto. Himmler freed a number of euthanasia gassing specialists of their previous responsibilities and transferred them to Globocnik at this time.[12] But the General Government would work as the main site for mass extermination facilities only if and when Himmler could be confident that the SS and police could control the entire process.

Another option for receiving German Jews was the existing ghetto at Lodz, in the Wartheland, which was not in the General Government. But Lodz was already crowded. Initially, Himmler wanted to send sixty thousand Jews there temporarily, promising that they would later be pushed farther east. Various difficulties emerged, so that between October 16 and November 4 only about twenty thousand German, Austrian, and Luxembourgian Jews and five thousand Gypsies were transported and squeezed into Lodz, over the protest of the district governor. Himmler had the man sent on vacation. Lodz, however, could only be a small part of the solution.[13]

Auschwitz was in the midst of a major expansion. The first experimental gassings there were conducted in early September 1941, but the gas chambers constructed at nearby Birkenau did not begin functioning until the spring of 1942. Auschwitz was eventually to become the central killing site for Jews deported from all across the continent, but in September 1941 Birkenau could not easily liquidate masses of German Jews. To hold German Jews at or near Auschwitz did not make sense either, for that too was now German soil (in the annexed portion of Upper Silesia).

There are indications that Heydrich had previously thought of the Soviet Union as the preferred site to conduct liquidations of Jews from elsewhere.[14] He and his subordinates—Heinrich Müller of the Gestapo and Adolf Eichmann of its Jewish section—had primary responsibility for getting Jews out of Germany and to somewhere else. The lack of immediate alternatives made the Soviet territories the best bet. They had plenty of room, and greater secrecy was possible there. SS and police authorities had already surmounted at least the initial obstacles to mass liquidations and had demonstrated their effectiveness.

The extraction and deportation of Jews involved legal and financial matters that required the support of various government agencies.[15] Could they be brought to cooperate? Himmler wanted complete control of the Jews—and for this he had to have leverage over a number of unwieldy bureaucracies in Germany.[16] Shipping Jews by train from Germany or elsewhere into the Baltic area or Byelorussia required the assistance of the Transportation Ministry. Getting trains in the midst of war involved a substantial effort, and the army might object, but these were not insurmountable obstacles—not when Himmler and Heydrich threw their weight around. At most, train shortages would only slow down the deportations.

It was appropriate, Heydrich declared at an October 10 meeting in Prague, to send Jews farther east into the operational (military) area, where they could go into camps for Russian prisoners of war. Referring specifically to Arthur Nebe and Otto Rasch, heads of Einsatzgruppen B and C, he showed that he wanted his own subordinates, who had already executed more than one hundred thousand Jews, to handle the German Jews as well.[17] With that comment, Heydrich also made the fate of the deportees transparent.

But Heydrich's promotion in late September to Reich Protector of Bohemia-Moravia—a capacity in which he was directly subordinate to Hitler—and his aggressive pursuit of Jewish policy stirred up old and new animosities between him and Daluege.[18] One way for Daluege— and Himmler—to avoid overdependence on Heydrich and his organizations was to make use of the Higher SS and Police Leaders in the East to receive the transports of German Jews. Himmler tended to discuss with Daluege, not Heydrich, the appointments of Higher SS and Police Leader Korsemann and of SS and police leaders in Minsk (Carl Zenner), Lublin (Globocnik), and Galicia (Fritz Katzmann).[19] And of course, Daluege's links with Jeckeln, Bach-Zelewski, Prützmann, and Korsemann had grown over the summer. Order Police battalions had become the main forces for them, and they relied on the Order Police communications network; also, the Order Police administration handled financial and personnel matters for them.[20] In practice, then, Daluege and the Higher SS and Police Leaders relied increasingly on each other. On one occasion, Daluege enlisted the support of Oswald Pohl, head of the SS Budget and Construction Office (and later of the SS

Economic-Administrative Main Office), to treat the Higher SS and Police Leaders as his subordinates, but Himmler refused to ratify the agreement.[21]

The Higher SS and Police Leaders, directly subordinate to Himmler, had control of a variety of reception sites in the East. As they had in Poland, German authorities established ghettos in some major cities and towns in the Baltic region and Byelorussia for the Jews not killed immediately. Military and civil authorities alike agreed with the SS and police to cordon off portions of cities and towns for this purpose, moving out the non-Jewish residents. Some of the larger ghettos were properly sealed with walls and barbed wire; others were more makeshift, relying primarily on guards. Jews, automatically considered a threat to security, could not be allowed free movement or unregulated contact with the rest of the population.

The two Higher SS and Police Leaders most efficient at disposing of Jews were Bach-Zelewski and Jeckeln. So it was probably not a coincidence that in mid-October Himmler ordered Jeckeln and Prützmann to swap positions. Jeckeln arrived in Riga on October 26; he did not have much time to prepare for new challenges there.[22]

On October 23, Adolf Eichmann chaired a meeting in Berlin regarding Hitler's order to "evacuate" fifty thousand Jews from Germany and the protectorate of Bohemia-Moravia to Minsk and Riga. Half-Jews, Jews with foreign citizenship, Jews doing skilled labor (and their relatives), and Jews over sixty years old were supposed to be exempt. All the directions Eichmann gave out about what the Jews might bring with them were a ruse to convince the deportees that they were being resettled in the East. Their passports and identity cards were to be stamped EVACUATED.[23] This was to be the first step in the deportation of all German Jews, except those still married to Germans and the half-Jews, whose fate was still up in the air. The Gestapo would load Jews onto the trains and have a representative accompany them in an advisory capacity. The municipal police (*Schutzpolizei*), one officer and fifteen policemen for each thousand Jews, would control security during the transports.[24] Heydrich's and Daluege's organizations each got a share, just as they each would have a share once the Jews arrived at their destinations.

On the day Eichmann announced the transports, Himmler flew off to visit Bach-Zelewski once again, this time at his headquarters in Mogilev. He toured the new forced-labor camp under Bach-Zelewski's control, where that day 279 Jews were executed. Four days earlier police had killed 3,726 Jews from the Mogilev ghetto, where fewer than 1,000 now remained alive. Max Montua complained during Himmler's two-day stay that the continuing massacres of Jews endangered the morale of his men and the other troops involved. According to Bach-Zelewski's adjutant, who was present, Himmler promised that other solutions would come soon.[25]

Himmler returned from Mogilev to his East Prussian headquarters on October 25 and met with Odilo Globocnik, SS and Police Leader in Lublin, who briefed him on recent, and apparently difficult, discussions with Governor Frank in Poland. That evening Himmler also discussed Poland with Higher SS and Police Leader Krüger.[26] He had already approved the construction of extermination camps in Globocnik's region,[27] but it was obvious that they would not be ready in time for the imminent expulsion of German Jews. Himmler decided to postpone his request to Hitler for a new decree giving Himmler superordinate powers over officials in the General Government. It, too, would take too long to push through.[28] He would wait until he was more confident of his leverage. Meanwhile, he had alternatives elsewhere.

Bach-Zelewski apparently had high hopes of making his region into a major killing center for German and European Jews and of improving the process of mass extermination. He had pressed Himmler in mid-August in Minsk about the psychological problems caused by mass shootings, with some effect. He also had got Himmler's approval for a large budget for urgently needed provisions. But he had to pry the money loose from the SS bureaucrats, which took time.[29]

In 1946, Bach-Zelewski falsely testified that a commission from Hamburg came to Mogilev in 1943 (!) with an order to build a gassing facility. He said that he demanded an order from Himmler before proceeding and that his insistence stymied the project. He said that he had no previous knowledge of gassings.[30] Himmler's 1941 appointment book, however, helps to correct some of the falsifications: the Higher SS and Police Leader for the North Sea region (in Germany), Rudolf Querner (who lived in Hamburg), accompanied Himmler to Mogilev in late October 1941 and met with Himmler at least once during his visit.[31] The discussion of gassing occurred in the fall of 1941, and German radio messages (intercepted by the British) offered some traces of it. Upon his return to Germany, Querner placed an order with the Hamburg corporation Tesch and Stabenow for a large supply of Zyklon—the commercial insecticide based on prussic acid already tested for its ability to kill humans at Auschwitz.[32] This order was not just for Bach-Zelewski, since Dr. Bruno Tesch, the head of the firm, went off to Riga to give directions to Jeckeln's medical officer on how to use the poison safely and effectively.[33] Jeckeln had just arrived in Riga, Prützmann was still there, having delayed his departure for the Ukraine, and Bach-Zelewski was on the way. It is clear at least that the three men met together around the beginning of November.[34]

Another order for Zyklon, this one to be sent to Riga, was placed on November 5. The shipment was delayed, however, for lack of suitable transport. Because of military needs, trains to the East were in very heavy demand. Jeckeln's office radioed Querner and suggested sending it by truck or express train to Königsberg; Jeckeln would have it flown from there to Riga. Meanwhile, Tesch wanted his mail forwarded to Jeckeln's office.[35] Tesch might well have taken pains to please. The order was for seven hundred kilograms of Zyklon, a substantial amount. At the time, Auschwitz had ordered only five hundred kilograms.[36] Some later shipments of Zyklon went directly to the SS hospital at Minsk, in Bach-Zelewski's region.[37]

Police radio messages implicated Higher SS and Police Leader Querner in the use of Zyklon in the East. After going with Himmler to Mogilev in late October, he served as intermediary for the Higher SS and Police Leaders in the East, relaying their orders of Zyklon to Tesch and Stabenow and coordinating other arrangements with the firm. But historians did not know of Querner's involvement with projected gas chambers in the East until the 1990s, and the evidence about shipments of Zyklon appears here for the first time.[38]

Partly because of limitations in the text of the radio messages (or in the decodes of them), there are uncertainties about just how far plans for the use of Zyklon went at this time. Zyklon had various concentrations, labeled A, B, C, D, E, and F, each suitable for different targets or situations. Zyklon D was the normal pesticide, Zyklon E was for specially resistant vermin or for gassings in wooden barracks, and Zyklon B had been used on humans at Auschwitz.[39] A radio message referred only to a shipment of Zyklon. But would Tesch himself have gone to Riga just to teach the Higher SS and Police Leaders how to fumigate properly? There is also independent evidence—a chemist named Herbert Kallmeyer was sent to Riga, for example—to suggest that the SS had plans to construct an extermination camp with stationary gas chambers there, which for various reasons did not come off.[40]

These visits were not the only instances of training SS personnel in the use of Zyklon. In mid-October, Himmler transferred SS-Sturmbannführer Franz Magill from the Second SS Cavalry Regiment to Bach-Zelewski's staff in Mogilev. For a time Magill had served as acting commander of the regiment while it was slaughtering Jews in the Pripet Marsh region of northern Ukraine. Although an experienced officer and a good organizer, Magill was judged too weak a leader and too prone to alcohol, making him unsuitable for permanent command.[41] But Bach-Zelewski was glad to take Magill onto his inner staff in November 1941 and use him for what Bach-Zelewski called the tasks of the Waffen-SS.[42] On December 15, Magill was sent to the Oranienburg concentration camp to receive instruction from Tesch and Stabenow personnel regarding the use of Zyklon.[43] (The only evidence of the posting comes from a radio message decrypted by the British.)

Bach-Zelewski may not have been able to afford top-of-the-line gas chambers. Himmler had given him only 100,000 marks, and the cost of the gas-chamber apparatus later built at Auschwitz-Birkenau was about 310,000 marks.[44] There was the option of converting an existing building into an improvised gas chamber (using Zyklon B), and there were gas vans—specially converted vehicles that recycled the exhaust forward into a large, sealed freight compartment, so that the passengers died of carbon-monoxide poisoning. Their use in the East had been under consideration since early October, but these vans had limited capacity and other disadvantages.[45]

In mid-November, the SS Main Office for Budget and Building in Berlin placed an order with the Topf Company of Erfurt to build a huge crematorium—an oven with four cremation chambers—in Mogilev. The cost was billed to Bach-Zelewski's building administration.[46] On November 28, Bach-Zelewski's staff radioed an urgent request to this SS administrative office in Berlin asking that ten technicians and architects be sent immediately for great tasks (grosse Aufgaben) that Bach-Zelewski had assigned them. The crematorium, shipped in segments, arrived on December 30, 1941.[47]

Decades later, one writer would argue implausibly that this crematorium was built to dispose of the bodies of German soldiers and Soviet prisoners of war who died of typhoid fever.[48] The number of Germans ill with typhoid fever did not exceed three hundred per month. The number of Soviet prisoners of war who caught it was larger, nearing five thousand in December 1941. Most Soviet prisoners of war who died in German hands in 1941 or early 1942, however, starved or froze because of German indifference to their survival. The capacity of the crematorium was to be three thousand corpses *per day*.[49] Clearly it was intended to deal with the large number of dead bodies automatically considered a source of infection, and Soviet Jews, as well as Jews from Germany and other parts of Europe, would supply them. But high SS officials would have approved of using typhoid fever as a cover story.

Of course, the shootings could continue for quite some time. If the existing killers were worse for wear, then bring in new ones. The reinforcements came in three varieties: individual policemen from Germany who were reassigned to rather different functions in the East; entirely new Order Police battalions; and non-German auxiliaries, in conjunction with stationary police outposts or, more commonly, Order Police battalions.

In the late summer and fall of 1941, a good number of Order Policemen were transferred individually to the East in a process that makes it difficult to trace or reconstruct any general patterns. Gendarmerie Lieutenant Max Eibner, for example, was sent to Minsk in early October and then to Baranowicze, as district chief of gendarmes. He testified later that the various towns and villages in the region had German outpost chiefs, a handful of German constables (some older police reservists) serving under them, and Byelorussian auxiliary police subordinated to them. By the end of 1942, the number of Order Policemen assigned to stationary duty either in the cities or in rural areas of the Soviet territories had reached almost fifteen thousand.[50]

Some of these Order Police performed functions critical to the Final Solution. After German authorities forced Riga's nearly thirty thousand Jews into a ghetto in late October, they used some sixty German municipal policemen to man the twenty-eight posts around the ghetto. The Security Police and SD (Heydrich's men) could enter the ghetto and do what they chose with its inhabitants, with occasional executions and miserable conditions the result, but the Order Police controlled the perimeter. Jeckeln had on his staff in Riga five officers from the German municipal police and thirty-six policemen.[51]

In August, Jeckeln's predecessor in the North, Prützmann, had corresponded with Himmler regarding use of Reserve Police Battalion 11 in his region. This battalion was first used to supervise and restrain the Lithuanian auxiliaries guarding the Kowno (Kaunas) ghetto, while Einsatzkommando 3 gradually extracted groups of Jews from the ghetto and, with Lithuanian assistance, liquidated them in several of the forts ringing the city. When more pressing matters arose for the Order Police battalion, Einsatzkommando 3 suggested bringing in more German municipal policemen for the ghetto guard.[52]

Reserve Police Battalion 11 soon graduated to more visible and active tasks. On October 3, most of it was ordered to assemble three days later in Kowno with the Second (later renamed Twelfth) Battalion of the Lithuanian auxiliary police (Schutzmannschaften). Major of the Municipal Police Franz Lechthaler, his staff, and two German companies —a total of 284 German policemen and 463 Lithuanians—appeared as required in the early-morning hours of October 6. Most of the German battalion was composed of activated members of the police reserve— men in their forties. They and the Lithuanians rode southeast into Byelorussia and arrived later that day in the former capital, where they made quarters in local army barracks. Their orders were to combat "partisans" in the Minsk-Slutsk-Borisov area for three to four weeks.[53]

The SS and police authorities wanted the territory around Minsk as "secure" as possible. Partisan activity in the thick wooded areas and swamps of Byelorussia was a more serious concern than in Lithuania. German army authorities agreed with the SS and police to work jointly against all actual and suspected enemies. Later, General Gustav von Bechtolsheim (Baron von Mauchenheim), military commandant of Byelorussia, would specify that the Security Police and SD were primarily responsible for actions against Jews; the army itself could carry out reprisals to ensure security, conduct executions if it had special units available, or turn Jews over to the SD.[54]

Bechtolsheim reported that on October 8 Reserve Police Battalion 11 and two Lithuanian police companies shot 9 Soviet partisans, a Red Army man, and 630 other "suspicious elements without identity cards, Communists, and Jews" in the area of Uzlany-Rudensk. The Lithuanians also participated in the killing of 800 partisans, Communists, Jews, and "suspicious rabble" during the next several days in Rudensk. The German battalion shot a total of 1,341 Communists, partisans, and Jews on October 13–14 in the villages of Kliniki and Smilovichi.[55]

In his weekly report Major Lechthaler stated that two Lithuanian companies had liquidated 625 Communists in Minsk on October 15– 16 and one Lithuanian company killed another 1,150 Communists on October 18. Meanwhile, Einsatzkommando 3 killed 3,050 Jews from the Minsk ghetto during late September and the first half of October, and the Order Police played a role in these actions too.[56] In addition, two German companies from Reserve Police Battalion 11 and two

Lithuanian companies moved into the town of Koydanov, southwest of Minsk, and on October 21 they liquidated 1,000 Jews and Communists there.[57] The Lithuanians carried a significant part of the burden of this kind of work.

They sometimes went too far. On October 27, Germans from Reserve Police Battalion 11 and the Lithuanian auxiliaries hauled thousands of Jews and some non-Jews from their apartments in the town of Slutsk in such a brutal and indiscriminate way that the German civil administrator complained. It was not just an action against the Jews anymore, he charged; it looked rather like a revolution.[58] But the killing actions continued.

On November 6, Major Lechthaler and his two German companies returned to Kowno according to the initial plan; the Lithuanian auxiliary battalion remained behind, and the SS and Police Leader and the commander of the Order Police for the region took charge of them.[59] That same day an SS lieutenant and his forces rounded up members of the Minsk Jewish Council, the Jewish ghetto police, and skilled workers, taking them to the concentration camp. The next morning the SS and police, accompanied by both Lithuanians and Byelorussians, marched into the ghetto and brutally herded men, women, and children into Jubilee Square. The elderly and feeble were shot on the spot. Other Jews were lined up, and the Lithuanians gave them red Soviet flags and banners celebrating the anniversary of the great Socialist October Revolution. Then they were taken to the storehouses of the former Sixth Soviet Secret Police (NKVD) Division, where large numbers of Jews were crammed in so tightly that those who fainted could not fall. After two or three days, those still alive were removed, taken to prepared pits, and executed. The Minsk Jewish Council learned that approximately 12,000 had died in this way, although a German document credits only 6,624 Jewish victims to Einsatzkommando 1b during November 7–11.[60] Other German and Lithuanian forces may have claimed additional victims. In any case, this action created plenty of room for incoming Jews.

The first transport of roughly one thousand German Jews (from Hamburg) arrived in Minsk on November 10, many of them under the illusion that they were being sent to colonize the East. According to one Einsatzgruppen report, they felt like pioneers.[61] SS and police officials kept the newcomers in a separate "special" ghetto. Other trains brought Jews from Düsseldorf, Bremen, Frankfurt am Main, and Berlin during the next week. A Jewish survivor of the Minsk ghetto later wrote that even after wild Latvian auxiliaries had thrown the arriving Jews out of the train cars and they had seen Russian Jews miserably incarcerated in the main ghetto nearby, they expected that they would be treated better.[62] They did not have a glimmer of what awaited them. To be sure, liquidations of Byelorussian Jews occurred first—there was another killing action on November 20.[63] Then the oncoming winter conditions—the ground was too hard to dig pits—helped most of the German Jews to last until mid-1942.[64]

Before leaving the Ukraine, Jeckeln placed temporary authority in the hands of Obersturmbannführer Herbert Degenhardt, appointing him as "ordinance officer" on his operational staff. Degenhardt had served with Jeckeln in France, and Jeckeln trusted his organizational ability and ruthlessness. In case Degenhardt had any difficulty getting others to cooperate, Jeckeln wrote out a carefully worded authorization, which he later described: Degenhardt had the task of carrying out necessary actions "according to the usages of war in keeping with instructions given to him orally." He would have the use of the guard platoon of Jeckeln's operational staff, and he would also work together with Police Regiment South. Degenhardt later termed his activity as combatting bands (partisans) and Jews in Berditschev, Krivoi Rog, Kiev, and Krementschug.[65]

Based on the sequence of events and on a note in Himmler's appointment book, it appears that, in a private meeting on November 4, Himmler notified Jeckeln of what share Riga would receive of the deportations of German Jews and the projected schedule of the transports there.[66] The existing population of the Riga ghetto would have to be liquidated before the transports arrived; Jeckeln could not wait for the construction of gas chambers. The scheduled date of arrival for the first transport was November 10, as one of Heydrich's subordinates had already told Reich Commissar Hinrich Lohse. Perhaps Himmler also warned Jeckeln about past difficulties with the civil authorities, for Lohse had stressed the economic disadvantages of simply liquidating Jews and Reich Minister for the Occupied Eastern Territories Alfred Rosenberg had also clung to outmoded solutions for the "Jewish problem."[67] A small concession to Lohse and Rosenberg, sparing some Jewish workers and forcing through rapid liquidation of the rest, might even capture some needed revenue.[68]

Jeckeln tried to prepare carefully. He needed a site that was easily reached, somewhat isolated, and, because the water table around Riga was high, elevated. Following his example or his orders, in late November some fourteen men from his staff drove to a small area screened by pine trees less than a quarter mile from the Rumbuli railway station, a local stop on the line from Riga to Daugavpils. On the other side was a highway connecting the two cities. The soil was sandy and soft. An architect among them received the order to prepare to excavate the pits. Soviet prisoners of war guarded by German soldiers followed the architect's directions, digging about five pits, ten meters long by ten meters wide and about three meters deep. A ramp at one end of each pit made it possible to march the victims in. The architect later testified that all the Germans present, including the army soldiers, knew that Jews would be shot and buried here; there was open discussion of it around the pits. The digging went on all day, and more pits were added during the next day or two. The total capacity was set for about twenty-eight thousand bodies.[69]

Jeckeln's preparations in and outside Riga did not proceed swiftly enough to accommodate the schedule of transports from Germany. The civil authorities also raised some obstacles. So five convoys of German Jews from Munich, Berlin, Frankfurt, Vienna, and Breslau were diverted from Riga to Kowno, where Einsatzkommando 3 and Lithuanian auxiliary police had of course already massacred tens of thousands of Lithuanian Jews in several of the forts surrounding the city. Between November 25 and 29, the Jews from the five transports were liquidated en masse in Fort 9.[70]

In Riga, on or around November 27 there was a meeting of SD and Order Police commanders at the Order Police headquarters. The Latvian auxiliary police were also represented. This meeting established the schedule for the ghetto operation of November 30 and parceled out roles for all the participating police organizations. On November 28, the SS and police authorities ordered the removal of as many as four thousand adult male Jews whom they considered capable of labor and sent them into a separate section of the ghetto, which they barricaded off. They also separated three hundred female Jewish workers and sent them to a prison. Some other groups were quickly added, so that the total number destined for the small ghetto may have reached five thousand. Most of the Jews from the ghetto, however, were ordered to assemble on November 30, allegedly for resettlement to a new camp, Salaspils, nearby. They were permitted to bring luggage with them, a ruse to sustain the notion of resettlement.[71]

A transport of about one thousand Jews from Berlin arrived in Riga on the evening of November 29. They were left overnight at the railway siding and marched to the pits in the early morning. They became the first victims at Rumbuli, but their liquidation was a mistake of sorts. This transport included a number of decorated World War I veterans, who according to prior SS decisions should have been sent to the special camp at Theresienstadt for prominent or decorated elderly Jews. When Himmler found out about their presence on the train, he tried to cancel the killing, calling on Heydrich to intervene; but the action had already taken place.[72] Himmler was furious at this breach of instructions and political insensitivity. On December 1, he sent out a radio message to Jeckeln: "The Jews resettled into the territory of the [Reich Commissariat] Ostland are to be dealt with only according to the guidelines given by me and the Reich Security Main Office acting in my behalf. I will punish unilateral acts and violations."[73]

The ghetto action of November 30 began at 4 a.m. Snow had fallen the previous evening and was still on the ground. About seventeen hundred Order Police, the SD, and Latvian auxiliaries—this last, the largest group—moved from block to block, house to house, waking up Jews and forcing them to assemble. Many Jews refused to go, and the first killings took place in their residences. Others went outside, but then tried to escape and hide. The authorities needed a substantial force to carry out the operations effectively. In the street Jewish men, women, and children had to remain standing under guard in columns of roughly one thousand each for hours. Then the march began, the first column at 6 a.m., other columns following periodically. Trucks carried the aged and infirm who could not march, but under the conditions hundreds of others could not keep up and were shot in the ghetto or along the way, staining the snow with blood. The Jews in the first column reached Rumbuli around 9 a.m. There they were forced to strip and enter the pits, where they were shot to death.[74]

Jeckeln had ordered his staff to participate in and oversee this mass execution, and he watched the proceedings for a time himself. There is some testimony that Reich Commissar Lohse and District Commissar Otto-Heinrich Drechsler, both of whom had previously raised objections to SS policy on the Jewish question, were also present for a time. Reserve Police Battalion 22 cordoned off the site and prevented efforts to escape. A gauntlet of German SD and Order Police and Latvian auxiliaries under the command of Viktor Arajs funneled the Jews to the pits, and a small execution squad, perhaps no more than twelve men, did the shooting with Russian automatic weapons set on single shots. Members of Jeckeln's staff, already proficient at shooting Jews from their experience in the Ukraine, did much of the killing, although after the war German policemen testified that the Latvians did the most. The death toll that day was about fourteen thousand; it was all the executioners could dispatch by nightfall during the short winter day. Afterward, the participants all got schnapps. Some Jews in the pits were only wounded, and a unit of Latvian auxiliaries was sent to guard the area and shoot any survivors who crawled out.[75] The execution of the remaining thirteen thousand Jews in the large ghetto was postponed until about a week later.

The strain on the executioners and other participants may have led to this postponement, which caused some logistical problems at the pits, but there is also evidence that orders came from above. Himmler sent a radio summons to Jeckeln to meet him in East Prussia. When Jeckeln asked about the agenda, he was informed that Himmler would tell him when he arrived and that Himmler wanted to know immediately when he was coming.[76] These were signs that Himmler did not want a written record of the subject and that it was urgent.

Too many people had witnessed the preparations or the slaughter itself on November 30. An eyewitness account reached the Interior Ministry, and another account came to Admiral Wilhelm Canaris, head of German military intelligence (the Abwehr). Canaris, by one account, went to Hitler to complain. Hitler is supposed to have replied: "You're getting too soft, sir! I *have* to do it, because after me no one else will!"[77] According to Jeckeln's postwar testimony, Himmler told him that shooting was too complicated an operation; it was better to use gas vans.[78] (There were as yet no such vans in Riga.) The gas chambers using Zyklon B were a big technological advance over the vans, but Jeckeln neglected to tell his KGB interrogators about the projected construction of such facilities in the East. In any case, there were no immediate alternatives; the killing of the remaining Jews in the Riga ghetto on December 8 more or less duplicated the procedures of November 30.[79]

One of the municipal police officers wrote a very detailed account of his mid-December convoy of 1,007 Jews from Duisburg, Krefeld, Düsseldorf, and other Rhineland sites to Riga. The planning was poor. The Jews had to assemble at 4 a.m. on December 11, but the train did not leave until 9 a.m. The Jews were overloaded in some cars. There were delays at many stops, and lack of heating, food, and water did not improve matters. At one station the manager was extremely uncooperative with a police officer who thought he was one of those Party

comrades accustomed to solicitude for "those poor Jews." Two and a
half days after the start, near midnight, the train arrived in Riga, where,
the policeman noted, Latvians particularly hated Jews. But the Latvian
railway personnel could not understand why Germans were sending
their Jews to Latvia instead of exterminating them in Germany.[80]

Minor protests continued in the Reich Commissariat Ostland (the
German administrative structure for the former Baltic States and much
of Byelorussia). The military commander there complained about the
damage to the war economy from the liquidation of Jewish laborers;
the civil authorities in Riga, meanwhile, could not even clear away
Jewish property from the ghetto before more transports of German Jews
were to arrive. The immediate outcome was that the SS and police
took charge of this Jewish property and used the temporary camp at
Jungfernhof for the arriving German Jews, although some later transports went into the ghetto.[81] Wilhelm Kube, General Commissar for
Byelorussia, wrote to his superior decrying the SD's failure to distinguish between the subhuman local Jews and the German Jews who
were "from our cultural circles." Kube asked skeptically if he should
entrust the slaughter to Latvians and Lithuanians.[82] It turned out that
he did not have much say about it. At a private meeting a month earlier,
Himmler had already, none too gently, made Reich Minister Rosenberg realize what the Führer wanted. With Rosenberg on board, subordinate civil authorities could get nowhere with objections, and Kube
later went along.[83]

The shooting itself remained a problem—among other reasons, because it bothered Himmler. In testimony years later a member of
Jeckeln's staff explained that sometime around the end of 1941 or early
1942 the Einsatzgruppen received an order from Heydrich to begin
using "disinfection [probably an allusion to Zyklon B] or gas vans" to
dispose of enemies. Each Einsatzgruppe was to receive four gas vans.
The staff man claimed to have seen Heydrich's order, which used as its
justification the fact that the shooters had suffered too many psychological problems, some turning to alcohol to obtain relief.[84] No copies
of this order have survived, but Heydrich would have been the proper
authority to take care of the needs of the Einsatzgruppen.

In any case, Himmler reinforced his previous expressions of concern
about the handling of mass shootings. On December 12, he composed
a secret SS order addressed to all Higher SS and Police Leaders and
their subordinates, as well as to SS offices in conquered territories in
the East. He stressed that commanders and superior officers had a "holy

duty" (*heilige Pflicht*) to ensure that their men did not suffer damage to their character or spirit from carrying out just death sentences on enemies of the German people. A combination of strict discipline during the event and camaraderie at evening gatherings following the executions would help. Under no circumstances should the commanders allow misuse of alcohol at these sessions. (Himmler was aware of the problems here.) Some music, speeches, and the pleasant atmosphere of German spirit and feeling should occupy the men's minds during these hours.[85]

This order, dated December 12, did not reach Higher SS and Police Leader Jeckeln's office until January 8, 1942, despite regular courier service, which suggests that Himmler delayed sending it out. The section about social gatherings in the evening was well within his purview—he had provided all this advice before orally. But the first paragraph contained fairly blunt language about eliminating every shred of opposition without mercy and administering death sentences in the sharpest form to enemies of the German people behind the front. Perhaps it was best to check with the highest authority first.

On December 18, Himmler met privately with Adolf Hitler, and the first item on the agenda was the Jewish question. The issue was apparently not what to do about the Jews: more than four hundred thousand had already been killed; additional deportations from Germany were in progress; and the first deportations from occupied France had already been announced. The Final Solution was well under way. Nor was the main question how to kill Jews in the future. The extermination camp at Chelmno had begun operations a week and a half earlier, and other extermination camps were by then under construction. The addition of new technology was at hand. The gas vans would relieve some pressure on the SS and police in the interim, and the non-German auxiliaries could handle much of the heavy work, too. The real point was how to present the extermination of the Jews to, among others, the German policemen who would continue to do some of the killing. Himmler and his subordinates also had to say something to more and more German officials, whose cooperation was needed. (Some of the highest government officials would meet soon—on January 20, 1942 —in the Berlin suburb of Wannsee to hear Heydrich explain the Final Solution of the Jewish question.) Finally, there was the problem of leaks of information to the outside.

Himmler summarized Hitler's comment as "Exterminate Jews as partisans."[86] Any Jew was automatically suspected to be a partisan or a source of support for partisan activity. It was as close as Hitler ever came to a written endorsement of a policy he had long approved in substance. There was no danger that the enemy would intercept an order in this form, but one enemy was able to conclude roughly what the policy was anyway.

# 6

✳

# BRITISH RESTRAINT

GREAT BRITAIN SUCCEEDED in code breaking during World War II where Germany generally failed. Hitler's arrogant assumption of German racial and military superiority translated into an insufficient appreciation for the value of intelligence and counterintelligence and an underestimation of the enemy.[1] From the beginning, however, the hard-pressed British placed the utmost emphasis on discerning Nazi Germany's intentions, movements, and use of resources. Desperate defenders needed quick wits and quick responses.

Some of what the British code breakers extracted from German radio messages went to the highest level of the British government. Winston Churchill had a long-standing tie with decoding operations and an appreciation for the potential benefits. As First Lord of the Admiralty in 1914, he had ordered a naval officer to study German messages "with a view to finding out the general scheme of the enemy, and tracing how far the reports of the telegrams have in the past been verified as recorded facts." After cryptographers and analysts demonstrated that decodes of messages sent by wireless telegraphy could provide valuable intelligence in time to make use of it, Churchill himself wrote the rules and procedures for processing and distributing decodes.[2]

British code-breaking successes against Turkey and Germany followed. The results with Germany were the most spectacular—British disclosure of a German telegram to Mexico (known as the Zimmermann telegram) helped to persuade the United States to enter the war.[3] The Turkish theater was also an area of major interest, even though good intelligence did not necessarily lead to good results. By one ac-

count, Churchill disregarded intercepts indicating how Britain might
have bribed Turkey to break with Germany and allow the Royal Navy
through the Dardanelles. He soon paid a huge penalty, when the Ot-
tomans humiliated an Allied force at Gallipoli, a disaster for which he
himself was held responsible. In 1922, however, British decodes of
Turkish diplomatic messages enabled Churchill, Lord Curzon, and
Prime Minister David Lloyd George to block impending Turkish aggression at Smyrna.[4]

During the period between the wars, Britain also penetrated the
codes of Italy, the Soviet Union, Japan, Spain, Portugal, and the United
States. In 1937, British experts managed to decipher some German air
force and police transmissions for the first time, setting the stage for the
much larger code-breaking operation at Bletchley Park, near Woburn,
during World War II, which came about partly through an outside
breakthrough. In 1939, Poland's secret service duplicated Germany's
sophisticated coding machine Enigma. A great deal of skillful work by
Polish cryptanalysts, a visit to Warsaw by top British intelligence officials, and the transfer of one Enigma to Britain supplied the intellects
gathered at Bletchley Park with a major head start in decoding operations.[5]

Shortly after Churchill became Prime Minister on May 10, 1940, he
requested and began to receive regular decrypts of German radio messages, along with intelligence interpretations. It was perfect timing, for,
as the historian Christopher Andrew has written, Churchill had more
faith in, and fascination with, secret intelligence than any of his predecessors. The original code name for the decrypts was "Boniface," and
Churchill sometimes continued to refer to "Boniface" documents,
which he kept in a locked buff-colored box, even after the name
changed. But he also called them the "Most Secret Sources."[6] The
name that stuck was Ultra, but "Ultra" technically meant the decrypts
of the sophisticated codes produced by the German Enigma machines.

The British began to read German Order Police messages on a regular basis in September 1939, and by the time Churchill came into
office, decoding Order Police hand-based codes was already well advanced. According to a brief history of the German Police Section at
Bletchley Park, Brigadier John Tiltman made the first substantial break
in the coding system, although the French and Poles also made progress.
The coding system, called Double Transposition, was relatively simple,[7]
and the Germans regularly placed the address at the start of a message
and the signature at the end. Once the British and French established

who was located where, the breaking of each day's code was not difficult, provided there was enough intercepted text to work on.[8]

Radio sets in France could pick up many more signals than those in
Britain, so in February 1940 the British sent a mission to work with a
French team under the auspices of the Deuxième Bureau (the French
secret intelligence service), in the village of La Ferté-sous-Jouarre.
There was some tension between the two allies about this work, but it
was managed in part by an agreement that the French would decipher
on even days of the month, and the British on odd days. If one side
failed on a given day, the other side took a shot. The system worked
well; failures were uncommon.[9]

It soon became clear that these police signals would not yield much
information of tactical military value but that they did detail what was
going on within Germany and German-occupied territories. If nothing
else, they might reveal when Germany was experiencing difficulties that
the Allies could then exploit. The Order Police also had many men,
and how the Germans used manpower was an important issue. Finally,
the police decodes furnished much factual information that could be
used for cryptographic and analytical work with other, more sophisticated codes.[10]

The cryptanalysts in France were so absorbed in their work that the
German invasion of the country in May 1940 caught them by surprise.
Cryptographic work suffered during the ensuing weeks and the June
1940 evacuation of the cryptanalysts from Bordeaux to Britain.[11] Some
of the transcripts of German messages from this early period were lost
in the process.[12] At the beginning of August 1940, the section of British
intelligence working on the German police was reestablished in the
main building at Bletchley Park. Although the Germans had learned to
complicate their codes—among other ways, by placing the addresses in
the middle of the text rather than at the beginning—the British cryptanalysts by then had accumulated enough experience and feel for the
traffic that they still had little trouble. During the last five months of
1940, more than 10,600 individual messages were intercepted, and the
analysts broke the codes on all but twenty-six days.[13]

Well before the German invasion of the Soviet Union, then, the
British police cryptanalysts in France and at Bletchley Park picked up
an array of information about the German occupation of Poland and
about the deployment of manpower and resources generally. The first
analyst was a man named Lucas, who took pains to master the material
and summarize the salient points. He was succeeded by a Captain

Crankshaw in MI 8, whose work ran into criticism, and the job passed
to others. It soon became clear that the cryptanalysts themselves had a
feel for the substance of the messages on which they had spent so much
time, so they wrote up brief summaries. Any intelligence analyst who
needed more details could get the full text of the decodes. The translated excerpts and prepared summaries included mentions of transfers
of Poles and Jews into Germany's newly established General Government of Poland, a requirement for executions to be reported to the
appropriate Higher SS and Police Leader, and German exchanges of
population with their (then) Soviet allies. The analysts noted some signs
of friction between the army and the SS and police but cautioned
against exaggerating their significance.[14]

British analysts also perceived that deportations of Jews into the Lublin region created congestion that interfered with the repatriation of
Volhynian Germans from the Soviet Union, a relationship historians
would discover decades later.[15] Such difficulties, accompanied by clashes
between the SS and police and the German civil authorities in the
General Government of Poland, contributed first to new timetables for
the resettlement of Jews and then to new plans entirely.[16]

By March 1940, British analysts had gathered a good appreciation of
the involvement of the German Order Police battalions (which they
sometimes mistakenly called the *Verfügungspolizei*) in helping to exert
control over conquered peoples and to regulate the mass movements
of people in the East, immigration of German Balts, and displacement
of Poles and Jews.[17] This assessment overestimated the Order Police's
jurisdiction in some respects, because the British analysts had no cor
responding decodes of Security Police messages. Nonetheless, they
knew more about the range of Order Police functions in the East at
the time than historians would for decades.

The German invasion of the Soviet Union introduced changes into
the Order Police transmissions and the British monitoring of them. The
Order Police adopted a separate key (set of codes) and a new frequency
for use on the Eastern front, which meant that the British code breakers
had double the work. They were aided by their prior knowledge of
Nazi officials, addresses, and titles; as long as these were included in the
communications, the British had a good head start on breaking each
new code. But they succeeded only when they had intercepted enough
coded messages on a given day. At first, they "broke" less than half the
time; for a period during August 1941 (when the Germans used two
keys per day for Russian-area signals), the percentage of decodes de-

clined to twenty-five.[18] But even the minority of messages deciphered contained valuable information, including some of military significance.

From their previous work British military intelligence analysts knew that Nazi officials tended to use euphemisms and a terminology of camouflage for extreme measures. They recognized almost instantly what it meant when, on July 14, 1941, Nazi officials tried to find film equipment to help the police troops prepare for their "special duties." Likewise, they recognized that, for police units, "pacification" of an area involved execution of enemies.[19]

To be sure, they grasped only a fraction of the Nazis' activities and policies in the East. But their decodes from the summer and fall of 1941 did include dozens of open reports of mass killings directed by the Higher SS and Police Leaders and carried out by the Order Police and Waffen-SS.[20] With Bach-Zelewski boasting on August 7 that the total number of executions carried out in his region exceeded thirty thousand,[21] it was hardly possible, even without totaling all the body counts, to miss the scale of the massacres. The British analysts commented:

> The tone of this message suggests that word has gone out that a definite decrease in the total population of Russia [sic] would be welcome in high quarters and that the leaders [i.e., the Higher SS and Police Leaders] of the three sectors stand somewhat in competition with each other as to their "scores."[22]

This deduction about the Nazis' seeking to reduce the non-German population stands up well to historical scrutiny.

The historian F. H. Hinsley has indicated that Britain's Secret Intelligence Service (SIS) chief "C" or Sir Graham Stewart Menzies sent weekly English-language summaries of police activities in the Soviet territories to Prime Minister Churchill. (The summaries recently made available in the Public Record Office are at monthly intervals or longer, not weekly.) Since the declassification in 1993 of some intelligence files of the Prime Minister's office, historians have also known that selected items from the German police decodes were included in Churchill's daily written intelligence briefings.[23]

There is some evidence of Churchill's early reactions, although it leaves a number of key questions unanswered. On August 24, 1941, the Prime Minister broadcast a speech about the massive conflict in the East, stressing that the Soviets were fighting magnificently and taking a heavy toll of German soldiers:

The aggressor is surprised, startled, staggered. For the first time in his experience mass murder has become unprofitable. He retaliates by the most frightful cruelties. As his armies advance, whole districts are being exterminated. Scores of thousands—literally scores of thousands—of executions in cold blood are being perpetrated by the German police-troops upon the Russian patriots who defend their native soil. Since the Mongol invasions of Europe in the sixteenth century [sic], there has never been methodical, merciless butchery on such a scale, or approaching such a scale.

And this is but the beginning. Famine and pestilence have yet to follow in the bloody ruts of Hitler's tanks . . . We are in the presence of a crime without a name.

This segment of Churchill's speech contained forceful rhetoric and strong emotion, and it is easy to force today's perspectives on his wording. In his volume on the early part of the war, Churchill's official biographer, Martin Gilbert, quoted these lines without commentary. Elsewhere, however, he suggested that this portion of the speech was a direct if restrained (because of secrecy considerations) reaction to the first phase of the Holocaust, during which "special SS killing squads" murdered as many as a million Jews.[24] The accepted figure for the first wave of killings of Jews is actually roughly half a million,[25] and more than just the SS were involved. Beyond that, Churchill's "crime without a name" was not the Holocaust.

The text of Churchill's speech indicates that he did not yet focus on the Jewish dimension. First, Churchill linked Nazi "atrocities" to stiff Soviet resistance and to the military campaign generally. He connected the killings of scores of thousands of "Russian patriots" to the Nazis' frustration because of heavy German military casualties (for the first time). This explanation of mass murder as the result of frustration might have had some surface plausibility in 1941, but we know today a great deal more about the advance Nazi planning and directives for the murder campaign. Churchill was wrong, even if he had a good (political) motive for emphasizing the strength of Soviet resistance. Second, he denounced the extermination of whole districts, which was at that time at least a rhetorical exaggeration. He said nothing about Jews whatsoever.

Some have argued that Churchill could not have denounced Nazi killings of Jews without betraying the secret of Britain's code-breaking successes.[26] But Nazi hostility toward Jews was known throughout the world. And his speech did include a specific reference to German police troops, which revealed precise knowledge based on an excellent source. Churchill certainly did want to preserve the secrecy of Britain's code-breaking successes, but he would have given away less by denouncing the mass killings of Jews than by identifying the German forces involved in the murder campaign. Why did he specify the perpetrators but fail to identify the prime victims?

One reason is that, as of August 24, he did not have enough clear information from the police decodes about the Nazi focus on killing Jews in the Soviet territories. Early reports of executions came largely through messages from Higher SS and Police Leader Bach-Zelewski,[27] whose practice of qualifying or disguising the targets of the shootings as Jewish plunderers, Bolsheviks, or partisans, perhaps in accordance with Himmler's instructions,[28] undoubtedly caused confusion or un-certainty for those in Britain trying to decipher the events, not the texts. The detailed intelligence summary and analysis of police decodes issued on August 21—three days before Churchill's speech—mentioned but did not stress the executions of Jews; it placed these in the broader context of Nazi measures to reduce the Soviet population generally. Isolated items from Jeckeln's communications, identifying Jews as the victims of mass executions, reached Churchill *after* August 24.[29]

Perhaps with his speech of August 24, Churchill wanted to send a message to Nazi leaders and followers that their crimes were not un-detected. He certainly wanted to call attention to Soviet suffering and resistance as well as to solidify convictions at home and abroad about the righteousness of the war against Nazism. An emotional and impul-sive man, he was very likely angered and horrified by what he had read. He wanted to do something, but he could hardly react to what he did not have enough information to grasp.

New reports of executions flowed in immediately following his speech. On August 28, Churchill learned that Police Battalion 314 had shot 367 Jews; he circled the total. Two days later he read that Battal-ions 45 and 314 shot a total of 355 Jews, and the Police Squadron another 113. On August 31, the First SS Brigade killed 283 Jews, and Police Regiment South was credited with 1,342. Churchill again circled the latter figure. Part of the even larger Kamenets-Podolsk action and some of the Berditschev killings of Jews were reported to him as well.[30] So he may have and should have recognized the direction of the reports, with increasing numbers and percentages of Jewish victims, but only after August 24.

British intelligence had other sources of early information about killings in the Soviet territories. Paul Thümmel, an official of the Abwehr who was secretly working with the Czechoslovakian government-in-exile in London, told the Czech resistance in late July 1941 that German forces in the Ukraine were resolving the Jewish question in a radical way. They arrived at a locality, separated the male Jews, had them dig trenches supposedly to be used as fortifications, and then shot them into the trenches. Thümmel's source was the chauffeur of the head of the Gestapo in Prague, and his information reached the British through the Czech government-in-exile in London.[31]

Thümmel, whose code designation was A-54, had begun working with Czechoslovak intelligence in 1937, at first for payment, and later supposedly out of idealism alone. His advance information about German military plans and intentions was generally correct, although he forecast a military coup against the Nazi regime in 1938 that never came off. Just before the German takeover of Bohemia-Moravia in March 1939, Czech intelligence managed to transplant its operations and some of its officials abroad. From their base in London, General Frantisek Moravec, the head of Czech intelligence, managed to re-establish contact with Thümmel through the Czech underground, and he indirectly became a British source. After he delivered German plans for the offensive against France, Menzies is said to have commented: "A-54 is an agent at whose word armies march."[32]

The ousted President of Czechoslovakia, Edvard Beneš, used information from Thümmel and Czech underground sources to impress Foreign Minister Anthony Eden and Churchill and to procure recognition from the British for his government-in-exile.[33] The Czech leaders had to worry about the survival of their country after the war and about keeping up contact with the Czech underground through radio messages. No one is known to have jumped when Thümmel delivered the report about Nazi killings of Jews in the Ukraine, and there is no evidence that this specific information reached Churchill. There is also no mention of this particular report from Thümmel in the official history of British intelligence, but A-54 does appear in another context.[34]

Although they probably lacked access to reports from agents and informants in Europe, the British analysts of police decodes could and did infer Nazi policies from the decodes alone. Even with the ambiguous and camouflaged terminology for the victims, the number of Jews reported killed was staggering—and produced some skepticism. Between August 23 and August 31 alone, British decodes revealed that the German SS and Order Police units (not the Einsatzgruppen, the details of whose activities were probably still unknown) killed 12,361 Jews. The intelligence summary issued on September 12 contained a disturbing projection: the actual number of executions was probably double the recorded number, because the code breakers had succeeded only about half of the time, it said. A short but pointed paragraph followed:

> The execution of "Jews" is so recurrent a feature of these reports that the figures have been omitted from the situation reports and brought under one heading (3.d). Whether all those executed as "Jews" are indeed such is of course [!] doubtful; but the figures are no less conclusive as evidence of a policy of savage intimidation if not of ultimate extermination.[35]

Perhaps this analyst was or these analysts were not particularly familiar with Nazi racial thought, or perhaps he/they did not want to believe that the SS and police forces in the field took pains to separate Jews from other nationalities before the mass shootings. Whereas it was quite conceivable that the Nazis wanted to get rid of large numbers of people, there was something uncomfortable about concluding that they were isolating and executing Jews—hence the use of quotation marks and the note of doubt. Still, the analyst(s) recognized that the reports of Jews killed—accurate or not—were extremely significant, for at the very least they demonstrated "that this is the ground for killing most acceptable to the Higher Authorities."[36] Through this circuitous route, the analyst(s) concluded that the Nazi regime had an official policy of destroying Jews in the U.S.S.R.

On September 12, 1941—the same day the intelligence summary was issued and the day before Daluege ordered the Higher SS and Police Leaders to cease sending execution reports by radio—the SIS staff explained that future briefings for the Prime Minister would not contain such material: "The fact that the Police are killing all Jews that fall into their hands should by now be sufficiently well appreciated. It is not therefore proposed to continue reporting these butcheries specially, unless so requested."[37] This comment referred to Nazi treatment of Jews only in the conquered territories of the Soviet Union, not in all of Nazi-dominated Europe. Thus, almost three months before the start of operations in the first extermination camp and more than four months before the Wannsee Conference, British intelligence had a basic grasp of Nazi intentions toward Jews in the Soviet territories.

There are only hints of what brought about the decision not to send further reports of executions of Jews to Prime Minister Churchill. To the stated reason—that British intelligence now knew what was going on—we must add that the police analysts and perhaps also higher SIS authorities feared that Churchill's speech of August 24 had tipped the Germans off. A contemporaneous British summary indicated this· "General Daluege[,] alarmed perhaps by our evident awareness of the unspeakable activities of his police in Russia, sent the following message [about radio secrecy] . . ."[38] An internal history of the German police section noted more specifically that the Prime Minister's speech may have increased Daluege's anxiety about secrecy. Not only did Daluege issue his warning about what kind of information could not go by radio; the Germans also soon abandoned Double Transposition as a coding system and adopted Double Playfair in its place.[39]

To send information to Churchill that he might think useful for his speeches was not the foremost priority of the SIS. Official London was preoccupied with the war, not with the beginning of the Holocaust. German bombing had made life miserable and dangerous for urban Britons for more than a year. Germany had conquered and occupied Poland, Denmark, Norway, Belgium, the Netherlands, France, Yugo-slavia, and Greece in short order. In two months, German troops had inflicted massive damage on Soviet forces, and the United States had still remained formally neutral, staying out of the fighting. In the sum-mer and fall of 1941, the immediate British concern was whether the Soviet Union could withstand the German onslaught. Relatively few British experts predicted its survival. By one account, only three officials in Whitehall (plus Churchill) initially expected the Blitzkrieg to fail.[40] Sir John Dill, Chief of the Imperial General Staff, claimed, "The Ger-mans will go through the Russians like a knife through butter."[41]

If Germany triumphed in the East, then Hitler presumably would turn back to his plan for an invasion of the British Isles. The British Joint Intelligence Committee gradually began to qualify and then revise this view of an imminent Soviet collapse and a threatened German invasion of Britain, but it met with resistance from the British military hierarchy.[42] Under these circumstances, British intelligence paid careful attention to what was taking place in the territories of the U.S.S.R., and the most critical intelligence in those summer weeks was information about German military movements and strategy, not about Nazi occupation policies.

Daluege's warning of September 13 to the Higher SS and Police Leaders certainly reduced the flow of "atrocity" information sent by radio, but it hardly stopped Nazi executions or allusions to them in radio messages. After quoting Daluege's message, British analysts explained the effect of it:

> . . . from the 14th [of September] onwards [situation reports] contained the enigmatic phrase "Action according to the usage of war" under the heading which had formerly contained the figures of executions. If there were any doubt as to the meaning of the phrase[,] it is dispelled by a slip on the part of the Higher SS and Police Leader South, who in his situation report on the day before the General's [Daluege's] order, reports . . . "Police Regiment South: Action according to the usage of war, (3) *Successes*; Police Regiment South liquidates 1,548 Jews."[43]

Each time this euphemism *Aktion nach Kriegsgebrauch* appeared subsequently, British analysts knew what it meant.

Occasionally, the analysts misread the significance of messages. When Himmler angrily instructed Higher SS and Police Leader Prützmann to use the Second SS Brigade for cleansing operations in early September, not for trying to conquer Leningrad, the decode was partly garbled. The British thought this brigade would be used for cleansing actions for two weeks and then for trying to conquer Leningrad. A slightly more significant error came when the British monitored messages from Jeckeln's subordinate Herbert Degenhardt, who arrived in Krementschug in late October 1941 and prepared an initial action "with 300." In all likelihood, he meant three hundred Jewish victims, but the intelligence analysts thought he meant three hundred executioners and that the killing went on all through the night of October 30–31.[44] They overestimated the death toll in this particular incident and misunderstood when the executions were carried out (in daylight).

On the other hand, the British caught a good sense of the harmonious cooperation between the SS and police, on one side, and the German Army, on the other, during some of the killing actions in the South. The Seventeenth Army had requested liquidation of the Jews in Krementschug because of several cases of sabotage. When Degenhardt prepared the action, he solicited the approval of the commander of Rear Army Area South, which he got and which the British noted. General

Erich Friderici was so pleased with the results of the ongoing executions that he requested that Jeckeln's staff company remain in Krementschug and not follow Jeckeln to Riga.[45]

An extraordinary act of army–SS cooperation and inhumanity came after German troops reached the city of Novgorod near Lake Ilmen, about one hundred kilometers southeast of Leningrad. In a hospital there, most of the (Russian) patients were suffering from dysentery. The German troops needed the building as quarters, but what could they do with the patients? A senior physician with the Army High Command by the name of Freyberg knew that a special unit under the command of Herbert Lange (based in Posen) had disposed of unwanted patients elsewhere with a mobile gassing van. Freyberg put in a request that Lange, five subordinates, and the gas van be sent from Posen on a military transport plane to Novgorod. Higher SS and Police Leader Wilhelm Koppe in Posen relayed this request to Himmler himself. The Reich Führer SS quickly gave his permission, and Lange was sent off immediately. The British read the whole exchange (which comes to light here for the first time).[46] The army did not have to involve itself in the messy work of murdering hundreds of patients.

It took German historians several decades before they were able to discredit the myth that the regular German Army had little or nothing to do with the Holocaust or crimes against humanity generally. And some of those responsible for such crimes, like the ones in Novgorod, were never punished.

The British also were able to follow some transports of German Jews to the East. Because the Order Police were involved in the deportations and were in charge on the trains themselves, the police authorities sent radio messages about the transports through the Order Police system. Transport train DO 26 left Berlin on November 17 at 6:25 a.m. for Kowno (Kaunas) with 944 Jews, 2 Gestapo officers, and 15 municipal policemen. An officer named Exner was in charge; he had a list (in duplicate) of the passengers. The provisions for the trip were listed, too. Transport DO 56 left Bremen on November 18 headed for Minsk with 971 Jews, accompanied by a detachment of Bremen's municipal police under the authority of Police Master Bockhorn.[47] And British intelligence knew a fair amount about what had already gone on in Minsk.

How much about Nazi killings of Jews and other victims did Britons know in late 1941 and early 1942 from other sources? Strenuous efforts by SS and police officials to ensure secrecy meant that there were usu-

ally few eyewitnesses to the slaughter other than the perpetrators themselves.[48] Scraps of information, usually about particular incidents, nonetheless filtered out to the West. In October 1941, the Jewish Telegraphic Agency correspondent in Zurich wrote an article based on a Ukrainian newspaper article that the Nazis had expelled Jews to an unknown destination, and that in Zhitomir only six thousand out of fifty thousand Jews remained.[49] *The Jewish Chronicle* in London reported in late October and early November that thousands of Jews in the Ukraine had died in pogroms.[50] The Polish government-in-exile's delegate in Poland, operating underground, sent a report at the end of August about the killing of six thousand Jews at Czyzew near Lomza (in the former Soviet zone of eastern Poland) that reached London in mid-October. The government-in-exile released it to the press, and the Jewish Telegraphic Agency played that up as well.[51]

A German-language newspaper in London called *The Apocalypse* published a report in late October, based on a Swedish Social Democratic publication, that Jews deported from Germany to conquered Soviet territory were to be killed one way or another in a program of premeditated mass murder; this account quickly appeared in *The Times* of London as well. It was something in the nature of a prediction, since the deportations were just then beginning.[52] In late October and November, the mainstream British press widely reported the deportations of Jews from Germany and Austria to the East, giving the impression that all Jews would have to go.[53]

Gerhart Riegner, a young lawyer who had left Germany after Hitler took power and ended up in Switzerland as the representative of the World Jewish Congress, wrote up a bleak assessment for his superiors in late October 1941.[54] There were accounts leaking out of ten thousand Jews killed here, ten thousand there. How many Jews would be left in Europe by the end of the war? Hoping not to be Cassandra, Riegner urged Congress leaders to work on Britain and the United States to give maximum publicity to the desperate situation of European Jews.[55] In February 1942, the World Jewish Congress in London sent to the Foreign Office a 160-page report titled "Jews in Nazi Europe: February 1933 to November 1941," which included documentation of Nazi persecution.[56]

In November 1941, Riegner's ally in Geneva, Richard Lichtheim of the Jewish Agency for Palestine, reported ominous news to Chaim Weizmann, president of the Jewish Agency. (Weizmann had been instrumental in bringing about the Balfour Declaration of November 1917 in which Britain pledged support for a Jewish homeland in Palestine. Of all the Zionist leaders, he had the best ties with the British government.) Lichtheim told him that the trainloads of Jews deported from Germany, Austria, and the protectorate of Bohemia-Moravia were going to Lodz, and from there to other points, possibly all the way to Minsk. Lichtheim urged a worldwide campaign of publicity; declarations by statesmen and intercessions by neutral countries with Germany might have positive effects in some cases.[57]

Within the Ministry of Information, British postal and telegraph censorship officials, who scrutinized press reports and private overseas correspondence for relevant, useful information, had already begun a special, confidential series titled "Reports on Jewry." The third such report, dated January 22, 1942 (two days after the Wannsee Conference), began with a stark introduction to the excerpts from articles and private letters: "The Germans clearly pursue a policy of extermination against the Jews . . . [An official German document states] the only things Jewish that will remain in Poland will be Jewish cemeteries."[58]

These various published reports, documents, and private assessments offered Britain a potential opportunity. If the government had wanted to react publicly to Nazi killings of Jews, it did not have to reveal its "Most Secret Sources." It could simply have highlighted and supported what others were claiming and sometimes publishing. But who knew enough to confirm other reports?

A very limited number of government offices received copies of the decodes—military intelligence experts in MI 8, the intelligence specialists on Germany in MI 14, the Air Ministry, the Ministry of Economic Warfare, along with the Joint Intelligence Committee.[59] The Foreign Office did not even receive copies of Ultra or police decodes at this time, although one Foreign Office official, Victor Cavendish-Bentinck, chaired the Joint Intelligence Committee and therefore had access. None of the recipients apparently had any interest in following up what they had received from Bletchley. (I write "apparently," because some of the files of these agencies remain classified.) Of course, the Foreign Office received information from other sources that might have led to similar conclusions, such as a despatch from the British minister in Bern, based on information from a Polish source, that 1.5 million Jews in the former Soviet zone of Poland had simply disappeared; nobody knew what had happened to them.[60] If the implication was that they had been killed, the report was exaggerated—or premature. Still, it should have established that Nazi killing of the Jews in the Soviet territories was part of a broader pattern.

Neither the decodes nor other sources of information about the killings and disappearance of Jews elicited much reaction in London. The British government had already established a course of relative silence about Nazi policies, specifically toward Jews. Since the war began, the Foreign Office especially had shown reservations about any emphasis on Nazi atrocities and strong reservations about public statements regarding Jewish victims. A White Paper on German atrocities issued in late 1939 over the objections of some Foreign Office officials dealt with Nazi anti-Semitic actions and persecution of the churches. The Foreign Office evaluated it as ineffective, with neutral countries considering it "stale and tendentious propaganda on our part." A November 1939 Ministry of Information circular discussing propaganda themes for the Middle East listed "Jewish persecution" as undesirable.[61] In 1940, the government deterred George Bernard Shaw from denouncing Nazi persecution of the Jews in a radio broadcast because it would have a negative effect on public opinion, particularly in the United States. And in July 1941, the Ministry of Information advised that, in order to make the Nazi threat credible to the British people, it should not be made to seem too extreme: "horror stuff . . . must be used very sparingly and must deal always with treatment of indisputably innocent people. Not with violent political opponents. And not with Jews."[62]

A British Political Warfare Executive (PWE)—a forced merger of portions of the Ministry of Information, the Special Operations Executive, and the British Broadcasting Corporation (BBC)—began to function in August 1941. This ill-coordinated PWE was responsible for overt and covert propaganda to all enemy and enemy-occupied territory. The Foreign Office could intervene regarding the foreign-policy matters on propaganda to enemy territory; the Ministry of Information and the Ministry of Economic Warfare also shared supervision of this new body, which issued directives to the BBC and monitored BBC broadcasts.[63]

The British cabinet failed to agree on the broad lines of propaganda, or even on a clear statement of war aims that could be used as the basis for propaganda to occupied Europe. There were also specific disagreements about Germany—how much to blame Hitler, the Nazi Party, or the German people for the war. Should the PWE offer Germans hope for the future or threaten retribution?[64] If the Germans were to be offered a better future, why harp on their responsibility for Nazi crimes? But the supposed involvement of the German people in the killing of Jews could also serve as a reason—or a rationalization—for the British not to discuss the crimes in radio broadcasts. In July 1942, Foreign Office official A. David declined to endorse publicity for an eyewitness account of a mass execution of German Jewish deportees:

> I cannot understand why it should be necessary to send broadcasts to the Germans about persecution of the Jews, on the grounds that they know very little of what is happening. The movement is surely tolerated and even encouraged by many, and is certainly known to all Germans—since they are forced to participate.[65]

Although a historian of British wartime propaganda maintained that the PWE repeatedly issued directives calling for attention to German crimes in news reports and broadcasts, all the examples he listed came after August 1942. A good number of them also dealt with crimes against non-Jews.[66]

It would be highly revealing to compare information the BBC received about Nazi killings of Jews with the contents of BBC broadcasts into Germany during 1941. The BBC had a considerable degree of autonomy during the war.[67] Unfortunately, the records of the BBC's German service have been, according to one source, "unaccountably lost."[68] But some evidence survives. A private 1940 BBC memo circulated among those who worked in the European service division asserted that Germans were in general not susceptible to moral arguments. In February 1941, the European service wrote to a listener: "For a German audience we do not use, rightly or wrongly, appeals for sympathy on behalf of Jews, as a propaganda line."[69]

From his exile in the United States, Nobel Prize–winning author Thomas Mann wrote and then recorded a series of addresses to Germany, which the BBC broadcast. A partial collection, published in 1943, reveals several early allusions to crimes against Jews but no sense of the overall picture. In September 1941, Mann warned that Himmler had openly declared he would physically exterminate the Czech nation; in contrast, Nazi "accomplishments" with regard to Poles and Jews "belong to those reasons for which it will indeed be no pleasure, after this war, to be a German." In January 1942, he announced that the Nazis had brought four hundred Dutch Jews to Germany to use as subjects in poison-gas experiments; in June he corrected the number to eight hundred and revealed that they had died at Mauthausen.[70]

There is some evidence about the BBC's broadcasts in the form of periodic surveys of audience reactions in various European countries. (These surveys, carried out by the BBC's European Intelligence section on the basis of letters to the BBC from abroad and other sources that reached the government, analyzed the effectiveness both of German propaganda efforts within Germany and of British broadcasting to Germany.) The surveys indicate that the BBC had a large German audience interested primarily in accurate information about the war but also in events in Germany not generally known, such as mercy killings and the confiscation of church properties.[71] A British official in Switzerland discussed the BBC's broadcasts with "an eminent German domiciled in Switzerland who is in constant touch with well-placed persons in Germany." (This individual may have been Joseph Wirth, Chancellor of Germany in 1921–22 and a member of the former Catholic Center Party, who then lived in Zurich and fits the description.) In the spring of 1942, this German émigré complained that Moscow was broadcasting reports about Nazi atrocities, whereas the British were not—did "Chamberlainism" still rule in London?

> The respectable German wishes to hear that throughout the world there is the same horror as he feels at the Nazis against crime and sadism and he is infuriated at the embarrassed silence of the people in London on the question of the persecution of the Jews.[72]

Historians have divined a variety of reasons for British reluctance to discuss Nazi crimes against Jews early in the war. Beyond doubt, false Allied propaganda during World War I had left a broad legacy of suspicion about reports of enemy atrocities. Joseph Goebbels himself cited the World War I experience in an effort to discredit later Allied claims of Nazi crimes.[73] The British public did not react positively to the late 1939 White Paper on German atrocities, feeling that the government was seeking to manipulate them. But its description of concentration camps in Germany established a frame of reference and a limit that was then, consciously or unconsciously, applied to later information; whether or not the information about prewar camps was entirely reliable, few could believe that Nazi inhumanity would or could get worse.[74]

Government officials, as well as some currents of British public opinion, tended to doubt information emanating from Jewish sources, because Jews allegedly had an interest in exaggerating the suffering of their own kind or a tendency to fear the worst.[75] This skepticism came easiest to those who were themselves anti-Semitic, but it was not limited to them. Many Britons (and Americans) also resisted deviation from a liberal paradigm in which the Nazi regime had various enemies and represented an assault on civilization generally. There was a peculiar notion that singling out or emphasizing Jewish victims was to concede the Nazis' point—that Jews were a separate people. For the British, that stance had dangerous implications for their country's balancing act in Palestine.[76] Any further nod to an increased Jewish presence there ran the risk of stirring up Arab disorders.

In its White Paper of May 1939, issued in part to quell Arab violence against the British mandate in Palestine, Britain had, among other things, explicitly rejected the concept of a Jewish state in Palestine and had limited future Jewish immigration to seventy-five thousand people over the next five years. At that point the Arab population could veto any further Jewish immigration.

Britain had to contend with both immediate and longer-term issues in the Middle East. In late 1941, Germany had the prospect of striking east from Italian-held Libya to the Suez Canal (and Palestine). Alternatively, German forces might break through the Caucasus Mountains region of the Soviet Union into the Middle East, or they might try to cross neutral Turkey. German attempts to enlist Arab support against British rule in Palestine and Egypt had made headway among some Arab leaders, and there were many Muslims in the British armed forces.[77] In the long run, Britain wanted to remain an imperial power in the region, which required some consideration of Arab concerns.

To give official confirmation to Jewish casualties, some believed, would have been to narrow the anti-Nazi cause—and in wartime, perhaps also to endanger it, given the existence of widespread anti-Semitism in Europe and Arab hostility toward Jews. Attention to Jewish issues would have given Nazi propagandists evidence to support their claim that the Allies were fighting a war on behalf of the Jews.[78] Finally, the stakes of the military conflict were so high that many government officials and private citizens wanted to focus all efforts and attention on the overall task. They paid little attention to anything else, particularly if it might complicate winning the war as quickly as possible.

Churchill certainly did not share some of his colleagues' emotional distaste for Jewish issues; he was pro-Zionist.[79] But he did not do more than stretch the limits of a wartime government consensus in his public speeches or broadcasts. He exploited one opportunity to raise the conditions in the East obliquely. On October 25, 1941, President Roosevelt issued a statement denouncing German executions of innocent hostages in France as revolting and terroristic. In a separate statement Churchill joined him, then used what he called the butcheries in France as an illustration of what the Nazis were doing elsewhere—in Poland, in Yugoslavia, in Norway, in Holland, in Belgium, and above all behind the German fronts in Russia. It surpassed "anything that has been known since the darkest and most bestial ages of mankind . . . Retribution for these crimes must henceforward take its place among the major purposes of the war."[80]

This declaration went somewhat further than his speech of August 24, and again Churchill drew on evidence he had received from police decodes. But again he placed Nazi crimes in a very broad framework, and again there was no specific mention of killings of Jews. This general approach could not very well indicate the fate of Jews in the East to anyone, and The New York Times actually indicated that Churchill's signal of postwar retribution was directed at crimes against innocent Frenchmen.[81]

In November, Churchill sent a message to The Jewish Chronicle on the occasion of its hundredth anniversary that gave somewhat more prominence to Jewish victims of Nazism:

> None has suffered more cruelly than the Jew the unspeakable evils wrought on the bodies and spirits of men by Hitler and his vile regime. The Jew bore the brunt of the Nazis' first onslaught upon the citadels of freedom and human dignity. He has borne and continues to bear a burden that might have seemed to be beyond endurance. He has not allowed it to break his spirit: he has never lost the will to resist. Assuredly in the day of victory the Jew's suffering and his part in the struggle will not be forgotten. Once again, at the appointed time, he will see vindicated those principles of righteousness which it was the glory of his fathers to proclaim to the world. Once again it will be shown that, though the mills of God grind slowly, they grind exceedingly small.[82]

This was a sympathetic statement in a medium of very limited and select circulation by a head of government and a politician to one of his constituencies. And on the last point, Churchill turned out to be wrong: the mills of God did not grind small in this case, at least in this world.

Elsewhere, the picture was little different. In January 1942, the governments-in-exile of nine Western and Central European countries occupied by Germany met at St. James's Palace in London to sign a resolution denouncing Germany's regime of terror, characterized by "imprisonment, mass expulsions, execution of hostages, and massacres." Picking up on President Roosevelt's statement of October 25, and the accompanying statement by Prime Minister Churchill, both endorsing war-crimes trials as a principal aim of the war, the governments-in-exile called for judicial punishment of those guilty for ordering or carrying out crimes against civilians in occupied territories. But the signatories ignored a request from the Board of Deputies of British Jews and the Anglo-Jewish Association to make some specific reference to the suffering of Jews and the part they played in the common struggle. Britain had earlier rejected the notion of a formal endorsement of postwar trials of Nazi criminals, and, along with the Dominion countries, the United States, and the U.S.S.R., merely signed the St. James's Declaration as an observer.[83]

British military options ranged from limited to nonexistent. In the fall of 1941, Britain was unable to defend all its overseas possessions and was awaiting the next German blow, hoping that the Soviets could hold on and that the Americans would enter the war sooner rather than later. Only then could London see a realistic way to defeat Germany. Selection of some civilian or military German target as a stated retaliation against Nazi policy toward Soviet Jews when Britain itself was in grave jeopardy would hardly have struck a realistic British politician as the right priority. The foremost need was to redress the military imbalance by whatever steps the military thought necessary.

Even in mid-1942, by which time Britain was better situated militarily, the notion of retaliatory bombing as a response to "atrocities" had little support. A Conservative M.P. wanted the British to react to the destruction of the Czech town of Lidice by threatening that, for every innocent person murdered in occupied territory, the Royal Air Force would obliterate an undefended German town or village. Churchill responded that there were not enough German villages to go around but that Allied bombers would attack where they could be most effective. Frank Roberts, acting First Secretary in the Central Department of the Foreign Office, noted that there was already heavy bombing of German cities—let the Europeans draw their own conclusions about why.[84] The resistance in this case had nothing to do with fear of raising Jewish issues.

The idea of sending relief to starving Jews in Polish or Soviet ghettos was not beyond question, but it would not have stopped the Nazis from liquidating the ghetto populations. And the British government had already made up its mind to force Germany to feed and support all its conquered peoples. As it had told the United States in July 1940, in the context of suggestions to send relief into occupied France, Belgium, and the Netherlands:

> His Majesty's Government appreciate to the full the humanitarian ideas which inspire the desire now becoming apparent to supply relief to the stricken territories, [but] they are convinced that it would be entirely mistaken policy to lengthen the war by allowing Germany to be assisted in the difficulties which confront her and which are of her own creation. Painful as the decision is, they have, therefore, decided that no exemption from contraband control can be accorded for relief goods. . . . His Majesty's Government realise that their decision may lay them open to criticism, the sincerity of which is beyond question. But their intention is to win the war in the shortest possible time and so to liberate the peoples from Nazi oppression.[85]

There was no inclination in London to break with this general policy for the sake of European Jews in late 1941 or thereafter.

It was certainly possible, however, to release and use information. Britain was already engaged in what was then called political or psychological warfare, especially in the form of radio broadcasts into enemy and neutral countries. At a time when the Nazi regime was still killing Jews in the Soviet territories and was beginning to deport German Jews into the conquered areas of the Soviet Union, and at a time when many of those Jews had little idea what deportation meant, it would have been valuable and moral to send *them* a signal. It would have been worth sending the gist of the information the government had obtained from decodes and from other sources, suitably camouflaged, into Germany and German-controlled territories to alert Jews and non-Jews alike. The Nazi officials themselves were so determined to preserve the secrecy of their program of mass extermination precisely because they feared that release of information would interfere with their objectives and damage their interests.

The British government did distribute and exploit some information obtained from other decodes. When intelligence analysts decoded information sufficiently useful to merit distribution to government offices and commands in the field, they disguised the origin to keep the secret as tightly as possible. Creative memo writers invented a source looking over the shoulder of a German commander or filching a document from a wastepaper basket.[86] When the decodes identified locations of German ships or other potential targets, British authorities sent reconnaissance planes out to "spot" them and serve as the official source. Ultra decodes supplied the original information as to where the planes should look. In the summer and fall of 1941, Britain gave some high-grade Ultra intelligence to the Soviet Union in an effort to help it survive the German onslaught. The Ultra items were "wrapped" up with other, less sensitive material and misattributed to sources, such as reliable and occasional agents.[87] In short, when there was a strong enough reason, the relevant authorities could usually figure out a way.

Intelligence was and is meant to be used. Sometimes the best use of intelligence is quietly to take military countermeasures: the original information and the response come to light only decades after the events. Sometimes, in a democracy, intelligence is leaked or publicly announced to help mobilize public opinion. Insofar as we can judge, British intelligence about the beginnings of what we now call the Holocaust, whether obtained from police decodes or other sources, was simply hoarded. Few persons within the upper ranks of the British government, whether they had access to the police decodes or not, felt that there was a strong reason to distribute this kind of information publicly, let alone to consider possible responses to it.

British intelligence certainly had some legitimate concern about any use of the decodes that might reveal British successes to the Germans, who then could change their codes. Churchill had already given the public speech on August 24, 1941, in which he had drawn, a little too obviously, from the police decodes. There was, however, an unusual sequel to German concerns with the security of its codes. As I have noted above, following Daluege's warning of September 13, the Order Police began to shift their coding system from Double Transposition to Double Playfair, and they completed the process on November 1. The changeover, however, made it possible for British experts to break all but four of the keys used for communications from the Reich and all but two of the keys used for communications from the Soviet territories; the number of unbroken keys had been higher before. The British intelligence analyst noted the irony, quoting a French expression: "The best is often the enemy of the good."[88] In retrospect, it appears that Britain could have publicized Nazi killings of Jews in the East without in the least impairing its code-breaking successes.

# 7

✳

# AUSCHWITZ
# PARTIALLY DECODED

THE GERMAN POLICE DECODES gave British intelligence analysts a cross section of many aspects of the war in the East. In December
1941, stiff Soviet military resistance and the savage Russian winter
caught the German forces unprepared. To stem its losses and to prevent
Soviet breakthroughs, the German Army called on the SS and police
authorities for help. As a result, the soldiers in Waffen-SS units and
even older men such as the policemen of Reserve Police Battalion 11,
previously used to scour conquered territory for Jews and suspected
partisans or, in conjunction with the Lithuanian auxiliaries, to carry out
mass executions of Jews, suddenly found themselves involved in serious
military combat and taking major casualties. Bach-Zelewski complained
heatedly, and his relations with Daluege began to deteriorate—a development the British regarded as a barometer of increasing tension.[1]

The police decodes in 1942, however, contained much less detail
about mass killings of Jews and other victims in the Soviet territories
than they had in the summer and fall of 1941. The warnings about the
vulnerability of signals communication had reduced radio indiscretions
considerably. Here and there Higher SS and Police Leaders, in the
course of reporting major sweeps against actual partisan units, mentioned executions of groups of Jews.[2] Most of the time they referred
to how many were killed by using euphemisms such as "finished off,"
given "special treatment," or shot according to martial law. Generally,
they did not identify the category of the victims.[3]

If one looks closely at the decodes for clues to the evolution of the
Final Solution in 1942, some subtle shifts emerge. The prolific murder

organizer Herbert Degenhardt went from Riga to Mogilev in February or March, where he helped to fill a vacuum.[4] Bach-Zelewski had undergone a serious intestinal operation, aggravated by something close to a nervous breakdown brought on, in the opinion of the chief SS doctor, Dr. Ernst Grawitz, partly by the effects of all the executions; recuperating in an SS hospital in Berlin, he was reliving the shootings of Jews he had conducted.[5] The British were aware that his preoperation pain led him to use opium; they also knew that he was in Berlin for the operation and recuperation. They did not, however, learn of Dr. Grawitz's precise diagnosis.[6]

Degenhardt was temporarily attached to Bach-Zelewski's office in Mogilev. Not coincidentally, Himmler visited Mogilev again. Three gas vans were in operation in the city at this time.[7] Himmler sent back a friendly radio message to assist Bach-Zelewski's recovery: everything was in the best order; he was thinking of his good old friend.[8]

Degenhardt's activities in Mogilev were part of a broader pattern. SS and police forces in the Soviet territories had begun a new sweep for Jews in early 1942. By the summer, major liquidations took place in many remaining ghettos, and the pace of executions remained very high well through the fall.[9] Himmler ordered the collection of data regarding the activities and casualties of all police battalions since June 22, 1941, the results to be presented to Hitler, and he reported actual totals of executions to Hitler.[10] But this data did not appear in the British decodes. British intelligence read occasional items, such as one German radio report about the execution of seven hundred Jews incapable of labor in the area southwest of Kamenez in the Ukraine,[11] which provided clues about general Nazi policy.

The decodes also picked up numerous indications of another German problem—severe shortage of labor, partly the result of the horrendous mortality among Soviet prisoners of war, so badly handled by the German Army. The large-scale shipment of Polish laborers to factories in Germany helped alleviate labor problems there, but created a scarcity in Poland.[12] This constraint apparently contributed to a decision to make use of those Jews capable of hard labor or skilled labor, rather than execute them immediately, but the SS insisted on direct control of that labor.[13]

Hitler himself issued an order (passed along by radio and read by the British) allowing the use of Jews as forced laborers for the construction of roads in the northern Soviet sector, but in some other cases requests for the use of Jewish labor were denied.[14] The tension between ideology and practical needs could lead to serious conflicts. Nine months later Rudolf Höss, commandant of Auschwitz, sent a message to Adolf Eichmann through the SS Economic-Administrative Main Office (WVHA). He wanted to be sure that transports of Dutch Jews would not stop in Kosel, in Silesia, where other authorities might commandeer them for labor. The Schmelt organization was already using thousands of Jews there for construction of war-related factories.[15] Höss wanted them routed directly through to Auschwitz, and the British got the message.[16] If some of these Jews temporarily were spared from the gas chambers, they certainly were under SS control.

The expansion and evolution of Auschwitz exemplified a broader shift in the geography of the Final Solution during 1942. Chelmno and Auschwitz were in Polish territory formally annexed by Germany in 1939. In general, it was easier for the SS to operate in the East than in Germany proper, but the regional civil administrators and Gauleiters in the Wartheland (where Chelmno was located) and Upper Silesia (where Auschwitz was) were cooperative. Auschwitz was particularly well located for rail transport; Jews from many parts of Europe could be sent by train to its gates. By comparison, Mogilev could not be reached from the West by rail at all. It would have been necessary to ship Jews along rivers for part of the journey, and military priorities in the central sector interfered with trainloads of Jews even to Minsk. Ambitious SS potentates sometimes had to bow to practical realities. Three more crematorium ovens, which Bach-Zelewski had fought to get and had paid for, were diverted to Auschwitz in August 1942.[17] But the SS continued to run a "small" extermination camp at Maly Trostinets outside Minsk, although there was little or no information about it in the German police decodes.[18]

The extermination camps of what was called Operation Reinhard— named after Reinhard Heydrich, whom Czech agents had assassinated in mid-1942—also enjoyed some geographical and practical advantages.[19] Once Himmler and his subordinates were able to resolve most of their difficulties with the civil administration in the General Government of Poland and to monopolize control of Jewish policy and property there,[20] and once the gas chambers and crematoria at Belzec, Sobibor, Treblinka, and Maidanek were ready to function, it was efficient to use them for Polish Jews and some transports from outside.

From its headquarters at Oranienburg, outside Berlin, the WVHA— which oversaw the array of extermination camps, concentration camps, factory camps, labor camps, other types of camps, and SS economic enterprises—liked to use radio communication. As opposed to the Order Police, most branches of the SS used the sophisticated Enigma coding machine, but the British were able to break at least one Enigma key used by the WVHA beginning in December 1940 and read the communications, with many ups and downs, until late in the war.[21] In the process, they got a glimpse of activities related to the Holocaust.

The same concerns about communications secrecy prevailed in the SS, despite the Enigma. Top secret information went only by courier, not by radio. But one WVHA radio instruction was itself a revealing indicator of the nature of activities at the camps. On June 11, 1942, one or more of the concentration-camp commanders who had received previous instructions about radio secrecy learned that reports of executions carried out were no longer to be considered top secret (*Geheime Reichssache*), but only secret.[22] It meant that the camp commanders could report executions by radio to the WVHA, and it implied that there was something considerably more sensitive than simple shootings of prisoners going on.[23] The decodes picked up traces, often garbled, of meetings between Eichmann, who was in charge of removing and transporting Jews, and various concentration- and extermination-camp officials.[24]

SS and Police Leader Odilo Globocnik, in charge of Operation Reinhard, disclosed relatively little in radio messages about the extermination camps at Belzec, Sobibor, and Treblinka. But he did send a radio message to one of Adolf Eichmann's subordinates about "evacuation" of Rumanian Jews by rail to Trawniki; from there they would be distributed to the appropriate camps. (By then the British analysts knew what "evacuation" meant.) The WVHA also inquired by radio about the watches and other personal items recovered during Reinhard.[25] It happened that a cut in his gasoline allotment made it difficult for Globocnik to carry out his "special tasks," the approved euphemism Globocnik used in a letter to refer to (but disguise) the mass murder of Jews. Globocnik turned to Himmler's military adjutant for assistance in getting more fuel, but Himmler suggested shipping off the valuables by railway freight car, instead of trucks, with guards to prevent theft, thereby conserving gasoline (for the engines churning out carbon monoxide for the gas chambers at Belzec, Sobibor, and Treblinka).[26] But these written messages did not emerge in the decodes.

Substantial information about Auschwitz was made available in signals communications in part because it was a collection of camps with different purposes, some less secret than others. Auschwitz had started out as a concentration camp mostly for various categories of Poles; it began a dramatic expansion in 1941. Auschwitz II (Birkenau) became the center of mass extermination in 1942; and an I. G. Farben synthetic-rubber (Buna) factory at Monowitz, Auschwitz III, absorbed many of those prisoners capable of hard labor.[27]

Auschwitz, particularly Auschwitz III, needed laborers, and that kind of information could go out by radio. The Reich Security Main Office stated that unexplained internal political reasons made it impossible to ship some thousand German Jews capable of labor to Auschwitz on June 3 and 4, 1942,[28] but the Nazi puppet state of Slovakia cooperated to fill the gap. New transports of Jews from Slovakia to Auschwitz began on June 16; the purpose was deployment for labor.[29] From March 1942 on, trainloads of Slovak Jews were among the first to undergo "selection" at Auschwitz—the able-bodied spared temporarily for hard labor; the children, elderly, and weak sent to the gas chambers. The transports of June 16–20, however, consisted of adults apparently needed and used as laborers—for the time being.[30] In November 1942, the British learned that 396 prisoners were involved in construction at the Buna camp, and 1,568 worked in the Buna factory itself. (In his famous memoir, Primo Levi describes his activities in the Buna plant.)[31] Information about Birkenau and the factory-style process of mass murder was more difficult to locate in the decodes, but it was there. In a partially garbled decode in June 1942, SS-Brigadeführer Dr. Hans Kammler, the head of construction for the WVHA and the builder of camps and camp installations, alluded to a chimney for the crematorium.[32] At that time additional gas chambers and crematoria were under construction at Birkenau.[33]

The decodes also picked up reports of a number of meetings between WVHA chief Oswald Pohl and Rudolf Höss and between Kammler and Höss.[34] These meetings apparently were connected with high-level dissatisfaction with the pace of resolving the Jewish question, complications caused by transportation bottlenecks in hindering shipments of Jews, and construction of new extermination facilities.[35] Himmler himself went to Auschwitz for a two-day inspection on July 17–18, 1942, and he observed the gassing of one selection of Jews. He then authorized a major expansion and gave commandant Höss a promotion. Following that visit, he went straight to Lublin and observed operations in at least one of Globocnik's extermination camps, Sobibor.[36] Neither trip apparently showed up in the decodes. In any case, it would have been very difficult for British analysts to make a connection in mid-

1942 between transports of Jews to Auschwitz and the new installations there from these decodes alone, and there is no sign that British intelligence did so. More suggestive was a November message that Auschwitz urgently needed six hundred gas masks to equip its new guards, but that, too, was only one little piece of the picture.[37]

Himmler and his subordinates had a liking for good records and for statistics. In early 1943, the WVHA passed along to the various camps an order from Himmler to compile the prisoner population each year since 1933 by category: political prisoners, criminals, Jews, Poles, Spanish Communists, and Russians. Himmler wanted to know how many each camp had released each year and how many had died.[38] If the returns were sent by radio (which is most unlikely), reports of them have not survived or have not been declassified.

During 1942, however, a number of camps, Auschwitz among them, reported by radio almost daily the number of additions and subtractions to the camp prisoner population. Following instructions, they also broke down their total number of prisoners by the major categories—Germans, Jews, Poles, and Russians. With one big exception (explained below), British intelligence could and did, with some delay, track the changing population and mortality at Auschwitz.[39] In January–March 1942 the number of Jews was in the hundreds. Beginning in April, it moved into the thousands, reflecting the arrival of deportees from Slovakia, and by late July it exceeded ten thousand. The peak number was just more than twelve thousand in August; then the official Jewish population began to decline. In August 1942, 6,829 men and 1,525 women died in the camp. From September 1 on, "natural" deaths were no longer to be sent by radio—only in writing.[40]

These statistics covered only the number of prisoners registered at the Auschwitz camps. The death total included those shot or beaten to death as well as those who died of disease or starvation. They *omitted* all Jews (and the smaller number of Gypsies) selected for the gas chambers immediately upon arrival. This omission—was it, too, a cloaking device?—might have imposed a critical handicap on interpreting Auschwitz's role, but other forms of intelligence could and should have compensated for it.

From early in the war, British intelligence read German railway decodes, and from February 1941 on, a Railway Research Service within the Ministry of Economic Warfare analyzed German rail transportation, too.[41] (If they still exist, these decodes apparently remain classified.) Some WVHA messages also referred to shipments of categories of Jews to Auschwitz. A mid-July 1942 message explained that a particular transport from France was not filled with Jews, the implication being that the others were. An October 1942 message referred in passing to transports of Jews from Polish, Czech, and Dutch territory.[42] The railway decodes must have contained even more detailed information, so British intelligence analysts must have known about the scale of deportations. They also knew from the data that the Auschwitz camp population was not taking in Jews in numbers comparable to what the transports must have brought and that Jews were not departing. Had Auschwitz become one of the largest cities of Europe? There was only one logical conclusion about the fate of Jews transported there. But specific British intelligence conclusions about Auschwitz-Birkenau either have not survived or remain classified.[43]

The British also received through the intelligence organization of the Polish government-in-exile a series of reports from Polish agents and couriers about activities at Auschwitz and other extermination camps. (For present purposes, what mattered most were Polish reports passed to the British and the Americans, not the larger body of information that reached the Polish government-in-exile.) Information from human sources, especially escaped prisoners, took much longer to reach London and contained hearsay as well as eyewitness testimony. Nonetheless, the Polish underground reports were an important complement to, and confirmation of, British signals intelligence.

A Polish agent based in London, Tadeusz Chciuk-Celt, parachuted into Poland twice. His first visit came at the end of December 1941, and he remained through mid-June 1942. He went from Poland to Budapest and sent a report to London in the fall of 1942 about mass executions and the expansion of Auschwitz's capacity to absorb victims. Chciuk-Celt's original reports were lost or remain classified, but he wrote up some of his experiences for publication in 1945 and afterward.[44] His account also is consistent with the pattern formed by those contemporary documents not still classified.

On November 15, 1942, the Polish underground reported that tens of thousands, mostly Jews and Soviet prisoners of war, had arrived at Auschwitz "for the sole purpose of their immediate extermination in gas chambers." This information reached the Polish government in London by November 27.[45] The Directorate of Civilian Resistance in Poland reported on March 23, 1943, that a new crematorium was disposing of about three thousand persons per day in Auschwitz-Birkenau, of which most were Jews.[46] This report was very close to what postwar reconstruction would establish as the actual situation at that time. Crematorium IV had begun to operate on March 22—one day earlier—and Crematorium V started up about two weeks later. Together they had the capacity to deal with three thousand bodies per day.

The report of the new crematorium, sent by Stefan Korbonski in underground Poland to London, appeared in April 1943 in a Polish bulletin called *Poland Fights* along with other related information. Through the middle of 1942, according to this publication, there had been 63,340 prisoners registered at Auschwitz-Birkenau, but another 22,000 persons had arrived at the camp, not been registered, and were simply liquidated. Among the unregistered were 4,000 Poles, 10,000 Jews, and 8,500 Soviet prisoners of war. Also included was another estimate that 57,000 people had died at Auschwitz-Birkenau of illness, exhaustion, or execution.[47]

On April 18, 1943, the day before the Warsaw ghetto uprising began, a Polish underground courier who had made his way to London drafted a long report about his stay in Poland and Europe from roughly November 1941 until October 1942.[48] He made some errors in his report, and there were some overly optimistic comments about the current relationship between Poles and Jews in Poland, but he also had detailed information about Auschwitz:

I lived in Oswiecim [Auschwitz] for a number of weeks. I know the conditions well, because I investigated them . . . I had the most detailed information of what is going on there from people [Polish prisoners] who were freed. When I left Oswiecim at the end of September [1942], the number of registered prisoners was over 95,000 . . . Among the [unregistered were] 20,000 Russian prisoners of war who were brought there in the summer of 1940 [1941] as well as masses of Jews brought there from other countries. The POWs died from starvation. Jews were exterminated en masse.

On the basis of information I collected and [obtained] on the spot, I can ascertain that the Germans applied the following killing methods. a) gas chambers: the victims were undressed and put into those chambers where they suffocated; b) Electric chambers: Those chambers had metal walls. The victims were brought in and then high-tension electric current was introduced; c) the so-called Hammerluft system. This is a hammer of the air [presumably some sort of air-pressure killing]; d) shooting, often killing every tenth person.

The first three methods were said to be the most common.

Obviously, there were false elements (the electric chambers and Hammerluft system) and deductions in this account, gathered from a variety of sources. Nonetheless, the courier left little doubt that large numbers of Jews were being gassed at Birkenau:

> Gestapo men stood in a position which enabled them to watch in gas masks the death of the masses of victims. The Germans loaded the corpses and took them outside Auschwitz by means of huge shovels. They made holes where they buried the dead, and then they covered the holes with lime. Burning of victims by means of electric ovens was seldom applied [in this period]. This is because in such ovens only about 250 people could be burned within twenty-four hours.[49]

This Polish courier met in London with Dr. Ignacy Schwarzbart, a member of the Polish National Council and a representative of the World Jewish Congress. On April 27, Schwarzbart sent a report about this meeting and about this document to the Representation of Polish Jews in the United States within the World Jewish Congress. He asked his recipients to keep the information strictly confidential. But the U.S. government had this information, too, because its Censorship Office inspected all transatlantic mail, summarized relevant and useful information, then sent it on its way.[50] The British must have had this information from Polish intelligence or even through a direct debriefing of the courier. The information remained unpublished at the courier's request, but the Western governments had it. In arguing that the killing operations at Birkenau remained secret, Martin Gilbert commented on this document: "There is no evidence, however, that its revelations made any impression or that it was quoted or mentioned again."[51] But do we have access to all British intelligence records about this report?

On May 18, Polish military intelligence in London prepared another report on conditions in Poland that was sent by diplomatic pouch to Washington; a copy in Polish was given to the Joint Chiefs of Staff in June. Again there was updating of information regarding Auschwitz-Birkenau, this time from new underground sources. The total number of people killed at Auschwitz–Birkenau through December 1942 was now said to be 640,000—65,000 Poles, 26,000 Soviet prisoners of war, and 520,000 Jews.[52]

In May 1943, the Polish embassy in London gave the British Foreign Office another firsthand (largely accurate) account of the killing process

at Treblinka, which the author thought was the center for the extermination of Europe's Jews. Nonetheless, the report mentioned other
such killing centers, and Auschwitz (Oswiecim) was listed.[53]

In late August 1943, the Polish government informed the British of
information recently received concerning the systematic depopulation
of part of the province of Bialystok and virtually all of the province of
Lublin. Hundreds of thousands of people in Lublin were said to have
been deported or exterminated, with women and old men put to death
in gas chambers, and some children sent to Germany to be brought up
as Germans or sold to German settlers. A British Foreign Office official,
Roger Allen, objected to British endorsement of Polish conclusions
based on scanty evidence and specifically to the notion of Poles being
put to death in gas chambers. What was the advantage of a gas chamber
over a machine gun anyway? he asked skeptically.

This question elicited a revealing comment from Victor Cavendish-
Bentinck, chairman of the Joint Intelligence Committee, who had access to the German Police and SS decodes. Cavendish-Bentinck first
deplored Polish and Jewish information about atrocities: both groups
(to a far greater extent, the Jews) sought to "stoke us up" and seemed
to have succeeded, he thought. He in effect wrote off information
supplied by Polish and Jewish sources. Cavendish-Bentinck then challenged several aspects of this most recent Polish report, particularly the
claim of Poles being gassed. There was more evidence, he argued, about
Russians murdering Polish officers at Katyn, in the former Soviet-
occupied zone of Poland. (In the spring of 1943 German troops discovered the mass graves of about ten thousand Polish officers in the
Katyn forest, near Smolensk. The Soviet Union and Germany each
blamed the other, but even during the war the evidence available suggested Soviet responsibility. We now know that Stalin made the decision, confirmed by the Politburo, in the spring of 1940, to kill these
Poles and that the Soviet executioners used German bullets sold to the
U.S.S.R. in the 1920s and 1930s.[54]) Ultimately, Cavendish-Bentinck
conceded British knowledge of the fact that Nazi Germany was out to
destroy Jews of any age unless they were capable of manual labor. But
he compared some stories about gas chambers to World War I stories
about the use of human corpses to manufacture fat, which turned out
to be mendacious Allied propaganda.[55]

Cavendish-Bentinck was correct that some Polish and Jewish reports
were exaggerated or partly inaccurate;[56] but particularly with regard to
the Jews, he acknowledged the essential point: one way or another the

Nazis were murdering most Jews. Still, in a handwritten postscript, he added: "I feel certain that we are making a mistake in publicly giving credence to this gas chamber story."[57] It is not clear whether his skepticism about reports of gas chambers also covered reports of their use to dispose of Jews.

The flow of information about Auschwitz continued. A December 1943 Polish military intelligence report from a Polish woman, code-named Wanda, reached London at the end of January 1944. Wanda had apparently also written about Auschwitz-Birkenau earlier and was believed to be completely reliable. Her report was given to the U.S. liaison to the Allied governments-in-exile and to the American military attaché in London, with the request to publicize it as widely as possible. Copies were sent to the Office of Strategic Services (OSS) in London and eventually to Washington. Wanda claimed that, through September 1942, 468,000 non-registered Jews had been gassed at Auschwitz-Birkenau. Then during the next eight months, 60,000 Jews had arrived from Greece; 50,000 from Slovakia and Bohemia-Moravia; 60,000 from Holland, Belgium, and France; and 11,000 from other areas—98 percent of the recent arrivals were gassed. So Wanda's grand total as of early June 1943 was 645,000 Jews gassed.

She, too, described the processes of selection and killing:

> Each convoy arriving at Auschwitz is unloaded. Men are separated from women and then packed haphazard in a mass. Children and women are put into cars and lorries and taken to the gas chamber in Brzezinka. There they are suffocated with the most horrible suffering lasting ten to fifteen minutes, the corpses being thrown out through an aperture and cremated. Before entering the gas chambers, the condemned must be bathed. At present, three large crematoria have been erected in Birkenau-Brzezinka for 10,000 people daily which are ceaselessly cremating bodies and which the neighboring population call "the eternal fire."

Wanda also mentioned that the overwhelming majority of Gypsies from Greece and southern France were gassed immediately.[58]

In his 1981 work, *Auschwitz and the Allies*, Martin Gilbert argued that the West lacked information about the gas chambers and crematoria disposing of huge numbers of Jews at Auschwitz until four prisoners escaped in April–May 1944 and their accounts filtered out to the West in June:

From the first week of May 1942 until the third week of June 1944 the gas chambers at Auschwitz–Birkenau had kept their secret both as the principal mass murder site of the Jews of Europe and also as the destination of so many hundreds of deportation trains from France, Holland, Belgium, Italy, Greece, and elsewhere.[59]

But as we have seen, such information was available, though some British officials with access to it chose not to examine it or not to believe it. British intelligence analysts may have had some difficulty for a time untangling the various functions of the Auschwitz camps, but historians cannot examine how they tried to do so, given that relevant British documents are still classified.

It is certainly true that the very detailed report about Auschwitz and Birkenau compiled by two escapees, Rudolf Vrba and Alfred Wetzler, and distributed in mid-1944 gave Western governments many new details and brought fundamentally new information to the public in Britain and the United States.[60] But for those British intelligence officials who had had access to the decodes or to Polish intelligence, the Vrba–Wetzler report was not the first to reveal that huge numbers of Jews were being killed at Auschwitz–Birkenau or that poison gas was an essential part of the process.

Gilbert conceded that a few fragmentary reports of Auschwitz as a killing center for Jews did leak out earlier, but, he contended, none of them made an impact.[61] If he meant that none made an impact on Western governments, he got the last part right. The sources and extent of American contemporary knowledge of the Holocaust and the interaction of British and American officials regarding the Holocaust, however, require more detailed investigation.

# 8

*

# AMERICAN ASSESSMENTS

THE UNITED STATES, like Great Britain, was in a favorable position to get information about Nazi secret crimes, but not with high technology. Technically neutral in the war until December 1941, the United States had reporters and diplomats in Germany during the first wave of the Holocaust. Even if they had nothing so revealing as the German police decodes, American observers could pick up substantial information about Nazi measures against Jews from public sources, insiders within the regime, and opponents of it. Some of this information reached the American government and the public, but little of it was broadcast to Nazi-controlled Europe, even after Pearl Harbor and America's entrance in the war. Although the United States did not have the problems of direct rule over Arabs brought about by the British mandate in Palestine, some officials in Washington shared other British political considerations and calculations.

Following Germany's invasion of the U.S.S.R., the Jewish-American press was, in general, quick off the mark. Yiddish newspapers in New York City reported in July 1941 that the Nazis had killed hundreds of Jews in Minsk, Brest-Litovsk, Lvov, and elsewhere. The Yiddish press had a circulation of about four hundred thousand, more than half of which was in New York City. The Jewish Telegraphic Agency (JTA), a news service, issued a *Daily News Bulletin*, which was the main source for most English-language American Jewish weeklies and periodicals. JTA items occasionally reached the mainstream press as well.[1]

Other relatively early newspaper accounts of killings and atrocities stemmed from Soviet and Polish sources that did not emphasize Jewish victims. On October 26, however, *The New York Times* carried a story about a German and Ukrainian massacre of fifteen thousand Jews in Galicia, some of whom had been deported from Hungary. The sources were letters reaching Hungary and eyewitness testimony from officers present. In mid-November, the *New York Journal American* featured a story about the Rumanian killing of twenty-five thousand Jews in Odessa; the actual total was considerably larger. A couple of weeks later it also printed a story based on Soviet information about the killing of fifty-two thousand people in Kiev (where the victims included more than thirty-three thousand Jews liquidated at Babi Yar).[2]

American reporters also wrote extensively about the deportations of Jews from Germany; some even witnessed early departures of Jews crammed into railcars. The destination of German Jews was said at first to be ghettos or camps in Poland, not the Soviet territories. At the end of October, Louis P. Lochner, the Associated Press's senior German correspondent, wrote that total elimination of Jews from European life was "fixed German policy" and that the fate of Jewish deportees from Germany was unknown. When the *New York Herald Tribune* carried a story in late November 1941 about the condition of Jews in the Soviet territories, it accepted the accuracy of reported deportations (for example, twenty thousand Jews sent into the Pinsk marshes) but was non-committal about more extreme measures: "some reports received here from Central Europe speak of massacres of Jews by Germans."[3] This was the beginning of a trend in the mainstream American press of treating reports of mass killings of Jews skeptically.

In September 1941, American diplomats noticed an intensification of Nazi propaganda against Jews, including renewed charges that world Jewry sought the destruction of the German people. The Nazi press explained that the Jewish question had to be solved "without any sentimentality." A few weeks later the American embassy in Berlin picked up rumors of mass deportations of German Jews to Lublin, Lodz, or Warsaw, part of a policy to "remove all Jews in Germany to Poland and other eastern areas as rapidly as is feasible." Later despatches explained that shortages of trains had slowed down the process.[4] According to the diplomats, the deportation policy was unpopular:

> . . . the Berlin populace is showing increasing sympathy with the Jews as the scope of the present action becomes more widely known. Several

cases have been noted of people being reprimanded for showing kindness on the street and in shops to elderly persons wearing the Jewish star or for criticizing the present drastic measures in public.[5]

By late October, the American embassy expected that all Jews in Germany would be deported within a few months, and in mid-November, it added that able-bodied Jews were being sent from Germany to Russia for forced labor.[6] Meanwhile, the American military attaché in Berlin reported separately at around the same time that there was no question that SS units were killing Jews in many occupied localities in Russia. The *normal procedure* for the Nazis upon taking over a city, he said, was to establish local commandos, to separate the Jews, and to shoot them. He also correctly revealed atrocities and mistreatment of Soviet prisoners of war.[7] A logical conclusion was that the deportees would also be killed in the East. The diplomats knew that deportations of Jews to the East would bring grave hardships; they cited rumors filtering back to Berlin of deaths of Jews from disease, cold, starvation, and outright massacre.[8] But they did not indicate clear knowledge of the fate of the deportees.

In mid-November, Propaganda Minister Joseph Goebbels, using his own name, wrote an article that was published in the paper *Das Reich* under the title "The Jews Are to Blame"; this blame allegedly included responsibility for the war. Hence Germany would, under the law of retribution, fulfill Hitler's prophecy of January 30, 1939, that a war would result in the annihilation of the Jewish race in Europe. Goebbels condemned Germans who allowed themselves to be duped by Jews into sympathizing with them: among the greatest weaknesses of Germans, he declared, were their magnanimity and forgetfulness. He found it remarkable that every measure taken against Jews in Germany was reported in the British and American press the next day. Jews must have some secret means of communication with enemy foreign countries, he claimed.[9] Side by side with ideological and emotional rationalizations of a Holocaust, here were signs of some nervousness about the leakage of specific information, particularly since liquidations of German Jewish deportees were about to commence in Kowno, Riga, and Minsk.[10]

Germany's declaration of war on the United States just after Pearl Harbor radically altered the situation for American observers in Germany. Most American reporters who had not left the country, along with remaining embassy staff and a few American military officials, were interned as enemy aliens in Berlin; then they traveled on a guarded train to the resort of Bad Nauheim, north of Frankfurt, where they were held at the abandoned Jeschke's Grand Hotel. During their enforced idleness of roughly five months, and in spite of the presence of a Gestapo officer, the Americans managed their own affairs and activities much of the time. With the aid of a secret battery-operated radio, they listened each night to the BBC (and some other foreign broadcasts) and generally kept in touch with events.[11]

In February or early March 1942, the American military attaché distributed a questionnaire to the newsmen at Bad Nauheim and asked them to produce individual analyses of the climate of opinion in Germany, the strengths and weaknesses of various countries' wartime broadcasts, and recommendations for future American information policies. The military attaché, Lieutenant Colonel W. D. Hohenthal, summarized the findings, concluding that "propaganda" was vital to weaken the morale of the German people and deplete their war effort. The principal objective of propaganda, he wrote, should be to drive a wedge between the German people and the Nazi leadership, as well as between the regular armed forces and the Nazi Party.[12]

Given the difficulties of measuring popular attitudes in a police state,[13] the reporters' detailed responses are worthy of some attention. They also reveal something of the reporters' attitudes about both the climate in Germany and what the United States could or could not do to influence the situation. P. C. Fisher of the National Broadcasting Company (NBC), for example, believed that American propaganda had to reach the German intelligentsia first; the intellectuals could and would pass on the message to others. Fisher wanted American broadcasts to stress, among other things, the corrupt Nazi judicial system, the outrages perpetrated by the Gestapo, barbaric pogroms against the Jews, and ruthless outrages committed by the SS in Poland and other occupied countries. But he also warned not to give the Jewish question a prominent place in American propaganda and not to allow Jews to write or disseminate American propaganda, adding: "I say this not in bigotry or any dislike for the race, but merely because I know that anything which smacks of the Jewish angle or has a Jewish ring will be suspected and will not be well received in Germany."[14]

J. M. Fleisher of the United Press cautioned that the evidence and proof of atrocities should be so convincing when reported that there could be no doubt of authenticity: "in general, I believe it would be better to ignore the atrocity idea because it became quite generally discredited as a result of world war [I] practices."[15] Louis Lochner, who had spent twenty-one years in Germany, expressed grudging respect for the effectiveness of Nazi propaganda. Germans slowly began to repeat what they heard over and over again on the radio and in the press, he said:

> people who in 1933 wanted to be fair to the Jew now repeat the same arguments that the press brings for their complete despoliation and elimination. I often could not refrain from saying to German acquaintances, who thoughtlessly repeated the popular slogans and arguments, "Have you lost all power of thinking?"

Lochner also noted that the September 1941 introduction of the yellow Star of David, which German Jews were required to wear, was unpopular with decent Germans but that the Propaganda Ministry had put out false word that it was retaliation for Americans requiring Germans to wear swastikas, which placated some. (An American diplomat had previously reported that the regime spread this swastika story but claimed that ordinary Germans gave it little credence.) Lochner did not express an opinion about the use of atrocities against Jews in American broadcasts.[16]

Frederick Oechsner of the United Press advised against impassioned defenses of the Jews.[17] Only Glen Stadler, also of the United Press, specifically recommended not only a media campaign of accusations against the Gestapo but also the use of statistics on concentration camps and death rates in them. Stadler wanted discussion of the Nazi treatment of the Jews to be part of an approach based on truth, accuracy, and sympathy for the German people.[18] Alvin Steinkopf of the Associated Press, however, warned against allowing Jews to prepare anti-Nazi propaganda, cautioning against threadbare stories from Jewish immigrants, who had their own reasons for hating and misjudging Germans.[19]

Many of the correspondents recommended pursuing the line that Nazism was un-German. Several newsmen specifically advocated using stories about the Nazi "euthanasia" program, even spreading rumors that severely wounded soldiers might be put to death. It was certainly possible to argue that revelations of Nazi killings of Jews and other victims might widen a split between Germans of conscience and the Nazi regime and that an American supply of factual information might counter the effects of Nazi anti-Semitic propaganda. But most of the newsmen preferred to leave the subject alone or to give it a subordinate position in any American broadcasts. The military attaché went with the majority when he concluded that it was inadvisable to defend or champion the Jewish cause vigorously.[20]

Formulating their recommendations, the newsmen were reticent about what they actually knew of the Nazi persecution of Jews. They may have feared that German authorities would seize their papers. Joseph Grigg of the United Press mentioned in passing that he had made a special study of the Jewish question in Germany and of German attitudes toward Jews, but he included hardly any specific comments about persecution in his responses to the questionnaire.[21]

In the spring of 1942, the interned Americans were exchanged for German nationals similarly caught in the United States, which soon removed constraints on what the reporters said and wrote. In the interim, important information had reached the American press from other sources. In March 1942, the JTA and *The New York Times* both reported that the "Gestapo" had murdered 240,000 Jews deported from Germany and other parts of Central and Eastern Europe into the Ukraine. Deportations were continuing, the articles asserted. This information was obtained by S. Bertrand Jacobsen, an official of the American Jewish Joint Distribution Committee who had served in Budapest for two years. Jacobsen had talked to Hungarian soldiers who had served in the conquered Soviet territories, and when he returned to New York, he held a press conference.[22]

At the beginning of June 1942, Joseph Grigg issued a bleak, detailed survey of events during the past year in the Baltic region. In Latvia, SS troops and Latvian irregulars had killed fifty-six thousand Jewish men, women, and children in several days over the summer of 1941. In Lithuania, special "cleanup" squads that came from Nazi-ruled Poland disposed of thirty thousand Jews, and Grigg described the process of machine-gunning victims in prepared graves. In Poland, the total number killed was at least eighty thousand, a high percentage of them Jews. Grigg estimated the total number of Jewish victims as at least two hundred thousand. In a 1942 book he wrote about his experiences, Frederick Oechsner put the total killed by Nazi execution squads between the outbreak of war in the East and the spring of 1942 at at least two hundred thousand; the precise total, he wrote, would never be known. Stadler put the total at more like four hundred thousand.[23] Both turned out to be low. In contrast, Lochner did not mention killings of Jews but did describe the deportations and also condemned the Nazis' barbarous behavior.[24]

Grigg connected the killings with Hitler's public declaration to the German Reichstag on January 30, 1939, that if the Jews succeeded in forcing Germany into a war it would lead to the destruction of the Jews themselves: "those of us who lived in Germany know that he and his agents have done everything to make the prophecy come true."[25] The pattern was becoming clear to those who had a feel for the events and the climate in Nazi-controlled territory.

In June 1942, new reports through the Polish underground also reached London, and they substantially raised both the death counts and the visibility of Nazi killings of Jews. Some of this material was publicized in the United States as well. The most critical report to reach the public came from the Jewish labor organization in Poland known as the Bund. Dated May 11, 1942, it left Warsaw on May 21 and reached the Polish government-in-exile in London, with the aid of Swedish businessmen traveling between Warsaw and Stockholm, in less than two weeks. The Bund's report summarized Nazi actions against the Jews of Poland and put the number already dead at seven hundred thousand. The rest were in dire danger:

> The above facts prove unquestionably that the German government has begun to implement Hitler's announcement that five minutes before the end of the war, whatever the end, he will kill all the Jews in Europe. Millions of Jewish citizens of Poland face the threat of immediate extermination.

The Bund requested an immediate Allied response.[26]

The BBC carried the thrust of this story on June 2 and issued a general directive on June 24 to emphasize it. On June 6, the Polish cabinet delivered a note to the Allies protesting German crimes in Poland, including extermination of the Jewish population. Szmul Zygielbojm, the Bund's representative in London, was able to get a major story based on the Bund report into *The Daily Telegraph* the next day. It mentioned the Nazi use of mobile gas chambers.[27]

On June 29, Ignacy Schwarzbart, the representative of the Zionists on the Polish National Council, held a press conference in London at which he announced that one million Jews had already died. *The Times* of London and other British newspapers highlighted the story and the number.[28] A high official in the Polish Ministry of Information told Schwarzbart: "Hitler murdered many Jews, but you exaggerate the numbers." Polish Foreign Minister Edward Raczyński was also dubious, influenced in part by the attitudes in the British Foreign Office: "we had to be absolutely precise and very cautious not to meet with the criticism that we exaggerated."[29] American reaction was more low-key and also skeptical. Some American newspapers picked the stories up without giving them much prominence; others attributed them to Jewish sources.[30] In a late June Columbia Broadcasting System (CBS) news broadcast from New York City, however, Quincy Howe cited a World Jewish Congress estimate that the Germans had already massacred more than one million Jews since the fall of 1939.[31]

Around the same time, another secret account, complementing the Bund report, emerged from Poland. A number of British soldiers trapped in Warsaw had found shelter in the ghetto. In mid-June 1942, one of them escaped and managed to get to neutral Lisbon within two weeks. Presumably, British officials debriefed him in Lisbon and later in Britain, but those records are not known to be available. An American official in Lisbon, however, talked to the escapee and wrote up a summary of his experiences and conclusions. (Circumstantial evidence suggests that the American was Gerald M. Mayer, a former newsman for NBC fluent in German, then on his way to Switzerland to run an outpost for the American Office of War Information.[32]) The American report began:

> Germany no longer persecutes the Jews. It is systematically exterminating them. The new racist policy, which in cold calculated cruelty surpasses the horrors of Magdeburg [destroyed during the Thirty Years' War] or Carthage, was revealed to me by a British officer who escaped the hell of the Himmler ghetto in Warsaw. For several months now, the Third Reich has been brutally destroying the Jewish population by two effective means: starvation and mass execution.

The remainder of the five-page document recounted some of what the officer had experienced and much that he had heard. There were exaggerations, some inaccuracies, and major gaps. The officer reported a trial shooting at Sobibor, but he could not have known of gassings there—they had not yet begun when he escaped. He assumed that the ghettos were themselves the major sites of destruction, working through starvation, disease, and occasional shootings. Still, the officer learned that Himmler had visited Warsaw that spring and insisted on complete extermination of the Jews. Himmler had allegedly said that they were not disappearing fast enough to please the Führer.[33]

This officer's comments made their way from the American in Lisbon to American intelligence officials, and they presumably reached British intelligence as well. But there is no sign of an immediate effect. The information was not, apparently, used to affect Allied policy toward the fate of Jews then being deported from Western Europe into Poland. The American official in Lisbon followed up, however, with another article on Nazi extermination of the Jews several months later —this one written from a spot (presumably in Switzerland) on the German frontier:

> The exact date when Hitler decided to wipe the jews [sic] from the surface of Europe in the most literal sense of the word, namely by killing them, is unknown. Evacuations and deportations accompanied by executions date as far back as the Polish campaign, but the organized wholesale slaughter of whole communities and trainloads of jews appears to have been practised not before the German attack on Russia.

This account culminated with a description of the killing of Jewish women and children outside Minsk in gas vans, though the author thought that phosgene gas, not carbon monoxide, was the killing agent.[34]

During the summer of 1942, American diplomats and officials of international welfare organizations, such as the American Friends Service Committee, also sent detailed descriptions of the barbaric round-ups, imprisonment, and deportations of Jews from the unoccupied zone of France, where the French (Vichy) government still held sovereignty. High Vichy officials and the French police chose to cooperate with German requests that foreign Jews be turned over, first supposedly as punishment for French resistance attacks on German servicemen and then, from late June on, for what was said to be labor service in Eastern Europe. Deportations of some French Jews followed. From July on, trainloads of Jews from the German-occupied zone and from Vichy France rolled regularly to the East. Vichy gave out the story that these Jews were headed for an ethnic "reservation" in Poland, and other observers simply stated that the ultimate fate of the deported Jews was unknown.[35] After he made a fruitless effort to dissuade Premier Pierre Laval from cooperating with these deportations, the American chargé d'affaires, S. Pinkney Tuck, urged Washington to protect and admit into the United States four thousand Jewish children in France left behind in initial deportations. He described them as de facto orphans, because the Nazi authorities intended for their deported parents not to survive. An Assistant Secretary of State, however, wrote in his diary that deported Jews were being used as laborers in the East.[36]

There were major barriers to getting Americans to believe in a Holocaust. Nazi barbarism was geographically distant. The Final Solution was not merely unprecedented but almost literally incredible. It was hard for human beings to conclude that members of the same species were capable of such behavior. It took more than reading some stories, particularly if they were cast in qualified or skeptical terms, to dent this conviction. Who was in a position to say for sure what was happening? Some organizations and individuals were particularly disinclined to accept the claims of Jewish spokesmen.

Nonetheless, a few Washington officials became interested in mid-1942 in highlighting Nazi war crimes. Allen Dulles, soon to head the new Office of Strategic Services (OSS) outpost in Switzerland, suggested an Allied "tribunal" of distinguished jurists from Allied and neutral countries that would immediately examine all evidence about Nazi, Fascist, and possibly Japanese perpetrators of violence and spoliation. The tribunal could make public its findings and generate a continuous flow of publicity. Dulles's superior, William J. Donovan, about to become head of the OSS, was skeptical: how could one have a trial conducted only by one side and without the defendants? Dulles suggested that the procedure might be more like a grand jury hearing than a trial and that the publicity itself might deter other enemy criminals. He continued to lobby in Washington circles for some version of this plan.[37]

It was as hard to coordinate publicity and information policy in the Roosevelt Administration as it was in the British government. In 1941, Donovan headed an office called the Coordinator of Information, but there was also a small organization called the Office of Facts and Figures, headed by the poet-playwright and Librarian of Congress Archibald MacLeish. (In mid-1942, part of Donovan's empire, MacLeish's organization, and some other stray parts merged into the Office of War Information, or OWI.) The guiding philosophy of the Office of Facts and Figures was to combat the enemy with a strategy of truth.[38]

MacLeish established an interagency body called the Committee on War Information Policy, which considered the possible use of evidence about Japanese atrocities in Nanking. One official noted that President Roosevelt had encouraged a writer to tell the story of his horrifying experiences in China, which then appeared in an article in *The Saturday*

*Evening Post* accompanied by a statement that Roosevelt had approved release of this information.[39]

Edgar Ansel Mowrer, former Berlin correspondent for the *Chicago Daily News* whom the Nazis had expelled in 1933, contended that the most effective soldiers against the Axis so far—the Soviets, the Chinese, and the Royal Air Force—were all motivated by fanatical fervor against the enemy. Mowrer wanted to use information to show Americans the nature of the enemy. Assistant Secretary of War John J. McCloy cautioned that some officials in the War Department feared that release of atrocity material might cause attacks on alien groups in the United States and subsequent enemy retaliations against American prisoners of war. Still, he said that there was guarded sentiment in favor of "proper use" of atrocity material. Former newsman Lowell Mellet, head of the Office of Governmental Reports, a clearinghouse for information about government activities, argued that Americans did not need to hate in order to fight well, and another official thought that atrocity stories worked better if they included heroism on the part of a victim or victims. MacLeish concluded that it would be government policy not to go easy on the use of atrocity material that clearly showed the barbarism and inhumanity of the systems under which the enemies operated but not to use material fabricated or trumped up in any way. The government needed carefully documented facts so as to leave no doubt of their accuracy.[40] But even in mid-1942, the Americans did not yet have the documentation about Nazi killings of Jews to meet that standard.

In June 1942, the Nazi killings at the Czech town of Lidice—a reprisal for the Czech assassination of Reinhard Heydrich—and the complete destruction of the town unleashed new indignation in the West. MacLeish, now deputy director of the new OWI, decided to undertake a campaign to develop Lidice as a symbol of "German oppression."[41] The White House and the State Department also became more interested in public discussion of the enemy's atrocities and of Allied countermeasures in the form of statements about postwar trials.[42] But official statements contained very limited information about Nazi actions against Jews.

On the evening of July 21, one day before the Jewish commemoration of the destruction of the ancient Temple at Jerusalem, about twenty thousand people attended a rally at Madison Square Garden in New York City sponsored by the American Jewish Congress, B'nai B'rith, and the Jewish Labor Committee to protest Hitler's atrocities.

President Roosevelt sent a message to the gathering, one portion of which drew from news reports:

> Citizens, regardless of religious allegiance, will share in the sorrow of our Jewish fellow-citizens over the savagery of the Nazis against their helpless victims. The Nazis will not succeed in exterminating their victims any more than they will succeed in enslaving mankind. The American people not only sympathize with all the victims of Nazi crimes but will hold the perpetrators of these crimes to strict accountability in a day of reckoning which will surely come.

There was no clear recognition here that Jews were a special Nazi target, and there was certainly no hint of interest in rescue action during the war, but Roosevelt did use the term "exterminating."

Prime Minister Churchill's message to the gathering contained some references to his statement of October 25, 1941, and to the need to make retribution for war crimes one of the major purposes of the war. He also rephrased his November 1941 message to *The Jewish Chronicle*: "The Jews were among Hitler's first victims and ever since they have been in the forefront of resistance to Nazi aggression." Churchill recognized the support of ten thousand Jews from Palestine who were serving with the British armed forces in the Middle East but avoided mention of some Jewish calls for an army composed of Palestinian and stateless Jews.[43] The head of the government that knew more about Nazi killings and plans said less about it.

A message read at the same meeting from the American Jewish Committee, often more restrained and more conservative than other Jewish organizations, condemned the barbarous mass murders of civilian populations: "Hundreds of thousands of defenseless Jews—men, women, and children—have been and are being murdered in violation of all laws of modern warfare by the Nazis, who openly proclaim their intention to destroy the Jews throughout Europe."[44] The President and the Prime Minister might have made such a statement, which would have given more visibility and credibility to reports of Nazi killings. But political caution and calculation dominated on both sides of the Atlantic.

Neither Roosevelt nor Churchill spelled out reasons for restraint, but there is evidence from lower-level officials as to what kind of thinking prevailed. In July, the British Political Warfare Executive opened an office in New York to collect information, and representatives from it and the British Ministry of Information began to meet in Washington with high-level representatives of the OWI to coordinate information policies. (OWI representatives did much the same in London.) At the beginning of September, Harold Butler, from the British Ministry of Information, noted that both governments had been cautious about the use of atrocity reports. He wondered whether there should be any distinction between the treatment of Germany and Japan, and he suggested a common approach by the two governments. MacLeish said that the United States had tended to repress official statements because of adverse reaction to a statement issued at the time of the Japanese bombing of Manila, but the American interagency Committee on War Information Policy was about to discuss the issue again.[45]

The next day MacLeish presented a draft statement to the American committee that drew a clear distinction between the rulers and people in enemy countries. He wanted to release authenticated information about militaristic and Fascist rulers (individuals and parties) in enemy countries when the effect would be to clarify public and world understanding of the enemy's character and purposes:

> . . . It is generally agreed that atrocity material relating to atrocities perpetrated upon citizens of other countries may produce in the minds of our people morbid results rather than desirable results . . . Under such a policy as this, barbarous actions and cruelties not serving to directly illuminate the nature of the enemy, but merely to excite horror and hatred of all members of the races guilty of such actions, would not be released.

MacLeish also expressed concern that American emphasis on enemy atrocities might bring about reprisals by enemy countries on American prisoners.[46] MacLeish's proposal to the committee went unchallenged. Other committee members were supposed to study it and react later, but the interagency committee disbanded shortly thereafter, perhaps eclipsed by the new joint British-American committee.

In his memoirs, Mowrer offered a none-too-flattering portrait of the Committee on War Information Policy. MacLeish and a number of others were brilliant, and they all had opinions of their own that they steadfastly defended. But the basic purpose of the committee was far from clear; only the military representatives seemed to know what to do. The military preferred to restrict the flow of information that might affect the war effort.[47]

Pending further discussion with the British, OWI continued to exercise restraint in releasing information about Nazi killings of Jews. In October 1942, the OWI Overseas Branch, which operated semi-autonomously (under the direction of Robert Sherwood), issued its central directive for American broadcasts to Europe. Sherwood and OWI wanted to interfere with German recruitment of laborers in occupied countries by means of a "manpower campaign." They explained that use of foreign labor in Germany was part of a planned depopulation of conquered countries; by separating men from their families, Hitler reduced the birthrate. Executions and deaths fit into this context:

> Hitler wants to make sure that even if he loses the war, the Germans will dominate Europe by sheer weight of numbers. The more German casualties grow (use a figure not in excess of four and a half million), the more he must murder non-Germans and prevent their having children. (There is plenty of material to keep this theme going through the winter. Every story out of Poland provides evidence.) The extermination of the Jews is openly avowed by the Germans, but extermination of the Poles, Czechs, French, and Greeks, which is not openly avowed, is equally demonstrable.[48]

The last sentence indicated either that Sherwood and the OWI Overseas Branch had no grasp of what extermination really meant or that they were determined not to distinguish the mass murder of Jews from the suffering of others.

The American government monitored radio broadcasts to prevent release of any information that might undermine the war effort. In November 1942, the theologian Paul Tillich, a German who had come to the United States in 1934, tried to broadcast a warning to the German people against participating in the persecution of the Jews. The gist of his statement was that, if persecution of the Jews did not cease, the Germans might be treated similarly. OWI censors in New York City barred him from making the statement.[49]

The American government was interested in broadcasting "atrocity reports" only if they helped to mobilize the public and the outside world to win the war. Some Allied officials thought that coverage of the Jewish plight hampered psychological warfare. Foreign Jews were not among the most popular groups in the United States or, for that matter, in other parts of the world. Nazi radio propaganda and other media outlets were charging daily that the Allies were fighting this war only on behalf of Jews, and the American government did not want to seem to support this charge any more than Britain did.[50] In retrospect, both governments limited their coverage to stories they believed would work against the Nazi regime in the occupied countries, in Germany itself, and with the neutrals. They had ambiguous evidence of attitudes in Germany, from which most drew far-reaching conclusions. They were not concerned enough with simply reporting what was happening.

Too many present and former newsmen, brought into government, or regulated and influenced by it, were seduced by this prospect of boosting morale at home and conducting psychological or political warfare abroad. With few exceptions, their calculations of what would work overshadowed what the Nazis were actually doing, and they failed to bring out to the American people (and to the German people through their broadcasts) the true nature of Nazism. They were not much concerned with reporting what was happening to the Jews. They also failed to display effectively the values of Western democratic societies.

# 9

\*

# BREAKTHROUGH
# IN THE WEST

NEITHER INTELLIGENCE DATA nor press reports caused Western governments to react publicly to what the Nazis called the Final Solution of the Jewish question for more than a year. But during the last five months of 1942, additional information from a range of different sources brought about a significant breakthrough on both sides of the Atlantic. Information not only came in increasing volume, but it offered a clearer picture of the overall Nazi scheme. Vivid and horrific information from a prominent, but secretly anti-Nazi, German industrialist and a Polish underground courier reached governments as well as Jewish organizations; those sources had the biggest impact on Western governments, and both men later regretted how little the West did in response. Their two different messages were by no means the only evidence of the Holocaust that emerged in the late summer and fall of 1942, though they reinforced each other at a particular and crucial moment in late November 1942.

The stories of the senior German industrialist and the courageous young Pole have already been told separately.[1] There has been, however, some continuing controversy about the German source who supplied information to the World Jewish Congress; some have also questioned the value of his information. Additional evidence is now available about both points. Similarly, new documentation sustains the long-accepted version that the Polish courier provided timely information about the Holocaust, answering recent skeptics. Finally, we must now reassess the process in which both governments reacted to these two messengers in light of Great Britain's Secret Intelligence Service's prior knowledge about Nazi mass killings of Jews obtained from the decodes.

On July 30, 1942, a German industrialist from Breslau named Eduard Schulte met with a Swiss business associate in Zurich. Schulte revealed that at Hitler's headquarters a plan was being considered to concentrate all Jews from Germany and German-occupied territories in the East and to exterminate them through the use of prussic acid. It would resolve the Jewish question once and for all. All together, he said, some 3.5–4 million Jews would be killed in this operation, which was set for the fall. A giant crematorium would dispose of the bodies.

The plan was in fact not under consideration; it had already begun. The undertaking was so large that it could not occur suddenly, as Schulte thought, or as quickly as the Nazi leadership hoped, but would take many months. Nonetheless, the Breslau businessman, whose company had mines not far from Auschwitz, had uncovered a good portion of the Final Solution. After insisting that his identity be withheld (for he was returning to Germany), Schulte urged his business associate to get this information to Churchill and Roosevelt immediately.[2]

What Schulte thought was the beginning of a program was actually a shift into high gear. Later critics argued either that Schulte's report was not the first such report or that it was hardly definitive.[3] Schulte's information was clearly not the first report of massive Nazi killings of Jews, but it was the first report from a well-placed German source of the intent and plan to destroy the Jewish people entirely. Previous conclusions were deductions. Even if Schulte's report contained some inaccuracy, the fact remains that, because of other circumstances, his message had a much greater impact on Western governments than earlier information.

The historian Christopher Browning has recently put Schulte's message into the proper German context. What Schulte uncovered was an effort, spearheaded by Himmler in mid-1942, to speed up the killing of Jews, partly through the construction of additional gas chambers and massive crematoria. There was a strenuous effort to rid Poland entirely of Jews, except for small numbers in labor camps run by the SS, by the end of 1942. In addition, the Reich Security Main Office (RSHA) ran a massive program of deportations of Jews from various parts of Europe to the extermination camps during late 1942. Browning termed Schulte's information "true in its basic message about the fate of Europe's Jews" and accurate in the particular details that Himmler and his entourage must have discussed during their July 17–18, 1942, visit to Auschwitz.[4]

Within days, Schulte's warning reached Benjamin Sagalowitz, head of the information bureau of the Association of Swiss Jewish Communities. Sagalowitz quickly told Gerhart Riegner, the representative of the World Jewish Congress in Geneva. Riegner had been sending Washington and London regular reports of Nazi atrocities and killings of Jews in Eastern Europe and of deportations of Jews from Western Europe to the East. This new information complemented what Riegner knew from other sources about the brutality of the deportations. He consulted his mentor, the distinguished law professor Paul Guggenheim, who urged Riegner to delete from the message he wanted to send the reference to a giant crematorium. Guggenheim also persuaded Riegner to insert into the message a note of caution about his inability to confirm the information. After doing so, Riegner went to the American consulate in Geneva and asked Vice-Consul Howard Elting, Jr., to inform the American government and to pass the report on to Rabbi Stephen S. Wise, the president of the American Jewish Congress.[5] Riegner also went to the British consulate, where he asked officials to transmit the same message to Sidney Silverman, a Labour Party member of the House of Commons who was also the British representative of the World Jewish Congress.

Although he was skeptical of the revelation, Elting dutifully wrote up a memo for his superiors at the American legation in Bern. Elting assessed Riegner as a serious and balanced individual who would not have come forward if he had not believed the story. Legation officials sent Riegner's message to Washington but with an accompanying despatch questioning its accuracy. American Minister to Switzerland Leland Harrison thought that Nazi treatment and miserable conditions were decimating Jews but not that the Nazis had a plan to kill all of them. State Department officials, summarizing the despatch for the Office of Strategic Services (OSS), called Riegner's message "a wild rumor inspired by Jewish fears."[6]

The dominant view in the State Department was to sit on this unconfirmed allegation, not to pass it on to Rabbi Wise. Even if it were accurate, what could they do about it? They did not want others to publicize this information, and there was an effort to stop reports being sent through the diplomatic pouch to third parties (such as Rabbi Wise) in the United States. Word went back to Riegner that he would need corroborating information.[7] The State Department's reaction and response indicated not only that previous information and published reports of Nazi killings of Jews had made just a limited impression but also that the European Division at State had little inclination to pursue the matter.

Riegner had better luck with the British, but only because of fortuitous circumstances. The intended recipient of Riegner's telegram in London was Sidney Silverman. A sensible Foreign Office official did not simply bury a message to a member of Parliament. Frank Roberts wrote on August 15: "I do not see how we can hold up this message much longer, although I fear it may provoke embarrassing repercussions. Naturally we have no information bearing on the story."[8] (Some of the decodes from June 1942 discussed the crematorium at Auschwitz;[9] Roberts was unaware of them.) In general, Foreign Office officials reacted skeptically to Riegner's information, despite their awareness of previous reports of massacres in Poland.

In early June, Polish Prime Minister Władisław Sikorski had given a speech on a BBC broadcast to Poland, in which he referred to executions of Jews at Wilna and Lvov and predicted that the Nazis intended to "slit the throats of all Jews, no matter what the outcome of the war." On June 24 the BBC, as we have seen, had instructed news writers to feature a story about executions of Jews in the Wilna, Lodz, and Lublin regions. Zygielbojm, the Bund's representative on the Polish National Council, had announced the basic elements of the Bund's report—that seven hundred thousand Jews in Poland had already died —in a broadcast on June 27 (apparently the first Yiddish broadcast on the BBC).[10] The next day a London rabbi declared on the BBC European service that systematic mass murder of the Jews was in full swing and said others would also be targeted.[11] According to one study, the BBC was more tolerant of such disclosures in foreign broadcasts than on the BBC home service—the first report of mass killings of Jews in Poland came on the home service on July 9. When the fiercely anti-German British diplomat Sir Robert Vansittart had declared on the BBC home service in September that thousands of Jews, including children, were being gassed each day in Poland, BBC officials thought he had gone well beyond what the facts justified.[12]

Following the publicity of June and early July 1942,[13] Jewish organizations in Britain had increased their lobbying efforts through a number of channels to induce the British and U.S. governments to try to put an end to Nazi mass murders, if necessary by adopting new policies.

On July 5, the Council of Polish Jews in Britain had convened a meeting of many Jewish organizations, one outcome being a report on Nazi atrocities against Jews in Poland submitted to all members of both houses of Parliament. One M.P. had asked the government whether Britain would commit, through neutral channels, food and medical supplies to Jews in Polish ghettos to ensure that they were not worse treated than prisoners of war. Foreign Minister Anthony Eden had stood by previous decisions to consider food relief only when it would not impair the effect of the blockade on the enemies' war effort. Eden had said the government was willing to assist delivery of medical supplies, in the strict sense of the term, to occupied territory.[14]

On July 8, the Polish National Council had passed a resolution that denounced the "systematic destruction of the vital strength of the Polish Nation and the planned slaughter of practically the whole Jewish population." The next day Polish and Polish Jewish representatives released new evidence at a press conference held at the Ministry of Information. Introducing the speakers, the Minister of Information, Brendan Bracken, a close confidant of Churchill, expressed horror and indignation at Nazi crimes in Poland and particularly atrocities committed against Jews. He adhered to the standard line—retribution would take place after victory—but added some specific elements: the Allied governments should collect names of those responsible, they should be brought to justice quickly, and the punishment should suit the crimes. The BBC broadcast his statement the next day.[15]

The Council of Polish Jews in Britain had then called for Britain and America to find means, during the war, of paralyzing the terror unleashed by the Germans and the planned slaughter of the Jewish population. Prime Minister Churchill also asked the Royal Air Force to consider the feasibility of obliterating a German town as explicit retribution for Nazi atrocities, but despite the practice of heavy bombing attacks, the government rejected the idea of such an announcement.[16]

In this context, Riegner's telegram from Geneva in early August seemed not only to confirm and extend previous information but also to make the need for Western action during the war even more urgent. It was not welcome news for those who wanted the West to focus solely on military goals. Silverman accepted Riegner's report as reliable and asked Foreign Office permission to send it to Rabbi Wise in New York City, which he got. He also asked the Foreign Office to give its opinion about publicizing the information. Another Foreign Office official, Denis Allen, accepted the notion that large numbers of Jews had died in Poland and that there had been executions. He summarized the Nazi policy as eliminating "useless mouths" but making use of able-bodied Jews as slave laborers, which had a small kernel of truth. But he rejected the notion of "extermination at one blow" as a wild story.[17]

At his August 21 press conference, Roosevelt summarized information recently received from the governments-in-exile of several European countries about barbaric Nazi occupation policies that "may even lead to the extermination of certain populations." He then welcomed the submission of additional reports from any trustworthy source: "In other words, we want news—from any source that is reliable—of the continuation of atrocities."[18]

After receiving Riegner's telegram (via Silverman in London) on August 29, Wise sent it to Undersecretary of State Sumner Welles, President Roosevelt's trusted number-two man in the State Department, with a cover letter vouching for Riegner. Welles telephoned Wise, conceding that Riegner's information could be correct but arguing that it would be illogical for the Nazis to kill large numbers of Jews when they needed laborers. Wise asked Welles to have Minister Harrison meet with Riegner and gather additional evidence. Welles urged Wise to refrain from any publicity until further investigation confirmed or refuted the story.[19]

Decades later, there would be harsh charges that Wise did not do enough in response to Riegner's telegram.[20] The criticism is at least overstated; not all the critics paid attention to what Wise actually did or what he knew or did not know at the time. Wise did contact Supreme Court Justice Felix Frankfurter and ask him to pass Riegner's telegram to the President.[21] After receiving, on September 4, a second cable from Switzerland about Nazi killings of Jews from the Warsaw ghetto—this one originating from Recha and Yitzchok Sternbuch of the Agudas Israel (Orthodox Jewish) organization and delivered through representatives of the Agudas Israel in New York—Wise attended and chaired a meeting of representatives of major Jewish organizations in New York. He informed them of his discussion with Welles and of Welles's request for no publicity until further information could confirm or refute the story. They considered various suggestions for action if or when the information was confirmed.[22] Wise adhered to Welles's request, and so did the other Jewish organizations.

The following week Wise went to Washington twice and conferred with government officials about the plight of Jews in Nazi Europe. He spoke to Secretary of the Treasury Henry Morgenthau, Jr., and asked his advice—should he make the information public?[23] He continued to hear the version put out previously by the Polish ambassador in Washington: the Nazis were capable of killing all Jews, but they were presently deporting Jews from the Warsaw ghetto to the eastern frontier to build fortifications.[24] Wise did not know which version was true. On September 17, he drafted a cable to send to Alexander Easterman of the World Jewish Congress in London: "Doing everything possible[,] continuous conferences government authorities STOP[.] Washington believes deportations from Warsaw ghetto for building purposes not massacre."[25] Wise must have been tempted to hold to the less alarmist version prevalent in Washington.

The very well informed assistant solicitor general in the Justice Department, Oscar Cox, was among those to whom Wise sent copies of Riegner's cable and the one from Agudas Israel. Cox sent copies to the Polish ambassador and wrote: "If the facts are true, something ought to be done about it." He added, "It seems to me the problem should be handled not as a Jewish problem but as part of the whole atrocity problem." The Polish ambassador responded that he knew of these cables already and left the impression that he knew about the liquidation of the Warsaw ghetto population.[26]

Under the circumstances, Welles's request for time to investigate did not seem unreasonable, and Wise's decision to withhold publicity about the telegram was logical for the time being. It did not prevent him from publicizing other reports and holding rallies, however. If the Jewish organizations wanted quick government action, they would not get far by defying one of the few sympathetic men (and the most powerful one) at State. Unlike members of the European Division in the State Department, Welles took a serious interest in the question of Nazi policy toward Jews, and he launched an American investigation, centered largely in Switzerland, the details of which have been presented elsewhere.[27] The inquiries there, however, took considerable time, much longer than Wise and others expected.

In later decades, some writers would maintain that everyone all across Europe knew what was happening to Europe's Jews during the war, but no one in the West could do anything about it. One version, written by the president of the Franklin and Eleanor Roosevelt Institute, not a professional historian, appeared in *The New York Times Magazine*:

Within months of Churchill's receipt of the intercepts, Roosevelt, Eisenhower, Marshall, the intelligence services of the Allied nations, every
Jewish leader, the Jewish communities in Great Britain and America, and
anyone who read a newspaper knew that Europe's Jews in colossal numbers were being murdered.[28]

The implication here was that withholding information from the British
decodes of German police messages made no practical difference.

In reality, as late as September 1942, probably the most powerful
man in the State Department doubted that there was a Nazi Final Solution. The President of the United States had publicly requested information from reliable sources of the continuation of Nazi atrocities,
but there is no sign that British intelligence had made their sources
available to American counterparts. The president of the American Jewish Congress himself was uncertain whether the information he had
received in late August and early September 1942 from Gerhart Riegner
in Geneva was correct. Others more distant from the situation and less
well informed could not have easily recognized the truth.

Key British officials had more information. Simultaneously with the
Americans, on October 7 Sir John Simon announced in the House of
Lords the formation by the Allies of a war-crimes commission (referred
to at the time as the United Nations War Crimes Commission because
"United Nations" was the term used for the countries fighting the Axis
powers), and he briefly referred to Nazi persecution of Jews.[29] The next
day, Victor Cavendish-Bentinck notified the Permanent Undersecretary
in the Foreign Office, Sir Alexander Cadogan, that the two most reliable sources of information about Nazi crimes could not be used until
after the war: the first was the tape recordings the British were making
of conversations among German prisoners of war; the second was "the
intercepted police messages between S.S. brigades etc. and Headquarters. These have in the past contained accounts of wholesale executions, etc." Cavendish-Bentinck recommended that two Foreign Office
officials sift through the material to come up with good evidence for
the international commission at the appropriate time, and Cadogan
agreed.[30]

This decision brought three more Foreign Office officials—Cadogan
and two subordinates—into the secret of the German police decodes
and the unimpeachable evidence of wholesale Nazi killings of Jews in
the East. (It also created the file of documents, a copy of which ended
up, much later, in the United States and eventually in the National

Archives there.[31]) One of the two subordinates was Denis Allen, who in August had thought the Nazis were merely eliminating "useless mouths" and who had rejected the notion of extermination of European Jews at one blow as a wild story.

The American investigation of Riegner's report proceeded entirely independently. Myron Taylor, the American emissary to the Vatican, was unable to gather much information there, but the American minister in Bern, Leland Harrison, began to send back information in October, which was passed on to Rabbi Wise.[32] By late November, the State Department had gathered enough information from other sources to convince Welles, who summoned Wise to Washington and told him that his deepest fears were confirmed. Wise then arranged for press conferences in Washington and New York and made public what he knew. The Associated Press carried the story, which appeared in the *New York Herald Tribune* on November 25 under the headline: "Wise Says Hitler Has Ordered 4,000,000 Jews Slain in 1942." The publicity was greater than anything generated previously, but it was not a lead story for most of the mainstream American press.[33]

On the same day this article appeared, a Polish underground courier code-named Karski arrived at a Royal Air Force base outside London. He had left Poland at the beginning of October, made his way through occupied France to Spain, and then to Gibraltar. His information actually preceded his arrival in London. He had carried microfilm concealed in a key, which was flown to London on November 17. Polish officials in London had condensed the information about Nazi killings of Jews into a two-page report in English. On the evening of November 25—the day Karski had arrived and the day the articles about Riegner's telegram appeared—they gave a copy to Alexander Easterman of the British section of the World Jewish Congress.[34]

The World Jewish Congress in London did not miss the fact that Riegner's telegram (publicized November 25) and Karski's report (received November 25) reinforced each other. On the morning of November 26, Sidney Silverman and Alexander Easterman called on Richard Law, Parliamentary Under-Secretary in the Foreign Office, and lent him their copy of the Polish report. They also pointed out that the State Department now accepted the veracity of these stories: they knew of Welles's confirmation of Riegner's telegram.

Law gave away very little, judging that the State Department did not likely have more information than the Foreign Office. Given what was known about the Nazi regime, the stories perhaps seemed consistent

with Nazi ideology. This assessment was in effect a complete discounting of the evidence that Karski had just given to him in the Polish
summary. Law understood the link between Karski's information and
Riegner's report, but he was also skeptical about the latter. He told
Silverman and Easterman that the British consul in Geneva had also
seen Riegner but had not been able to get from him the facts on which
his evidence was based. The two World Jewish Congress delegates
pressed for a four-power declaration about the Nazi extermination plan.
Law doubted that it would do much good, but he pointed out to the
Foreign Office that they would be "in an appalling position" if the
stories turned out to be true and they had done nothing. He also observed that Silverman and his friends could make considerable trouble.[35]

Neither Law nor the other Foreign Office officials he communicated
with had access to the decodes of German police and SS messages that
might have ended their skepticism about the reliability and sufficiency
of evidence about Nazi plans and actions. To be sure, access to such
irrefutable evidence would only have increased their political dilemma,
since they had already convinced themselves that nothing much should
be done about Nazi treatment of Jews; they thought there were few
remedies available to the Allies, and these were perceived to impair the
war effort.

Silverman and Easterman pressed on. Making specific reference to
Riegner's telegram, they again contacted (among others) American
Ambassador John G. Winant, who reported to Washington:

> Each time I have brought the matter to the attention of Mr. Eden, as I
> was requested to do. The Foreign Office told me that they had no def-
> inite information on such a [Nazi] program. Last week [end November–
> early December] I was asked to petition my own government to
> intervene.[36]

The Jewish organizations needed outside assistance, and some of it came
from the Polish government-in-exile—itself much more willing to intervene after Karski's report.

One scholar has recently raised questions about whether Karski
stressed the desperate situation of Polish Jews in late 1942. He was a
non-Jew, and the Polish underground had plenty of troubles of its own
with the Nazi occupation. Perhaps Karski dealt with Polish problems
first and the tragedy of Polish Jews months later. The Polish government had a long history of not considering Polish Jews full citizens.[37]

It would help historians to have access to the microfilm, to the twenty-page Polish report prepared from it, or to British interrogations of Karski. The microfilm and the twenty-page report have not been located, and the British War Office file that probably contains Karski's debriefing is scheduled to be declassified in the year 2018.[38]

There are, however, at least four good, if imperfect, accounts available, three from 1942 and one undated, but apparently from early 1943, of the information Karski presented in London about the Final Solution in Poland. The first account was actually a British summary that may have blended Karski's information with other related sources. On December 2, 1942, the Political Intelligence Department of the British Foreign Office issued its weekly intelligence summary, and the section on Poland came largely from a detailed report "written in a very sober style" from a reliable source that was given to the Polish government-in-exile. The British document described the Polish report as confirming views expressed in previous British weekly intelligence summaries that the German government had a policy of wiping out the Jewish "race" in Poland. (Those views were based on evidence other than the decodes of police and SS communications. Previous Political Intelligence statements about Nazi policy had not had much effect on higher officials of the Foreign Office.)

As summarized in this document, the Polish report retraced some of the history of executions of Jews in Poland since the fall of 1941. In March 1942, Himmler was said to have visited the Government General and to have issued an order for the liquidation of at least half of the remaining Jews by the end of 1942. In July, Himmler paid another visit to Poland to maintain the pressure. The preparations for deportations from the Warsaw ghetto "to the East" were recounted in some detail, and the report also described the suicide of Adam Czerniakow (misspelled Czerbiakow), head of the Jewish council in the ghetto, when he was faced with organizing deportations in July 1942. The intelligence summary explained that many elderly and ill were shot in Warsaw but that the majority were squeezed onto freight trains. The probable destinations were Treblinka, near Malkinia on the Warsaw-Bialystok line, Sobibor in the Lublin region, and Belzec in eastern Galicia:

> In those three places "camps" have been established which are believed in Poland to be in nearly all cases only places of execution for those Jews who have survived the terrible and protracted journey. It is obviously very difficult for the Poles in Warsaw to get first hand news of what

happens in those "camps," but according to the report which forms the basis of this summary, only two small parties, making 4,000 persons in all are known to have been sent in the direction of the German-Russian front [for construction purposes].[39]

Here Karski correctly identified the extermination camps of Operation Reinhard and discredited the notion that Jews were being used systematically for forced labor.

A second, near-contemporary account of Karski's message came after he hurriedly dictated, on November 30, a detailed account of what he had learned about the Nazi extermination policy. On December 2, he was to meet with the two Jewish members of the Polish National Council in London, Zygielbojm and Schwarzbart. In preparation for the meeting, Schwarzbart received and read one day earlier the text Karski had dictated. He immediately sent off a telegram to the World Jewish Congress in New York, saying, among other things, that deportations exceeded in horror the worst fears, that Jews in Poland were almost completely annihilated, and that death camps existed at Belzec, Treblinka, and Sobibor.[40]

The most detailed account came after the December 2 meeting. It is likely Zygielbojm's and Schwarzbart's reconstruction of what Karski said and wrote, and it may also contain quotations embellished for publicity purposes or modified to avoid endangering Polish and Jewish sources in Poland.[41] Karski himself was the unnamed, impassioned narrator:

> I cannot relate all I saw: it is beyond the power of any human being to describe all that I witnessed personally. Moreover were I even able to depict all[,] I fear you would not believe me. Shortly after I had crossed the Polish border I got in touch with a number of diplomatic representatives of Great Britain and told them what I had witnessed. They listened to me politely, showed a great deal of sympathy, but gave me to understand that in view of my horrifying experience it was my overwrought imagination that was painting macabre pictures, and all that I related could be only partially true . . .
>
> Of the three and one half million Jews in Poland and the five to seven hundred thousand who were brought there from other Nazi-occupied countries[,] only a small number remains alive. It is not any longer a question of oppressing Jews, but of their complete extermination by all

kinds of especially devised and perfected methods of pain and torture . . .

In Warsaw I saw the first part [of the deportations] . . . and later on the outskirts of Belzec the second and last part. From Warsaw the Jews are driven to the railroad tracks on the outskirts of the city where a long train of cattle cars is already waiting for them. Before they reach the tracks[,] however[,] many are shot for one reason or another. Particularly those who lag behind. The whole route is literally strewn with corpses . . . Then they are loaded onto cars, [a] hundred people in a car, and the first lap of the journey which lasts from two to eight days, begins. Not once during the journey are the doors of the cars opened[,] with the result that many die before they reach the "sorting point" . . . which is located about fifty kilometers from the city of Belzec.

In the uniform of a Polish policeman I visited the sorting camp near Belzec. It is a huge barracks, only about half of which is covered with a roof. When I was there about five thousand men and women were in the camp. However[,] every few hours new transports of Jews, men and women, young and old, would arrive for the last journey toward death . . .

The guards keep on shooting at the throng. Corpses are scattered everywhere. Convulsively moving men step over the corpses barely noticing the dead. Every few minutes the guards pick a number of men to clear the dead which are piled up alongside the fence. This, too, is done without any emotion, without a single expression on their faces as though they are completely oblivious of what they are doing. They are no longer normal human beings but one large convulsive mass breathing its last.

According to this account, Karski went on to describe how the Nazis crammed Jews into cattle cars and simply left them to die there or else took them to nearby Belzec, where they were murdered by poison gas or the application of electric currents. He did not actually see the gas chambers, but he heard about the process. The account concluded with a message from an unnamed spokesman of the Bund (later identified as Leon Feiner):

what is happening to us is altogether outside the imagination of civilized human beings. They [in the West] don't believe what they hear. Tell them that *we are all dying*. Let them rescue all those who will still be alive when the Report reaches them. We shall never forgive them for not having supplied us with arms so that we may have died like men, with guns in our hands.[42]

Despite their anguish, the Bund leader and a Zionist leader in Warsaw made other specific suggestions: a public declaration by the Allies that preventing the extermination of the Jews was one of their war aims; a propaganda offensive to convince the German people of what was taking place and tell them which German officials were responsible or involved; a public appeal to the German people to put pressure on the regime to stop the slaughter; a declaration that, if genocide continued, the German people would be considered collectively responsible; and the initiation of Allied reprisals through bombing important cultural sites and executions of Germans loyal to Hitler in Allied hands. Karski apparently conveyed these demands (despite his reservations) in London, but they got nowhere. In fact, suspicious British counterintelligence officials detained Karski for several days, until they were satisfied that his overall story checked out.[43]

The fourth account, a memorandum of December 9 from the Polish government-in-exile, presented evidence from a range of Polish sources to the British and American governments. This document again stressed the significance of Himmler's visits to Poland and drew heavily on Karski's description of deportations from the Warsaw ghetto. It suggested that of the 250,000 Jews deported from Warsaw through September 1 only 4,000—those designated for hard labor—were still alive. The trains took others to extermination camps at "Tremblinka," Belzec, and Sobibor. Overall, this note stated that more than a million Polish Jews had perished since 1939.[44]

Some Foreign Office officials and their State Department counterparts continued to express skepticism about evidence of a Final Solution,[45] as did BBC officials. Discussing the recent reports in late November, the BBC's Foreign and Home News boards deliberated over the evidence of a "plan" for mass murder but recommended soft-pedaling it for the time being.[46] The information was beginning to reach a broad public and higher political levels, however. When American Jewish representatives announced a day of mourning and prayer on December 2 (held in other countries as well), New York Mayor Fiorello La Guardia took part, half a million Jewish union workers ceased work for ten minutes, and the National Broadcasting Company aired a nationwide memorial service. The lead editorial in *The New York Times* declared that five million Jews faced extermination.[47]

At the end of November, a small group of American Jewish leaders sought to gain an audience with President Roosevelt to present him with their accumulated information of a Final Solution. Welles helped

Wise and four other American Jewish leaders surmount the obstacles and schedule an appointment with Roosevelt for December 8. By the time they reached the White House, the situation in London was more favorable toward an official Allied statement.[48]

In a December 1 letter to British Foreign Minister Eden, Polish Foreign Minister Raczyński stressed the Nazi murder of Jews. He highlighted the significance of Himmler's mid-July visit to Poland and the deportations from the Warsaw ghetto from July 23 on. He also mentioned three destinations for all the deportations: Tremblinka [sic], Belzec, and Sobibor, which were described as extermination camps, and he stated that they used various means of killing, including poison gas and electrocution.[49] The next day Soviet Ambassador Ivan Maisky weighed in with his personal endorsement (having received no instructions from Moscow) of an Allied declaration denouncing Nazi killings of Jews. In addition, Polish Prime Minister Sikorski met with Undersecretary of State Welles in Washington on December 4 to explain how the Nazis were resolving their Jewish problem. Polish officials urged a joint protest of all concerned governments against the crimes committed on the Jewish population in Poland.[50]

On December 6, Ambassadors Winant and Maisky discussed with Eden the plight of Jews across all of Europe. By then William Temple, Archbishop of Canterbury, had published a letter to the editor in *The Times* as well. The new information and the combined internal and external pressure moved Eden to notify the British ambassador in Washington on December 7 that he now had little doubt about a German policy of gradual extermination of all Jews, except highly skilled workers.[51]

The next day London transmitted a draft declaration on behalf of the British, American, and Soviet governments that accepted the reality of a Final Solution. The German authorities were said to be now carrying out Hitler's oft-repeated intention to exterminate the Jews of Europe and were transporting Jews from all territories under their control to Eastern Europe. The draft mentioned the Nazi practices of working able-bodied Jews to death and leaving the infirm to die of exposure or starvation. It confirmed mass executions of Jews but omitted any reference to gas chambers or crematoria. After condemning these Nazi actions, the draft had the Allied governments reaffirm their pledge to punish those responsible and urge all freedom-loving peoples to overthrow Hitlerite tyranny.[52]

Also on December 8, Maurice Wertheim of the American Jewish

Committee, Adolph Held of the Jewish Labor Committee, Henry Monsky of B'nai B'rith, Israel Rosenberg of the Union of Orthodox Rabbis of the United States, and Stephen Wise gave President Roosevelt a memorandum titled "Blue Print for Extermination," which included a special section on Hitler's order to exterminate Jews and which quoted sections of Riegner's telegram. Wise appealed to Roosevelt to bring the extermination program to the attention of the world and to try to stop it. Roosevelt said that the government was familiar with most of the facts—confirmation had come from American representatives in Switzerland and other countries—but that it was hard to find a suitable course of action. Hitler and his entourage represented "an extreme example of a national psychopathic case," but the Allies could not act as if the entire German people were murderers or agreed with Hitler's actions. He agreed to release another statement denouncing mass killings, and he referred again to postwar punishment: "The mills of the gods grind slowly, but they grind exceeding small."[53] It was the same metaphor Churchill had used in his message to The Jewish Chronicle a year before.[54]

Churchill and Roosevelt were both well-educated men as well as good politicians. Churchill had won the Nobel Prize in Literature, and he would likely have been familiar with this old English proverb that came from Greek and Latin prototypes. Roosevelt could have come across Henry Wadsworth Longfellow's translation of the nineteenth-century German poet Friedrich von Logau or found the line in a good dictionary of quotations.[55] Their renditions were slightly different—for example, Roosevelt had the "mills of the gods" (not God)—but the reappearance of this phrase indicated that Churchill and Roosevelt were handling Jewish requests in virtually the same way. They both wanted to concentrate on winning the war as quickly as possible. The threat of postwar retribution was the only diversion they would consider, and it turned out that Roosevelt was more enthusiastic about that approach than Churchill.[56]

There was one symbolic but important difference in the way the two leaders handled Jewish requests. Roosevelt met with a Jewish delegation, even if he spent much of the half hour on peripheral issues. A week later James de Rothschild requested that the Prime Minister receive a group of leading British Jews to discuss the situation of European Jews. Churchill's secretary John Miller Martin gave the appeal to the Foreign Office, accompanied by the following instructions:

As you will see, Mr. Churchill has referred this to the Foreign Secretary. No acknowledgement is being sent from here and I should be grateful if you could ensure that in any communication to the Board of Deputies [of British Jews] it is made clear that Mr. Eden is handling the matter at Mr. Churchill's request.[57]

Churchill's direct involvement was limited. After he received the December 10 Polish note, he requested further information from the Foreign Office.[58] Since the Secret Intelligence Service had ceased to report executions of Jews to Churchill in mid-September 1941, more than a year before, Churchill apparently had not received or requested reports about the plight of European Jews. He had allowed the Foreign Office to handle matters related to the Holocaust, and the Foreign Office had shown little inclination to believe the worst reports, let alone to recommend action in response.

In the second week of December 1942, Churchill's show of interest eliminated any chance that mid-level opposition (in the Foreign Office and State Department) would prevent a joint Allied statement.[59] Based on the chronology, however, it is unlikely that Churchill's request significantly influenced either Eden or Roosevelt, both of whom had revised their positions earlier.

On December 14, Eden presented a summary of the information to the War Cabinet, confirming massacres in Poland and deportations of Jews to Poland: "it might well be that these transfers were being made with a view to wholesale extermination of Jews." The cabinet approved the idea of a joint declaration, and with only minor changes the British draft of December 8 became the joint Allied Declaration of December 17—the first official Allied statement during the war denouncing Nazi killings of Jews. Sidney Silverman, the initial recipient of Riegner's telegram, put a question to the government in the House of Commons, and Eden read the Declaration in response. James de Rothschild then spoke with deep emotion of Jewish suffering in Europe, and the House of Commons rose and observed a moment of silence.[60]

Until there was this acceptance of the facts, no one in authority would even think about changing existing policies or adding new ones. The Allied Declaration made no mention of rescue efforts. It was, however, a necessary precondition to any official consideration of what Western governments might do to mitigate the slaughter. It came about only because Jewish organizations and the Polish government-in-exile had their own sources of information—not as detailed as the German police and SS decodes, but good enough to grasp the general picture. An official of the British Foreign Office described the Polish government as the driving force behind the declaration, though the British Foreign Office, he complained, had to do most of the work.[61] In reality, Jewish organizations on both sides of the Atlantic had a role, too. They had enough leverage to gain a hearing at the highest levels of the British and American governments.

In the House of Lords on December 17, Viscount Herbert Samuel thanked the government for participating in the Declaration and observed that the only remotely parallel event in history was the Turkish massacre of Armenians during World War I. Samuel then raised the question whether the West might now do something to save Jewish lives, suggesting that the cooperation of neutral countries might produce positive results.[62] Samuel was quite right, but neither Britain nor the United States would effectively pursue this strategy during the next twelve months.

# 10

\*

# REACTIONS TO
# PUBLICITY

IN DECEMBER 1942 and January 1943, the British Political Warfare Executive (PWE) decided to emphasize Nazi atrocities against Jews, with repeated coverage in BBC radio broadcasts and other efforts. How such information affected the German public was difficult to gauge at the time and remains so in retrospect, but the impact was not negligible. Nazi authorities certainly did their best to block this flow of outside information about their policy of mass extermination as well as to dissipate or counteract the potential effects of breaches of secrecy.

On the day World War II began, Propaganda Minister Joseph Goebbels had issued an ordinance making it illegal for Germans to listen to any foreign radio broadcasts, including those of Germany's allies. Violators (the British called them "blacklisteners") could be sentenced to hard labor; those who spread news from foreign broadcasts could be sentenced to hard labor or to death for grave offenses. The biggest target of this regulation was the German-language service of the BBC, which for years had been the single most important source of outside information and which became Germans' most popular provider of illicit news during the war.[1] Nearly sixteen million households in Germany had licenses for radios, and some others managed to acquire sets without paying the required license fee. (Five million of these households had shortwave sets, something of a status symbol; the remainder had long- and medium-wave receivers.)[2] Foreign broadcasts offered Germans an alternative picture of reality, free of Nazi distortions, and some provided a reasonably accurate flow of information about the course of the war, which many Germans felt they lacked. So they took the substantial risk of breaking the law, which was in fact harshly enforced, with sentences published to deter others.[3] The German newspapers and radio broadcasts also sought to persuade Germans not to listen to foreign broadcasts, claiming that they were in effect pure poison. Nazi authorities justified the ban and punishments on the ground that they could not correct foreign distortions because they did not want to reveal military secrets.[4]

There were also regular German efforts to jam British and American broadcasts and to superimpose German broadcasts on the same frequencies. But the BBC's shortwave broadcasts were almost immune to jamming, and its broadcasts on other ranges could be received by all but the smallest German radios when jamming was only partial. The BBC's intelligence division concluded that, in general, most eager German listeners could manage to receive audible broadcasts on one frequency or another. Foreigners and diplomats who spent time in Germany confirmed this.[5]

A Gestapo official was supposed to have estimated at the end of 1941 that the German-language service of the BBC had an audience of about one million. BBC intelligence judged that this figure probably overestimated the number of habitual German listeners but certainly greatly underestimated the number of those who listened at one time or another. In addition, substantial numbers of middle- and upper-class Germans were thought to listen directly to the regular BBC home service broadcasts in English (which had less propaganda): the Polish underground also preferred them to BBC broadcasts in Polish.[6]

On December 10, 1942, the PWE issued a central directive emphasizing Hitler's plan to exterminate the Jews of Europe and predicting a "solemn pronouncement" by the Great Powers based mainly on Polish evidence; whether or not such a pronouncement occurred, PWE wanted to present the facts fully to Europe.[7] One week later, the next central directive was even more explicit and emphatic:

> In giving the facts soberly, stress: i) The deliberate plan of Jewish extermination. The one war aim Hitler still hopes to achieve in the few months [!] remaining to him. ii) The civilized world will judge Germans and the vassal peoples by their attitude to Hitler's plan in the coming months. iii) Main languages should include this week at least one message of encouragement to the Jews.[8]

Several times a day for a week the BBC's European service read the Allied Declaration of December 17 and the related statement by the Polish National Council in London.[9] This activity was unprecedented and very significant: it undoubtedly saved lives by encouraging some Jews to hide or escape, and perhaps also by encouraging some non-Jews to assist them.[10] In addition, following requests from British Jewish representatives to Foreign Minister Eden and Richard Law, Parliamentary Under-secretary in the Foreign Office, the Royal Air Force also dropped 1.2 million flyers about the Nazi extermination program during January 1943 bombing raids. Some 150,000 copies of one flyer, which included a lengthy quote from the Allied Declaration of December 17, 1942, were dropped on Berlin alone.[11]

The Office of War Information (OWI) and American broadcasts to Europe did not conduct a mid-December campaign (like the British one) emphasizing Nazi extermination of Jews.[12] Following the accumulation of evidence in London, Edward R. Murrow of the Columbia Broadcasting System (CBS) made one unusually explicit radio broadcast to the United States describing the murder of millions, mostly Jews: "The phrase 'concentration camp' is obsolete, as out-of-date as 'economic sanctions' or 'non-recognition.' It is now possible to speak only of 'extermination camp.' " CBS also reported the Allied Declaration of December 17, 1942.[13] But these reports went to an American audience, not to a German one.

The Voice of America (VOA) was by this time broadcasting via shortwave directly to Europe, and British transmitters relayed VOA programs on long and medium waves. The PWE had established a close working relationship with OWI and the VOA, and it is possible that British influence resulted in some VOA mention of Nazi extermination policy.[14] In general, however, American information officials were uncomfortable with this topic. An early January 1943 memo offering guidance on atrocity and terror stories from the OWI Overseas Branch showed some ambiguity, declaring that the primary consideration, as it had been before, should be what effect a story would have on the morale of friends and enemies:

2 a) Any act of violence or oppression committed by our enemies . . . is a story worth using if the act of resistance [on the part of our friends] can be played up as the primary part of the story. It is not a useful story if it simply builds up the terror and tends to show that those who commit acts of resistance are ruthlessly punished.

b) Any story which substantiates one of the main themes of our directives, such as the wilful [sic] depopulation of Europe by the Germans, is a useful story. Such stories are likely to concern large groups of individuals rather than small groups.

3) One of our primary purposes is to make the enemy conscious of his guilt and aware of our knowledge of his guilt. It is important to bring home to the German people what their leaders are doing to the Poles, the Jews, the Greeks, etc. It is doubtful whether much of this is known in Germany.

4) In the last analysis it all depends upon how the stories are treated . . . The mere reporting of atrocities is likely to do nothing more than build up the terror.[15]

This concern with propaganda having the proper effects seemed to override any idea of informing the German people as to what the Nazis and their followers were doing. On top of all other problems, OWI's various considerations were contradictory: refraining from mere reporting of atrocities precluded making the German people aware of what was taking place. And again, there was little distinction made among Nazi persecutions of different groups.

Soon after December 17, the PWE also tried, in slightly different fashion, to link the Nazis' killings of Jews with atrocities against other groups. By doing so, they hoped to make their reporting directly relevant to more listeners:

The sufferings of the Jews should now be merged in the wider picture of Nazi persecution . . . We should bear in mind that i) the Jewish persecution has in all countries occupied by the Nazis been the prelude to the persecution of other sectors of the population; ii) that apart from its physical brutality, it is a subtle form of political warfare aimed at breaking human ties between different groups and individuals in all countries and destroying any feeling of common citizenship where persecution of the Jews is set on foot.[16]

Along these lines, the first PWE directive for 1943 maintained that the Nazis were now engaged in the extermination of the Polish people,[17] an interpretation that was by no means correct: despite massive Nazi killings and barbarities directed against Poles, the Jews and Poles were (in the words of a well-known study) "unequal victims."[18]

Foreigners who left Germany, Germans who were able to travel abroad (and willing to talk), and those who ventured to write abroad agreed that the BBC broadcasts received considerable attention in Germany and that Germans were generally aware of Nazi persecution of Jews.[19] But there were sharp differences of opinion over the effects of such knowledge. A German journalist in Sweden said that British propaganda made the public determined to fight on, that the Germans greatly feared a Russian takeover of Germany—in part because they knew about German behavior in the East, had guilty consciences, and expected retaliation—but that they also feared the British and Americans would avenge the killing of Jews. The Nazi regime played on these fears in the hope to sustain solidarity—a kind of strength through fear *(Kraft durch Furcht)*.[20]

A non-Nazi German diplomat told a British source in Spain that only a minority of German intellectuals plus the victims of persecution really understood what the Third Reich was like; the majority held loyal to Hitler's regime. Yet a Spanish architect who had spent time in Berlin said in early 1943 that German morale had declined and there was widespread longing for peace. He recommended that the British stress their desire to destroy the regime but not the German people.[21]

A thirty-five-year-old Guatemalan, having lived in Germany for seven years and married a German from an elite family, had plenty of exposure to many Germans during the Nazi years. After leaving Germany in March 1943, he said that most Germans had negative feelings about Jews but that nearly everyone thought by early 1943 that the Nazi regime had gone too far on the Jewish question.[22]

Any diagnosis of prevailing German sentiments toward Jews would be based on too small a sample to be anything more than suggestive. But the reality of widespread though limited anti-Semitism would help explain why a good number of Germans had helped the Gestapo to enforce racial laws from 1935 on or used the Gestapo to help settle scores against particular Jews by denouncing them for making negative comments about the Nazi regime. From March 1933 on, Nazi Germany had laws and regulations making it possible to prosecute even those who privately criticized the state or Party, and denunciations of Jews were common during 1933–41. (Private motives were also a factor in some of these denunciations.)[23] In any case, how many Germans in a police state would take risks during the war on behalf of those they did not care for or had come to dislike as the result of Nazi propaganda?

Still, the presence of widespread anti-Semitism did not mean that all Germans were eager and willing executioners.

BBC surveyors assumed that the continuous Nazi accusations against Jews had credibility in Germany. As much as Nazi leaders believed in the iniquity of Jews, they would not resort to so much anti-Semitic propaganda if they did not think it effective in mobilizing the public: "a large segment of the public is behind the regime in its determination to make Jews a scapegoat." Besides, they observed, there were no signs that public opinion, which had some influence on the regime in certain other areas, had modified the Nazis' anti-Semitic policy.[24]

These BBC intelligence judgments may have given too much weight to the German public's ability to limit application of critical tenets of Nazi ideology and Hitler's personal beliefs. The Nazi regime adjusted its methods—but much less often its goals and policies—to suit what it thought the Germans could take. The German public's discontent with the Nazi "euthanasia" program had had some effect, for example, but euthanasia killings nonetheless continued in more decentralized and secret fashion.

To be sure, Nazi leaders worried about German morale. In a September 1942 speech in the Propaganda Ministry to some sixty German journalists and editors (which an informant for Polish intelligence attended), Goebbels showed considerable concern about the German people's ability to withstand military hardship. He argued that they were still suffering from the psychological burden of the revolution of November 1918, which Goebbels, like Hitler, saw as the reason for Germany's defeat in World War I. Whereas the Germans were politically immature, the British people had a proud imperial tradition that helped them to withstand hardship, he noted. Without that consciousness and solidarity in difficult times and without the memory of Germany's collapse in 1918, Britain might have given way after the fall of France.[25]

But Goebbels showed no sign of uncertainty or concession when it came to the Jews. Warning the journalists to maintain silence about some matters because the Germans were so susceptible, Goebbels nonetheless declared:

> There are still 48,000 [Jews] in Berlin. They know with deadly certainty that as the war progresses they will be packed off to the east and delivered up to a murderous fate. They already feel the inevitable harshness of physical extermination and therefore they harm the Reich whenever possible while they live.[26]

This kind of explicit statement about mass murder being in progress was bound to raise some comment, and it could not have helped the cause of secrecy. But Goebbels was seeking to justify the policy of killing Europe's Jews, not to bend to public opinion. Still, perceptions of German attitudes could and did affect Nazi decisions about the Final Solution on the margins. The one real example of private citizens' attenuating Nazi policy and even changing it was the March 1943 protest of Berliners very directly and personally affected: (non-Jewish) Germans married to Jews.

As Gauleiter of Berlin, Goebbels had long wanted to clear the capital of all Jews,[27] and Hitler agreed. The problem was that some Jews, as essential skilled workers, had managed to gain temporary exemptions from being deported, and others whom Nazi racists considered Jews were spared because they were counted as privileged mixed breeds. Still others had German spouses, many of whom, despite heavy pressure from the Nazi regime, had refused to divorce their Jewish spouses. Until early 1943, high Nazi and government officials felt that deportation of Jewish spouses in existing marriages was too sensitive politically. It would have driven Germans to ask all kinds of questions about the location and fate of their spouses. Even Hitler was inclined to think that resolution of the delicate problems of mixed breeds and Jews married to Germans would have to wait until after the war.[28]

Toward the end of 1942, Germany suffered a number of highly visible military setbacks. In late October, British forces broke through German defenses at El Alamein in Egypt, and in early November, American and British forces landed and took control of territory in French North Africa. In the East, Leningrad continued to hold out against a sustained but costly German siege. Although Germany's southern forces penetrated to Stalingrad, the Soviets launched a well-planned counteroffensive in mid-November. But deterioration of Germany's military position did not prevent (and may well have stimulated) further Nazi actions against the Jews.

The official line toward Jews in mixed marriages changed in late 1942, part of a general tendency to rid Germany of all Jews by early 1943. Industrialists received instructions, based on Hitler's own decision, to replace their Jewish workers with foreign ones. Some of them tipped off the Jewish workers, who went into hiding. Jewish spouses in marriages without children also became a target, particularly in Berlin, where Goebbels and officials of the Reich Security Main Office (RSHA) agreed on a tougher line. In late February 1943, Hitler gave a speech, promising again that the war would destroy European Jewry; this could not have discouraged the Nazi radicals about the Jewish question.

To achieve the separation of families, Goebbels wanted a massive show of force, and he engaged the Waffen-SS division Leibstandarte Adolf Hitler to help the Gestapo and municipal police to carry out arrests and to transport Jews to the stables of the Hermann Göring barracks on Rosenstrasse: from there they were to go to Auschwitz. Some were in fact shipped off. But almost immediately German spouses (largely wives) and relatives began to gather outside the barracks, initially to seek information. As the roundup stretched over a number of days, the crowds grew, and the gathering came to resemble an implicit protest. Eventually, the decision to deport Jewish intermarried spouses was canceled; "overzealous subordinates" were blamed for the roundup. Some of the Jewish husbands deported to the labor camp at Auschwitz were even returned, more than seventeen hundred Jews were released, and the Jewish spouses elsewhere in Germany were spared, since their deportation would have become too public, perhaps too unpopular, and would have jeopardized the security of the whole process.[29]

There were undoubtedly a number of reasons why this protest came about—among them, the high concentration of German-Jewish intermarriages in Berlin and the courage and devotion of those who flocked to Rosenstrasse day after day. Knowledge of what the deportation truly meant undoubtedly contributed to individual decisions to gather and to protest, just as they contributed to some Jews' willingness to go into hiding rather than accept what the Nazis had prepared for them in the East.

Here and there, in reports compiled by Heydrich's SD about public opinion, there were other signs of German complaints, disgust, or depression about Nazi atrocities generally—though not much to indicate a widespread tendency or a serious problem.[30] In mid-1943, the German public did not respond positively to a new wave of Nazi charges about Bolshevik and Jewish atrocities, because it brought to mind what they had heard one way or another about German practices in the East. Some Germans even rejected the (accurate) Nazi charges that the Soviets had previously murdered tens of thousands of Polish officers and buried them in the forest at Katyn; they believed the bodies were German-killed Polish and Soviet Jews.[31] They did not want to hear Nazi propaganda on the subject, because it brought up troubling issues. A middle-aged Bavarian woman said in the fall of 1943: "Do you think that nobody listens to the foreign broadcasts? They have loaded Jewish women and children into a wagon, driven out of the town and exterminated *(vernichtet)* them with gas." She was sentenced to three years in prison.[32]

At a minimum, then, the British information campaign, despite its limitations, neutralized Nazi propaganda and helped to make more Germans aware of vast crimes.[33] Although it is almost impossible to establish direct cause-and-effect relationships, the British efforts in December 1942 and early 1943 also undoubtedly contributed in some measure to saving the lives of some Jews.

It was no surprise that Nazi authorities tried to block the influx of foreign publicity about the Final Solution. Almost schizophrenically, they mixed bombastic threats against Jews with efforts to preserve the secrecy of the Final Solution. Outbursts of official anti-Semitic rhetoric had some practical purposes: they helped to rally the Party faithful into action and preserve a sense of revolutionary dynamism. Images of the Jew as bacillus or vermin spoke in part to those who already believed anything negative about Jews, but the propaganda also exploited and sought to radicalize the more limited anti-Semitism present in various sectors of German society, particularly among conservative nationalists.[34] For years some high officials had stated that the war would lead to severe punishment of Jews within German reach.[35]

During 1941, Nazi public accusations had included the charge that American Jews had developed plans to sterilize all Germans under the age of sixty,[36] so that virtually any punishment meted out to Jews would seem justified. While this particular claim might seem bizarre, it apparently had some effect; looking at a range of indicators of German public reaction, the BBC's intelligence surveyors concluded that threats of horrible treatment of all Germans upon Germany's defeat, common in official Nazi propaganda and in semi-official rumor campaigns, helped to keep the German people behind the war and the government. They specifically cited the sterilization plan.[37]

Sometimes the activities the Nazi leaders pinned on Jews were visions of what Nazi ideologues wanted to do to Jews: a phenomenon psychiatrists call projection. For example, in a private speech to the SS elite in November 1938, Himmler had maintained that the Jews wanted to starve and butcher all Germans, whether or not they supported the Nazis.[38] Fears that this might be true served to justify anti-Jewish policy.

But with some exceptions,[39] official Nazi propaganda about the Jewish menace and the need to eliminate it went to the point of indicating the ultimate elimination of Jewry but not beyond. In an October 1942 instruction to Nazi Party officials, Martin Bormann, head of the Nazi Party chancellery, codified the limits of official discourse. He did not criticize Goebbels's indiscretion, but explained that circulation of information about the Final Solution was a problem:

> In the course of working on the final solution of the Jewish Question, we have heard of recent discussions among the population in various regions of the Reich about "very strict measures" against Jews, especially in the Eastern territories. These findings revealed that such ideas—mostly distorted and exaggerated—are spread by persons on leave from various units stationed in the East who have had occasion to witness such measures. It is conceivable that not all citizens fully appreciate the necessity for such action, especially not those segments of the public which have not had the opportunity to form their own opinion of Bolshevik atrocities.

Since the next generation of Germans might not understand the necessity of eliminating millions of Jews from the European economic area, Bormann said, Germany's leaders had to act now: "these somewhat difficult problems can only be solved with ruthless severity."[40] That comment was both a justification and an announcement of how much it was appropriate to reveal.

Szmul Zygielbojm, who was on the Polish National Council in London and maintained contacts in Nazi-controlled territory, noted in mid-February 1943 that German radio jamming of the BBC had been especially heavy for the past five weeks. The Nazi regime did not want Germans to hear about the "monstrosities" in Poland, "for it is feared that if the average Germans get to know of the facts and believe them, they will be afraid of being made to pay for these misdeeds and their 'morale' may thus be broken."[41]

Western publicity also pressured Nazi leaders to adapt in small but telling ways to a new situation. On November 30, 1942, Himmler had written a short letter to Heinrich Müller, head of the Gestapo, regarding what Rabbi Stephen Wise was saying. At his press conference of November 24, Wise had claimed, among other things, that the Nazis were making soap from the flesh of Jews who were gassed, as well as fertilizer from bones.[42] Himmler knew that his extermination-camp commanders were not supposed to be doing anything of this nature but feared that some zealous subordinate might have overstepped the bounds. Moreover, he wanted to remind Müller of the importance of camouflage. His own letter was an example of it. Himmler wrote:

> In view of the large emigration movement of Jews, I do not wonder that such rumors come to circulate in the world. We both know that there is present an increased mortality among the Jews put to work. You have to guarantee to me that the corpses of these deceased Jews are either burned or buried at each location, and that absolutely nothing else can happen with the corpses at any location.
>
> Conduct an investigation immediately everywhere whether any kind of misuse [of corpses] has taken place of the sort as listed in point 1, probably strewn about in the world as a lie. Upon the SS-oath I am to be notified of each misuse of this kind.[43]

The two men both knew very well that the gas chambers and execution units were the prime forces behind increased mortality of Jews, but they also knew that this kind of information should not be committed to paper. The next generation might not understand, just as the current one apparently did not.

Müller was in charge not of the actual killing of Jews but of a portion of the cover-up. Beginning in June 1942, he had directed the concealment operation carried out by special units known by the numerical designation 1005. Müller had instructed Paul Blobel, former head of an execution unit known as Sonderkommando 4a, to erase traces of the shootings of Jews in the East. Blobel testified after the war that he was ordered to go to occupied territories and eradicate mass graves from Einsatzgruppen operations—while preserving absolute secrecy and putting nothing on paper. Blobel actually began, however, with the bodies at the extermination camps Chelmno and Auschwitz-Birkenau, which up until then had been buried. Burning (with or without crematoria) replaced burial. Then he proceeded to the extermination camps at Sobibor, Belzec, and Treblinka, where there were a great many buried corpses. Only then, in the fall of 1942, did Blobel go to the conquered Soviet territories to destroy the evidence of genocide there.[44] He and his men could and did exhume and burn hundreds of thousands of bodies. They did not know of and, of course, could not touch the documentary evidence of the mass killings that by then had accumulated at Bletchley Park.

During early December, Himmler's Personnel Staff Office noted and passed on to appropriate offices several other foreign comments about

Germany's Jewish policy. There was the Archbishop of Canterbury's suggestion, reported in *The Times* of London, that the Allies take in all Jews who made it out of Nazi-controlled territory. He also recommended a threat of postwar punishment of all those who directly and indirectly took part. A note about this went to the RSHA.[45] A copy of a Reuters dispatch from London about the extermination of Jews went to the SD, as did a statement by Lady Reading of the World Jewish Congress.[46] No direct evidence of Himmler's reaction to the Allied Declaration of December has been located, but the Declaration and Allied broadcasts based on it can only have reinforced his earlier concerns about the information leaking. The publicity must have emphasized the importance of destroying all traces of the corpses and reminded those involved in the Final Solution just how deeply they were committed to the cause. They could not go back now.

The PWE surmised that the Allied Declaration had embarrassed the Nazi leadership.[47] Goebbels wrote in his diary:

> [Rothschild] delivered a flood of sob-stuff bemoaning the fate of the Polish Jews. At the end of the session the House observed a minute of silence . . . That was quite appropriate for the British House of Commons which is really a sort of Jewish exchange. The English, anyway, are the Jews among the Aryans.[48]

Name-calling allowed Goebbels to dismiss the criticism, but his propaganda machine had to figure out ways to counteract the effects of this information in Germany.

New problems caused by Western publicity about Nazi extermination policy could not, however, change the way Hitler, Himmler, Goebbels, and their direct subordinates looked at the relationship between the war and the Final Solution. In the peculiar Nazi view of the world, Jews were behind all Germany's troubles, including its current problems of flagging morale at home and the insufficient effort being made by its allies. Information reaching Himmler around this time continued to point to Jews as the source of Germany's problems with Hungary, for example: Gottlob Berger, chief of the SS Main Office, reported on a conversation with the former Archduke Albert of Hungary, who told him that the Hungarian government was unwilling to undertake action on the Jewish question. The Regent of Hungary, Admiral Miklós Horthy, supposedly under Jewish influence, was hedging on his commitments to Germany until it became clear which way the war would go.[49]

From the perspective of the Nazi elite, military setbacks were no reason to change course on the Final Solution but, rather, a reason to continue with it. Himmler undertook a series of initiatives to drive the Final Solution onward in December 1942 and January 1943—just when Germany was losing the battle of Stalingrad, the largest battle in world history. He pushed for the transportation and "emigration" of Jews in France (including the Italian zone of occupation) to the East.[50] But the Italians were unwilling to permit deportation of Jews from its territory, and Himmler feared that this gave other European countries a reason to resist cooperation with the Germans on the Jewish question. If Germany's own ally would not go along, why should they?[51] He also asked Transportation Minister Albert Ganzenmüller for more trains to transport Jews, who in Nazi eyes were always the source of support for partisans, from the Bialystok region and the Soviet territories, as well as from Western Europe.[52] Although he did not say so, the destinations for Jews and all people suspected of being partisans or helping partisans were Auschwitz and Maidanek.[53]

Still, Western publicity did raise one new option for the Nazi regime. If the Allies really were concerned about the lives of European Jews, perhaps Germany could gain some economic-military leverage by sparing select groups of Jews. In agenda notes Himmler prepared for his meeting with Hitler on December 10, 1942, he had cautiously raised the possibilities of releasing some Jews in exchange for ransom (an idea he said he opposed) and holding some Jews as hostages. Hitler had responded that Himmler could approve releases if they really brought in substantial amounts of foreign exchange. During the same meeting, Himmler suggested a special camp for those Jews with connections in the United States, and he recorded Hitler's approval with a check mark. (This discussion was in all likelihood the original and most basic reason for the 1943 creation of Bergen-Belsen—initially, a camp designed to keep some ten thousand or so Jews alive.[54])

Foreign criticism of Nazi Germany's Jewish policy also tempted Himmler to try to expose the emptiness behind foreign expressions of sympathy for Jewish victims. After hearing that Switzerland and Spain had objected to removing some Jews with Swiss and Spanish citizenship (along with all other Jews) from France, Himmler suggested to Foreign Minister Joachim von Ribbentrop that the French might dump some of them over the Swiss and Spanish borders. That would really test two neutral countries' attitude toward Jews, the implication being that they might then stop criticizing Germany's actions.[55]

In short, foreign publicity about Nazi extermination policy encouraged the Nazi leadership to consider a few experiments with holding Jews for ransom or as hostages, and perhaps to release some small numbers of them as a stimulant to anti-Semitism abroad. Himmler was willing to spare a limited number of Jews if Germany (and particularly the SS) could derive specific benefits from doing so—accelerating the progress of the Final Solution, earning some money, and stirring up divisions among Germany's enemies.

After Foreign Minister Anthony Eden read the Allied Declaration in Parliament, he wrote in his diary: "It had a far greater dramatic effect than I had expected."[56] But the political effect, which was to stimulate widespread complaints that Britain's efforts to save the victims of persecution were inadequate, rapidly turned into a sizable problem for Eden and the Foreign Office.[57] Unable to devise an acceptable British solution, London quickly turned to Washington, partly to discuss and help provide some small remedies and, even more, to share responsibility for the government's refusal to act in ways that British public opinion and various pressure groups called for.

The Foreign Office told its embassy in Washington that the Allied Declaration had "made a unique and profound impression on the British Parliament and public opinion,"[58] which, led by the Archbishop of Canterbury and some members of Parliament from all parties, now favored some sort of British action beyond mere denunciation of Nazi policy. Five days after the Allied Declaration, one official in the Foreign Office wondered how Britain could simply hold to its previous policies: if it were not willing to take steps to save Jewish lives, why should any other country act?[59] The most frequent request was for the Allies to facilitate the escape of Jews into neutral countries and to make possible the reception of more escapees by extracting and resettling refugees already in neutral lands.[60]

As a result of the change in public opinion, on December 23, the cabinet established a new War Cabinet Committee on the Reception and Accommodation of Jewish Refugees, consisting of the Foreign Secretary (Eden), the Home Secretary (Herbert Morrison), the Secretary of State for the Colonies (Oliver Stanley), and some of their subordinates. Its mandate was to consider possible arrangements for Jewish refugees who escaped or might emerge from enemy-occupied territories. But at its first meeting, on December 31, this committee rejected most of the ideas raised by members of Parliament and others for re-settling refugees presently in neutral countries. Stanley also argued against making any distinction between Jewish refugees and other refugees, and the committee deleted the word "Jewish" from its title.[61]

Morrison's comments may have had some bearing on that last decision:

> The Home Secretary said that the Home Office would not refuse to take a limited number of refugees, say, from 1,000 to 2,000 [into Britain], but certainly not more, . . . and on the condition that they were sent to the Isle of Man and stayed there as long as he thought it necessary. He could not, however, agree that the door should be opened to the entry of uncategorised Jews. It should be borne in mind that there were already about 100,000 refugees, mainly Jews, in this country and that the accommodation problem was already most difficult and would become critical in the event of renewed air attacks.
>
> The Home Secretary added that there was considerable anti-Semitism under the surface in this country. If there were any substantial increase in the number of Jewish refugees or if these refugees did not leave this country after the war, we should be in for serious trouble.[62]

On the same day, Prime Minister Churchill brought the British military authorities into the discussion. At a meeting of the Chiefs of Staff Committee, Churchill asked Air Chief Marshal Sir Charles Portal to consider a request from Prime Minister Sikorski to bomb certain targets in Poland as reprisal for German persecutions. He also urged two or three heavy raids on Berlin, in the course of which the Royal Air Force should drop leaflets warning that these bombing raids were reprisals for Germany's persecution of Poles and Jews. Portal agreed to consider the first request but warned that it was a long way to the suggested targets in Poland. The Chiefs of Staff Committee supported the prospect of one or two heavy raids on Berlin but did not comment about explicit warnings to Germans that the bombing was a reprisal.[63]

In a follow-up note, Portal expressed opposition to an announced reprisal raid on several grounds: it might call into question the legitimacy of Britain's normal attacks on cities as military targets; it might evoke comparisons with German brutality; it might lead to an avalanche of requests from the governments-in-exile of other conquered nations; and it might induce the Germans to take reprisals against captured British airmen. Eden had different objections: the Germans might massacre even more Poles and Jews; or they might refrain from such killings and demand a cessation of bombing. Churchill was persuaded not to press the notion.[64] In mid-January 1943, a Foreign Office official noted that reprisal statements had been considered but ruled out, and another commented that they would send a stock denial to all future calls for reprisals.[65]

After British diplomats in Turkey had reported, at the end of December 1942, that Rumania might be willing to release as many as seventy thousand Jews, one refugee specialist in the Foreign Office called this a "frightful prospect" but one they would have to face if they wished to avoid reproaches from the archbishops. As it turned out, Rumania did not put Britain to the test.[66] Another exchange in early January 1943 also illustrated the prevailing feeling in the Foreign Office: the Home Office asked if it could, when refusing visa applications from Jewish refugees to Britain, explain that negotiations with other Allied governments were currently under way to resolve Jewish refugee problems. The Foreign Office hedged:

> we feel that we should at all costs discourage the building of exaggerated hopes upon the recent declaration in Parliament and that we should emphasise the obvious (to us, though not, it would appear, to the public) difficulties of the situation. For that reason we would prefer the substitution of the word "consultation" for "discussions" . . . The formula should also, we think, hold no promise of any announcement of the result of such consultation, and it might be better if, instead of mentioning a "joint [Allied or American-British] scheme," you said [that the Allies were consulting to see] "whether there is any prospect of overcoming the great difficulties in the way of any substantial relief."[67]

It seems reasonable to conclude that "consultations" (and later, actual negotiations) were meant to provide a justification or cover for inaction or for minimal steps to assist Jews on the Continent.

There were very real difficulties. The Nazi regime was not going to release large numbers of Jews simply because the Allies requested it. Less rigid, however, were Germany's allies and associates—independent governments that had treaties with Germany, participated with Germany in the war, or had to contend with German military presence on their territory. The governments of France (headquartered at Vichy), Rumania, and Slovakia had to decide to turn over their Jews to Germany. The examples of Italy and Hungary—formal German allies—as well as the less attached governments of Bulgaria and Finland showed that countries under some obligation to Germany could limit or withhold their involvement in the Final Solution. The formidable M.P. and writer Eleanor Rathbone emphasized the opportunity for the West to exert countervailing pressure on German "satellites" in Europe, making them willing to evacuate Jews to safe havens.[68] But British officials feared that the Nazis or the satellites *might* release large numbers of Jews. During an early January conversation with Richard Law in the Foreign Office, Alexander Easterman of the World Jewish Congress expressed the hope that the Nazis might release one hundred thousand Jewish children if the Allies pressed for it. Law responded that, in his opinion, the Nazis really believed in their Jewish campaign: the worse things went for them on the battlefield, the more they would push for victory over the Jews; "not everyone, however, would agree with me and we could not take the risk of the Germans calling our bluff."[69] An influx of Jews into Britain or into Palestine would create major political problems with the Arabs, and so it was safer for Britain to avoid unilateral initiatives. This was the consistent Foreign Office line.[70]

The requests for action continued to pour in during early 1943, some too emotional and highly placed to dismiss or to ignore. On January 16, Lady Reading wrote Prime Minister Churchill:

You know, better than any words of mine can describe to you, the horrible plight of the Jews at the mercy of the Nazis. I have said to myself what can I do, who can help. And the answer is clear, only Mr. Churchill can help and I can at least write and beg him to do so. In other days I would have come to you in sackcloth and ashes to plead for my people; it is in that spirit I write. Some can still be saved, if the iron fetters of the red-tape can be burst asunder . . . England cannot surely sink to such hypocracy [sic] that her members of Parliament stand to show sympathy to the Jewish dead and meanwhile her officials are condemning those same Jews to die? You cannot know of such things. I do not believe you would tolerate them. There are still some 40,000 certificates for Palestine even under the White Paper regulations. Mr. Churchill, will you not say they are to be used now, for any who can escape, man woman or child. Is it possible, is it really possible, to refuse sanctuary in the Holy Land?

I am your very ardent admirer and most obedient servant. V. Reading.

Churchill's office asked for Eden's views, and the Foreign Office experts drafted a reply, which Eden then approved. The situation called for delicate wording and, as one official put it, a sympathetic tone:

> . . . we are at present giving our urgent consideration to the whole vast problem of rescue and relief for both Jews and non-Jews under the enemy yoke. I can assure you that we fully realise the urgency of the situation, but, I must emphasise the great difficulties we are encountering and shall continue to encounter. Even were we to obtain permission to withdraw all Jews (I leave aside for the moment non-Jewish refugees) transport alone presents a problem which will be difficult of solution. The lines of escape pass almost entirely through war areas where our requirements are predominantly military, and which must therefore in the interests of our final victory receive precedence.
>
> These difficulties are very real, and I fear cannot be dismissed as "fetters of red-tape"; but we shall do what we can.[71]

By the time this response came through, the government had made another statement to Parliament stressing that an Allied victory was the only real remedy for the Nazis' racial and religious persecution.[72]

The British government refrained from significant unilateral initiatives, even with neutral countries such as Switzerland and Sweden. Notifying its legation in Stockholm about the domestic political pressures, the Foreign Office mentioned that neutral countries were the focus of many rescue schemes. After observing that geography would seem to "protect Sweden from any considerable influx" of refugees, the Foreign Office inquired how many refugees were there already. In any case, Britain would not approach Sweden to do more on its own; it could only be done as part of an international effort.[73]

Although concern about Palestine was not nearly so strong in Washington as in London, some American foreign-policy officials had similar, if more combative, views about the dangers of efforts to save Jewish lives. In fact, the prevailing sentiment in the State Department was that Rabbi Wise had played fast and loose with the facts and needed to be curbed.

Wise's point of contact at the State Department was Undersecretary Sumner Welles, who had asked various American diplomats to investigate Gerhart Riegner's August 1942 telegram about the Final Solution. Later, Welles had obtained enough supporting evidence from American sources, as well as through Riegner, to give Rabbi Wise a confirmation, which Wise then publicized. One critical piece of evidence was an affidavit with information derived from Carl Burckhardt, a high official of the International Red Cross (who had personal experience of previous negotiations with Hitler and many high-level contacts in Germany).[74] But Welles did not record his findings or his conversation with Wise. He did not instruct the specialists in the European Division, the Visa Division, or the Special War Problems Division (which included refugee matters) to acknowledge the truth of reports about the Final Solution. Welles's lapse made it easier for mid-level officials at State to hold on to their prevailing views—that reports about Nazi extermination policy were unconfirmed and that, even if true, nothing much could be done.[75]

Just before and even after the Allied Declaration of December 17, some State Department officials opposed the idea of such a declaration and criticized Wise for having mentioned that the State Department had confirmed the reliability of his information. The European Division told the British embassy in Washington on December 30 that, had they seen the affidavit with Burckhardt's information before it was given to Wise, they would have added a rider that they took no responsibility for its contents. One refugee specialist at State, Robert Borden Reams, at first argued that an Allied Declaration against Nazi mass killings of Jews might actually intensify Nazi barbarities. Then he complained in an internal memorandum:

> If Rabbi Wise had treated this communication [supporting evidence provided by Riegner] as an unofficial report received from his own representative and transmitted through the good offices of the Department of State, little harm might have been done. However, he gave great publicity to the information contained therein and attributed it to official State Department sources . . . It should again be stressed that all of these reports are unconfirmed. It is obviously impossible to secure confirmation of German activities in the various occupied countries . . . It cannot be doubted that the Jewish people of Europe are oppressed and it is certain that considerable numbers of them have died in one way or another since the war started. Whether the number of dead amount to tens of thousands or, as these reports state, to millions is not material to the main problem . . . Our main purpose is the winning of the war and other considerations must be subordinate thereto.[76]

In addition, in another January 1943 memo, Elbridge Durbrow of the European Division called Wise's use of Riegner's report a misrepresentation. There was no doubt that the Nazis were carrying on a ruthless campaign against the Jews in Poland, he claimed, but "the State Department has never received any information from official sources and therefore it is not in position to furnish official confirmation to these allegations."[77]

State Department officials had no hint of the details about Nazi killings of Jews that Bletchley Park had already made available to British intelligence. Intelligence analysts in London could easily have refuted the notion that it was impossible for the West to discern what the Nazis were doing in occupied Europe; they had a good picture, but only select officials could see it. Since October 1942, at least three Foreign Office officials had received from Bletchley precisely the kind of "official" evidence that Durbrow said the State Department lacked: original German radio messages.

There were some unpleasant side effects to the State Department's officially uninformed and largely negative stance: people working in the Visa Division complained that they had received some Christmas cards in 1942 calling them murderers.[78] Since it was thought that Wise had caused "problems" for the State Department, one solution was to cut off—or greatly impede—his access to information from Riegner in Geneva. In February 1943, an official in the European Division drafted a telegram to the American legation in Bern, discouraging it from accepting reports for transmission to private parties in the future: "It is felt that by sending such private messages which circumvent neutral countries' censorship we risk the possibility that neutral countries might find it necessary to curtail or abolish our official secret means of communication."[79] This was a rather thin pretext for disposing of an unpopular messenger. True, the Swiss government did not wish to antagonize Germany by publishing or allowing the distribution of atrocity reports from Switzerland—a policy that hindered Jewish organizations in Switzerland and moved them to seek assistance from sympathetic Western diplomats.[80] But if Switzerland was afraid to antagonize Germany, it would have been at least as reluctant to antagonize the United States by interfering with its diplomatic communications.

The next time Riegner tried to send a cable to Wise through State Department channels, Leland Harrison, who had previously asked Riegner to help gather information, was forced to explain that new instructions prevented him from passing it on to Wise, although he was willing and eager himself to send Riegner's information to the State Department. When Harrison suggested that Riegner telegraph Wise directly, Riegner explained that the telegrams contained highly confidential information: he could not risk an uncoded telegram, which the Germans might decipher. Harrison said he would try to clarify the situation in Washington, and he asked the State Department not to cut Riegner off. The European Division eventually agreed, but only if it had full discretion whether or not to send messages on to Wise. Even Undersecretary Welles, now aware of the dispute, explained to Wise that he should not refer to the source of information or the means of transmission if he made the messages public.[81]

As it happened, the cable Riegner wanted to send Wise (of March 10) concerned the Nazi roundup of fifteen thousand Jews in Berlin in late February and early March (including the privileged Jews in mixed marriages), part of the reported plan to remove and exterminate all Jews in Berlin by the end of March. After consulting with Willem Visser't Hooft of the World Council of Churches, who had supplied him with some of the information, Riegner urged Allied rescue efforts in every way possible. He specifically recommended the exchange of Jews for German civilians held in the Western Hemisphere or in Allied countries; American and British guarantees of food for refugees in neutral countries and eventual removal of refugees there; and daily BBC broadcasts warning Germans and others not to collaborate in the Nazi extermination program. The American consul in Geneva sent the cable to the legation in Bern, not knowing whether or when it would get through to Wise.[82] It turned out that the German spouses of Berlin Jews in mixed marriages acted more quickly.

The Foreign Office was also, in a more limited way, sensitive about further publicity concerning the Final Solution. In May 1943, Riegner's ally in Geneva, Richard Lichtheim, tried to send a message from Geneva to the Jewish Agency representative in London with details of the persecution of Jews in Bulgaria and Rumania. He urged that the information be published and requested BBC broadcasts about it with warnings to the Bulgarian and Rumanian governments that they would be held accountable later for their treatment of Jews. The Foreign Office transmitted the telegram to the Jewish Agency after *deleting* Lichtheim's suggestion of publicity. In an internal memo, a Foreign Office official stated that it was better not to put such ideas into the heads of the Jewish Agency in London.[83]

Events in London and Washington following the Allied Declaration of December 17, 1942, conformed to a similar, but not identical, pattern. Publicity about the Final Solution in the West resulted in pressure for remedial action by Western governments. Public opinion led by some forces in Parliament and in the Anglican Church was a more significant and earlier factor in Britain; in the United States, much of Congress was unsympathetic, and Jewish organizations, divided among themselves about means and priorities, had few powerful allies. But even in the United States, publicity elicited more and more calls for rescue, which caused some State Department officials to try to cut off the flow of information.

If Western governments had officially recognized Nazi extermination policy earlier, the calls for rescue and relief measures would have come earlier and have generated more political pressure.

# 11

❋

# COMPETITION AND
# COLLABORATION

ON JANUARY 20, 1943, the Foreign Office sent an aide-mémoire to Washington that was intended to create common ground and begin a British-American dialogue on refugee problems. This British initiative explicitly rejected treating the refugee situation as a wholly Jewish problem, on the grounds that many other peoples were suffering and there would be much criticism if the Allies showed preference to Jews. The Foreign Office foresaw a rise in anti-Semitism wherever foreign Jews were introduced. Germany or its satellites might flood other countries with alien immigrants. The aide-mémoire concluded by asking whether the United States considered joint action advisable and whether it would participate in a private, informal United Nations conference on the subject.[1] It was, in effect, an invitation to the U.S. government to join forces against critics of the official line in both countries.

About a week later, a high official in the British embassy in Washington asked Undersecretary Sumner Welles for an indication of the American stance on refugee problems. Welles declined to comment until he could do so definitively.[2] The American reaction was reserved, in part because some State Department officials feared that the British invitation was a trap and in part because Welles was still smarting from some other foreign-policy disagreements with the British.[3] The Foreign Office had hoped for a quick response, since signs of a joint policy would convince Parliament not to rush into action.[4]

On February 3, some members from both houses of Parliament met privately and agreed to raise a motion to support "immediate measures on the largest and most generous scale compatible with the requirements of military operations and security for providing help and temporary asylum to persons in danger of massacre." By February 23, more than 260 M.P.s had signed this motion in Commons, and the Archbishop of Canterbury had agreed to introduce it in the House of Lords.[5] Eden alerted the War Cabinet that it was difficult to tell Parliament that Britain was involved in international negotiations about refugee problems when the United States showed no sign of interest.[6] On February 24, during Commons' discussion of the motion (which passed), an M.P. asked Eden whether Britain was doing all it could on its own and whether he could expedite multilateral action. Eden responded that Britain had a good if not perfect record of its own but that the question of multilateral action was "rather baffling in some respects." Eden could not say it, but he was referring to the delay in the American response to Britain's invitation to a conference. The political correspondent of the *Manchester Guardian*, however, viewed the situation more critically. He reported that the British government had "thrown up the sponge" (Americans would say "thrown in") about Jewish refugees. In a misguided moment, the War Cabinet decided that, before Britain took any action, it would have to get other countries, especially the United States, involved.[7]

The next day the State Department refugee experts sent the British embassy in Washington a proposal. Although agreeing that the refugee problem should not be treated as a strictly Jewish one, the State Department said it preferred to have a conference to strengthen the long-dormant Intergovernmental Committee on Refugees rather than to plan bilateral steps. This was doing the British strategy one better and creating plenty of protection against demands for unilateral American rescue or relief action. The document also listed (in exaggerated form) all the positive steps the United States had taken in the past, and it was composed to resemble an original proposal, not a response. On March 3, the State Department released the American stance to the press.[8]

British Minister Ronald Campbell complained to Undersecretary Welles about the delayed response and about publication of the American note. Welles not only defended American actions but launched a withering counterattack:

> the British Government was allowing the impression to be created that the British Government was the great outstanding champion of the Jewish people and the sole defender of the rights of freedom of religion and

of individual liberty, and that it was being held back in its desire to undertake practical steps to protect the Jews in Europe and elsewhere and to safeguard individual rights and liberties by the reluctance of the United States Government and the unwillingness of the United States itself to take any action . . . other than words and gestures.[9]

British foreign-policy officials thought that Welles was attacking British propaganda efforts more than British foreign policy, but they also perceived that he was more liberal on refugee matters than some of his State Department colleagues and was somewhat frustrated.[10]

Although at first taken aback by Welles's attack, the foreign-policy officials needed American cover so much that they overlooked the extraordinary slight. After Britain and the United States had agreed to meet,[11] the Foreign Office was able to deflect further demands, including one from the Board of Deputies of British Jews, that Britain take bold new steps in refugee policy by simply referring to the upcoming conference in mid-April.[12] In a peculiar rendering of events, it blamed British public opinion for the whole difficulty, telling the British embassy in Washington that M.P.s and prominent figures had demanded consultation (rather than British action):

His Majesty's Government took every possible measure 1) to discourage the hope that very far-reaching measures of relief were practicable at the present crisis of the war; 2) to avoid invidious comparisons with the United States. It was impossible, however, to oppose a complete negative to the idea of United Nations action and accordingly the approach to the United States Government . . . was made. We felt that if broad lines of policy could be agreed between us, common United Nations action could be worked out without great difficulty. Our hope was not only that United States Government might be able to announce hospitality to refugees (on this we fully appreciate American domestic complications) and assist in providing an outlet in North Africa (which we realise to be primarily a matter of military security) but, even more important, that United States would join us and other United Nations in assurances to neutral Governments which seemed to offer chief hope for the maintenance and increase in reception of refugees.[13]

These comments were not exactly accurate; they were a kind of diplomatic code for a harsher truth: that Britain expected the United States not to announce hospitality to additional refugees, a refusal that would then provide cover for a similar British one.

To emphasize Allied assurances to neutral countries receiving refugees was in effect to reject any British commitment to these neutral countries. One day earlier, the Swiss legation in London had asked the Foreign Office how the Anglo-American discussions would affect Swiss interests. Switzerland's minister in London had already asked for a guarantee that it would not have to support refugees beyond the end of the war, and Alec Randall explained that this issue was the kind of thing the British and Americans might discuss. The Swiss official stressed anxiety about the constant stream of refugees into Switzerland. Randall was reassuring: the discussions would be informal and preliminary. There was no question of committing Switzerland to anything without appropriate consultation.[14]

When Foreign Minister Eden arrived in Washington to discuss a range of issues and problems in the management of the wartime alliance, he told the Foreign Office, in reply to an inquiry, that he would not initiate any discussion of refugee issues during his trip.[15] It was not the first time he had tried to avoid the subject. On February 4, he had met for thirty minutes with Jan Karski, who had been so important in bringing information about the Final Solution to London in 1942.[16] Karski had given Eden a presentation about the Polish underground and the plight of Polish Jews. But when he had recommended dropping leaflets and carrying out retaliatory bombing raids in an effort to halt the killing of Jews, Eden cut him off: "The Polish report on atrocities has already reached us," Karski remembered him saying. "The matter will take its proper course."[17] In Eden's memorandum about this conversation for distribution to the War Cabinet, there is but one passing mention of Jews: Karski had said, he reported, that the whole population of Warsaw, including the remaining Jews, was united not only in its hatred of the Germans but also in its resistance to them.[18]

Eden's disinclination to discuss in Washington the problem of Jewish refugees forced Parliamentary Undersecretary Richard Law to telegraph Eden and explain the political problem in unusually candid terms:

I am sorry to bother you about Jews but we are going to be faced with [an] ugly position if Cranborne [Viscount Cranborne was Secretary of State for the Dominions and a government spokesman] has nothing whatever to say about conference when matter is debated in Lords on

proposed March 23rd. It will be very high-powered debate with Archbishop of Canterbury in person and other churches by proxy . . .

I know what a bore this is but about fortnight will have passed since
we accepted the invitation to a conference and it will be extremely difficult to confess that nothing whatever has transpired since the acceptance
of the invitation. I think it will look very queer, too, if you, after the
demonstration following your statement in the House, come back here
and say that you have never mentioned the subject [while in the United
States].

There would obviously be no need for you to go into the problem
in any detail. What we would very much like Cranborne to be able to
say is something on these lines: "I am confident that the problem is very
much in the Foreign Secretary's mind and he will no doubt take any
opportunity which offers itself to expedite the proposed discussions."[19]

Eden got the point. On March 22, he met with Secretary of State
Cordell Hull and Ambassador Lord Halifax. According to the American
record, apparently the only surviving one, Eden spoke of British efforts
to move thirty thousand Jews from Eastern Europe to Palestine. Hull
inquired about the Arab reaction, but Eden explained that these Jews,
if they materialized, would fall under Britain's quota for Jewish immigration to Palestine. He pressed the Americans for assurances to Spain,
Portugal, Switzerland, and Sweden that they would not have to support
refugees indefinitely. The British government also wanted to announce
the forthcoming conference on refugees, and subordinate officials on
both sides met to draft an appropriate statement, which was sent to
London immediately.[20]

The next day the House of Lords debated Archbishop Temple's motion calling for admission of all refugees able to reach Britain and for
prompt British action. In response, government spokesman Viscount
Cranborne rejected the idea of unilateral British action, citing food and
shipping constraints, but he read the British-American statement, which
had just arrived, about the two countries working out solutions for
refugee problems at a mid-April conference on the island of Bermuda.[21]
Eden's efforts had served their main purpose.

On March 24, Nahum Goldmann of the World Jewish Congress,
along with Moshe Shertok of the Jewish Agency and Rabbi Maurice
Perlzweig, lobbied William Strang, a Foreign Office official who was
with Eden in Washington, for an Allied statement pledging to receive

all Jews who left Axis territory. Undersecretary Welles then helped Joseph M. Proskauer, of the American Jewish Committee, and Rabbi Wise, who were co-chairs of the Joint Emergency Committee for European Jewish Affairs, to get an appointment with Eden. He made available half an hour on Saturday, March 27.[22] Wise and Proskauer urged an Allied declaration asking Hitler to permit Jews to leave occupied Europe. Eden called the idea "fantastically impossible." He also rejected shipment of refugees from Spain and Portugal to Palestine because of danger in the Mediterranean. Adult Jews could not go from Bulgaria to Turkey because "Turkey does not want any more of your people." (British diplomats had recently reported a high level of anti-Semitism in Turkey, but Britain had made no effort to induce Turkey to accept more Jewish refugees.[23]) Eden threw cold water on the notion of shipping food to starving Jews still in Europe and dismissed every other suggestion. The discouraged Wise and Proskauer then went to Welles, who promised to do what he could.[24]

Later that day Eden met again with Secretary of State Hull and Welles; Harry Hopkins, Lord Halifax, and Strang were also there. Unlike the mid-level State Department officials, the Americans in this group were not in tune with the British approach. According to Hopkins's record, Hull urged Eden to do something about the sixty or seventy thousand Bulgarian Jews threatened with extermination.[25] Eden responded that if the Allies set a precedent Jews throughout the world would demand similar action for Polish and German Jews: "Hitler might well take us up on any such offer and there simply are not enough ships and means of transportation in the world to handle them." He claimed that Britain was willing to take tens of thousands of Jews into Palestine but that transportation and security posed great problems—Germany would insert agents among the refugees. He warned the Americans against making expansive promises.[26] But in general, Eden did not welcome Jewish immigration into Palestine. In April, his private secretary wrote in his diary: "Unfortunately, A. E. is immovable on the subject of Palestine. He loves Arabs and hates Jews."[27]

Welles, however, looked favorably on some opportunities for rescue. Ten days before the Bermuda Conference, he expressed hope for schemes to evacuate Bulgarian Jews to Turkey and British-controlled Egypt. He also said he welcomed further mass meetings in the United States designed to rally support for rescue and relief measures; he added that only President Roosevelt could reverse the unfavorable attitude in the government toward an appeal to Germany to release all Jews. (Even if it accomplished little with the Nazi leaders, such an appeal would have spread public knowledge of the Final Solution in Germany and occupied Europe and perhaps encouraged noncooperation with the extermination program. In any case, it would have once again warned the remaining Jews of the illusion of "resettlement.") Welles judged that the Bermuda Conference would be a success if it saved fifty thousand lives.[28]

Following a visit to Stockholm by Saloman Adler-Rudel of the Jewish Agency, Rabbi Wise told Welles that the Swedish government might admit a substantial number of Polish Jews, particularly if the United States asked it for humanitarian assistance. Wise asked if the American Minister in Stockholm, Herschel Johnson, might raise the issue with Sweden, and Welles so instructed Johnson.[29] Johnson learned that Sweden had already approached Germany about taking in Norwegian and Dutch Jews; Germany had rejected both offers. The only exceptions to blanket German refusals had come when people were willing to pay large sums of money as ransom for specific Jews. Sweden was not optimistic about Germany's willingness to release Jews without burdensome conditions, but it was willing to try.[30]

On April 15, the Swedish cabinet discussed the possible admission to Sweden of twenty thousand Jewish children. The proposal was received favorably, in part because the government thought it would make a good impression in London and Washington. The cabinet approved the measure, providing that Britain and America paid the costs of maintaining the children, allowed additional imports of sufficient food for them, and pledged to remove them at the end of the war. Erik Boheman, Secretary-General in the Swedish Foreign Office, told Adler-Rudel that Sweden preferred to take Jewish children from the Low Countries rather than Poland but that this was not a condition of acceptance.[31] This Swedish decision came only days before the British-American conference opened in Bermuda on April 19, and it might have had some bearing on its deliberations, but the delegations moved in a different direction.

Assistant Secretary of State Breckinridge Long and his refugee specialist Robert Borden Reams had handled the American preparations for the conference, which in part explained why the Americans ended up with a relatively low-level and inexperienced team of outsiders and politicians in addition to the State Department delegation.[32] Parliamentary Undersecretary Law—Eden's handpicked choice—headed the British delegation (Eden had arranged to return to London and confer with Law before the latter set off for Bermuda).[33]

At the closed-session working discussions at Bermuda, each side in

effect agreed to respect the other's sensitive areas: the British did not
want anything that might inflame Arab opinion in the Middle East,
anything that involved negotiating with Germany for the release of
Jews, or any shipment of food through the Allied blockade; the United
States did not want anything that would compromise its tight immigration policy.[34]

On the third day of the conference, Law sent a candid interim assessment to Eden personally:

2. . . . It is going well in the sense that the Americans have not come
here in order to throw the onus of failure upon us. I do not think that
they will try to embarrass us about Palestine . . . I think . . . that they
are seeking our support to enable them to state unpalatable facts to their
own public opinion. It should be correspondingly helpful to us to be
able to enlist their support against our own Archbishops. From this negative, but not unimportant point of view, I think that some good may
come out of Bermuda.

3. I confess that I feel less hopeful on the positive side. You can look at
the map for hours on end and still there seems to be no solution. I fancy
that the people here would be prepared to recommend North Africa,
but there is no guarantee (and in my opinion very little likelihood) that
such a recommendation would be accepted in Washington. It may be
that I am unduly pessimistic and the situation may clarify itself when we
get down to business. On the assumption that it is as stated the main
preoccupation of the Americans to pass the baby to us, it is to their
interest as much as ours that there should be some positive result.

4. At present, I am inclined to think that our principal objective ought
to be to establish, at the earliest possible moment, some form of intergovernmental machinery to handle the problem. If we here can define
the problem in terms of practical possibilities (i.e. in thousands rather
than in hundreds of thousands) and if we can put in train some machinery
which will exploit those possibilities, (charter a neutral ship here and
there and find a haven for a few hundred of these wretches in this territory or that) we shall have done something . . .

6. I understand that there is to be a refugee debate on the 4th May [in
Parliament] . . . The best I can hope for is that [before then] we could
get some formal agreement about what is impossible, i.e. that we cannot
ask Hitler to send us his Jews, that we cannot exchange dangerous Nazis
or POWs for German Jews, that we cannot send food in through the
blockade to feed the Jews; and some formal agreement that we are setting
up immediately some kind of inter-governmental machinery.[35]

Law regarded the most important goal of Bermuda as joint agreement on what should not be done; he wanted to shift the locus of responsibility for action to an international body.

Not surprisingly, the Bermuda Conference agreement involved very small projects. In the end, neither Britain nor the United States supported a bilateral declaration pledging to assume responsibility at the end of the war for refugees who had been taken in by neutral countries; each side, while expressing tribute to the humanitarian contributions of the neutrals, preferred to wait for a guarantee by all the Allied nations. The two delegations issued a press release but agreed to keep the agreement itself secret—apparently to deflect criticism of the limited results. And following the conference, first Churchill and then Roosevelt had to intervene to override the various obstacles and bring about the construction of small camps for Jewish refugees in North Africa—one of the conference's recommendations.[36]

Shortly after the Bermuda Conference ended, Archbishop Temple wrote to Eden in support of Sweden's reported willingness to approach Germany about accepting twenty thousand Jewish children. The Swedish government thought the offer might have some chance if it pledged to resettle these Jews outside Europe, and it asked for British assurances to this effect, as well as additional food for the refugees. Eden generally approved the idea, he wrote, but he declined to endorse resettlement outside Europe, partly on the grounds that the children's parents would no doubt want them back in Europe at the end of the war! In any case, any guarantee was a matter for the Allies as a whole.[37] In a follow-up discussion with the British Minister in Sweden, Secretary-General Boheman warned again that resettlement outside Europe was the only bait likely to interest the Nazi leaders; he was disappointed that Britain had not offered such reassurance. The American reaction was only slightly more flexible. After (or despite) some encouragement from Sumner Welles, the State Department was willing to promise to try, after the surrender of the enemy, to ensure that these people could return home. Sweden then cooled on the idea of approaching Germany.[38]

Yet the original Swedish suggestion was not impossible, as another episode at that time showed. In May 1943, the Swiss government conveyed a British request to Germany to allow five thousand Jewish children from the General Government of Poland and other Nazi-occupied lands in Eastern Europe to go to Palestine. In response, Himmler laid down the binding principles and the degree of flexibility in the German response to such offers. In general, he was opposed, but he might approve if it was part of an exchange for young interned Germans, perhaps four Germans for every one Jew.[39] The German Foreign Office added to Himmler's stipulations: if released, the five thousand Jews could not go to Palestine because the Arabs would object; they could, however, go to Britain if Britain was willing to give Germany something in return (such as interned Germans) and if the House of Commons was willing to sanction this bargain officially. In late June, Himmler and Ribbentrop jointly endorsed these terms, but, of course, they recognized the British were not likely to accept.[40]

The Nazi leaders would consider the release or exchange of some thousands of Jews only if they left Europe and became wards of the Allies. Such a move would still have allowed them to pursue their goal of completely eliminating Jews from Europe, and it also offered the prospect of stirring up anti-Semitism and potential political trouble in Allied countries. They had little interest in a simple agreement to allow limited numbers of Jews to leave for havens in neutral countries. (A new proposal to allow some French and Belgian Jewish children to go to Sweden collapsed when Germany said it could not spare the transportation.) The diplomatic exchanges dragged on unsuccessfully into 1944.[41]

Undersecretary Welles was frustrated by British opposition to evacuating Jews to sites in the Near East. In late June, he warned Lord Halifax that there was a need to remove Jews quickly from Bulgaria; further delay might miss the window of opportunity, and the Allies would be held responsible. But Halifax wanted to wait for the construction of concentration camps, as he called them, in North Africa for refugees from Europe.[42] These camps (recommended at Bermuda but not yet approved) were not designed for the numbers Welles had in mind or Eden had mentioned during his March visit to Washington.

In a May 4 speech in Boston, Assistant Secretary of State Adolf Berle, a former speechwriter and adviser to President Roosevelt, drew what seemed to be the consequences from the limited achievements at Bermuda. Known for his intelligence but hardly for his tact,[43] Berle did not deny the facts or dress up Allied policy. Germany had organized the extermination of the Jews and coerced its satellites to cooperate in it, he declared. It was the first time in modern history that a civilized country was carrying out a program of national murder, and he warned the German people that they would be held responsible. At the same time, he declared, immediate relief to those under the Nazi yoke was impossible: "Nothing can be done to save these helpless unfortunates except through the invasion of Europe, the defeat of the German arms and the breaking of German power. There is no other way." A refugee specialist in the British Foreign Office commented approvingly that U.S. official circles now recognized the difficulty of the refugee problem.[44]

A stark acceptance of continued Nazi killings of Jews might have been endurable in the West if the war had been going badly. But by mid-1943, the military outlook was considerably brighter, which meant that more and more people, even in the United States, could not simply resign themselves to accept Berle's line. Once it became evident how little the Bermuda Conference had accomplished, the pressures for British and American action resumed and then intensified.

In April, another British-American meeting took place besides the one in Bermuda, and it had nothing to do with Nazi extermination policy and the possibilities of saving those Jews who still remained. In the very lack of a connection—and in previous British policies regarding the distribution of intelligence—lies a relevant story.

On April 25, three American intelligence officials—William Friedman, Colonel Alfred McCormack, and Lieutenant Colonel Telford Taylor—reached London on their way to Bletchley Park. Friedman, fifty-one years old, was a self-taught code breaker who had become the preeminent figure in American cryptology—in one knowledgeable estimation, the greatest cryptologist. But he had already experienced one nervous breakdown and was on a reduced work regimen.[45] McCormack, a lawyer, had little experience with cryptanalysis. Taylor, a very young lawyer, had five months of service with the Army's Special Branch, and he was available to help sustain Anglo-American intelligence cooperation.[46] Their visit had important and lasting consequences for British-American intelligence cooperation, but it had been a long time coming.

British-American intelligence collaboration during World War II was an outgrowth of a growing British-American diplomatic and military partnership that had begun well before the United States formally entered the war.[47] The two intelligence communities had their own character and peculiarities so that at times they were poorly synchronized with the political relationship.[48] Intelligence organizations traditionally keep secrets they uncover and exploit—they do not share them. The Americans knew nothing of the early British breakthroughs against the hand ciphers used by the German police or the Enigma codes used by the German armed services, and at first they had no glimmer of the

large (and unified) British decoding and analysis operation at Bletchley
Park. The United States had its own cryptographers and cryptanalysts
divided—sometimes very divided—among the armed services and the
Federal Bureau of Investigation.

Army cryptanalysts had managed to reproduce a Japanese coding
machine and, in September 1940, to break a Japanese diplomatic code
called Purple. This intelligence received the name Magic, more or less
the counterpart to the British Ultra. A U.S. Army representative quickly
told the British Chiefs of Staff about their progress against Japanese and
Italian ciphers and proposed an exchange of intelligence information.
In October, War Department officials ratified this idea, and the President and Secretary of State were informed.[49] In January 1941, a U.S.
Army-Navy mission went to Britain, bringing a Magic machine that
was to be extremely useful for the British in monitoring Japanese activities in the Far East. According to the historian Bradley F. Smith,
this was one of the most generous initiatives in the history of modern
cryptanalytic relations.[50]

The American team received in return a brief tour of Bletchley Park,
a very general lecture on British cryptanalytic methods, and an understanding of the basic division of labor there (the now famous "Hut"
system, a team of specialists located in each of the Nissen huts on the
estate). But the British at that time had made only limited progress
breaking the Enigma codes, and the Americans were not shown an
Enigma machine, let alone given one; the Americans did not even
know of the existence of such an apparatus or of the machine (called a
bombe) the British used to calculate the wheel settings of the Enigma.
They also did not get a detailed enough picture to know how crucial
Bletchley Park would soon become to the war effort.

Based on the limited evidence available, Smith suggests that Graham
Stewart Menzies, head of the Secret Intelligence Service (SIS), perhaps
reinforced by Prime Minister Churchill, was responsible for treating the
Americans with reserve, in part because of concerns about breaches of
security on the other side of the Atlantic. The Americans did in fact
have security problems, as well as serious inter-service rivalries. But the
result of British reserve was that American military and intelligence
officials perceived that they had given far more than they had received.
Subsequent American resentment added to the difficulties of working
out closer intelligence cooperation with Britain.[51]

The British decodes of the German police hand ciphers were not as
sensitive as the Ultra decodes, but they remained hostage to the general

Allied intelligence relationship. Gradually, the British provided some Ultra information in disguised form to help American ships avoid German U-boats in the Atlantic during the second half of 1941,[52] and they provided additional assistance on the codes of Italy, France, French colonial states, Brazil and some other South American states, Portugal, and Sweden by late 1942. At least one British intelligence official regarded the relationship as lopsided in the Americans' favor.[53]

The Americans had no need to know about German police activities—or so the British apparently thought. And Menzies and his deputy, Nigel de Grey, were generally opposed to sending any of Bletchley Park's products to Washington. Only after the British ran into a number of technical problems for which they needed American assistance did the SIS bend: if the American army was prepared to send representatives to England, they could see everything.[54]

That offer led to the late April 1943 meeting. The three-man American delegation got a tour of Bletchley Park and was stunned by the size (about five thousand people) and productivity of the operation. Taylor stayed on in London, at first gaining access to the diplomatic decodes produced in a separate British intelligence office at Berkeley Street under Alastair Denniston, the former head of Bletchley Park.[55]

On May 17, high British and American intelligence officials signed a formal intelligence-sharing agreement for finished intelligence but not for the exchange of raw intelligence (such as the encoded radio intercepts). The net effect was that the United States would specialize in the interception and decoding of non-German messages, especially Japanese ones, and that the British would continue their near monopoly of work on German messages, as well as carry out other decoding work. Shortly thereafter, Taylor was able to move to Bletchley Park and to learn in detail what was produced there.[56]

The first team of American cryptanalysts arrived at Bletchley Park in July 1943 to assist their British counterparts. Among them was Arthur Levinson, a native of Brooklyn trained in mathematics and with several years' experience in the Army Signal Corps. (He later had a long and successful career with the American National Security Agency.) Levinson found the atmosphere at Bletchley Park upbeat, confident, and egalitarian. The whole operation was charged up with bright people who had been successful and expected further successes in the future. They had a mission, and they enjoyed one another's company. Polishing his code-breaking skills on German Enigma messages, Levinson deciphered no messages dealing with Nazi killings of Jews. References to such activity must have been quite rare in the radio messages of the German armed services.[57]

A British cryptanalyst named Walter Eytan, who had worked on German Enigma naval ciphers at Bletchley Park since early 1941, however, received a message in late 1943 or early 1944 that a German-commissioned boat was transporting Jews from the island of Rhodes to the Final Solution. Eytan, who by birth was a German Jew—his name had been Ettinghausen—had never seen or heard the expression Final Solution before, but, as he recalled later, he knew instinctively what it meant. He did not comment about it to others on duty at the time.[58]

The cryptanalysts at Bletchley Park never broke the Enigma key used by the Gestapo for its most secret communications, which would have had information about the Einsatzgruppen and perhaps also about the deportations of Jews from various countries to the extermination camps. But they did apparently break other Gestapo and SD codes, which may have had some information about these subjects.[59] Those records have apparently not yet been released.

It is worth remembering that decoding Enigma-based messages was a difficult process, starting with the use of large receivers to intercept the radio messages, with multiple coverage of each frequency, and radio operators with keen ears to identify the individual letters. The more people listening to the same message, the better the chance of ending up with a clean (uncorrupted) code text. So success in decoding the text depended in part on the number of people and the amount of time assigned to it. High officials had to establish priorities and assign manpower; they could not cover everything.

The British received a major new source of information about past SS and police activities in the Soviet territories when, in October 1943, a plane carrying a Croatian Air Force captain and a German police escort landed behind British lines in Allied-occupied Italy. It happened that the German policeman, an Austrian named Robert Barth, had served previously in Einsatzgruppe D (Einsatzkommando 10b) and was frightened enough to talk about it. (Only the initial summary of Barth's comments to British intelligence has been released so far.)

Barth described the formation of the Einsatzgruppen in May 1941 and their tasks—fighting partisans and Communism and carrying out general intelligence duties. He admitted that commissars and leading Communists were arrested and shot but misleadingly claimed that the Order Police ("Schupos") and Waffen-SS did the shooting. (They did, but the Einsatzgruppen did even more.) Barth revealed that Jews were almost invariably shot and in later stages gassed. He then discussed the 1943 activities of Einsatzgruppe E in Serbia and Croatia.[60] After the war, he gave American interrogators interested in prosecuting the heads of the Einsatzgruppen a much more detailed picture of events in Germany and the Ukraine in 1941,[61] but it is unclear just how much detail he offered the British in late 1943.

The Order Police messages in hand ciphers, which the British easily decoded, and the deciphered SS Enigma messages conveyed in small but significant ways some of the specific operations Nazi Germany was carrying out against the Jews of Europe. If there had been any Allied disposition to interfere with Nazi killing operations or to undertake or arrange rescue efforts, these police decodes and the SS decodes would have provided essential details about locations and activities. On October 15, 1943, for example, the British learned that seven hundred Jews had just broken out of the Sobibor camp and that countermeasures were under way. The text of the message gave the location of Sobibor: five kilometers from the Bug River, between Cholm and Wlodawa, in the Lublin district.[62] Whatever the immediate possibilities in this particular case, such detailed messages could have been used at least to plan future steps when military circumstances permitted them. But there was no move in that direction.

For a while longer, the British government alone had this option. Since the Anglo-American intelligence-sharing agreement dealt with only the highest-grade enemy ciphers, such as Ultra and Magic, and excluded field intelligence from the hand ciphers,[63] the Americans had no formal claim on the German police decodes. Even in late 1943, therefore, Taylor did not receive copies of the current police decodes,[64] let alone the back files. But in 1944 arrangements loosened up, and Taylor began to get current copies.

At the war's end, Taylor became involved in planning the International Military Tribunal at Nuremberg, and he served on the American prosecution team. Decades later, he wrote a personal memoir about the Nuremberg trials, in which he commented that he first became aware of the Holocaust during his exposure to the relevant witnesses and documents at Nuremberg during the second half of 1945.[65] That was rather late. And the documents he saw and used then did not include the German police decodes from 1941–42, with their many reports of mass killings of Jews.

# 12

✳

# THE TREASURY DEPARTMENT'S
# OFFENSIVE

THE MOST IMPORTANT CHANGE in American refugee policy during the war was the establishment of the War Refugee Board, and several elements in the history of this agency are relevant to this study.[1] A clash between the State Department and key officials of the Treasury Department exposed the same kind of political attitudes that prevailed in London—anything to do with the rescue of Jews obstructed the war effort. But the Treasury's initiative with the War Refugee Board profoundly altered British-American interaction over Jewish refugee problems, and it created significant differences between London's approach and Washington's. The Board then took some steps that had been considered earlier but never taken. One lesson of its history is that certain kinds of effort would have been possible if a committed Western government agency had had access to early intelligence about the Final Solution and if it had taken seriously the Allied Declaration of December 17, 1942.

On October 6, 1943, four hundred Orthodox rabbis, in conjunction with a flamboyant Palestinian Jew named Peter Bergson, who ran the Emergency Committee to Save the Jewish People of Europe, marched from the Capitol to the White House as a gesture of protest against American inaction with regard to the Holocaust.[2] This demonstration in Washington reflected a months-long trend: Jewish and liberal forces willing to use public pressure and demonstrations were taking charge from those who preferred to try to persuade behind closed doors.

This rising tide of American opinion in favor of action—despite a high level of anti–Semitism and anti–immigration sentiment—stood in contrast to declining British hopes for action. The British historian Tony Kushner has suggested that British activists, long struggling against the imperviousness of the Foreign Office, had faltered by mid-1943.[3] But American Jewry and its allies, with little support within the government, were no more likely to force changes in government policy than Jews and humanitarian groups had done in London. British officials believed that anti–Semitic and anti–immigration forces were more organized in the United States than in Britain and, consequently, that the Roosevelt Administration was unlikely to change course radically.[4] It was an assessment that turned out to be wrong. Shifts of opinion and influences within the American government did, in fact, bring about a major change of American policy before the end of the year.

There had been earlier signs of American openness to the issue of sending food and medicine into Nazi territories. In March 1943, Undersecretary Sumner Welles had backed a proposal for relief for women and children in Belgium and Norway and had alluded to other plans of this kind that the United States was anxious to carry out. Welles urged the President to contact Prime Minister Churchill directly about relief; otherwise the British government would continue its rigid opposition.[5] In June, a State Department official named Francis Sayre had told Clarence Pickett of the American Friends Service Committee about a recent conversation between Roosevelt and Churchill concerning this matter. Roosevelt reportedly did his best to persuade Churchill to allow further humanitarian exceptions to the blockade of Europe, but with no success. Churchill said that nothing must hinder the war effort. Sayre added: "The public reason given is that Germany would probably interfere, but the actual reason is not that. It is Churchill's insistence on the primacy of the military consideration."[6]

Sayre's account is consistent with other evidence. One of Churchill's strategic visions was to use Allied bombing, a tightening ring around German-held territories, and economic privation to starve Germany into collapse and surrender, minimizing Allied casualties.[7] Churchill and Roosevelt had spent much time together in May 12–25, discussing the strategy for mounting a near-term invasion of Italy and planning the cross-Channel invasion of France for mid-1944. In his address to Congress on May 19, Churchill warned against relaxing a "single fibre of our being" or tolerating "the slightest abatement of our efforts."[8] And a year later Churchill and Eden bluntly told Undersecretary of State

Edward R. Stettinius that there were to be no shipments of food through the blockade to occupied Europe. Eden added that Britain historically depended on blockade as a principal weapon of war.[9]

The implications of this strategy, if pursued to the limit, were severe. Imports of food and medicine that could conceivably allow Germany to reallocate resources for its war effort would delay the collapse. Any suggestion to evacuate children, the ill, or the elderly would relieve Germany of its obligation to sustain those who were economically un-productive, and if the Allies took part of the burden from Germany, Hitler might then seek to unload more. According to this view, simply to fight the war and to do little to alleviate suffering was the right policy.

At Bermuda, the American and British representatives had, among other things, agreed on only a vague verbal encouragement of human-itarian action to neutral countries and had called for a guarantee of repatriation of refugees by all the countries fighting the Axis powers.[10] This step was a weak substitute for direct American and British pressure on the neutrals to admit Jewish refugees, and not much happened. The Allies also neglected some diplomatic opportunities to move Jews in jeopardy to safer locations in neutral sites.

In July 1943, representatives of the World Jewish Congress asked the British government to lend support to a proposal for Switzerland to take in up to one hundred thousand refugees escaping or evacuated from Germany, France, and Italy. The British Minister in Bern, Clifford Norton, thought the Swiss were unlikely to be accommodating if most of the refugees were adult Jews, even if the Allies provided additional food and fuel. He decided not to approach the Swiss at that "inop-portune" moment.[11]

Mussolini's government—itself no secure protector of Italian Jews—fell later that month. When the new Badoglio government decided to leave the Axis and the war in September 1943, Germany flooded the country with its own forces, and German police began to deport Italian Jews to Auschwitz and to a new killing center at San Sabba, in Trieste.[12] It turned out to be less opportune to try to extract Jews from the hands of the SS and police than from the Italians.

The World Jewish Congress, meanwhile, pushed the idea of subsi-dizing relief and rescue of Jews in Rumania and France. Because the Allies did not permit funds to be sent to Europe for use in occupied territory, Gerhart Riegner and others suggested an alternative: deposit the funds into blocked bank accounts in Switzerland or the United

States, accounts that could serve as collateral (or guaranteed repayment after the war) for loans that friendly sources within France and Rumania could then make; no outside money would enter occupied Europe until the war ended. Riegner confirmed that wealthy Rumanian Jews would lend money on this basis.[13]

In the midst of discussions of this project, including one Rabbi Wise had with President Roosevelt, Jan Karski, now in the United States, was able to see the President on July 28. Although Roosevelt was interested in the Polish and Jewish underground and many other subjects, Karski was able to steer the conversation around to the concentration camps and eventually to Nazi treatment of the Jews, which he described as fundamentally different from the treatment of other peoples, since Nazi policy was to destroy the group's very biological substance. If the Allies did not intervene, Polish Jewry would cease to exist. After thanking Karski, the President said his story was important and that he was thrilled to hear about the Polish underground.[14]

Five days earlier, Roosevelt had told Wise to "go ahead" with his plan for the relief and evacuation of Jewish refugees in Rumania and France. That was not quite evidence of Presidential backing, although Wise certainly got the impression that the climate was favorable; he followed up with a letter to the President, and Roosevelt, shortly after his meeting with Karski, asked the Treasury Department about the status of the matter and asked it to respond to Wise. This small initiative was nonetheless significant—and it is consistent with Treasury official John Pehle's later recollection that Karski's visit and conversation with the President changed the climate. Roosevelt's August 14 letter to Wise, drafted by the Treasury, said that Treasury had approved the plan and that only some exchanges between the State Department and the American legation in Berlin were needed to complete the details.[15]

But the climate in the State Department was not transformed. About two weeks later a State Department official, responding to a citizen's inquiry about a New York Times article regarding extermination of Jews at Treblinka, conceded that the State Department had received information from reliable sources about murders of Jews in Europe but said it had no authentic figures regarding the numbers killed nor the means used.[16] No one was particularly looking for such evidence at the State Department, and neither British intelligence nor the British Foreign Office had sent over anything convincing.

In early September, a State Department official in the Visa Division drafted a response to another appeal to the President for rescue and relief actions made by the Emergency Committee to Save the Jewish People of Europe. The draft maintained that the Allies should avoid giving the enemy any opportunity to negotiate with them in return for worthless promises to alleviate the plight of their victims. Repeated warnings about barbarities had had little or no effect, so there was not much chance that further ones would be useful. A sharply worded conclusion contained an implicit attack on Jewish protesters:

> Appealing petitions have been addressed to this Government by persons who are interested in the plight of European Jews. Some of these appeals are of a sentimental nature and have come from persons who are themselves refugees from Europe and who have found safety after their admission into the United States. Large numbers of those whom we have sheltered are, however, engaged in activities more directly calculated to bring about the early defeat of our common enemies. I am confident that when this war shall have ended we will have no cause to regret that we extended to such persons the traditional asylum and hospitality of our country and that the presently helpless victims of Nazi tyranny will recognize their true deliverers.

In other words, the number of refugees in the armed services was greater than the number of those who were stirring up trouble—a kind of backhanded compliment. This draft made the rounds within the State Department and was commended, but the consensus was to delete the conclusion, although it was perceived to be correct, because it raised controversial issues. In its place was a paragraph stating that the United States and the Intergovernmental Committee on Refugees would continue to do their best.[17]

There was a fierce battle within the State Department, and between State and Treasury, over the advisibility and feasibility of the World Jewish Congress's proposal to use blocked accounts to evacuate or support Jews in Europe. At State, the Foreign Funds Control Division favored it, but the refugee specialists, Assistant Secretary of State Breckinridge Long, the European Division, the Near Eastern Division, and James Dunn of Political Affairs were all opposed and delayed action. In the end, Herbert Feis, State's adviser on international economic affairs (and later a Pulitzer Prize–winning historian) and a Jew, had to take the proposal all the way to Secretary of State Cordell Hull to get it approved. Secretary of the Treasury Henry Morgenthau, Jr., had also cleared with Hull the Treasury's letter for the President to send to Wise.[18]

Sumner Welles was gone from the State Department by this time— the victim of an escalating personal and political rivalry with Hull and of his own sexual indiscretions.[19] When Robert Borden Reams briefed the new Undersecretary Edward Stettinius, he discouraged both any Allied offer to accept Jews and any schemes to ship food to Jews in Europe. The first posed the "danger" that Germany might turn over a large number of Jews to the United States and Britain for immediate transportation somewhere, which would raise military and shipping problems. The second might allow the Germans to divert food for their own use and would destroy the economic blockade.[20] This was a defense of the traditional negative Allied position, but the bureaucratic situation was now quite different since the Treasury had entered the discussion. Adolf Berle had accepted the Treasury's view, and Long (sometimes depicted as the main obstructionist at State) reluctantly recognized the significance of the President's approval. Long was, after all, a political appointee.[21]

The Treasury Department, not the State Department, claimed patronage of the proposal for rescue and relief of Rumanian and French Jews. Leland Harrison, in Bern, recognized not only that approval of this project was a change in policy but also that the State Department had reservations. Harrison worked for State, not for Treasury; he wanted specific instructions from his superiors. He also shared the information with his British counterpart in Bern, who wanted approval from the Ministry of Economic Warfare in London. When Treasury officials complained about delays, State countered that they should have cleared the project with the British first.[22] This game could be continued for some time.

The pace of action was quite different elsewhere. In November, the SS and police shot approximately forty-two thousand Jews in the area of Lublin within three days—an operation called Harvest Festival.[23] But rescue could also occur swiftly. On September 29, when the Swedish Foreign Office learned that Germany intended to deport all Jews from Denmark, its first reaction was to warn Germany that the move would have an unfortunate effect on Swedish public opinion, and it offered to accept the Jews in Sweden; if Germany feared they might have a harmful political effect, Sweden was willing to intern them. Germany did not respond,[24] but advance knowledge of the planned German sweep and a heroic Danish evacuation effort brought some eight thousand Danish Jews to Sweden.[25] By October 9, Stockholm was able to inform Washington that the purpose of the Swedish démarche, the transfer of virtually all Danish Jews to Sweden, was in effect achieved.[26] The success was so striking that it galvanized the Intergovernmental Committee on Refugees to prod London and Washington about the much discussed (but never issued) Allied guarantee to repatriate refugees in neutral countries after the war and to seek to resurrect the project whereby, under certain conditions, Sweden would take in twenty thousand more Jews.[27]

By November, continued American inaction ran significant political risks. Following months of public lobbying by Bergson of the Emergency Committee and private efforts by Oscar Cox, assistant solicitor general at the Justice Department, Congressman Will Rogers and Senator Guy Gillette of Iowa introduced (nonbinding) resolutions into the House and Senate calling on the President to create a rescue commission to save the surviving Jews in Europe from extinction.[28] On November 10, Roosevelt told Stettinius he was convinced that the United States could do more for Jewish refugees and suggested opening refugee offices in Algiers, Naples, Portugal, Madrid, and Ankara. When Stettinius presented this idea at State, Ray Atherton of the European Division objected that the United States would end up paying the bills if this was a purely American action. It was better to have an international approach. (International approaches usually slowed things down.) Stettinius continued to worry about growing political pressure and criticism of the State Department in Congress and in the press.[29] He did not yet know that the Treasury Department was to be even more scathing and more effective.

Secretary of the Treasury Henry Morgenthau, Jr., was the President's neighbor in Dutchess County, New York, and one of his political confidants. He was the only Jew in the cabinet and certainly one of the most prominent Jewish Americans in the country. He had encouraged Roosevelt to pursue refugee initiatives in 1938–39, but he had not done much since the war began. Under the influence of information from Rabbi Wise about the Nazis' plan for a Final Solution in September 1942 and private meetings with Bergson in 1943, Morgenthau had already begun to take an interest in rescue and relief measures. Then his subordinates accelerated his progress.

High officials in the Treasury Department—particularly John Pehle, Randolph Paul, Josiah DuBois, and Ansel Luxford (none of them Jewish)—reacted with frustration and then fury to the State Department's extensive delays of the World Jewish Congress's project. They persuaded Morgenthau to raise a series of problems with Hull, who responded by pushing some matters forward. Suddenly, the U.S. and British governments agreed, on December 10, to press all the governments-in-exile of the conquered countries for a declaration that at war's end they would readmit all nationals who were now refugees in neutral countries.[30]

Two separate developments in December undermined the State Department's effort to stay on top of the political pressure. It became public knowledge that Assistant Secretary Long, in responding to criticism, had earlier given Congress seriously inflated statistics about the number of Jewish refugees who had entered the United States since 1933.[31] More or less simultaneously, the British refused to drop their objections to the World Jewish Congress project and broadened their complaints to include political complications of proposed rescue actions. Where would seventy thousand Rumanian Jews go, and what difficulties would they cause? The Ministry of Economic Warfare told the U.S. embassy in London (which passed it on to the Treasury):

> The Foreign Office are concerned with the difficulties of disposing of any considerable number of Jews should they be rescued from enemy-occupied territory . . . They foresee that it is likely to prove almost if not quite impossible to deal with anything like the number of 70,000 refugees whose rescue is envisaged by the Riegner plan. For this reason they are reluctant to agree to any approval being expressed even of the preliminary financial arrangements.[32]

The Foreign Office had said much the same thing before but never "in plain text" to such an unsympathetic, influential audience.

At a Treasury strategy session, Pehle called the British position shocking; Luxford observed that, by doing nothing, the British were condemning these people to death; DuBois called the cable amazing. The Treasury group concluded that it was important to recognize that the British would not go ahead on anything to do with substantial numbers of Jewish refugees. Morgenthau then provisionally decided to back the idea of a new rescue commission composed of influential people and to raise the matter at a future meeting with President Roosevelt. The next day the Treasury group conferred with Cox, who gave them knowledgeable advice regarding both the politics of getting a refugee board approved and the actions it might take. Then they brought all of their evidence to Hull.[33]

Knowing there was trouble coming, Hull had already sent a cable to the American ambassador in London, saying that the British viewpoint had astounded them and that he should press the matter with Eden. On December 20, Hull conceded to Morgenthau that it had been difficult to get action approved in the State Department and said he had just personally approved and issued a license for the World Jewish Congress plan. Perhaps the most unusual exchange came when Long pulled Morgenthau aside and tried to blame a former official in the Foreign Funds Control Division—who had supported the project and supplied information to Treasury—for all the delay. The man was Bernard Meltzer, a Jew. Morgenthau responded that there were many around who thought that Long was an anti-Semite.[34] Long lost jurisdiction over refugee matters shortly thereafter.

One final development incited the Treasury group to a direct attack against the State Department and forced the establishment of a new government agency to handle refugee issues. Josiah DuBois had requested and secretly received a series of State Department cables regarding Riegner, and in the process he learned about the State Department's February 1943 instruction to the American legation in Bern not to transmit any more information from Riegner to private parties (Wise).[35] DuBois then spent Christmas Day 1943 drafting a document titled "Report to the Secretary on the Acquiescence of This Government in the Murder of the Jews." He charged State Department officials not only with gross procrastination but also with attempts to prevent action from being taken to rescue Jews. At a December 31 meeting, he reported that Rabbi Irving Miller of the American Jewish Congress had said, more or less, that American government behavior was such that it would indicate to Germany and its satellites that "we don't give a damn what happens to the Jews."[36] Morgenthau retitled the document "Personal Report to the President"; he probably did not pass along DuBois's threat to resign unless the White House took quick, decisive action, but he did warn Roosevelt of the danger of a scandal if dramatic changes did not occur.[37]

On January 22, 1944, President Roosevelt issued Executive Order 9417, establishing the War Refugee Board and instructing it to take "all measures within its [U.S.] policy to rescue victims of enemy oppression in imminent danger of death" and to provide "relief and assistance consistent with the successful prosecution of the war." The

Board was to be composed of the Secretaries of the Treasury, State, and War, but Undersecretary of State Stettinius handled the supervisory responsibility for Hull; John Pehle became the Board's executive director, which meant, as Randolph Paul commented, "The Treasury is in this business to the hilt and intends to see that something is done even if people have to be run over."[38] For the first time, a Western government agency aggressively sought to rescue or protect at least some of those the Nazis were committed to destroying.

The British ambassador in Washington, Lord Halifax, warned London that 1944 was an American election year and that the Jewish vote was important in the United States. The Roosevelt Administration would not countenance British decisions that American Jews would regard as inhumane. If the Foreign Office persisted, Britain would end up with full blame. In London, Eden soon got his reservations about the World Jewish Congress project on the record—both governments might end up being embarrassed by transport and accommodation problems—but he agreed to what the Americans had done after the fact.[39] The Bermuda Conference consensus was seriously undermined.

As it turned out, the establishment of the War Refugee Board was far more important than the specific World Jewish Congress project for Rumania and France. Neither the hopes nor the fears of a large Jewish evacuation proved justified; under German pressure, Rumania still would not formally allow many Jews to leave. But some support to keep Jews alive in Rumania emerged, and more than two thousand Jews made their way out of France to Switzerland and Spain with the costs covered by loans. The notion of creatively using blocked bank accounts spawned further rescue schemes and some successes in 1944–45.[40]

The British government quickly tried to get a sense of how far it had to adapt to the War Refugee Board and the new climate, inquiring whether the Americans contemplated using the armed forces for the rescue of victims. (This, of course, would have met major resistance— all the more because no one knew whether the Allied invasion of France, set for June, would succeed.) After the War Department indicated no interest in helping the new agency, the War Refugee Board carefully stated that no one expected to use combat units to rescue victims of enemy oppression unless it happened as a by-product of a military operation designed for a military purpose; still, the State, Treasury, and War Departments were prepared to cooperate in other ways. The Board suggested pointedly that the British make public the existence of their Cabinet Committee on Refugees (it had been secret), and it asked London to pledge itself to a refugee policy similar to its own.[41]

For London, such public declarations had drawbacks. In a note to the State Department, the Foreign Office explained that the World Jewish Congress had requested a new Allied declaration denouncing Nazi extermination of Jews. But it said that the original 1942 Declaration had been unsuccessful, and it had embarrassed the Allies and had aroused excessive expectations among Jews. The Congress might be seeking another declaration as evidence that Allied countries recognized Jews as having a separate national status. Before rejecting this request, however, Britain wished to obtain the view of the United States and some assurance of support if the same request reached Washington during an election year.[42] (British officials were aware that many American Jews wanted the U.S. government to intercede with Britain on behalf of a Jewish homeland in Palestine.) In another note, this one to the Cabinet Committee on Refugees, Eden also deprecated the creation of the War Refugee Board as a political maneuver.[43]

As it happened, the War Refugee Board was already pressing for a new Presidential declaration about Nazi killings of Jews. The State Department was hardly enthusiastic, and Reams went so far as to argue that the 1942 Declaration had itself accelerated Nazi persecution of the Jews. He recommended clearing any new statement with Britain and the Soviet Union (one of which would surely have killed it). At an interagency meeting on March 2, Myron Taylor, the American representative on the executive committee of the Intergovernmental Committee on Refugees, complained that the War Refugee Board had stepped into its territory and that nothing effective could be done without British cooperation. Robert Pell of the State Department advised against a propaganda offensive, saying that the Nazis would simply kill Jews all the quicker. Pehle saw opposition mounting, and he alerted Morgenthau to the danger. Morgenthau lobbied with Roosevelt, but, given all the opposition, the issue remained in doubt.[44]

On March 19, 1944, Germany sent troops into the territory of its wavering ally, Hungary. Suddenly, approximately 825,000 Jews—including converts defined as Jews by the Hungarian racial law of 1941 —and tens of thousands of Jewish refugees from other countries were in dire jeopardy. Pehle and Morgenthau again pressed for a Presidential statement. On March 24, at a press conference, Roosevelt released a statement denouncing systematic torture and murder of civilians by the

Nazis and the Japanese. The "wholesale systematic murder of the Jews of Europe" was relegated to the fourth paragraph (the War Refugee Board draft had it in the first), but it was still described as "one of the blackest crimes of all history." The statement warned that those who took part in deporting Jews from Hungary would share the punishment.[45] The opposition had diluted and delayed, but not blocked, this Presidential statement.

On March 30, the British Political Warfare Mission in Washington passed along corresponding British guidance for broadcasts on the BBC:

> His Majesty's Government associate themselves wholeheartedly with declaration issued by President of U.S., warning Germany and her satellites of consequences of further persecutions in their territories and appeal to men of good will everywhere to assist so far as they are able in protecting the victims of oppression, threatened with torture and death. His Majesty's Government are taking every opportunity of conveying to the countries and governments concerned their full agreement with the President's declaration, and their determination to cooperate in all measures consistent with efficient prosecution of the war designed to give assistance and refuge to all who can find means of escaping the Nazis and Nazi-inspired tyranny.[46]

Although the term "Jews" did not appear, Foreign Minister Eden issued this statement the next day.[47]

American officials were themselves divided about the wisdom of the exact wording of President Roosevelt's statement. The Office of War Information (OWI) issued its own guidance for American overseas broadcasts of the message in all languages, which included the explanation that the statement contained no changes in policy. In addition, the guidelines cautioned: "In regard to the President's special reference . . . to persecution of the Jews, do not give the impression that his denunciation was limited to this subject alone or that it was especially aimed at it."[48] But the American ambassador in Turkey, Laurence Steinhardt, and the War Refugee Board emissary there, Ira Hirschmann, told the Board that the President's statement was exceptionally well timed, that it had received much publicity in the local media, and that it had made a deep impression on people in the Balkan States. They recommended its daily broadcast, stressing the penalties for those who committed or aided the commission of atrocities against Jews or other minorities, and the dropping of leaflets; both of these were done.[49]

In late April, the War Refugee Board again requested OWI and American broadcasters to appeal to Hungarians to protect and shelter Hungarian Jews and Allied nationals in Hungary, and OWI complied.[50]

The West's knowledge of what was taking place in Hungary from May 1944 on was not as crucial a factor in events and in rescue considerations as it had been earlier. By this time, Western countries knew what to expect, because they now recognized Nazi Germany's general policy toward Jews—what the Nazis themselves called the Final Solution of the Jewish question—as Roosevelt's statement of March 24 indicated. In fact, even before the German invasion of Hungary, the War Refugee Board warned the Hungarian government not to take part in the Hitlerite policies of persecution. An outline of Hungarian deportation plans appeared in The New York Times on May 10, before the trains started to Auschwitz.[51]

Among Hungarian Jews themselves, more information about what deportation meant circulated than had been the case earlier with Jews in other countries. Western broadcasts to Hungary transmitted much information about Nazi atrocities and killings. In addition, Hungarian soldiers who had served in the East talked on visits home about what they had witnessed, and survivors of the Hungarian Jewish labor battalions also passed on information, as did Slovak Jews who had fled to Hungary. Despite postwar accusations that Hungarian Jewish activists had concealed essential information, it now appears that much information was available by the spring of 1944. Some Jews, no doubt, heard nothing and others only fleeting rumors, but many had good sources. Whether Hungarian Jews accepted it or forced themselves to make choices that could only be excruciating or tragic was another matter. They were caught in a trap, and only a small minority could escape.[52] Saving Jews who remained in Hungary required foreign assistance, support from sympathetic Hungarians, or luck.

Hungarian Regent Admiral Horthy, in a meeting with Hitler on March 18, gave permission for Germany to deport several hundred thousand Jews from Hungary for labor elsewhere. Adolf Eichmann's deportation specialists, key Hungarian government officials, and the Hungarian police concentrated quickly and deported roughly half of all the Jews in Hungary within two months.[53] The death mills at Birkenau disposed of most of them.

Near the start of the deportations, there was a curious episode that comes across as a Nazi diversion to some and as an abortive alternative to the Holocaust in Hungary to others. On May 18, 1944, two emissaries flew into Istanbul (in neutral Turkey) on special missions for high Nazi authorities. The first, Joel Brand of the Jewish Rescue Committee in Budapest, explained that he came with a proposal from Adolf Eichmann: if the Allies gave Nazi Germany ten thousand trucks for use exclusively on the Eastern front, as well as large quantities of tea, coffee, cocoa, soap, and assorted war matériel, Eichmann and Germany would spare the lives of the Hungarian Jews. Brand's traveling companion, Andor Grosz (alias Andreas Gyorgy), a Jewish convert to Roman Catholicism, a smuggler, and an agent for several intelligence services, claimed that he had a separate and more complicated mission from Hungarian-based officials of the SD: to contact Allied authorities and initiate peace negotiations between Nazi Germany and the West at the expense of the Soviet Union. After brief discussions with Jewish officials in Istanbul, Brand and Gyorgy separately crossed the border into British-held Syria, trying to reach Palestine. Suspicious of both men and their offers, British officials arrested them and sent them to intelligence headquarters in Cairo for extensive interrogation, which kept them out of action.[54]

The historian Randolph Braham has observed that Eichmann and his subordinates had no power to suspend the deportations of Jews from Hungary; they were willing to make minor concessions only to assure the ultimate success of the Final Solution. Although this conclusion remains in dispute, a subsequent study extends Braham's assessment of this strategy to Hitler and Himmler, who had made more than their share of insincere offers before.[55]

The authorities behind Gyorgy's mission remain opaque, and it is difficult to understand fully its origins and purpose.[56] It is clear that SD officials in Hungary were actively involved in events there, but few original documents about them have come to light. The historian Walter Laqueur wrote in 1981 that the British had read coded radio messages sent by the SD, and F. H. Hinsley's official history of British intelligence leaves that possibility open.[57] British code breakers did read at least some messages from and about Higher SS and Police Leader Otto Winkelmann in Budapest,[58] though so far the British government has not released decodes of SD messages. In any case, Allied governments wanted nothing to do with terms such as those voiced by Brand and Gyorgy. Ira Hirschmann was in favor of pretending to consider Brand's proposal, in the hope that it might lead the Nazis to suspend or reduce the deportations, but the British were unwilling to go even that far.[59]

As the deportations proceeded, the War Refugee Board orchestrated a series of warnings to the Hungarian government of the dire consequences for Hungary's future.[60] Horthy at first refused to halt the deportations but did ask Germany to allow specific categories of Jews to emigrate. Hitler decided as a concession to permit the emigration of four hundred Jews with Swedish protective papers, twenty thousand Jewish children to Palestine, and seven thousand additional Jews, provided that deportations (of the rest) continued.[61]

But in early July, Horthy ordered a halt to all deportations from Hungary. Braham noted the various pressures on him: a plea from the Pope on June 25, a demand from President Roosevelt the next day for an end to the shipments of Jews, a request from the King of Sweden on June 30, and a heavy American bombing raid on Budapest on July 2. After discussions within the Crown Council and the Council of Ministers in Budapest, these agencies managed to persuade Horthy to reverse course on July 7.[62]

Later, through the International Red Cross, Hungary offered to release Jews under the age of ten with visas for other countries, as well as all Jews who had certificates to Palestine. The War Refugee Board recommended a public American-British declaration of willingness to find havens for all Jews who left Hungary, but the British did not respond to this suggestion for several weeks—not until Secretary Morgenthau personally pressed the matter with Churchill and Eden in London. Meanwhile, the United States gave Hungary assurances through the Red Cross that it would arrange for the care of all Jews released by Hungary to neutral or Allied territory and that it would find temporary havens for them. After the United States had given its pledge, Britain agreed to a similar joint statement, but Germany did not permit substantial numbers of these Jews to leave.[63]

When Nazi officials forced Horthy to appoint a new pro-Nazi (Arrow Cross) government in October, the deportations and marches of Jews from Budapest resumed. Still, the three-month interruption in the murderous policy and the arrival of Soviet troops in January 1945, coupled with heroic efforts made in Budapest during preceding months by the celebrated Swedish emissary Raoul Wallenberg, Swiss Consul Charles Lutz, and others, saved more than a hundred thousand Jews there. American pressure on the Spanish government induced it to provide Spanish passports and letters of patronage to more than two thousand Jews of Spanish ancestry in Hungary; and the War Refugee Board induced Latin American governments not to interfere with the distribution of forged documents indicating that Jews were nationals of those countries.[64] Another few thousand Jews escaped from Hungary into Rumania and Yugoslavia. And 1,684 Hungarian Jews—as a result of still-controversial negotiations involving the Jewish Rescue Committee of Budapest, the Swiss representative of the American Jewish Joint Distribution Committee, and an SS emissary—were sent to Bergen-Belsen; thereafter, Himmler's men sent them to Switzerland in two stages as a sign of "good faith" in an effort to open negotiations with the Americans. Roswell McClelland, the U.S. representative of the War Refugee Board in Switzerland, played along with the Nazi illusion that releasing some Jews might gain Himmler something.[65] But any offers to release large numbers of Jews dissolved when (or by the time that) they were taken seriously in the West. Nonetheless, Western publicity and diplomatic efforts did make a substantial difference in saving a small minority of Hungary's Jews.

Much has been written (and more is still to come) about the requests made that Britain or the United States conduct bombing raids to interrupt the killings at Auschwitz-Birkenau, particularly in the summer and fall of 1944, and about both governments' rejection of these requests. Did British and American bombers have the range and precision to destroy the gas chambers at Birkenau, and could they have done so without killing many of the prisoners there? Heated debate continues, but it does not appear that such a bombing raid would have been easy.[66] Basic facts, however, have been buried in the thicket of controversy and technical detail.

As far as is known, the first proposal for a bombing attack on Auschwitz came from the Polish government-in-exile in August 1943. (It is possible that Polish officials in London suggested this site as a target even earlier.[67]) It claimed some support from the British Air Staff for the idea and wanted to couple it with an attack by the Polish underground on the camp to liberate the prisoners there, many of them Poles.[68] As we have seen, considerable information about Auschwitz was already available in the West by then.[69] But at that time, British bombers could not have reached the camp with an adequate load. The possibilities for bombing Auschwitz increased substantially in early 1944, after the Allies had bases and suitable equipment in Italy (at Foggia).[70]

The earlier a successful bombing raid was made on the gas chambers and crematoria, the more it would have impaired the efficiency of the

Final Solution. But there is no evidence that this would have forced Hitler, Himmler, or their subordinates into a fundamental change of course. Rather, it would have required them to switch the locations and/or methods of killing, and it probably would have slowed the frantic pace.

Following the escapes of several prisoners (especially Rudolf Vrba and Alfred Wetzler) from Auschwitz in the spring of 1944, many more details about the killing operations there emerged and became known to Jewish organizations and to the War Refugee Board. This new information about the specific mechanisms of killing, and its scale, led some Jewish representatives to propose ways to stop or interrupt the actions at Birkenau. These proposals reached some appropriate Western government authorities, but there is no sign that anyone seriously investigated the feasibility of bombing the gas chambers and crematoria, a task that some historians, starting in the late 1970s, took on with great thoroughness.

The War Refugee Board did, however, investigate the idea of bombing the rail lines and bridges leading to Auschwitz. But it came to the disappointing conclusion that, even if the bombing were successful, the Germans could and would repair the damage quickly and easily.[71] Proposals for bombing the gas chambers and crematoria never got far in 1944, for reasons that had little to do with technical difficulties. The Board had neither the jurisdiction nor the weight to force through a proposal of this kind: it had to renounce military options at the time of its birth.[72] And there were other political and military constraints on what it could recommend. The Secretaries of State and War could outvote Secretary of the Treasury Morgenthau—and that was only the first hurdle. The consensus in official Washington was to bring the war to conclusion as quickly as possible. The War Department would and did marshal its forces against anything that seemed to interfere with this goal—whether or not it did so. After receiving proposals for the bombing of Auschwitz-Birkenau, Pehle sent them on to the War Department without the urgency he had used on other matters. He must have known that this one represented a very long shot, and he did not want to ruin the climate for other projects.

Assistant Secretary of War John J. McCloy rejected the requests in a cursory manner, even though American planes were bombing factories and refineries near Auschwitz. Bombing such a specific target was not without complications, but there is no sign that the War Department wanted to examine the technical problems—or to suggest to American forces in the field that they do so. In this sense, the historians' debate about the range, load, and precision of various bombers misses the main problem at the time: McCloy, reflecting general War Department views, was opposed to the whole idea of a military mission for humanitarian purposes, and he stopped the War Refugee Board from pursuing it.[73] No one else in official Washington was likely to explore this possibility.

The same proposal went further and higher up in London. Churchill expressed approval of it, and Eden subsequently added his support. In fact, Churchill reacted to the information about Auschwitz-Birkenau on July 11 with a striking written comment to Eden (Churchill subsequently used it in his history of World War II):

> There is no doubt that this is probably the greatest and most horrible crime ever committed in the whole history of the world, and it has been done by scientific machinery by nominally civilised men in the name of a great state and one of the leading races of Europe. It is quite clear that all concerned in this crime who may fall into our hands, including the people who only obeyed orders by carrying out the butcheries, should be put to death after their association with the murders has been proved.[74]

(The scholar Raul Hilberg has cited this extended comment as a sign that the Prime Minister was concerned more with Germany's reputation than with the safety of Hungarian Jews.[75]) Churchill had told Eden four days earlier to "get everything out of the Air Force you can,"[76] but the British government did not bomb the gas chambers at Birkenau or even come close to approving such a mission. Though British military authorities (in particular, Sir Archibald Sinclair, Secretary of State for Air) expressed willingness to undertake a humanitarian mission, they, like the Americans, ruled out bombing the rail lines on grounds of efficacy. To bomb the gas chambers and crematoria, detailed topographical information was needed, which took a little time to procure. After considerable delay, the Foreign Office concluded that the Hungarian government's decision to halt the deportations and the technical difficulties of the mission made it no longer necessary, even though the topographical information was available. In the end, Parliamentary Under-Secretary Richard Law gave the final "no" in early September, stressing the absence of deportations from Hungary during the last month.[77]

As it happened, this was not quite accurate, and some British officials knew it. In August, Eichmann had been able to arrange a transport of Jews from the Sarvar camp in Hungary against orders from the Hungarian government, and the British had intercepted the message from the commander of the Security Police in Hungary to the Reich Security Main Office (RSHA), according to which 1,296 Jews from Sarvar were headed for Auschwitz. The British analyst drew the obvious conclusion about their fate, which was not specified in the radio message.[78] (The British data on the number of Jews involved in this transport were more precise than historians were able to come up with in their research from other sources in the 1990s.[79]) The larger significance was that Nazi Germany had not given up on its policy of killing the remaining Hungarian Jews, the Hungarian government's halt to the deportations notwithstanding.[80] And this should have been clear to anyone who had access to, or took the trouble to get, the best intelligence. Besides, deportations of Jews from other regions of Europe to Auschwitz-Birkenau also continued.

Except for this new information about the British decode, the story of how the British handled requests to bomb Auschwitz-Birkenau is not new. The historian Bernard Wasserstein unveiled much of the evidence in 1979, and both Martin Gilbert and Israeli scholar Michael J. Cohen have added further research. Each of these historians reached somewhat different conclusions about the reasons for British inaction. Wasserstein found the Foreign Office bureaucracy responsible,[81] whereas Cohen thought that the Air Ministry and the Foreign Office blamed each other for rejecting a project that neither one wanted.[82] Gilbert's account, although the most detailed, was also the most confusing, in part because he joined it to a chronological narrative of Brand's mission, the Allied reaction to it, and the American government's rejection of bombing proposals—all exceedingly complicated stories.[83]

In his conclusion, Gilbert insisted that Allied governments did not know the secret of Auschwitz-Birkenau until mid-1944; this alleged lack of knowledge gave him part of the explanation as to why the Allies never bombed the gas chambers there and why so many Hungarian Jews died: the information came relatively late.[84] Insofar as he apportioned responsibility for Britain's failure to bomb the gas chambers, he mentioned a few unspecified individuals in London (presumably Foreign Office officials) who had scotched the Prime Minister's directive, and he noted that Churchill was not always the final arbiter of policy. (However, he did not specify who was the arbiter in this case.) On the other side of the Atlantic, he blamed the War Refugee Board for with-holding its official support for the project until it was too late.[85] Cohen, however, objected to such a positive assessment of Churchill on this issue: The Prime Minister clearly knew how to get his way on many other matters. Why did he prove unusually ineffective or inattentive this time?[86]

In dealing with American handling of proposals to bomb the gas chambers, Richard Levy has recently extended a portion of Gilbert's argument, noting that relatively few Hungarian Jews were deported to Auschwitz after Horthy's July 1944 order to cease the transports, which he credits in good part to the (unrelated) American bombing raid on Budapest on July 2.[87] In other words, the proposals to bomb the gas chambers at Birkenau came so late that they could not have effectively interrupted the vast majority of the deportations from Hungary, even if a bombing mission had succeeded—which Levy doubts would have been possible. He concludes that the result of the American bombing of Budapest on July 2 "lends support to the view, often expressed at the time, that the most effective way to help the Jews was to win the war as soon as possible."[88]

This view was, in fact, the official Western line before the War Refugee Board was established, but Levy's example hardly demonstrates its validity. The American bombing of Budapest worked as a deterrent only because it was combined with repeated American threats against the Hungarian government and with other foreign pressure. This level of pressure was precisely what had been absent before 1944. Horthy's order to halt the deportations of Jews reinforces the points made earlier in this work: although the Nazi regime was relatively impervious to outside pressure, the German people, the Nazi satellites, and Germany's allies were not. Credible Western threats against those who collaborated in the Final Solution could have brought substantial results earlier.

Bombing the gas chambers in the summer or fall of 1944 would have been a more potent and convincing expression of concern about the slaughter of European Jews (and Gypsies) than anything the United States and Britain had said or done previously. But the time that West-ern governments had already lost—generally, from the fall of 1941 until the founding of the War Refugee Board—seems a more fundamental failure than their rejection of proposals to bomb Auschwitz.

# 13

✻

# THE MILLS OF THE GODS

WINSTON CHURCHILL and Franklin Delano Roosevelt both said that the Allies would punish those who had engaged in the mass murder of European Jewry, and at their June 1942 meeting Roosevelt gave Churchill a memorandum on the subject of Axis atrocities.[1] While British officials refrained from using the German police and SS decodes during the war, they did make some preparations to collect relevant evidence for eventual war-crimes trials. The fate of this evidence, however, demonstrates both the degree of their commitment to postwar judicial proceedings and their pervasive commitment to secrecy.

On October 7, 1942, in accordance with a simultaneous announcement by President Roosevelt, British Lord Chancellor Sir John Simon had suggested the establishment of a United Nations (i.e., Allied) War Crimes Commission that would gather evidence for postwar trials of those who had carried out atrocities and crimes against citizens of the Allied nations. Simon's statement had also mentioned Nazi persecution of Jews but had left open the question of whether the Allies would take responsibility for trying those who persecuted and killed people in Germany or without Allied nationality. Given the legal questions, some British officials preferred a governmental decision, not a legal process, to impose punishment on key enemy officials. But the War Cabinet did establish a special committee on the treatment of war criminals.[2]

British intelligence officials recognized in the fall of 1942, if not earlier, that the German police decodes contained important evidence of what soon was to be called "crimes against humanity." Graham Stewart Menzies agreed to a suggestion by Victor Cavendish-Bentinck that two reliable Foreign Office officials compile a dossier of evidence from the decodes. Military intelligence officers were instructed to translate the relevant decodes, with attention to Nazi euphemisms such as "special treatment." They were to assemble evidence about the number of people shot or maltreated, the specific officials responsible, and the police and SS or army units involved. The two Foreign Office officials, Denis Allen and a man named Campbell, received this evidence of past atrocities, suitably translated and explained, and they were supposed to obtain any relevant information from new decodes.[3]

Copies of the relevant police decodes, therefore, went to the Foreign Office, but they do not appear in the Foreign Office records available today. According to an archivist at the Public Record Office who consulted a detailed index of Foreign Office records, it appears that they were destroyed in routine sifting out of nonessential records. However, the Joint Intelligence Committee atrocities file from 1941–42, in the original German, survives.[4]

Some key British officials had little enthusiasm for the whole concept of war-crimes trials. In June 1942, Anthony Eden told the War Cabinet of his opposition to any form of international court or special judicial machinery. He wanted each Allied country to try cases against its own nationals, and he recommended either military tribunals or civil courts in other countries, using their existing laws and procedures. Eden was concerned about Britain's being saddled with the burden of trying huge numbers of war criminals and urged a quick disposition of the issue to facilitate the return to a peaceful atmosphere in Europe.[5]

This way of construing Britain's obligations in and of itself precluded significant British responsibility for trying those guilty of persecuting and murdering European Jews. The desire to rely on existing laws and procedures also overlooked the Nazi regime's perversion of Germany's legal system; the deportation and killing of German Jews was not in fact illegal in Nazi Germany. It is possible that, following Eden's inclinations, the Foreign Office ceased work on the decodes regarding crimes against people who were not British—and therefore no longer considered a priority—but we do not know.

From the beginning, future war-crimes trials were an American project. Some Washington officials considered the very announcement of trials in which offenders would be treated as common criminals, not political officers, an important element in a campaign of psychological warfare. The imminence of clear-cut mechanisms of law would appeal "to the legalistic German mind," it was thought, play on the guilt of those committing atrocities, and frighten some other Germans who might otherwise participate. Also, it was a way to punish the guilty without imposing indiscriminate collective punishment on the German people as a whole.[6] In other words, the likelihood of war-crimes trials would have beneficial effects as a deterrent on Germans during the war and would make possible fairer and more selective Allied punishment at war's end. An interdepartmental committee (which included White House political adviser Ben Cohen) was established to plan for the international prosecution of war criminals.

Meanwhile, Eden told the British embassy in Washington that there was no truth to the story that London was making such plans; an international war-crimes tribunal, he said, would be undesirable. Eden blamed the Soviet Union for the delay in following up Lord Simon's announcement,[7] but obviously that was only part of the story.

A memorandum prepared by the Joint (American–British) Committee on Information Policy reflected American inclinations. One British committee member then reported that very high quarters in London had assessed it unfavorably; he suggested withdrawing it.[8] In general, the British were opposed to making strong threats about war-crimes trials because of Foreign Office fears that Germany might retaliate against British prisoners of war. Churchill and Eden were inclined to impose sentences on select Nazi officials, not to try them formally.[9]

That left open several questions: whether any other Germans would be punished for crimes in Germany and occupied Europe, and if so, how many; who would impose punishment, and how. Lord Chancellor Simon wanted action through formal judicial proceedings and viewed the War Crimes Commission as responsible for collecting the necessary evidence.[10] This Commission was, however, unaware of the secret evidence that British intelligence and the Foreign Office already had, and Eden resisted extending the mandate of the Commission to deal with atrocities committed on racial or religious grounds in enemy territory. Later, the Foreign Office and the War Office each tried to pin responsibility on the other for dealing with the Commission.[11]

From 1943 on, there does not appear to have been any selection of relevant evidence from police and SS decodes for war-crimes trials involving offenses against Jews. British intelligence officials, especially the experts on Germany in MI 14, continued to receive, gather, and organize (and presumably analyze) information from all the decodes.[12] As of this writing, relatively few MI 14 records have been released. But the available records provide some good clues as to what did and did not happen.

The cryptanalysts did not falter. The code breakers had some difficulty with new German police codes introduced at the end of 1942, but before long in 1943 they were deciphering a substantial percentage of messages.[13] There was the old problem of secrecy and euphemisms in radio transmissions, but that problem had existed ever since Daluege's warning of September 13, 1941. Considerable specific information about deportations of Jews from France in 1944 came in, for example, and this continued even as Allied troops poured into the country.[14] And decodes of some SS Enigma messages also contained relevant information about the Holocaust in Hungary. But who highlighted it and urged others to take note? Was it relevant to anything that Britain intended to do?

At the Moscow Conference, which ended in early November 1943, Soviet Foreign Minister Vyacheslav Molotov, Secretary of State Cordell Hull, and Eden reached agreement on a declaration pledging to punish atrocities with war-crimes trials carried out in and by the countries where those crimes were committed. The major Axis criminals whose crimes had no particular geographical location would be punished by joint decision of the Allies. The rhetoric of the Moscow Declaration was in some respects far-reaching:

> Thus, the Germans who take part in wholesale shooting of Italian officers or in the execution of French, Dutch, Belgian or Norwegian hostages or of Cretan peasants, or who have shared in the slaughters inflicted on the people of Poland or in territories of the Soviet Union . . . will know that they will be brought back to the scene of their crimes and judged on the spot by the peoples whom they have outraged. Let those [not yet participating] . . . beware lest they join the ranks of the guilty, for most assuredly the three allied Powers will pursue them to the uttermost ends of the earth and will deliver them to their accusers in order that justice may be done.[15]

There was no mention of Jews in this declaration.

About two weeks before Churchill, in a memo to Eden, described the events at Auschwitz-Birkenau as the greatest and most horrible crime in world history,[16] the War Cabinet decided that the Allies should not assume formal responsibility for punishing atrocities committed on

racial, religious, or political grounds in enemy territory.[17] With this
cabinet position on the record, the evidence from German police decodes quickly faded into the background.

Some British intelligence experts on Germany had hoped to use information from the decodes in the postwar occupation.[18] The specialist
on the German police was Brian Melland, described by one of his
former colleagues as a theatrical character who, in the fall of 1943 and
early 1944, gave a series of spirited lectures to American and British
officers who were to enter Germany as part of the Allied forces.[19] Although he had a tendency to resort to stereotypes about national
character that was not uncommon at the time, Melland nonetheless
presented American and British officers with a careful, detailed analysis
of the importance of the German police within the Nazi system as it
changed over time, and he emphasized the role of the Order Police
battalions:

> It is perhaps a surprise to you to learn that battalions, regiments and even
> whole divisions of German police are being employed in this war as
> ordinary fighting troops or, more particularly and characteristically, as
> security forces along the lines of communication and in static occupied
> areas. In all their tasks these Police-soldiers collaborate very closely with
> Himmler's SS . . . This close affiliation of Police and SS under the
> leadership of Himmler cannot be sufficiently emphasized, for it consti-
> tutes the powerful backbone of the whole Nazi regime . . .
>
> I should just like to say however that the German police battalions
> and regiments, composed of men drawn from this barrack Schutzpolizei,
> and supplemented by police reservists, has a pretty black record for its
> share in repressive activities along the lines of communication and in
> static occupied areas. It has liquidated by plain straightforward butchery
> thousands of men, women and children and we should not lose sight of
> this fact when we come to deal with its members. Let us not assume that
> only the SS men in the Gestapo and SD are responsible for war crimes.
> We know that their partners have been these uniformed German police
> battalions. We know that for a fact.[20]

Melland did not reveal the secret of the German police decodes, but
he clearly had learned a good deal from them, and he obviously wanted
others to use this information in arresting war criminals. The lecture,
however, at least as written, contained only one passing reference to
Jews. A revised version of the same lecture, given in early 1944, men-

tioned the wholesale liquidation of civilians, the use of mobile gas vans, and the participation of the municipal police along with the Einsatz-kommandos. Again he made no specific mention of Jewish victims.[21]

This lecture received some compliments, and it was suggested that Melland prepare a kind of handbook on the German police. That suggestion appears to have been the impetus for a joint American-British handbook titled *The German Police* issued in April 1945 by the Supreme Headquarters Allied Expeditionary Force (SHAEF) Counter-Intelligence Division. The title page indicates that the London branch of the Allied military intelligence research section prepared this work in consultation with the War Office (MI 14d).[22]

With about 130 pages of text and hundreds of pages of appendixes, this study was extraordinarily detailed yet curiously partial. Melland's comments about the crimes of Order Police battalions in occupied territories did not appear. Instead, the SHAEF study listed the new wartime duties of the barrack police as guarding lines of communication, patrolling guerrilla-infested areas, operating against partisans, and maintaining law and order in cooperation with the SS, army, or other security organizations. It noted that, even where these battalions had been combined into regiments, they were not to be confused with the Waffen-SS and that their men were not necessarily SS members. The closest it came to describing Order Police involvement in mass murder was a statement that many battalions were among the most Nazified, fanatical, and brutal of the Nazi field units terrorizing Norway, Poland, Yugoslavia, Greece, Czechoslovakia, and Italy.[23] There was no discussion of mass killings by Order Police battalions in the Soviet territories and no mention of Jews in this context. Even the passages about the Jewish section of the Reich Security Main Office (Eichmann's) made no mention of Nazi killings of Jews.[24] Perhaps American participation in this project precluded use of information from the decodes, or perhaps the audience for the handbook was too broad. Discretion, in any case, prevailed.

In June 1945, SHAEF G-2 issued another report about the link between the SS and the Order Police, which noted that, one way or another, high officials in the police had become SS members. But the main body of the Orpo (Order Police) "has the distinction of seeming quite apart from the political life of the land, and therefore its individual rank and file members are considered harmless to our interests. The routine nature of the services performed by the Orpo leads to this conclusion."[25] This characterization helped Order Policemen to move more easily through the process of denazification, and it was probably made in good faith. British intelligence knew that a large number of Order Police in the East had made killing into a routine, but that knowledge did not pass over to SHAEF.

In September 1945, MI 4 and 14 distributed to Allied occupation authorities, the War Crimes Commission, and national military officers responsible for war-crimes proceedings a list of SS, police, and Nazi Party names. It began cautiously, with the warning that it was only a watch list: everyone mentioned was suspected either because of specific evidence or because of what was known about the office he had held. Still, it was "no more than a partial and fragmentary contribution toward a comprehensive black list of war crimes suspects."[26]

This list was indeed partial. Kurt Daluege, head of the Order Police, appeared only as the man responsible for reprisal killings in Czechoslovakia following the Czech assassination of Reinhard Heydrich. Adolf Eichmann was listed as responsible for rounding up and expropriating Jews and, specifically, for deporting Jews from Holland to Auschwitz. Erich von dem Bach-Zelewski was identified more or less correctly in terms of the positions he had held but accused only of razing the village of Borki in central Russia in June 1942. Friedrich Jeckeln was identified and accused of a series of crimes against Jews, Communists, and others in the Baltic States. There was nothing about Bach-Zelewski's or Jeckeln's other massacres in the summer and fall of 1941, which are plainly stated in the German police decodes.[27]

One is tempted to conclude that the author or authors of this blacklist did not know about or have access to the German police decodes, except for one inconvenient fact: the information about Bach-Zelewski and the razing of Borki did come from the decodes.[28] Jeckeln was accused of crimes known from other sources, though he was not accused of crimes in the Ukraine (killings of Jews), for which the best available evidence was his radio messages. It appears that there was already a Secret Intelligence Service decision or a disposition not to make use of the German police decodes for war-crimes trials.

At the beginning of 1946, the British War Office did establish a War Crimes Interrogation Unit; a predecessor organization had existed from 1940 on. This body gathered evidence of war crimes from interrogations of German prisoners and captured documents.[29] But the material from the German police and SS decodes—so painstakingly intercepted, deciphered, and in some cases translated and presumably analyzed—was still confined to secret files and not used.

The Government Code and Cypher School, however, decided at the end of the war to produce a (classified) history of various dimensions of the conflict, based solely on material decoded at Bletchley Park. Volume 13, written by Lieutenant E. D. Phillips, covered the German police. Phillips pointed out at the start that the ministries which had received copies of the decodes undoubtedly had a better standard for judging their importance, for they had other sources of information and better knowledge of the broader context.[30] Still, there was some value in summarizing just what the German police section (which operated independently until late 1943) and then Hut 3 at Bletchley Park had learned from the police decodes.

In an appendix, Phillips listed some of the incidents where Higher SS and Police Leaders had reported executions and the SS or police units that had carried out the shootings. The victims were most frequently labeled Jews or Bolshevists, but, Phillips added at the bottom, "It is probable that 'Jews' and 'Bolshevists' were convenient categories to account for any kind of execution."[31] This comment, made after the world had been shocked by photos and newsreels from concentration camps at Bergen-Belsen, Dachau, and elsewhere, and at a time when the International Military Tribunal was already under way, expressed a rejection of the known truth that the Nazis had liquidated huge numbers of Jews, a fact that Nazi officials themselves had reported openly.

Can one state that the absence of information from the police decodes affected postwar decisions? We can at least show that the decoded material was relevant to decisions about war-crimes prosecutions. For example, the British government decided to include Order Police officers among those Germans subject to automatic arrest in the British zone of occupation after the war. But consistent with the decision made by Allied prosecutors in the preparations for the International Tribunal at Nuremberg to prosecute the Gestapo and the SD as criminal Nazi organizations, the British placed Gestapo and SD officers into category 1, as potential major offenders, and high officers of the Order Police into category 2, as potential offenders.[32] There was some apparent logic to the argument that "ordinary" police, many of whom were not SS or Nazi Party members (except at the highest ranks) did not belong with the Gestapo's notorious figures, but those who devised these categories did not have the German police decodes showing the massive involvement of Order Police battalions in executions. In January 1946, the Allied Control Council for Germany issued a directive designed to remove and exclude Nazis and war criminals from official positions in postwar Germany. High police officials were listed, but Order Police lieutenants and below were not.[33]

Britain and the United States decided to hold off on trials of individuals in category 2 until they saw how well the first Nuremberg tribunal worked, and there was even some pressure to release the suspects in the meantime. Eventually, both nations decided to deal with the people considered criminal because of their membership in organizations through denazification proceedings, which were trials held in German courts under Allied supervision.[34]

The Americans tried to undertake a very extensive denazification program, beginning with the screening of the entire adult German population. This effort, probably a mistake in conception, since it diffused guilt too broadly, led to all kinds of errors and abuses in practice: few American officials had enough detailed knowledge about Nazi Germany to make good judgments about individual roles and culpability.[35] Why did they not focus first on the much smaller number of SS and police, whose units and assignments suggested their involvement in mass killings? At least that way, the worst offenders would have gotten proper attention. But did the Americans know which units and organizations were involved in mass killings? It was fairly obvious that concentration-camp officials and guards were a proper target, and then one (paper) copy of the Einsatzgruppen reports compiled in Berlin turned up to incriminate the officers and men in these detachments. But nothing comparable emerged for the Order Police battalions.

British denazification from the beginning was marked by a less crusading spirit and heavier economic constraints. Fewer Germans were automatically arrested in the British zone, and a substantial percentage of those who were arrested were quickly let go: the War Office decided to concentrate on what British occupation officials considered the most serious cases and to release the rest. Britain also declined to extradite suspected war criminals to countries where it was believed they would not receive a fair trial, such as the Soviet Union.[36] And British intelligence kept its police decodes secret.

Order Police battalion officers and men were rarely investigated and prosecuted in the Western zones of occupied Germany. There was a widespread tendency to believe that the murders and other atrocities were the work of only the SS—and even then, only of portions of that organization. West German investigations and prosecutions of Order Policemen were not uncommon from the 1960s on, but convictions were extremely rare. Lack of documentary evidence was part of the problem, a subject that merits an in-depth study of its own.[37]

For the highest SS and police officials, the Allies might still have held individual or group trials. The Americans successfully prosecuted some Einsatzgruppen officers but did nothing comparable for the Higher SS and Police Leaders or the Order Police battalion commanders. Since they did not have the German police decodes, it was hard to find evidence and correctly identify suitable targets for prosecution. Ironically, the lead American prosecutor in the Einsatzgruppen case was Telford Taylor, the very man who had spent so much time at Bletchley Park and received copies of Order Police decodes from 1944 on.[38] But he apparently had never received copies of the earlier decodes.

American forces arrested Kurt Daluege on the day Germany surrendered. Unlike the highest Nazi officials who committed suicide at the end of World War II (Hitler, Himmler, Goebbels), Daluege decided to test his luck. His main claim to notoriety was that, following the mid-1942 Czech assassination of his colleague and longtime police rival Reinhard Heydrich, he had directed German measures of retribution in what the Nazis called the Reich Protectorate of Bohemia-Moravia: the Nazis had responded by murdering all men in the Czech town of Lidice. Lidice's women went to concentration camps, eight children were judged suitable for Germanization, and the rest vanished. The occupiers destroyed all buildings in the town itself and eliminated the rubble. Lidice had disappeared from the face of the earth.[39]

The destruction of Lidice had shocked the West in 1942, but Daluege's colleagues who presided over extermination camps executed more people each week than all the Czechs killed in the crackdown following Heydrich's death. At the end of the war, revelations of horrors at Auschwitz, Belzec, Sobibor, Treblinka, Chelmno, and Maidanek, as well as so many concentration camps obscured Daluege's crimes. No one in authority considered including him in the first group of defendants brought to trial at Nuremberg; if Heydrich had lived, Allied prosecutors would have made him one of their most prominent targets.

In a rambling written statement for the Americans, Daluege explained that he had merely headed the green-uniformed Order Police whose men were now working without friction under the occupation authorities. His work, he said, never had anything to do with the concentration camps, the Jewish question, or the liquidation of opponents: all that was the province of the Security Police under Heydrich.

Daluege said he was no criminal; he had not even committed crimes in the most difficult years before 1933. In addition, he had suffered serious heart and blood illnesses in September 1943 and had essentially retired from active service at that point. (He later told Czech interrogators that he suffered from hereditary syphilis!)[40]

With the police decodes in hand, British intelligence knew a lot more, and someone wanted to learn more still. The Foreign Office put in a request to interrogate Daluege—it was eager to obtain certain information from him.[41] Any British interrogations of Daluege have not been released.[42] Still, American officials gave the Czechs access to and, later, control of Daluege. Although he tried to pass blame for Lidice onto Karl Hermann Frank, the Czechs had enough evidence for a court to have Daluege convicted and executed in 1946.

Higher SS and Police Leader Friedrich Jeckeln was captured by Western troops, which turned him over to the Soviets. In their interrogations the Soviets concentrated on Jeckeln's administration in the Baltic States, and Jeckeln tried to make it seem as if he had no previous experience with the Final Solution when he moved from the Ukraine to Riga. The Soviet Union executed him in early 1946.[43]

Erich von dem Bach-Zelewski was much luckier for some time. He fell into the hands of the Americans, and he began to talk, showing an adeptness for unveiling secrets from the inner circles of the SS without incriminating himself on the record.[44] He had a military background, and by 1943 he was in overall charge of actual anti-partisan warfare, not simply executing civilians. This military service and these combat activities apparently served as a cover for his other work, even though some of his military actions far exceeded international norms for battlefield behavior. His forces had suppressed the Warsaw uprising of 1944 with widespread murders and atrocities against civilians.[45] British intelligence had in hand his boast that his forces had executed thirty thousand people through August 7, 1941, and an intelligence analyst had summarized the salient points from the decrypts in a late 1944 or 1945 description of Bach-Zelewski's career.[46] Unknowing Allied prosecutors decided to use Bach-Zelewski as a prosecution witness at Nuremberg, and on January 7, 1946, he appeared in the dock there. The attorney who opened the questioning was none other than Colonel Taylor. One American described Bach-Zelewski on the witness stand as looking like a rather serious accountant. For the most part, Taylor gave Bach-Zelewski an easy time, eliciting testimony about the army's role (not the SS's) in atrocities. As Taylor later put it, "He was certainly no angel and did not claim to be, but he was thoroughly familiar with the army's conduct of the war on the Eastern Front and its involvement in war crimes, and he was willing to testify on these matters."[47]

When Taylor asked about his principal task as Higher SS and Police Leader, Bach-Zelewski responded that it was to fight partisans. When Taylor asked about the functions of the Einsatzgruppen, he explained that they were to annihilate Jews, Gypsies, and political commissars. He acknowledged that his anti-partisan operations resulted in unnecessary killing of civilian populations, but he blamed this on his subordinates and on German military authorities. The Russian prosecutor, Colonel Pokrovsky, was able to extract some sensitive information about general Nazi and SS policies but nothing particularly incriminating about Bach-Zelewski's activities.[48]

Bach-Zelewski's appearance and testimony provoked outbursts from some of the other Nuremberg defendants. Hermann Göring called him a swine, a skunk, and "the bloodiest murderer in the whole damn setup." In his history of the Nuremberg trial, Telford Taylor related this incident without any apparent awareness that Göring was very close to being correct, at least on the last count.[49]

Bach-Zelewski also testified subsequently in the preparations for the Einsatzgruppen trial in the American zone and other cases. According to *The New York Times*, American occupation authorities rewarded him for his cooperation by keeping him out of prison.[50] In 1951, a German denazification tribunal in Munich sentenced him to ten years' labor, but the sentence was suspended. He was not at ease, however, and in 1952 he denounced himself as guilty of mass murder. In 1961, he was tried and convicted for his involvement in the June 30, 1934, killings of Ernst Röhm and associates, and he received a brief prison sentence. In 1964, a West German court convicted him of having played a role in the deaths of six Communists. Although he received a life sentence, he was soon furloughed. After his release became public knowledge, there were protests and he was reimprisoned. He died in jail in 1972.[51]

Bach-Zelewski had kept a war diary of his activities, and he donated it to the *Bundesarchiv* at Koblenz so that scholars might properly appreciate what he had done in the East. There was, however, a slight problem. It later emerged that the entries covering the years 1941–42 were not the originals, and that they were heavily doctored. Bach-Zelewski claimed that the originals were lost.[52] He did not know that the original text of some of his incriminating radio messages in 1941–42 had survived in Prague and Britain, but neither did historians until the 1980s (for Prague) and 1996 (for Britain).

# CONCLUSION

DURING WORLD WAR II, Hitler and his key subordinates were determined, one way or another, to destroy the Jewish "race." In chapter 1, I have traced some antecedents of this determination. I do not wish to suggest that, from the 1920s on, Hitler and Himmler were so rigid and fixated on Jews that the history of Nazi Germany and the history of the Holocaust were nothing more than an unfolding of pre-arranged ideas and ideology. Even if this were true, there would be no satisfactory way to demonstrate it empirically. But *Mein Kampf* was hardly empty rhetoric. Himmler certainly took it (and Nazi ideology generally) seriously enough before and after the Nazi takeover of power on January 30, 1933.

Hitler had broad political and foreign-policy goals that took priority during the 1930s and in peacetime circumstances would influence how far he would and could proceed against Jews.[1] Elsewhere, I have tried to show the evolution of SS Jewish policy over time and how Himmler's hopes for a racial utopia involved all kinds of other changes.[2] Still, evidence indicates that before the war both men regarded the outbreak of war as the moment when Nazi Germany would cast off restraints in its campaign against its alleged international and racial enemy.[3] Although that evidence does not suggest a specific, full-scale plan for a Final Solution, the idea of mass murder of Jews did not erupt suddenly in the middle of the war. It was very early regarded as conceivable— and not just by Hitler.

The radicalism of their hostility to Jews and the sweep of their racial vision set many Nazi leaders apart from the substantial anti-Semitic portion of the German public. That gap makes it important to investigate how large numbers of the Order Police came to participate in mass executions. Through a case study and suggestive evidence, I have tried to show that popular anti-Semitism had some influence on police behavior, as it had some influence on German public reaction to the influx of information about genocide. But the authorities also heavily relied on orders, deception, and secrecy in handling both the police and the German public. If all German police had been "willing executioners," there would have been less official concern and far less urgency behind the push toward the use of gas chambers as a means of mass murder.

The first portion of this book contains a range of evidence, some of it available to Western scholars only in recent years, and certain British intelligence documents quite new, about the specific arrangements for the mass murder of Jews in Nazi Germany. This evidence modifies or complements our previous understanding of the Holocaust, most obviously by elevating the roles of several Nazi officials and the institutions they headed.

Nowhere else is Kurt Daluege considered a significant figure in the Final Solution, and other descriptions of the work of his Order Police have focused either on events and forces from 1942 on or on case studies of particular battalions. But it now appears that the Order Police was a major element even in the planning stage and that it clearly was a major element during the "first sweep" of Jews from the Soviet territories in 1941. This broad participation of non-elite units in the Germans' mass murders in the East raises some large political and philosophical questions.

The only substantial monograph on the Higher SS and Police Leaders concentrated on these officeholders within Germany.[4] But Jeckeln, Bach-Zelewski, and, to a lesser extent, Prützmann and Korsemann— all of them in the Soviet territories—helped to direct the first phase of the Holocaust, and this work also clarifies their relationship with Daluege and his Order Police battalions, which has not generally been understood.

The Nazi regime planned, through the Higher SS and Police Leaders in the East, to construct stationary gas chambers using Zyklon B gas and crematoria to liquidate Soviet Jews, as well as Jews deported from Germany and conceivably elsewhere.[5] It is not certain that these plans went completely unrealized: the methods used to liquidate Jews at some sites remain obscure and in need of further research.

Some scholars have argued that the goal of Nazi Jewish policy was for a time uncertain, that deportations to the East simply meant removing the Jewish threat within Germany and getting Jews out of the way, that the deportations evolved into the Final Solution only under later wartime pressures. But Nazi officials envisioned deportations of European Jews to the East from at least early 1941, and Himmler worked on the arrangements for deporting German Jews to the East beginning in September of that year.[6] The words and actions of Bach-Zelewski, Jeckeln, Prützmann, and others clarify what deportations of Jews meant—from the beginning.

This evidence tightens the intrinsic connection between the mass shootings of Jews in the Soviet territories and the assembly-line gassings of European Jews in the extermination camps, which only began at Chelmno at the end of 1941 and did not occur on a large scale elsewhere until mid-1942. In short, new evidence of Nazi plans for earlier extermination camps in the East fills a (partial) chronological gap in our reading of Nazi intentions and policies. This evidence suggests that the meaning of the term "Final Solution," used by Walter Schellenberg in May 1941 and again by Reinhard Heydrich on July 31, 1941, was exactly what it later became,[7] even if all the locations and methods of mass murder were not determined in advance. This book is about decodes in the strict sense of deciphering coded radio messages, but it is also about understanding evidence that is at times cryptic, partial, or even misleading on the surface.

Although I am no specialist in signals communication or cryptography, I have done my best to clarify how German forces in the Soviet territories communicated with high Nazi officials and vice versa. Much of this information is new, and this coverage had the side benefit of illustrating Nazi practices designed to maintain the secrecy of the Final Solution, as well as Britain's ability to penetrate Nazi cloaking devices.

Some decoding of the Allied response to the Holocaust is needed, too. The images of Winston Churchill and Franklin Delano Roosevelt remain so powerful and vivid that many people today tend to think of the history of British and American responses to the Holocaust primarily in terms of their individual reactions and policies. This tendency is not entirely sound: the history of any government policy in twentieth-century Western democracies must in good part be a study of bureaucracies. Still, we must look at the limited evidence about Churchill and Roosevelt themselves.

There are two explanations for the contrast between what Churchill said or wrote about Nazi killings of Jews and how British policy took shape: rhetoric is not always reality, and Churchill did not always (or even often) set British policy. Churchill's written comments are subject to more than one interpretation—something that becomes apparent if we think of them partly as the raw material for memoirs. High government officials not infrequently write their own memoirs or histories of events they were involved in (at times when others do not yet have access to the records they use), presenting themselves in the best possible light. Churchill once told his historical researcher Maurice Ashley: "Give me the facts, Ashley, and I will twist them the way I want to suit my argument." Although Ashley states that Churchill did not often follow through on this claim of twisting evidence, he admits that Churchill, in his writing, often presented his own case.[8]

The eminent historian Gerhard Weinberg has noted that Churchill, while serving as Prime Minister, probably expected to write a history of the war (his history of World War I was already well known), and it is quite possible that he tailored some comments he made during his term as Prime Minister for the historical record. He was still an active politician when he wrote his history of World War II, and by the time the last volume appeared, he was again Prime Minister. One should not expect objectivity under such circumstances.[9] Weinberg's general observations—not specifically aimed at Churchill's reaction to the Holocaust—are, I believe, relevant in this context.

Some of Churchill's statements suggest that he recognized at the time the moral and historical significance of Nazi policy toward the Jews, but he did not act as if he did, nor did Roosevelt. Both Churchill and Roosevelt, but particularly Churchill, deserve great credit for recognizing the evils of Nazism at an early date; and both men, especially Churchill, took tremendous risks to oppose Nazi Germany, but during the war they inevitably dealt far more with larger questions of military and diplomatic strategy and of the Allied partnership than with specific decisions about rescue of Jews. There were some exceptions—both men got involved with specific projects emanating from the Bermuda Conference—but the general statement still holds.

It is, of course, asking a great deal of wartime heads of government to recognize in the maelstrom of events the significance of a moral crisis and to initiate an appropriate response. Both men directly involved themselves in managing the military and diplomatic campaigns against the Axis. For the most part, they depended on subordinates and colleagues to handle Nazi killings of Jews and other civilians, and occasionally they ratified—or disagreed with—the recommendations that reached them from below. In settling bureaucratic conflicts and dealing with political issues, their behavior was more similar than dissimilar. This makes it all the more striking that Churchill enjoys a very positive reputation for his response to the Holocaust and Roosevelt a very negative one. Apparently, some believe that the buck and the pound stop at different locations.

On both sides of the Atlantic, foreign-policy officials failed badly. No Western action could have come close to stopping the Holocaust, but the Foreign Office and the State Department in general decided to act as if the Allied Declaration of December 17, 1942, meant less than nothing, that it was a move in the wrong direction which they had to correct. The Foreign Office's failure to use the information from the German police decodes either during the war or in postwar trial proceedings is consistent with this broader assessment. While British officials kept this irrefutable evidence secret, many State Department officials chose not to believe or to act on what evidence they had. With assistance from Jan Karski, the Treasury Department forced a major change of course in Washington in 1943, and President Roosevelt, with some limitations, accepted and followed it. But British refugee policy did not significantly alter even after decisive Allied military successes. If there is a distinction between Churchill and Roosevelt on rescue and relief issues, it is hard to see how it is in Churchill's favor.

Given the basic similarities of British and American foreign policy with regard to the Holocaust until 1944, what were the significant differences? There were some battles over Jewish issues within the State Department, particularly at the top, where Sumner Welles was more liberal than Cordell Hull (or than most of the specialists in the European Division and elsewhere). With Welles and Hull at odds and each distracted (Welles by a looming scandal and Hull by illness, as well as other issues of greater concern to him), influence moved elsewhere. Differences of opinion on Jewish issues within the Foreign Office, on the other hand, were apparently few, and Anthony Eden was a powerful foreign minister. Of all the officials mentioned in this and other studies of Western wartime policies, Eden had the most influence on his government's policies.

David Dutton's recent political biography of Eden, an excellent but selective account that unfortunately has little to say on Eden and Jewish problems,[10] presents him as a man hypersensitive to his image and often eager to adjust it favorably throughout his political career and in re-

tirement. He not only wrote three long volumes of memoirs but tried
to commission historians to write appropriately about him.[11] But there
are significant discrepancies between Eden's image and reality. The man
who gained a reputation as an opponent of appeasement—in part because of his resignation from Neville Chamberlain's government—had
apparently quarreled with Chamberlain about other matters, and on a
number of occasions Eden had expressed approval of the notion of
coming to terms with Nazi Germany. In 1937, Eden had argued that
Britain would join no anti-Communist bloc and no anti-Fascist bloc:
"It is nations' foreign policies, not their internal policies, with which
we are concerned." He also held a more favorable view of Hitler than
of Mussolini.[12] This orientation was quite different from Churchill's and
helps to explain some of what happened after Churchill made Eden his
foreign minister.

Whereas Churchill tried to make a close personal and political relationship with Roosevelt the center of his wartime strategy, Eden's anti-
American streak made him far more independent. Churchill was
impulsive; Eden was persistent and careful. According to Dutton, Eden
often took Churchill on and got his way.[13] Their political attitudes,
their personalities, and the nature of their relationship partly explain
why Churchill's occasional forays into rescue issues bore so little fruit.
He used Eden and the Foreign Office to insulate him from political
distractions, but a considerable price was paid for that strategy.

Victor Cavendish-Bentinck apparently represented Foreign Office
views of Nazi killings better than he exploited the intelligence on the
Holocaust that Bletchley Park made available. The police decodes, of
course, did not provide continuous data about Nazi killings: one needed
other sources to obtain an overall picture of the scale of Nazi policy.
Yet during the war, Cavendish-Bentinck decided that Polish and particularly Jewish sources were unreliable because they had an interest in
exaggerating the numbers of Nazi victims. Still, he wrote in 1943 that
the Nazis had a policy of eliminating Jewish women, children, and the
elderly, allegedly sparing only men capable of hard labor. This partial
perception should have led him to conclude that the number of Jewish
victims ran into the millions, an estimate for which Polish and Jewish
reports gave added support. Yet Cavendish-Bentinck criticized the Political Warfare Executive for publicizing allegedly dubious information
about Nazi atrocities.[14] Later, he explained that his prewar experience
of Germany had been limited,[15] but it seems obvious that he found

these conclusions politically inconvenient. Either he resisted the facts or he did nothing about them.

At the end of the war, Cavendish-Bentinck became British ambassador to Poland, and sometime thereafter he visited Auschwitz—a photo of him there appears in his biography, which is drawn largely from extensive interviews with him. He also related elsewhere that, after his visit to Auschwitz, when he told his Foreign Office colleagues that the Nazis had killed millions, they still did not believe him.[16]

Overall, it remains difficult to assess in detail the response of American and British intelligence organizations to the Holocaust. Some intelligence records may have been destroyed, and many others remain unavailable to most scholars. There are, however, enough declassified Office of Strategic Services (OSS) records to allow historians to address the American side, and some scholars have already made important contributions there.[17] The OSS, which had less information and less reliable information than London, was nonetheless able to get a reasonably accurate picture of the Final Solution, but probably not until late 1942. Even then, some knowledgeable people (such as the German émigré political scientist Franz Neumann) allowed ideological barriers to prevent them from understanding the obvious. The fact that two very committed American Jews (Charles Irving Dwork and Abraham Duker) worked in the Research and Analysis Branch of OSS helped to ensure attention there.[18]

Which other agencies in Washington might have taken information about the Nazis' killings of Jews seriously enough to consider or take action? The Office of War Information (OWI) was for a long time opposed to publicizing Jewish issues, as we have seen, and the majority of State Department officials did not wish to get involved in rescue and relief. This situation changed fundamentally after the creation of the War Refugee Board, which cooperated well with the OSS, both in general and in at least one field office (Stockholm).[19] Publicity was no longer taboo, and some rescue and relief measures received support.

To give an example of how government agencies might or might not react, the OSS representative in Switzerland, Allen Dulles, learned on May 18, 1944, that the Germans and Hungarians had just agreed on transportation arrangements for the deportation of about three hundred thousand Hungarian Jews to Poland "and to presumably their deaths." He immediately passed on the suggestion that Washington and London publicize this fact in radio broadcasts, warning that those who planned or carried out the deportations would be included among the war criminals.[20] This information added to the pressure for continuing American broadcasts and threats against the Hungarian government, which apparently had some effect in Budapest.[21]

It is still not possible to analyze the reactions of British intelligence in the way that others (and I) have done with the OSS, since many of the documents are not available. A study of British intelligence and the Holocaust should also cover intelligence specialists in MI 8 and MI 14, perhaps even the attitudes and reactions of Sir Stewart Menzies. One official who served in MI 14, Noel Annan, has written very interesting memoirs,[22] but memoirs are not a substitute for original documents.

In a 1997 work based on little archival research, the historian William Rubinstein argued flatly that the Allies could not have saved any more Jews from the Holocaust.[23] It was certainly possible to argue that some of the rescue schemes proposed at the time were unrealistic—particularly because they ignored the essential (but not absolute) rigidity of Nazi policy toward the Jews and also because they overlooked the difficulties and trade-offs involved in Allied military action for nonmilitary purposes when major battles were still raging.

In a larger sense, however, Rubinstein's argument is fundamentally misleading and methodologically flawed. The history of the American War Refugee Board, founded as late as January 1944, shows failures but also quite a few successes and partial successes. How much more difference would it have made if there had been a War Refugee Board and a comparable British one years earlier?

History is not a laboratory science, and we cannot give a precise answer to that question. But I have presented some of the nonmilitary ways in which Western governments could have made a considerable difference in saving Jewish lives earlier if there had been the will to do so. The mere distribution of information about Nazi killings itself had some positive effects.

Leon Kubowitzki, who worked in the Rescue Department of the World Jewish Congress, spoke in mid-1944 about a conspiracy of silence that had existed within OWI and that was reversed under pressure only after considerable time. New warnings broadcast to the satellite countries were, he said, very effective in Rumania in bringing about the cessation of killings there.[24] But even after Kubowitzki's statement, OWI continued to be ambivalent about and somewhat resistant to the War Refugee Board in this regard. As late as December 1944, OWI told its London office: "Playing up atrocities that have been committed by the Germans may, on the part of the Germans, increase fear, feelings of guilt, and thus resistance . . . the advantage of our showing moral indignation does not outweigh this risk."[25]

Before the founding of the War Refugee Board, there were a few positive Allied rescue efforts, such as an American and British effort to save five thousand Jewish children in France in late 1942. The British Political Warfare Executive and the BBC did for a time distribute essential information to Germany and Europe about the Final Solution and in general did a better job than their American counterparts.[26] The high officials of the U.S. Treasury Department deserve special mention for their efforts in late 1943 and thereafter. But the record generally shows that in 1942 and 1943 the U.S. government and the British government did not try to do what might have worked. This makes it very difficult, long, long after the fact, to demonstrate that saving more Jews had been impossible.

# EPILOGUE

IN A COMPETITIVE WORLD, governments may need to keep current and recent discussions and deliberations secret. The same considerations rarely apply to documents more than several decades old. Yet official secrets and government restrictions on the declassification of historical documents continue to affect how much of our past we are able to decode and properly understand, including the Holocaust.

The history of this book is relevant to the events described in it and to its themes. So it may be worthwhile to relate some recent, personal stories here. In the beginning, I was simply prospecting for sources, for material that other historians of Germany and I could use. For a number of years, I served as chair of the Archives Committee of the Conference Group for Central European History, a subdivision of the American Historical Association (AHA). The Conference Group is an organization of some six or seven hundred American scholars, most specializing in German and Austrian history. It holds a business meeting once a year during the AHA's convention. A significant portion of the attendees are drawn to the beer party and socializing that follows the business meeting, but the annual gatherings actually do accomplish something.

Prompted by Professor Gerhard Weinberg of the University of North Carolina, the world's leading authority on the foreign policy of Nazi Germany, in January 1994 the Conference Group passed a resolution asking its Archives Committee to seek declassification of captured World War II records pertaining to cryptography. Weinberg knew that the U.S. and British governments had seized many German cryptographic records that were not yet declassified or available to scholars in the U.S. National Archives. A Presidential executive order exempted cryptographic records from declassification—but only for fifty years. 1994 was forty-nine years after the end of World War II, and it was almost time for the government to deliver up the material. Or so we hoped.

As chair of the Archives Committee, I had the job of conveying to the National Archives and to relevant government agencies the comments, reactions, requests, and resolutions of my colleagues. Resolutions are nice, but at best they can help to persuade. I sent the Conference Group's resolution to the almost invisible National Security Agency (NSA), but I also filed a Freedom of Information Act (FOIA) request for this material. That gave my request a legal claim and forced the agency to respond.

I did not know just what NSA held or what Weinberg was most interested in, so I asked NSA to declassify "all German records decrypted [decoded] by the Allies and still held by NSA." I then sent Weinberg a copy of my FOIA request. A few days later, he called to explain that I had misunderstood his target. He knew that during World War II the Germans had broken some Allied codes and had managed to decipher some Allied transmissions and coded documents. He believed that those decoded messages and related German intelligence documents were still in NSA's hands. Since these were technically German records, not American and British records, the U.S. government had no reasonable grounds for keeping them secret. These German records had nothing in them that could significantly affect American national security.

I apologized for misinterpreting the resolution and promised to file a new FOIA request for German decrypts of Allied transmissions and documents. But I asked Weinberg whether NSA also held American and British decrypts of German transmissions and documents. Weinberg replied that it was possible but that he did not know. I decided to let my FOIA request stand and supplement it with a second one corresponding to Weinberg's original goal.

NSA quickly acknowledged my two FOIA requests, but it took nine months for me to learn something substantive about the agency's collection of World War II documents. An NSA archivist called to explain that the agency held some German decrypts of Allied messages, as well as some Allied decrypts of German messages. But there was a very large volume of World War II cryptographic material, and downsizing of NSA staff had made it extremely difficult to handle large requests. It would also have to charge me for the costs of searching for and photocopying the huge number of documents covered by my requests, which might amount to a considerable sum of money. When I suggested that my university might be willing to provide financial support for this project, the archivist indicated that the costs might be beyond what a modest grant could cover. I rethought the matter: American University was not Harvard, and I could not draw on the tiny treasury of the Conference Group either. There had to be another way.

The NSA archivist asked what I personally wanted to see. I identified my prime target on the Allied side as anything related to the SS and German police, for I was looking to fill in gaps uncovered in my research for previous books on the Holocaust. If I could find intercepted and decoded radio transmissions about mass killings or concentration-camp activities, I could go back and fill in evidence to add to, confirm, or refute what I had written previously. Or perhaps the new evidence would lead me in a different direction entirely. The archivist thought that NSA held a manageable number of records in this area; there was, however, some question about whether it could release them, even under a FOIA request. It might require the consent of another government.

I remembered that I was not just representing myself and the Holocaust specialists but acting on behalf of a community of scholars interested in World War II. In a later telephone conversation, I suggested what the Conference Group for Central European History had initially called for. I did not really need a personal copy of all these documents. Why should NSA not simply declassify all the material and turn it over to the National Archives? The archivist said that he would check with higher authorities. Once a decision was made to review and release a large portion of the documents, he could not have been more helpful.

NSA eventually turned over some 1.3 million pages of material, stored in 1,440 large archive boxes, to the new branch of the National Archives in College Park, Maryland. Processing and checking this huge collection took some time, but the NSA Historical Cryptographic Collection became available to researchers in April 1996. NSA even issued a press release to publicize the opening of the new sources, which covered a wide array of events and intelligence activities from before, during, and after World War II.

It was still an open question whether, even in this new collection, there would be any substantial new sources about the Holocaust. In late spring 1996, after checking many hundreds of boxes, I found an extensive set of German Order Police decodes for 1941–42, along with a few decodes for 1943, in box 1386 of this collection. The decodes were in German—or at least what the British analysts had managed to decipher of the German. Much of the information concerned mundane matters of supplies, appointments, and troop movements, but there were also reports of mass executions—some of which scholars knew about already, but others new. The reports from Nazi authorities in the U.S.S.R. radioed back to Heinrich Himmler and other high Nazi authorities covered a broad range of SS and police activities. These documents also showed exactly when the British code breakers had deciphered these transmissions and which British offices had received the information. As original documentation of Nazi policies and simultaneously of British knowledge of those policies, these stark and depressing German police decodes were unique.

The outline of this story—that British intelligence had managed to break Order Police codes and get some information about mass atrocities—was already known. In appendix 5 to volume 2 of *British Intelligence in the Second World War*, F. H. Hinsley had revealed that British intelligence obtained some information about the organization of concentration camps and mass executions carried out in the early phase of the Nazi campaign against the Soviet Union from decrypts (deciphered messages) of German Order Police radio transmissions. The German Order Police, with the outbreak of war, had formed battalions or regiments and collaborated closely with the SS as an army of occupation in conquered territories. Hinsley tallied at least seven references to police executions in the central Russian sector in the decrypts, with the victims described variously as Jews, Jewish plunderers, Jewish Bolshevists, and Russian soldiers. He cited Bach-Zelewski's boast that executions in his region now surpassed thirty thousand. He mentioned a total of seventeen cases of executions reported from the southern sector. He listed mass executions carried out on August 7 by the SS Cavalry Brigade (7,819 in the Minsk area) and on September 12 by Police Regiment South (1,255 Jews near Ovruch). All of Hinsley's examples had appeared in the late 1945 (partial) compilation of atrocities listed in the German police decodes carried out by Lieutenant E. D. Phillips for the Air and Military History series.[1] These particular examples, however, did not draw much attention to the role of Order Police, since the SS Cavalry Brigade was part of the Waffen-SS. Nor was it clear from the information provided that Jews were the primary Nazi target. Based on the documents I now had, Hinsley's tally of executions was also incomplete.

Hinsley did not indicate how this information might have helped the British government understand the sequence of killings at the time— or how it might have aided Holocaust scholars much later. "Jews" did not appear in the index of volume 2, and the treatment of the Order Police was limited to three pages in an appendix.

I already had enough detailed information to suggest a different focus and approach, and I had documents that, to the best of my knowledge, no one outside of government (with the possible exception of Hinsley's research team) had seen. Some of the factual information contained in the decodes was already known to historians from other sources, but some of it was not.

In the subsequent research for this book, I quickly ran into a number of perplexing questions. It was implausible that the British had been able to intercept and decode German police transmissions during 1941– 42, but not later. From other documents I soon turned up in the NSA Historical Cryptographic Collection and elsewhere, it became clear that what I had found was only part of what British intelligence had decoded at the time, even for 1941–42. Were the remaining decodes available somewhere in the files of NSA? How had these British documents come to the United States anyway? Did the British government share such intelligence information during the war with its American ally, or did the material arrive well after the events? Would Britain consider declassifying its own records about the SS and police? I had many questions but few answers.

My friend and colleague Konrad Kwiet of Macquarie University in Sydney, Australia, was then in Washington on a fellowship at the United States Holocaust Memorial Museum. A world-class expert on archival sources about the Holocaust, Kwiet had extensive experience working at the Military Archive in Prague, which had a collection of some file copies of SS and police radio messages, including some of the ones the British had intercepted and decoded. So I sought his advice at a dinner party.

After I showed him my copy of the German police decodes, I could hardly get him away from the documents to the dinner table. He thought that these documents represented a new and important source of evidence about the Holocaust, even if some of the information was available elsewhere. He urged me either to write something immediately or to go to the press. I knew that I could not quickly integrate these new sources with existing sources and write something that satisfied me. That left the media. He foresaw advantages there; I foresaw difficulties. As it turned out, we were both right.

Early newspaper stories about these documents contained much accurate information but also some facts relatively well known to scholars and some inaccurate information, the last supposedly drawn from other newly available documents that I had not discovered and had not read. (Regardless, the press quickly associated me with all the information. After the early stories were published, I spent a good portion of subsequent interviews trying to correct journalists' mistakes or misperceptions.) Journalists and broadcasters did not look at this material in the way scholars did, separating out which details were new and which confirmed other sources. For some, if the documents were newly available, the information was all "news." Certainly it was nothing new to maintain that the Holocaust first took the form of systematic shootings of Jews in the Soviet territories. (Some scholars still maintain, however, that the beginning of the war, September 1939, is a truer starting point.) But the public usually focuses on the extermination camps and was not fully aware of the extent of mass executions in the summer and fall of 1941. Some articles stressed it as news, and some scholars then responded that this "news" was not new. This, however, is not the place for an extended discussion of how the mass media handles the subject of the Holocaust.

Following the publicity, some survivors and relatives of Holocaust victims contacted me to ask questions or provide additional information. I tried to answer everyone and everything I could. A few explained that they or friends or relatives had gone into hiding after hearing foreign broadcasts of information about the Holocaust. Although there was already some evidence along these lines,[2] these comments strengthened my view that such broadcasts had saved lives and that earlier attempts might have saved many more lives. This feedback was very helpful, and let me again express gratitude to those who wrote to provide information.

A different sort of constructive reaction came in London. British scholar John P. Fox knew very well that the release of these documents was important and unusual, because he had already tried without success to obtain them in Britain. The Government Communications Headquarters had responded that it could provide no indication of when these particular records might be made available—it was likely to be "some considerable time."[3] After my success in Washington, on November 14, 1996, Fox wrote to the Prime Minister's office to push for declassification in Britain.[4] In addition, Lord Lester of Herne Hill, Q.C., saw a November 16, 1996, letter Fox had written to *The Times* of London about the matter and decided to put a question to the government in the House of Lords.[5]

Despite these developments, British journalist and historian John Keegan, in an Op-Ed column for *The New York Times*, called my statement that the documents contained new information about the Holocaust "either wrong or misleading or both." (At the time, it was unlikely that Keegan had seen the documents themselves, which were available only in the United States.) Keegan went on to explain and defend not only the need for British intelligence secrecy during the war but also Britain's postwar withholding of intelligence information that might have been used to convict war criminals: "But one must remember that immediately after the war Britain and America faced the growing hostility of the Soviet Union. Cipher superiority became a vital weapon of the cold war, and keeping Ultra secret from the Soviets was deemed vital."[6]

As I have already pointed out, the Order Police codes were a relatively primitive system from the World War I era that had nothing to do with the Enigma machine codes. They were not part of Ultra, although they did come out of Bletchley Park. Consequently, British postwar disclosure of success at decoding Order Police transmissions would not have surprised intelligence officials in any of the developed countries, least of all the Soviet Union.

There was, however, an even greater flaw in Keegan's argument. Britain worked out a trade of German police decodes with the Soviet Union in late 1941 or early 1942. Some information about this intelligence relationship had already appeared in print (and was available well before Keegan wrote his column). John P. Fox and I both located some additional details in the British archives.

In late June 1941, the British sent a military mission to Moscow headed by Noel Mason Macfarlane, and the Soviets sent a corresponding team to London. One task of each mission was to work out exchanges of intelligence. The original British estimates of the Soviet Union's capability to withstand the German invasion were so pessimistic that early British advice to Moscow included the suggestion to destroy anything that might be of value to the Germans and to scuttle the Soviet fleet. This attitude could not have made a good impression on the Soviets, who later told Mason Macfarlane that the British were talking too much and not fighting enough. Some British officials were Russian émigrés hostile to, or contemptuous of, the Communists; other native Britons did not much like the Soviet Union and let it show.[7]

Nonetheless, the two sides began to exchange intelligence. Although historians indicate that a trade of low-grade intelligence began in August 1941,[8] archival sources suggest that the police decodes were not included until early 1942. In March 1942, a Colonel Nicholls in the War Office (MI 8) instructed Major Edward Crankshaw of the Military Mission to turn over at once and unconditionally all German police decodes and literature about police ciphers to the Soviets. This gift was a sample of what Moscow might get in a broader collaboration. The British were willing to send to Russia every Eastern front police key within twenty-four hours after the Germans ceased to use them, and the British expected in return all messages intercepted (but not deciphered) by the Soviets.[9]

On April 15, 1942, Crankshaw notified the War Office (MI 8):

> At first formal meeting since start of police collaboration Russians yesterday showed genuine appreciation of our success and gratitude for help. They are pleased with what they get out of this traffic and showed less impatience than I expected at the high proportion of routine messages. They now propose to increase their cover[age] . . .
>
> We may justifiably call this experiment a success so far. My impression is that the Russians have passed from extreme scepticism of the efficiency of our Y. organisation to the reluctant conclusion that in some ways it is better than their own. They may well be a little more forthcoming in future because of this but suspicion and procrastination will remain.
>
> Please cable me average number of messages taken daily by you in both keys. I am today despatching Russian intercepts from April 5 to 12 inclusive.[10]

These comments indicate unmistakably that it was possible for British intelligence to detach the Order Police decodes from the more sophisticated Ultra information, which British officials kept "wrapped" or disguised whenever they handed individual items over to the Soviets. The British, however, gave the Soviets the original transcripts of their German police decodes.

The Soviets continually complained that the British were holding back on them. In September 1942, Crankshaw suggested that he give the Russians the whole set of German police decodes from July 1941 onward—the period in which there was detailed coverage of activities in the Soviet territories. It appears that he did so, but collaboration broke down in October 1942 anyway.[11] In other words, the British told the Soviets much more about mass executions of Jews and others in the Soviet territories than they told the Americans, and they revealed more to the Soviets about British decoding of German police traffic than they gave to the Americans until 1944.[12]

After the war Crankshaw turned his Russian experience to advantage, first writing a couple of books about the Soviet Union and its leaders.[13] In 1956, he published one of his best-known works, *Gestapo: Instrument of Tyranny*. Although concentrating on Heydrich's organizations, Crankshaw nonetheless showed (in passing) proper appreciation for the importance of Daluege and the supremacy of Himmler over Heydrich—conclusions undoubtedly facilitated by his wartime access to the British decodes of SS and police messages. Crankshaw even wrote that Daluege was responsible for many of the most dreadful crimes "loosely attributed to the Gestapo."[14] He did not cite his sources for this assertion, but some Soviet intelligence officials could have deduced what they were.

The British made another effort to resume the code-breaking partnership with the Soviets, offering in 1944 a selection of recently decoded police messages as enticement.[15] The evidence available (what I located among what has been declassified) does not reveal whether the Soviets accepted; but the Soviet Union could hardly have forgotten in 1945 or thereafter what it knew as recently as 1944—that Britain had a superb code-breaking capacity and that World War I–era codes were highly vulnerable. An additional reminder could have come from Leo Long, an efficient young officer who had assisted Brian Melland in MI 14 in the work on the German police. It turned out that Long was a Soviet spy.[16]

In any case, British intelligence knew that the Soviets knew, because the British had given them the non-Ultra police decodes. There was absolutely no way that the Cold War could have prevented the British from making use of the German police decodes in war-crimes proceedings, as Keegan had argued.

The day Keegan's article appeared, Morley Safer of CBS and *60 Minutes*, who had known Anthony Eden personally after the war, wrote me as follows (reprinted here with his permission):

As distinguished an historian as he [Keegan] is, he suffers from the same myopia of many of his countrymen . . . The real issue was one of passive anti-Semitism within the British establishment—sometimes not so passive . . .

Anthony Eden made his and the British government's position quite clear early on in the war: any attempt to negotiate the rescue of some Jews might result in Hitler "wanting us to take all Jews." His private memoranda were even more, shall we say, explicit . . .

Keegan's argument is both disingenuous and specious.[17]

These were strong statements, but they certainly served to counterbalance Keegan's judgments.

The next day, November 26, Lord Lester raised a pointed question in the House of Lords, asking Her Majesty's Government

Whether they will make available transcripts of the British Intelligence Enigma [*sic*] decrypts of German telegraphic traffic relating to Police and Security reports of Nazi mass killings of Jews in Russia and the Ukraine in the autumn of 1941; and if not, why not.

This question was too narrow, but it got a good part of the job done. A spokesman for the government indicated that there was a series of summaries issued between August 1940 and June 1945 related to acts of atrocities. The government was currently reviewing them and the transcripts on which they were based for possible release to the Public Record Office.[18]

The combined pressures of publicity, Fox's letters to government officials, and Lord Lester's interpellation finally bore fruit in May 1997—just after the British elections that brought Tony Blair and the Labour Party to power. Sixty-two "volumes" (files) of decodes of German police and SS transmissions became available on May 19, 1997, at the Public Record Office at Kew. For my purposes, this release produced even more relevant material than the NSA's had done, even if the NSA declassification was far larger in the aggregate. The British press found plenty of interest in the newly released British documents.[19]

I would like to express gratitude to all those who played a role in the British declassification, but especially to John P. Fox. He and I do not agree on all points of interpretation of Allied policies during the Holocaust. We do agree, however, on the importance of granting public access to important historical documents. We also agree that previous withholding of important evidence about the Holocaust has hindered historians from understanding the full dimensions of the tragedy.

The 1997 British release of decodes provided the outlines of an answer to the question, When and why did Britain give the United States copies of the decodes from 1941–42? I had originally assumed that the "gift" must have been made during the war—it might have served a purpose then, but what good could it have done later? Still, I decided to be cautious and say publicly that I did not know. The Public Record Office, however, revealed that Britain had given some of these records to the United States in 1982 for the purpose of war-crimes investigations.[20]

In 1981 or 1982, a man named David Marwell, then a staff historian at the Office of Special Investigations (OSI) within the U.S. Department of Justice, had a notion that the British government might have relevant information to help his agency. In 1979, the United States had established OSI to handle the investigation and civil prosecution of individuals alleged to have committed crimes against humanity during World War II. Under American law, they were not subject to criminal prosecution in the United States for their acts; but if they had lied about their wartime activities to procure entry to the United States, and if the government could clearly demonstrate that they had carried out acts of persecution, they could be denaturalized and deported. It required a team of trained historians as well as attorneys to amass the evidence and handle the complicated legal procedures.

Marwell's request went through channels and eventually made its way to London, where it was approved. The British government sent a set of decodes to NSA, where they were kept under strict security. Marwell had to get special clearance to see the documents, and, as it turned out, there was nothing immediately useful for the OSI cases in 1982.[21] But the copies, drawn from a file of the British Joint Intelligence Committee, remained with NSA. To my knowledge, no one else outside NSA saw the documents in the United States until they were declassified in 1996.

It would be nice to be able to conclude that the Allied governments, recognizing that they had given insufficient attention to the Holocaust during the war, had finally opened all their files about World War II and the Holocaust to scholars. As of this writing, however, they have *not* done so. I believe that at least some important information remains to be declassified in the United States, and a great deal more in Britain.

It happened that, while I was working on my study, Western government officials, Jewish organizations, and the media were focusing on Switzerland's role during the Holocaust. The American commission headed by Undersecretary of State Stuart Eizenstat managed to get a very large body of American government records declassified to help understand Swiss and (Allied) wartime policies. It is perhaps also relevant that British intelligence was reading Swiss government radio messages,[22] but those documents are still not available.

Even with regard to key perpetrators of the Holocaust, some Western documents are not in the public domain. One document is still classified and withdrawn from a British War Office file on Heinrich Himmler. It was listed "retained" as recently as 1994. An entire folder on Ernst Kaltenbrunner, head of the Reich Security Main Office from 1943 to 1945, remains withheld.[23] Absurdities are not lacking in the United States either. NSA reportedly has several hundred thousand more pages of documents (British and American) from the World War II era that are still classified. Some of my requests and appeals under FOIA for specific Office of Strategic Services documents have been pending (with the Central Intelligence Agency) for four years or more.

Governments that withhold critical information from the historical record and the public long after the events do their countries and the world no service. But the habit of secrecy is very hard to break. No democratic politician or official can in the end control future assessments of him or her by historians, but the longer critical sources are kept secret, the longer such control is possible. One of Anthony Eden's volumes of memoirs is titled *The Reckoning*,[24] but a full reckoning on this subject remains to be written.

# NOTES

## INTRODUCTION

1. Richard Breitman, *The Architect of Genocide: Himmler and the Final Solution* (Hanover, N.H., 1992).
2. As, for example, in a letter of Nov. 1941 to Quartermaster General Eduard Wagner, reprinted by Serge Klarsfeld, *Vichy-Auschwitz: Die Zusammenarbeit der deutschen und französischen Behörden bei der "Endlösung der Judenfrage" in Frankreich* (Nördlingen, 1989), 369–70.
3. An indispensable account of the activities of the Einsatzgruppen is Helmut Krausnick and Hans-Heinrich Wilhelm, *Die Truppe des Weltanschauungskrieges: Die Einsatzgruppen der Sicherheitspolizei und SD, 1938–1942* (Stuttgart, 1982). See also Ronald Headland, *Messages of Murder: A Study of the Reports of the Einsatzgruppen of the Security Police and Security Service, 1941–1943* (Rutherford, N.J., 1992), 105. Recent literature includes: Ralf Ogorreck, *Die Einsatzgruppen und die Genesis der Endlösung* (Berlin, 1996), and *Die Einsatzgruppen in der besetzten Sowjetunion 1941/42: Die Tätigkeits- und Lageberichte des Chefs der Sicherheitspolizei und des SD*, ed. Peter Klein (Berlin, 1997).
4. In his pathbreaking study, *The Destruction of the European Jews* (New York, 1985), vol. 1, 274–98 (original version 1961), Raul Hilberg described in great detail the composition and killing activities of the Einsatzgruppen in the conquered areas of the Soviet Union. In combing the reports about their operations, however, Hilberg found only selected items about Order Police participation. For example, he noted that Berlin sent a battalion of Order Police (about five hundred men) to reinforce the Einsatzgruppen, which were only three thousand men strong. The Order Police carried out most of the killings in Rowno, in the Ukraine, and a detachment of Police Regiment South helped Einsatzkommando 4a carry out the killings at Babi Yar. In the central sector, the Order Police executed about six thousand Jews

at Minsk and Mogilev. This scattered information suggested that Order Police played a significant role in the Holocaust, but Hilberg had Einsatzgruppen responsible for what he called the "first sweep," the first wave of Nazi mass killings in the U.S.S.R.

Christopher R. Browning, *Ordinary Men: Reserve Police Battalion 101 and the Final Solution in Poland* (New York, 1992), 10–18, found that twelve Order Police battalions totaling about six thousand men had "pacified" conquered areas in the East following the German invasion of the U.S.S.R. One of them was Police Battalion 9, whose members were distributed among the Einsatzgruppen as auxiliaries, but others were assigned to the Higher SS and Police Leaders and operated as compact units. Browning upgraded the numbers of Order Police involved in the early part of the Holocaust, even if most of his book covered only one Order Police battalion. But he underestimated Order Police involvement in the first phase of the Holocaust by about half.

Klaus-Michael Mallmann, "Vom Fussvolk der 'Endlösung': Ordnungspolizei, Ostkrieg und Judenmord," *Tel Aviver Jahrbuch für deutsche Geschichte* 26 (1997): 355–91, and Edward B. Westermann, " 'Ordinary Men' or 'Ideological Soldiers'? Police Battalion 310 in Russia, 1942," *German Studies Review* 21 (1998): 41–68, reached me too late to use in my work, but both substantially raised the importance of the Order Police in the Holocaust. An earlier work, Jürgen Matthäus, "What About the 'Ordinary Men': The German Order Police and the Holocaust in the Occupied Soviet Union," *Holocaust and Genocide Studies* 10 (1996): 134–50, was an important step in this direction.

5. Browning, *Ordinary Men*; Daniel J. Goldhagen, *Hitler's Willing Executioners: Ordinary Germans and the Holocaust* (New York, 1996).

6. Browning, *Ordinary Men*, 186.

7. Goldhagen, *Hitler's Willing Executioners*, 183–84.

8. Ibid., 103–28, 428–54.

9. Among the outpouring of reviews on this book, see Omer Bartov, "Ordinary Monsters," *New Republic*, 29 Apr. 1996, 32–38; Fritz Stern, "The Goldhagen Controversy: One Nation, One People, One Theory," *Foreign Affairs* 75 (Nov.– Dec. 1996): 128–38; Mitchell G. Ash, "American and German Perspectives on the Goldhagen Debate: History, Identity, and the Media," *Holocaust and Genocide Studies* 11 (1997): 396–411; István Deák, "Holocaust Views: The Goldhagen Controversy in Retrospect," *Central European History* 30 (1997): 295–307.

10. Browning, *Ordinary Men*, 188–89.

11. David Bankier, *The Germans and the Final Solution: Public Opinion Under Nazism* (Oxford, 1992), 4–10, has a good discussion of the major German sources and the problems with them. On the subject of German attitudes regarding Jews during the Nazi period, see also Ian Kershaw, "The Persecution of the Jews and German Popular Opinion in the Third Reich" and "German Popular Opinion and the Jewish Question, 1939–1943: Some Further Reflections," in *The Nazi Holocaust: Historical Articles on the Destruction of the European Jews*, ed. Michael R. Marrus

(London, 1989), vol. 5, part 1, 86–114 and 182–203; Otto Dov Kulka, "Public Opinion in Nazi Germany and the Jewish Question" and "Public Opinion in Nazi Germany: The Final Solution," in *The Nazi Holocaust*, vol. 5, part 1, 115–38 and 138–50; and Lawrence D. Stokes, "Otto Ohlendorf, the Sicherheitsdienst and Public Opinion in Nazi Germany," in *Police Forces in History*, ed. George L. Mosse (London, 1975), 231–61.

12. Walter Laqueur, *The Terrible Secret: Suppression of the Truth About Hitler's "Final Solution"* (Boston, 1980), esp. 3.

13. The Polish government-in-exile at times believed that the West would take Jewish claims more seriously than Polish claims. See David Engel, *Facing a Holocaust: The Polish Government-in-Exile and the Jews, 1943–1945* (Chapel Hill, N.C., 1993), 28. Examples of British dismissal or deprecation of Jewish and Polish sources appear below in chapters 6, 7, and 9.

14. Public Record Office, Kew, FO 371/34551, cited by Laqueur, *Terrible Secret*, 83.

## 1. FORESHADOWINGS

1. Gerald Fleming, *Hitler and the Final Solution* (Berkeley, Calif., 1984), 18–19; John Lukacs, *The Hitler of History* (New York, 1997), 47–49.

2. Oron James Hale, "Adolf Hitler: Taxpayer," *American Historical Review* 60 (1955): 831; Hermann Hammer, "Die deutschen Ausgaben von Hitlers 'Mein Kampf,'" *Vierteljahrshefte für Zeitgeschichte* 4 (1956): 163. The publication date on the first edition of the second volume was listed, however, as 1927.

3. Lukacs, *Hitler of History*, 65–75.

4. Hans Frank, *Im Angesicht des Galgens* (Munich-Gräfelfing, 1953), 45, cited by Hammer, "Die deutschen Ausgaben," 162. Frank was something of an authority on *Mein Kampf* in that he had handled Hitler's disputes with German tax authorities over royalties in the mid-1920s. See Hale, "Adolf Hitler: Taxpayer," 833–34.

5. *Hitlers zweites Buch: Ein Dokument aus dem Jahr 1928* (Stuttgart, 1961). For a summary, see Marlis Steinert, *Hitler*, trans. into German by Guy Montag and Volker Wieland (Munich, 1991), 213.

6. Adolf Hitler, *Mein Kampf*, trans. Ralph Manheim (Boston, 1943), 560–65, 575, 622–79.

7. Steinert, *Hitler*, 204.

8. Eberhard Jäckel, *Hitler's Weltanschauung: A Blueprint for Power*, trans. Herbert Arnold (Middletown, Conn., 1972), 52–61.

9. Jäckel, *Hitler's Weltanschauung*; A.J.P. Taylor, *The Origins of the Second World War* (London, 1961), 98. For a recent, perceptive summary, see Steinert, *Hitler*, 175–210.

10. See Gerhard L. Weinberg, *The Foreign Policy of Hitler's Germany*, vol. 1, *Diplomatic Revolution in Europe, 1933–1936* (Chicago, 1970), esp. 1–2; Sebastian Haffner, *The Meaning of Hitler*, trans. Ewald Osers (New York, 1979), 51–52; and generally, see Eberhard Jäckel, *Hitlers Herrschaft: Vollzug einer Weltanschauung* (Stuttgart, 1986).

11. Steinert, *Hitler*, 203.

12. Heinz Höhne, *The Order of the Death's Head: The Story of Hitler's SS* (New York, 1979). For a brief description, see Richard Breitman, *The Architect of Genocide: Himmler and the Final Solution* (Hanover, N.H., 1992), 12–13, 34–35.

13. Bradley F. Smith, *Heinrich Himmler: A Nazi in the Making, 1900–1926* (Stanford, 1971), 147, 169; Peter Padfield, *Himmler* (New York, 1990), 87–89.

14. Gelesene Bücher, item 276, Heinrich Himmler Collection in German Captured Documents Collection, Box 418, Library of Congress.

15. After he finished several chapters, Himmler recorded the dates. This book, in private hands since 1945, is to be donated to the Museum of Jewish Heritage. I am grateful to the donor for making a copy available to me.

16. Himmler's 1927 edition, 45.

17. Ibid., 44.

18. Ibid., 80.

19. Ibid., 33.

20. Hitler, *Mein Kampf*, 325, 562.

21. Himmler's 1927 edition, 344.

22. Hammer, "Die deutschen Ausgaben," 163.

23. For a good analysis of how the Nazi Party managed to attract voters, see Thomas Childers, *The Nazi Voter: The Social Foundations of Fascism in Germany, 1919–1933* (Chapel Hill, N.C., 1983), 119–269. For connections between Nazism and earlier right-wing appeals, see Peter Fritzsche, *Rehearsals for Fascism: Populism and Political Mobilization in Weimar Germany* (New York, 1990), 230–36. On Nazi Party organization, see Dietrich Orlow, *A History of the Nazi Party, 1919–1933* (Pittsburgh, 1969). For a very effective study of Nazism at the local level, see William S. Allen, *The Nazi Seizure of Power* (rev. ed., New York, 1984).

24. "The Nazi movement proved frequently and persuasively that Hitler's *Weltanschauung* was not the *Weltanschauung* of Hitler alone" (Hermann Graml, *Antisemitism in the Third Reich*, trans. Tim Kirk, Oxford, 1992, p. 79). Ian Kershaw, "Ideology, Propaganda, and the Rise of the Nazi Party," in *The Nazi Machtergreifung*, ed. Peter D. Stachura (London, 1983), 167, argued that anti-Semitism played only a secondary role in transforming the Nazi Party from a sect into a mass party. But Graml, *Antisemitism*, 85–86, emphasized that Nazi agitation did not play down expansionist and anti-Semitic goals to achieve popularity.

25. For a narrative of the events in January 1933 based on up-to-date scholarship, see Henry Ashby Turner, Jr., *Hitler's Thirty Days to Power* (Reading, Mass., 1996). Turner suggests that a military dictatorship was a more logical outcome of Weimar's crisis. Hans Mommsen, *The Rise and Fall of Weimar Democracy*, trans. Elborg Forster and Larry Eugene Jones (Chapel Hill, N.C., 1996), 490–544, presents an alternative account.

26. Karl Dietrich Bracher, Wolfgang Sauer, and Gerhard Schulz, *Die Nationalsozialistische Machtergreifung: Studien zur Errichtung des totalitären Herrschaftssystems in Deutsch-*

*land, 1933/34* (Cologne and Opladen, 1960), is still valuable and perhaps the most detailed account of the process.

27. Ibid., 143.

28. Ibid., 149–51.

29. "Mordanschlag gegen Adolf Hitler geplant," *Völkischer Beobachter*, 21 Mar. 1933, 1.

30. Hitler, *Mein Kampf*, 582.

31. Saul Friedländer, *Nazi Germany and the Jews*, vol. 1, *The Years of Persecution, 1933–1939* (New York, 1997), 17–23; Abraham Barkai, *From Boycott to Annihilation: The Economic Struggle of German Jews, 1933–1943*, trans. William Templer (Hanover, N.H., 1989), 13–17.

32. Messersmith to Secretary of State, 3 Apr. 1933, strictly confidential, George S. Messersmith Papers, item 133, University of Delaware; William E. Beitz Memorandum Concerning Boycott of Jewish Stores in Berlin on 1 Apr. 1933, Messersmith Papers, item 124.

33. Jesse H. Stiller, *George S. Messersmith: Diplomat of Democracy* (Chapel Hill, N.C., 1987), 29, 35.

34. Messersmith to Secretary of State, 25 Mar. 1933, strictly confidential, copy in Messersmith Papers, item 125.

35. Messersmith Memorandum of Conversation with Goering, 5 Apr. 1933, transmitted to Washington, 6 Apr. 1933, copies in Messersmith Papers, items 135–36.

36. Messersmith to Secretary of State, 23 May 1933, Messersmith Papers, item 186.

37. Messersmith to Secretary of State, 3 Apr. 1933, Messersmith Papers, item 133; Messersmith to Secretary of State, 22 June 1933, strictly confidential, Messersmith Papers, item 199; Messersmith to Secretary of State, 1 Nov. 1933, Present Status of the Anti-Semitic Movement in Germany, strictly confidential, Messersmith Papers, item 325.

38. Franklin L. Ford, "Three Observers in Berlin: Rumbold, Dodd, and François-Poncet," in *The Diplomats, 1919–1939* (Princeton, N.J., 1953), 438–47.

39. Rumbold to Sir John Simon, 28 Mar. 1933, *Documents on British Foreign Policy, 1919–1939* (hereafter *Documents*), ed. E. L. Woodward and Rohan Butler, 2nd series, vol. 5, 1933 (London, 1956), 3–6.

40. Rumbold to Simon, 30 Mar. 1933 and 5 Apr. 1933, *Documents*, 9–11, 19–24.

41. Rumbold to Simon, 28 Mar. 1933, *Documents*, 5.

42. Rumbold to Simon, 13 Apr. 1933, *Documents*, 41–42.

43. See Richard Breitman and Alan M. Kraut, *American Refugee Policy and European Jewry, 1933–1945* (Bloomington, Ind., 1987), 40–41.

44. Rumbold to Simon, 28 Mar. 1933, *Documents*, 5–6; Rumbold to Simon, 13 Apr. 1933, *Documents*, 40–41.

45. Messersmith to Secretary of State, 17 June 1933, strictly confidential; Messersmith to Secretary of State, 1 Nov. 1933, Present Status of the Anti-Semitic Movement in Germany, strictly confidential, Messersmith Papers, items 195 and 325; Mes-

sersmith to Phillips, 29 Sept. 1933, Messersmith Papers, item 312; Rumbold to Simon, 13 Apr. 1933, *Documents*, 39–44.

46. Rumbold to Simon, 26 Apr. 1933, *Documents*, 47–55, quote from 50.

47. James J. Barnes and Patience P. Barnes, *Hitler's* Mein Kampf *in Britain and America: A Publishing History, 1930–1939* (Cambridge, 1980), esp. 1–15.

48. Adolf Hitler, *My Battle*, abr. and trans. E.T.S. Dugdale (Boston, 1933), esp. chapter 11 of vol. 1 and chapters 13–15 of vol. 2; Barnes and Barnes, *Hitler's* Mein Kampf, 10–14.

49. Barnes and Barnes, *Hitler's* Mein Kampf, 21–49.

50. Ibid., 49.

51. Wesley K. Wark, *The Ultimate Enemy: British Intelligence and Nazi Germany, 1933–1939* (Ithaca, N.Y., 1985).

52. See A. J. Sherman, *Island Refuge: Britain and Refugees from the Third Reich, 1933–1939* (London, 1994); Louise London, "Jewish Refugees, Anglo-Jewry, and British Government Policy, 1930–1940," in *The Making of Modern Anglo-Jewry*, ed. David Cesarani (Oxford, 1990), 163–90; Marion Berghahn, *German-Jewish Refugees in England: The Ambiguities of Assimilation* (New York, 1984); Breitman and Kraut, *American Refugee Policy*; and David S. Wyman, *Paper Walls: America and the Refugee Crisis, 1938–1941* (Amherst, Mass., 1968). See also, Bob Moore, *Refugees from Nazi Germany in the Netherlands, 1933–1940* (Dordrecht, 1986); Paul R. Bartrop, *Australia and the Holocaust, 1933–1945* (Melbourne, 1994); and Irving Abella and Harold Troper, *None Is Too Many: Canada and the Jews of Europe* (New York, 1983).

## 2. PLANNING RACE WAR

1. "Kurt Daluege," in *Encyclopedia of the Holocaust*, vol. 1, ed. Israel Gutman (New York, 1990), 343–44. The author of the entry, Uwe Dietrich Adam, also described Daluege as short on intellectual ability.

A copy of Daluege's Nachlass (Papers) are available in the U.S. National Archives (NA), Record Group (RG) 242, Microfilm Series T-580. See esp. Rolls 219–29. These papers contain far more documents on the prewar period than on the war. In some wartime files, there are cover letters to documents, but what look like might have been incriminating documents are missing. See, for example, Himmler to Daluege, Heydrich, and Eicke, 25 Aug. 1939, Nachlass Daluege, NA RG 242, T-580/R 222, Ordner 66 (no frame numbers available). For additional evidence on what might have once been among Daluege's papers, see chapter 4 below.

2. The details of Daluege's career are available in his SS Personnel File, NA, Berlin Document Center (BDC), Microfilm A-3343, SSO-134. Correspondence there indicates a personal relationship between Daluege and Hitler. On the Stennes affair, see Shlomo Aronson, *Heydrich und die Frühgeschichte des SD* (Stuttgart, 1971), 50–

51; Richard Bessel, *Political Violence and the Rise of Nazism: The Storm Troopers in Eastern Germany* (New Haven, Conn., 1984), 62–63.

3.  Daluege's SS Personnel File, NA-BDC, A-3343, SSO-134.

4.  See George C. Browder, *Foundations of the Nazi Police State: The Formation of Sipo and SD* (Lexington, Ky., 1990), 80, 96.

5.  Aronson, *Heydrich und die Frühgeschichte*, 81.

6.  Ibid., 82. Browder, *Foundations of the Nazi Police State*, esp. 96, presents Daluege as a serious independent player in the maneuvers and shifting alliances, which is not my impression.

7.  See Browder, *Foundations of the Nazi Police State*, esp. 217–30.

8.  Die Deutsche Ordnungspolizei, Nachlass Daluege, NA RG 242, T-580/R 228/ Ordner 91, p. 3.

9.  George C. Browder, *Hitler's Enforcers: The Gestapo and the SS Security Service in the Nazi Revolution* (New York, 1996), 28.

10. Ibid., 30–31, 40–41. On Müller, see Aronson, *Heydrich und die Frühgeschichte*, 95–97, 108–10.

11. Browder, *Hitler's Enforcers*, 28, 44.

12. At the twenty-fifth course for SS-officer candidates in 1942, there were fifty-one participants, nine of whom failed the exam. The candidates were divided into groups of ten. In one group, five came from the SD, three from the Gestapo, and two from the Criminal Police. Exactly when these courses began is unclear, but there may have been three per year since the Nazi state began. See various documents about this course in NA RG 242, T-175/R 180/2715184-96.

13. Details about the teaching plan are in Heydrich to Commanders of the Officer School of the Security Police, 8 Feb. 1941, Center for the Preservation of Historical-Documentary Materials, Moscow (hereafter listed as Center-Moscow), 500-5-1. On Himmler's approval, see Himmler to Heydrich, 29 May 1941, NA-BDC, Heydrich's SS Personnel File, A-3343, SSO-095A.

14. Aronson, *Heydrich und die Frühgeschichte*, 81; Christopher R. Browning, *Ordinary Men: Reserve Police Battalion 101 and the Final Solution in Poland* (New York, 1992), 4.

15. Aronson, *Heydrich und die Frühgeschichte*, 82. The standard older work on the Order Police is Hans-Joachim Neufeldt, Jürge Huck, and Georg Tessin, *Zur Geschichte der Ordnungspolizei, 1936–1945* (Koblenz, 1957).

16. "Jewry and Penal Punishment," copy in Nachlass Daluege, NA RG 242, T-580/ R 220/Ordner 61.

17. Heydrich to Daluege, 12 Feb. 1940, Nachlass Daluege, NA RG 242, T-580/R 219/Ordner 60.

18. Information from Shlomo Aronson.

19. Die Deutsche Ordnungspolizei, Nachlass Daluege, NA RG 242, T-580/R 228/ Ordner 91, pp. 12–13, 26.

20. Very little has been written about the use of the Order Police in the Polish cam-

paign, but there is some discussion of Police Battalions 101–104 in Helmut Fang-man, Udo Reifner, and Norbert Steinhorn, *Parteisoldaten—Hamburger Polizei in "3. Reich"* (Hamburg, 1987), leaf between 86 and 87, 118–20. I am grateful to Jürgen Matthäus for this reference. For a brief summary of SS policies, see Richard Breitman, *The Architect of Genocide: Himmler and the Final Solution* (Hanover, N.H., 1992), 69–82. For an excellent case study, see Charles W. Sydnor, Jr., *Soldiers of Destruction: The SS Death's Head Division, 1933–1945* (Princeton, N.J., 1990). For Nazi policy generally in Poland, see Martin Broszat, *Nationalsozialistische Polenpol-itik, 1939–1945* (Stuttgart, 1961).

21. Helmut Krausnick and Hans-Heinrich Wilhelm, *Die Truppe des Weltanschauungs-krieges: Die Einsatzgruppen der Sicherheitspolizei und SD, 1938–1942* (Stuttgart, 1982), 36.

22. Sydnor, *Soldiers of Destruction*, 38 (on Eicke's title, HSSPF), and 21–22 (on Eicke and Heydrich).

23. Wolff to Daluege, Heydrich, and Eicke, 25 Aug. 1939, and handwritten comments in margin, Nachlass Daluege, NA RG 242, T-580/R 222/Ordner 66.

24. Rudolf Hoess, *Commandant of Auschwitz* (New York, 1961), 73, identified the audience as the replacement guards at the concentration camp. But see Sydnor, *Soldiers of Destruction*, 35, n. 86.

25. Hoess, *Commandant*, 73–74.

26. Krausnick and Wilhelm, *Truppe des Weltanschauungskrieges*, 48.

27. On Police Battalions 11 and 12 in 1939 and "special duties," see British intelli-gence Location List of Police Battalions, p. 2, Public Record Office (PRO) HW 16/1, and Summary of German Police Decodes, 3 July–14 Aug. 1941, p. 3, PRO HW 16/6, part 1.

28. Heydrich to Daluege, 29 Sept. 1939, responding to Daluege to Heydrich, 22 Sept. 1939, repr. in *Archives of the Holocaust: An International Collection of Selected Docu-ments*, ed. Henry Friedlander and Sybil Milton, vol. 11, part 1, *Berlin Document Center* (New York, 1992), 132–33. I am grateful to Charles Sydnor for calling my attention to this document. For the context and Heydrich's comments else-where, see Breitman, *Architect of Genocide*, 74–75.

29. Hermann Franz's SS Personnel File, NA-BDC, A-3343/SSO-219.

30. Die Deutsche Ordnungspolizei, Nachlass Daluege, NA RG 242, T-580/R 228/ Ordner 91, pp. 24–26, 31–32. Andrej Angrick, Martina Voigt, Silke Ammer-schubert, and Peter Klein, " 'Da hätte man schon ein Tagebuch führen müssen': Das Polizeibatallion 322 und die Judenmorde im Bereich der Heeresgruppe Mitte während des Sommers und Herbstes 1941," in *Die Normalität des Verbrechens: Bilanz und Perspektiven der Forschung zu den nationalsozialistischen Gewaltverbrechen* (Berlin, 1994), 367, n. 8. On the early 1941 total, see British intelligence Location List of German Police Battalions, PRO HW 16/1.

31. Op. Abt. An Gen. Qu. Abt. H Vers, 15 Jan. 1941, Bundesarchiv-Militärarchiv, RH2/v. 1325 (alt H 22/355), Barbarossa, Bd. 1, 7 Jan.–8 May 1941.

32. Breitman, *Architect of Genocide*, 105–15.

33. Ibid., 152. Richard Breitman, "Plans for the Final Solution in Early 1941," *German Studies Review* 17, no. 3 (Oct. 1994): 483–94. Schellenberg's memo, 20 May 1941, NA RG 238, Nuremberg Document NG-3104. At the time this memo was written, he was in the Gestapo and served on occasion as Heinrich Müller's deputy. Few historians have recognized that he was in a position to have good information about the planning of the Final Solution.

34. Heydrich's Aktenvermerk, 26 Mar. 1941, Center-Moscow, 500-3-795, cited by Götz Aly, *Endlösung: Völkerverschiebung und der Mord an den europäischen Juden* (Frankfurt am Main, 1995), 270–72. I am grateful to Charles Sydnor for a copy of this document, and I am following Aly's line of interpretation in part here.

35. Heydrich's Aktenvermerk, 26 Mar. 1941, Center-Moscow, 500-3-795.

36. Richtlinien für das Verhalten der Truppe in der Sowjetunion, 25 Oct. 1941, copy in U.S. Holocaust Memorial Museum, RG 48.004M, R 2/201382-404.

37. Ralf Ogorreck, *Die Einsatzgruppen und die "Genesis der Endlösung"* (Berlin, 1996), 27. The evidence about Heydrich and Brauchitsch comes from Picot to Künsberg, 10 Feb. 1941, NA RG 238, M-946/R 1/113. On the negotiations still being in progress, see handwritten notation based on information from Plötz at the end of Picot's memorandum, Einbau des Sonderkommando AA in die SS, 10 Feb. 1941, NA RG 238, M-946/R 1/109. On Heydrich and Himmler's discussion of the subject, see Himmler's appointments, 10 Mar. 1941, Center-Moscow, 1372-5-23, f. 522. I am grateful to Jürgen Matthäus for a copy of this document.

38. This is a short summary of a complicated set of events. For more details, see OKW, Richtlinien auf Sondergebieten zur Weisung Nr. 21, 13 Mar. 1941, International Military Tribunal, *Trial of the Major War Criminals before the International Military Tribunal* (Nuremberg, 1947), vol. 26, 53–57, 447-PS (hereafter, IMT, *Trial*); Helmut Krausnick, "Kommissarbefehl und 'Gerichtsbarkeitserlass Barbarossa' in neuer Sicht," *Vierteljahrshefte für Zeitgeschichte* 25 (1977): 685; Krausnick and Wilhelm, *Truppe des Weltanschauungskrieges*, 115–17; Jürgen Förster, "Das Unternehmen Barbarossa als Eroberungs und Vernichtungskrieg," *Das Deutsche Reich und der Zweite Weltkrieg*, vol. 4 (Stuttgart, 1983), 413–14; Förster, "The Relation between Operation Barbarossa as an Ideological War of Extermination and the Final Solution," in *The Final Solution: Origins and Implementation*, ed. David Cesarani (London, 1994), 89–91; Ogorreck, *Die Einsatzgruppen*, 24–31.

39. Himmler's appointments: 14 Mar. 1941, "Daluege: Einsatzfragen"; 15 Mar. 1941, "Daluege, Heydrich, Wolff: Einsatzfragen," Center-Moscow, 1372-5-23, f. 518–17.

40. Angrick et al., " 'Da hätte man schon,' " 328–29, reach similar conclusions through different reasoning.

41. For the agreement, see *Trials of War Criminals before the Nuremberg Military Tribunal*, vol. 10, 1 239–41, NOKW-2080. For analysis, see Krausnick and Wilhelm, *Truppe des Weltanschauungskrieges*, 129–30, 134; Förster, "Das Unternehmen Barbarossa," 415–17; Ogorreck, *Die Einsatzgruppen*, 37–38. On Himmler and Reinecke, see Himmler's appointments, 19 Mar. 1941, Center-Moscow, 1372-5-23, f. 515.

42. Himmler's appointments, 8 Apr. 1941, "Daluege: Einsatz Barbarossa," Center-Moscow, 1372-5-23, f. 497.

43. Daluege to Hitler, 21 Apr. 1941, Nachlass Daluege, NA RG 242, T-580/R 219/Ordner 57. On Hitler's approval, see also von Grolmann to Schmitt, 15 Oct. 1941, Gerret Korsemann's SS Personnel File, NA-BDC, A-3343, SSO-202A.

44. Himmler to Daluege, 9 Mar. 1942, Nachlass Daluege, NA RG 242, T-580/R 219/Ordner 57.

45. Angrick et al., " 'Da hätte man schon,' " 327–28; Ullmann to Daluege, Heydrich, and Jüttner, 21 April 1941, untitled, undated drafts, and Meine to Treusch, 21 April 1941, NA RG 242, T-175/R 123/2648762-68. The final version, largely unaltered, was sent out more widely. See Sonderauftrag des Führers, 21 May 1941, NA RG 242, T-175/R 123/2648739; Daluege's Vortrag über das Kräfte- und Kriegseinsatz der Ordnungspolizei im Jahre 1941: Dienstbesprechung der Befehlshaber und Inspekteure vom 1. bis 4. Februar 1942, Zentrale Stelle der Landesjustizverwaltungen, Ludwigsburg V/117. I am grateful to Konrad Kwiet for a copy of this last document.

46. For a sample letter of appointment, see Himmler to Prützmann, 28 June 1938, Prützmann's SS Personnel File, NA-BDC Microfilm A-3343, SSO-395A.

47. Ruth Bettina Birn, *Die Höheren SS- und Polizeiführer: Himmlers Vertreter im Dritten Reich* (Düsseldorf, 1986), 8–10.

48. Biographical information from Prützmann's SS Personnel File, NA-BDC, A-3343, SSO-395A. On 1 May 1941, Prützmann was appointed Higher SS and Police Leader for northeast Germany, and he was shifted to Higher SS and Police Leader for the Rear Army Area North seven weeks later.

49. Information from Bach-Zelewski's SS Personnel File, including Daluege's report of 14 June 1933, NA-BDC, A-3343, SSO-023.

50. Some of Bach-Zelewski's problems in 1935 are detailed in letters in his SS Personnel File. Bach-Zelewski's version of the affair in interrogation of 30 Oct. 1945, NA RG 238, M-1270/R 1/422-23. For Hitler's decision, see Himmler's Führervortrag (notes), 8 Oct. 1935, and Hitler's "bleibt.," NA RG 242, T-175/R 94/2613260.

51. Himmler's log of office correspondence: "Bach. Bittet um einen Fronteinsatz," 18 Mar. 1941, NA RG 242, T-581/R 45A.

52. Bach-Zelewski's SS Personnel File, NA-BDC, A-3343, SSO-023.

53. Biographical information and letter in Jeckeln's SS Personnel File, NA-BDC, A-3343, SSO-135A. Quote from Jeckeln to Richard, 23 Apr. 1941.

54. Himmler's Order of 1 May 1941, Jeckeln's SS Personnel File, NA-BDC, A-3343, SSO-135.

55. There is currently no documentary evidence of Himmler meeting privately with Prützmann, Jeckeln, or Bach-Zelewski before 12 June, but see n. 56.

56. Declaration von dem Bach, World Jewish Congress Records, Box C203, Folder Bach-Zelewski 1946, American Jewish Archives, Cincinnati. In *Architect of Genocide*, 147, 282 n. 11, 283 n. 12, I followed Bach-Zelewski's testimony at the

International Military Tribunal, where he dated this meeting as early 1941. That date, however, is unsupported by any contemporary documentation, whereas his Declaration contains the statement that the meeting occurred weeks before the invasion of the U.S.S.R., and 12–15 June more or less fits that description. For contemporary evidence of Himmler's meeting at Wewelsburg on 12–15 June, see Himmler's Office Log, 12 June 1941, NA RG 242, T-581/R 39A, and Center-Moscow, 1372-5-23, f. 445. I am grateful to Peter Witte for calling this first document to my attention.

Again, Bach-Zelewski's testimony here is credible because it is incriminating, not exculpatory, and because of independent documentation of the meeting at Wewelsburg.

57. Declaration von dem Bach, 13–15, 17, World Jewish Congress Records, Box C203, Bach-Zelewski 1946, American Jewish Archives. Bach-Zelewski stated, however, that Himmler originally intended to use all forces for this purpose but that fighting against partisans diverted the Waffen-SS and Order Police battalions, so only the Security Police remained. Here, Bach-Zelewski was trying to exculpate himself, Daluege, and other comrades and to place all the blame for executions on those who were dead. Contemporary evidence cited below indicates that Himmler did in fact use all three organizations to carry out a campaign of murder and destruction.

The Higher SS and Police Leaders did have influence over the Einsatzgruppen, but this was not convenient for Bach-Zelewski to reveal in 1946.

58. On the origins of the Kommandostab RFSS, see Yehoshua Büchler, "Kommandostab Reichsführer SS: Himmler's Personal Murder Brigades in 1941," *Holocaust and Genocide Studies* 1 (1986): 13–14. On Knoblauch, see his SS Personnel File, NA-BDC, A-3343, SSO-186A, and on interrogation of Knoblauch, see 30 Nov. 1946, NA RG 238, M-1019/R 36/412–15.

59. Interrogation of Knoblauch, 30 Nov. 1946, NA RG 238, M-1019/R 36/415–16. This account is more or less consistent with the war diary of the Kommandostab RFSS, which records Himmler's decision on 10 July. ". . . im rückwärtigen Gebiet der höhere SS-u Pol. Führer Verfügung über alles hat, was dem RF SS gehört. Was sich nicht im Gebiet der höheren SS-u.Polizeiführer befindet, ist nicht unterstellt. Auch für den SD gilt das Vorstehende. Die SS-Verbände sind dem SS-u-Pol. Führer erst dann zu unterstellen, wenn die Grenze überschritten ist" (Kriegstagebuch Nr. 1, Military Archive, Prague, RFSS KDS; copy also in U.S. Holocaust Memorial Museum, RG 48.004M, R 1). See also Angrick et al., " 'Da hätte man schon,' " 329. In practice, the Einsatzgruppen operated more independently of the Higher SS and Police Leaders than did the Order Police battalions.

60. The war diary kept by the Kommandostab RFSS includes only the activities of the Waffen-SS units. See Kriegstagebuch Nr. 1, 16 June–31 Dec. 1941, Military Archive, Prague, RFSS KDS; copy in U.S. Holocaust Memorial Museum, RG 48.004M, R 1. But see Kommandostab Reichsführer SS, Himmler Collection, Box 10, Folder 322, Hoover Institution.

61. It is, for example, still disputed what Heydrich told the heads of the Einsatzgrup-
    pen, Einsatzkommandos, Sonderkommandos, and some others at RSHA head-
    quarters on 17 June 1941 about their coming mission. It is also disputed whether
    Heydrich's subordinate Bruno Streckenbach or Heinrich Müller gave a speech to
    the policemen in these units at the Border Police school at Pretzsch, as well as
    what Streckenbach or Müller said. For a short summary of the controversy, see
    Breitman, *Architect of Genocide*, 163–64, 288–89. For a very recent, very detailed
    account with which I do not agree, see Ogorreck, *Die Einsatzgruppen*, 47–94.
62. Copy in NA RG 242, T-175/R 426/2955875.
63. PRO, Kew, HW 1/2212, C/4915. I am grateful to John P. Fox for a copy of
    this document.

## 3. A BATTALION GETS THE WORD

1. Konrad Kwiet, "Rehearsing for Murder: The Beginning of the Final Solution in
   Lithuania in June 1941," *Holocaust and Genocide Studies* 12 (1998): 1–3.
2. Korsemann had had a slightly checkered career, having stayed too long in the
   disgraced SA force. But he developed good relations with Daluege and eventually
   got command in 1940 of an Order Police battalion that served in Jutland. His
   appointment as Higher SS and Police Leader ran into budgetary problems and got
   delayed in mid-1941, but there was never much doubt that it would go through,
   which was why Daluege invited him to the briefing. See Korsemann's SS Personnel File, NA-BDC, A-3343, SSO-202A. See also Korsemann to Daluege, 5 March
   1940; Daluege to Himmler, 13 March 1940, Nachlass Daluege, NA RG 242,
   T-580/R 219/Ordner 60. For Himmler's Order of 25 Apr. 1940, see Prützmann's
   SS Personnel File, NA-BDC, A-3343, SSO-395A.
3. Heydrich's message of 2 July 1941, Center-Moscow, 500-1-25, copy in U.S. Holocaust Memorial Museum, RG 11.001M, R 183; Helmut Krausnick and
   Hans-Heinrich Wilhelm, *Die Truppe des Weltanschauungskrieges: Die Einsatzgruppen
   der Sicherheitspolizei und SD, 1938–1942* (Stuttgart, 1982), 150–57.
4. Krausnick and Wilhelm, *Truppe des Weltanschauungskrieges*, 150, notes the surface
   reason for Heydrich's instructions but not the broader conflict between Daluege
   and Heydrich.
5. Handwritten comment on memorandum compiled by Einsatzgruppe A regarding
   Reich Commissar Lohse's Guidelines, 6 Aug. 1941, Latvian State Archives, Riga,
   PSR CVVA-1026-1-4, 298, cited in *Herrschaftsalltag im Dritten Reich*, ed. Hans
   Mommsen and Susanne Willems (Düsseldorf, 1988), 467–71.
6. See n. 3 above.
7. This evidence has recently been pulled together by Ralf Ogorreck, *Die Einsatzgruppen und die "Genesis der Endlösung"* (Berlin, 1996), who in my view accepts it
   too uncritically. For earlier development of the theory that a general killing order
   of Jews came only in August, see Alfred Streim, "The Tasks of the SS Einsatz-

gruppen," *Simon Wiesenthal Center Annual* 4 (1987): 309–29, and the debate between Helmut Krausnick and Streim in *Simon Wiesenthal Center Annual* 6 (1989): 311–47.

8. Konrad Kwiet, "From the Diary of a Killing Unit," in *Why Germany? National Socialist Anti-Semitism and the European Context*, ed. John Milfull (Providence, 1993), 75–93; Andrej Angrick, Martina Voigt, Silke Ammerschubert, and Peter Klein, " 'Da hätte man schon ein Tagebuch führen müssen': Das Polizeibatallion 322 und die Judenmorde im Bereich der Heeresgruppe Mitte während des Sommers und Herbstes 1941," in *Die Normalität des Verbrechens: Bilanz und Perspektiven der Forschung zu den nationalsozialistischen Gewaltverbrechen* (Berlin, 1994), 325–85.

9. See chapter 2 above.

10. Angrick et al., " 'Da hätte man schon,' " 329; Kwiet, "From the Diary," 191.

11. Kwiet, "From the Diary," 79.

12. Montua's SS Personnel File, NA-BDC, A-3343, SSO-324A.

13. Angrick et al., " 'Da hätte man schon,' " 329–30.

14. Ibid., 330–31.

15. Kwiet, "From the Diary," 83; Ogorreck, *Die Einsatzgruppen*, 121.

16. Police Battalion 322's war diary, 8 July 1941, p. 38, Military Archive, Prague, Pol. Reg. Mitte; copy in U.S. Holocaust Memorial Museum, RG 48.004M, R 2.

17. Police Battalion 322's war diary, 8 July 1941, p. 39; Judenaktion der 8. Kompanie in Krassnopolje am 22.10.1941, Military Archive, Prague, Pol. Reg. Mitte; copy in U.S. Holocaust Memorial Museum, RG 48.004M, R 2.

18. Angrick et al., " 'Da hätte man schon,' " 331.

19. Bach-Zelewski affidavit, NA RG 238, M-1270/R 1/296; Declaration von dem Bach, 28–29, World Jewish Congress Collection, Box C203, Bach-Zelewski Statement 1946.

20. Angrick et al., " 'Da hätte man schon,' " 331–36.

21. Police Battalion 322's war diary, 9 July 1941, p. 41.

22. Kwiet, "From the Diary," 84; court testimony cited by Ogorreck, *Die Einsatzgruppen*, 122–23.

23. Riebel to Third Battalion, Police Reg. Center, 1 Sept. 1941, Military Archive, Prague, Pol. Reg. Mitte, copy in U.S. Holocaust Memorial Museum, RG 48.004M, R 2.

24. Richard Breitman, *The Architect of Genocide: Himmler and the Final Solution* (Hanover, N.H., 1992), 100, 242–43.

25. German Police Decodes, 14 July 1941, item 9, PRO HW 16/31.

26. Himmler's order, 30 Sept. 1940, NA RG 242, T-175/R 190/2727908. See also David Welch, *The Third Reich: Politics and Propaganda* (London and New York, 1995), 78; Stig Hornshøj-Møller and David Culbert, "Der ewige Jude (1940): Joseph Goebbels' Unequaled Monument to Anti-Semitism," *Historical Journal of Film, Radio and Television* 12 (1992): 41–46.

27. Welch, *The Third Reich*, 78. The actual relationship between the timing of the

film and the Final Solution seems more indirect. See Stig Hornshøj-Møller, *"Der ewige Jude": Quellenkristische Analyse eines antisemitischen Propagandafilms* (Göttingen, 1995), esp. 3–23.

28. German Police Decodes, 14 July 1941, item 13, PRO HW 16/31.

29. Angrick et al., " 'Da hätte man schon,' " 342–44.

30. Riebel to Third Battalion, Police Regiment Center, 1 Sept. 1941, Military Archive, Prague, Pol. Reg. Mitte; copy in U.S. Holocaust Memorial Museum, RG 48.004M, R 2.

31. Angrick et al., " 'Da hätte man schon,' " 344.

32. Kwiet, "From the Diary," 85–87; Angrick et al. " 'Da hätte man schon,' " 337–45. For Bach-Zelewski's explicit order to liquidate the Jews of Bialowies ("Wenn verbleibende Komp. zur Fortsetzung der Aktion nicht ausreicht, Aussiedlung bis eintreffen des neuen Btls. unterbrechen und Komp. einsetzen zur Liquidierung der Juden"), see Bach-Zelewski Funkspruch to Ustuf. v. Hertell, Police Battalion 322, 1 Aug. 1941, Military Archive, Prague, Pol. Reg. Mitte; copy in U.S. Holocaust Memorial Museum, RG 48.004M, R 2.

33. Kwiet, "Rehearsing for Murder," 82–85.

34. See Christopher R. Browning, *Ordinary Men: Reserve Police Battalion 101 and the Final Solution in Poland* (New York, 1992), and Daniel J. Goldhagen, *Hitler's Willing Executioners: Ordinary Germans and the Holocaust* (New York, 1996).

35. Angrick et al., " 'Da hätte man schon,' " 360–61.

36. Summary of German Police Decodes, 3 July–14 Aug. 1941, p. 9, PRO, HW 16/6, part 1.

37. "Crossing the Line in Nazi Genocide: On Becoming and Being a Professional Killer," Occasional Paper no. 2, Center for Holocaust Studies, University of Vermont (Burlington, 1997), 7–8.

38. Omer Bartov, *The Eastern Front, 1941–1945: German Troops and the Barbarization of Warfare* (New York, 1986), esp. 83–87 and 148–52, and Bartov, *Hitler's Army: Soldiers, Nazis, and War in the Third Reich* (New York, 1991), 28, argued that for the soldiers of the German Army, heavy casualties and frustration on the battlefield and the possibility of military defeat in December 1941 led to an increasing barbarization, making individual soldiers more willing to carry out the criminal policies inherent in Nazi ideology. Although there was certainly a difference between the police battalion members and the soldiers, my study does not support the notion that the military reverses of December 1941 changed German behavior in the East.

39. Bruce F. Pauley, *From Prejudice to Persecution: A History of Austrian Anti-Semitism* (Chapel Hill, N.C., 1992), esp. 79–88.

40. Himmler to Prützmann, Jeckeln, von dem Bach, Korsemann, and Globocnik, 25 July 1941, NA RG 242, T-454/R 100/699–700. It is likely that the same information was sent by radio, but no proof survives. The Einsatzgruppen had already recruited some non-Germans, but Himmler wanted the process expanded.

Ereignismeldung UdSSR #18, 10 Aug. 1941, NA RG 242, T-175/R 233/ 2721867.

41. Richard Breitman, "Himmler's Police Auxiliaries in the Occupied Soviet Territories," *Simon Wiesenthal Center Annual* 7 (1990): 23–39.

## 4. REPORTS OF ETHNIC CLEANSING

1. See Jürgen Förster, "Das Unternehmen Barbarossa als Eroberungs- und Vernichtungskrieg," in *Das Deutsche Reich und der Zweite Weltkrieg*, vol. 4 (Stuttgart, 1983), 440–47. On the need to cultivate relations with the military, see Daluege's comment that shifting Stahlecker to other tasks would bring disadvantages, because his successor would not have the same relationship with the military, and Himmler's recognition of this argument. German Police Decodes, 24 July 1941, items 13 and 31, PRO HW 16/31. The second message is only partly decoded.

2. Bormann to Lammers, 16 June 1941, NA RG 242, T-175/R 123/2648754-55.

3. See Martin Bormann's minutes of this meeting, which are extremely vague about the discussion of Himmler's functions, International Military Tribunal (IMT), *Trial of the Major War Criminals before the International Military Tribunal* (Nuremberg, 1947), vol. 38, 86–94, document 221-L. For a more detailed analysis, see Richard Breitman, *The Architect of Genocide: Himmler and the Final Solution* (Hanover, N.H., 1992), 181–84. See also Timothy Patrick Mulligan, *The Politics of Illusion and Empire: German Occupation Policy in the Soviet Union, 1942–43* (New York, 1988), 8–12. Mulligan sees Hitler as not only disregarding Rosenberg but also deceiving him.

4. Himmler went over his mail that day, according to Brandt's office log, NA RG 242, T-580/R 39A. He also held a conference, apparently with Heydrich, and made a number of promotions and appointments to posts in the East, one of them, Carl Zenner. Streckenbach Fernschreiben, 17 July 1941, Carl Zenner's SS Personnel File, NA-BDC, A-3343, SSO-020C. Breitman, *Architect of Genocide*, 184.

5. Erlass des Führers über die politische Sicherung der neu besetzten Ostgebiete, NA RG 238, T-1139/R 21/751, document NG-1688.

6. German Police Decodes, 14 July 1941, item 11, PRO HW 16/31.

7. German Police Decodes, 14 July 1941, item 11, PRO HW 16/31. German Police Decodes, 18 July 1941, items 6 and 15, NA RG 457, Box 1386.

8. For Himmler's trips, sometimes accompanied by Heydrich, see Breitman, *Architect of Genocide*, 170, 190–92, 194–96, 208, 211. Daluege's visits included stops at Bialystok (see chapter 3, pp. 46–47 above), Baranowicze, and Rowno on 28 July, Kowno on 29 July, Riga and Minsk in late August, and Berditschev in early September. German Police Decodes, 27 July, 28 July, and 29 July 1941, items 16, 6, and 14, respectively; PRO HW 16/32. German Police Decodes, 23 and 25 Aug. 1941, items 8 and 14, respectively; 2 Sept. 1941, item 17; all in NA RG 457, Box 1386.

9. Occasionally, the Einsatzkommandos also reported directly to Berlin. Interrogation of Kurt Lindow, NA RG 238, M-1019/R 42/472. Ronald Headland, *Messages of Murder: A Study of the Reports of the Einsatzgruppen of the Security Police and Security Service, 1941–1943* (Rutherford, N.J., 1992), 40.

10. Interrogation of Kurt Lindow, NA RG 238, M-1019/R 42/472. Headland, *Messages of Murder,* 40–41.

11. Helmut Krausnick and Hans-Heinrich Wilhelm, *Die Truppe des Weltanschauungskrieges: Die Einsatzgruppen der Sicherheitspolizei und SD, 1938–1942* (Stuttgart, 1982), 540. Gerald Fleming, *Hitler and the Final Solution* (Berkeley, Calif., 1984), 73–74.

12. Headland, *Messages of Murder,* 41.

13. German Police Decodes, 14 Aug. 1941, item 6, PRO HW 16/32. See Daluege's instruction to Police Regiment Center to submit a situation report every two weeks. Kriegstagebuch, 16–17 Oct. 1941, Military Archive, Prague, Pol. Reg. Mitte, KR 1 Folder A-3-1-7.

14. Fernsprech- und Fernschreibverkehr der Ordnungspolizei von und nach dem Ostraum, 29 Jan. 1942, copy in Nachlass Daluege, NA RG 242, T-580/R 222/ Ordner 73.

15. See Prützmann's telegram to Himmler's military adjutant Grothmann, 16 Sept. 1941, and Grothmann's telegram to Prützmann, 18 Sept. 1941, NA RG 242, T-175/R 112/2637729 and 2637744. On the transmitter, see Summary of German Police Decodes, 15–31 Aug. 1941, p. 5, PRO HW 16/6, part 1.

16. Kurierdienst in die Ostgebiete mit Flugzeugen der Ordnungspolizei, 25 June 1942, Nachlass Daluege, NA RG 242, T-580/R 222/Ordner 73. Summary of German Police Decodes, 1–30 Sept. 1941, p. 7, PRO HW 16/6, part 1. Summary of German Police Decodes, 1 Oct.–14 Nov. 1941, p. 8, PRO HW 16/6, part 1.

17. Interrogation of Ernst Sachs, 24 Oct. 1945, NA RG 238, M-1270/R 27/004–006.

18. Nachrichten Kp. 10984, 15 June 1941, and Croll to Gutjahr, 17 July 1941, Nachrichten Kp. 10984, Kommandostab Reichsführer SS, Military Archive, Prague, N 11079.

19. Interrogation of Ernst Sachs, 24 Oct. 1945, NA RG 238, M-1270/R 27/007. Among the Higher SS and Police Leaders, Jeckeln deviated somewhat in sending some reports also to Heydrich.

20. Interrogation of Ernst Sachs, 24 Oct. 1945, NA RG 238, M-1270/R 27/008. Robert Schlake's SS Personnel File, NA-BDC, A-3343, SSO-079B.

21. This description is somewhat simplified. For more details, see Explanatory Note, NA RG 457, Box 202, Study of German Police Traffic; and Noel Currer-Briggs, "Army Ultra's Poor Relations," in *Codebreakers: The Inside Story of Bletchley Park,* ed. F. H. Hinsley and Alan Stripp (Oxford, 1993), 209–18. But Currer-Briggs misdates the shift to Double Playfair. See Summary of German Police Decodes, 1–30 September 1941, p. 1, PRO HW 16/6, part 1.

22. German Police Decodes, 2 Dec. 1941, item 22, NA RG 457, Box 1386. Kommandostab Reichsführer SS to Higher SS and Police Leader Lublin, 17 Oct. 1941, NA RG 242, T-175/R 132/2659436.

23. Interview with Arthur Levinson, 19 May 1997. Levinson was among the first Americans who went to Bletchley Park and worked there during 1943–45.

24. Ernst Sachs's SS Personnel File, NA-BDC, A-3343, SSO-058B.

25. Currer-Briggs, "Army Ultra's Poor Relations," 209–18.

26. Summary of German Police Decodes, 1 Oct.–14 Nov. 1941, p. 2, PRO HW 16/6, part 1.

27. Interview with Arthur Levinson, 19 May 1997.

28. Breitman, *Architect of Genocide*, 6, 27, 29–30, 186–87.

29. IMT, *Trial*, vol. 33, 197, 3839-PS.

30. German Police Decodes, 29 July 1941, item 23, PRO HW 16/32; Breitman, *Architect of Genocide*, 192.

31. Himmler ordered Daluege to wait for him at the airport at Rowno. German Police Decodes, 28 July 1941, item 6, PRO HW 16/32.

32. Erwin Schulz Affidavit, 13 Aug. 1947, NA RG 238, NO-3644.

33. Reitende Abteilung, SS-Kav. Reg. 2, 1 Aug. 1941; copy in NA RG 242, T-354/R 168/3818936. For the denouement of this action, see Yehoshua Büchler, "Kommandostab Reichsführer SS: Himmler's Personal Murder Brigades in 1941," *Holocaust and Genocide Studies* 1 (1986): 15–17.

34. There is a collection of unpurged radio messages from the Kommandostab RFSS available at the Military Archive in Prague and on microfilm at the U.S. Holocaust Memorial Museum (RG 48.004M). For decades these documents were not available to Western scholars. For a large collection of Command Staff RFSS file messages that were purged of anything damaging, see NA RG 242, T-175/R 132/2659412, 2659439, etc.

35. Jeckeln to Himmler, von Roques, von Puttkamer, and Daluege, 1 Aug. 1941, NA RG 238, Nuremberg Document NOKW-1165.

36. German Police Decodes, 4 Aug. 1941, items 2 and 9, NA RG 457, Box 1386.

37. German Police Decodes, 7 Aug. 1941, item 24, NA RG 457, Box 1386. The British decrypt has the police battalion "evacuating" the male inhabitants of Jazyl; "evacuation" was a standard euphemism.

   On the message regarding Pinsk, see Fegelein's adjutant to Reit. Abt., 8 Aug. 1941, NA RG 242, T-354/R 168/3818930.

38. Historians have known about Himmler's visit to Minsk ever since Bach-Zelewski testified about it shortly after the end of the war. I have written previously about it in some detail, drawing on various sources, including Bach-Zelewski's accounts, Himmler's preliminary itinerary (NA RG 242, T-175/R 112/2637745), and police testimony. See Breitman, *Architect of Genocide*, 195–96. Since then, Himmler's itinerary for the trip has appeared in Moscow (I am grateful to Jürgen Matthäus for the copy), and it provides additional detail. Also, Abraham Peck supplied a

more detailed account by Bach-Zelewski, which is consistent with what he said elsewhere. Declaration von dem Bach, World Jewish Congress Collection, Box C203, Folder: Bach-Zelewski Statement 1946, American Jewish Archives.

39. Declaration von dem Bach, World Jewish Congress Collection, Box C203, Bach-Zelewski Statement 1946, 30–32. For Himmler's itinerary, see Center-Moscow, 1372-5-23, f. 434–35. Otto Bradfisch's testimony quoted by Fleming, *Hitler and the Final Solution*, 51. Ralf Ogorreck, *Die Einsatzgruppen und die "Genesis der Endlösung"* (Berlin, 1996), 182–83, drawing on Bradfisch and other testimony, presents Himmler as stating the policy of mass extermination of Jews *for the first time* in Minsk, which is debatable.

40. Breitman, *Architect of Genocide*, 87–88.

41. Bach-Zelewski's testimony of 8 July 1958, Fischer-Schweder Trial, quoted by Ogorreck, *Die Einsatzgruppen*, 182.

42. Breitman, *Architect of Genocide*, 87–88.

43. Bach-Zelewski to Wolff, 23 Aug. 1941, and Wolff to von dem Bach, 17 Sept. 1941; Heckstaller to Engelke, 5 Sept. 1941; all in Bach-Zelewski's SS Personnel File, NA-BDC, A-3343, SSO-023.

44. Declaration von dem Bach, World Jewish Congress Collection, Box C203, Bach-Zelewski Statement 1946, 32–33. For Himmler's itinerary, see Center-Moscow 1372-5-23, f. 433.

45. Police battalions specifically mentioned in the German Police Decodes shortly after the German invasion: Battalions 131, 306, 307, 309, 314, 316, 317, 322, and 507. The British intelligence Summary of German Police Decodes, 3 July–14 Aug. 1941, p. 3, mentions at least fifteen police battalions in the central sector. PRO HW 16/1, part 1.

46. German Police Decodes, 23 Aug. 1941, item 4, NA RG 457, Box 1386. On Himmler's orders, see Kommandosonderbefehl, 28 July 1941, NA RG 242, T-175/R 124/2598661. These orders specifically dealt with the cleansing of swampy regions, but they were applied more broadly.

47. Anklageschrift in der Strafsache gegen Rosenbauer, Besser, Kreuzer, Zentrale Stelle Ludwigsburg (hereafter, ZSL), I 4 Js 1495/65, 2010–11.

48. The file copy of these messages survived. Yad Vashem Archives, Jerusalem, 0-53-128/242-75, cited by Christopher R. Browning, *Ordinary Men: Reserve Police Battalion 101 and the Final Solution in Poland* (New York, 1992), 17, 196, n. 24. The British decoders failed to read the report of killing at Slavuta but got the rest. German Police Decodes, 23 Aug. 1941, item 4; 24 Aug. 1941, item 1, NA RG 457, Box 1386.

49. The British decrypt is not in the file, but the British did get this information at the time, since a 1945 summary of executions and atrocities lists it. GC and CS, Air and Military History, vol. 13, The German Police, NA RG 457, Box 92, p. 235.

50. German Police Decodes, 25 Aug. 1941, item 3, NA RG 457, Box 1386. Browning, *Ordinary Men*, 17, using the file copies of the messages, gave a total

of 1,324 Jews. One source or the other must have transposed the last two numbers.

51. Browning, *Ordinary Men*, 17. The British summary, however, gives the date as 26 Aug. See GC and CS, Air and Military History, vol. 13, The German Police, NA RG 457, Box 92, p. 235.

52. German Police Decodes, 27 Aug. 1941, item 1, NA RG 457, Box 1386.

53. Summary of the 25 Aug. 1941 meeting (written 27 Aug.), in Office of U.S. Chief of Counsel for Prosecution of Axis Criminality, *Nazi Conspiracy and Aggression*, vol. 3 (Washington, D.C., 1946), 210–13. The Supreme Army Command was also informed that Higher SS and Police Leader Jeckeln would deal with the problem of the deported Hungarian Jews. Kriegstagebuch von Roques, 24–25 Aug. 1941, NA RG 242, T-501/R5/000773. I am grateful to Wendy Lower for this reference.

54. Randolph L. Braham, "The Kamenets Podolsk and Délvidék Massacres: Prelude to the Holocaust in Hungary," *Yad Vashem Studies* 9 (1973): 141; Randolph L. Braham, *The Holocaust in Hungary*, vol. 1 (New York, 1994), 207–13.

55. German Police Decodes, 27 Aug. 1941, item 1, NA RG 457, Box 1386; Jeckeln to Kommandostab RFSS, 29 Aug. 1941, Military Archive, Prague, copy in U.S. Holocaust Memorial Museum, RG 48.004M, R 1; German Police Decodes, 30 Aug. 1941, item 1; 31 Aug. 1941, item 1, NA RG 457, Box 1386.

56. Jeckeln to Kommandostab RFSS, 29 Aug. 1941, Military Archive, Prague, RFSS KDO 1A 10909 KR2; Ereignismeldung #80, 11 Sept. 1941, translated copy in *The Einsatzgruppen Reports*, ed. Yitzhak Arad, Shmuel Krakowski, and Shmuel Spector (New York, 1989), 129.

57. Braham, "The Kamenetz Podolsk and Délvidék Massacres," 141–42.

58. German Police Decodes, 2 Sept. 1941, item 2; 6 Sept. 1941, item 2, NA RG 457, Box 1386.

59. German Police Decodes, 2 Sept. 1941, item 17, NA RG 457, Box 1386; Shmuel Spector, "Berdichev," in *Encyclopedia of the Holocaust*, vol. 1, ed. Israel Gutman (New York, 1990), 184. Report of the killing in Operational Situation Report, no. 88, 19 Sept. 1941, cited by Raul Hilberg, *The Destruction of the European Jews* (New York, 1985), vol. 1, 298.

Police Regiment South as a whole executed 4,144 Jews on 4 Sept., and Jeckeln's staff company carried out 1,303 of those executions. That left plenty for the police battalions in the area. See Jeckeln's Funkspruch, 4 Sept. 1941, Bundesarchiv Koblenz R 70/SU 18/1130; Jeckeln's Fernschreiben of 5 Sept. 1941, Military Archive, Prague, copy in U.S. Holocaust Memorial Museum, RG 48.004M, R 1.

60. Spector, "Berdichev," 184. A recent biography of Vasily Grossman has valuable information about Berditschev, but because the authors draw on wartime Soviet investigative reports, they are inaccurate about numbers killed, dates, and the identity of the executioners. See John Garrard and Carol Garrard, *The Bones of Berdichev: The Life and Fate of Vasily Grossman* (New York, 1996), 23–24.

61. German Police Decodes, 6 Sept. 1941, item 2, NA RG 457, Box 1386.
62. Interrogation of Anton Paul, 20 Apr. 1967, ZSL, Ermittlungssache gegen Rosen-bauer et al., ZSL I 4 Js 1495/65. This interrogation is vague about the numbers involved, but Police Battalion 45 must have accounted for some portion of the twenty-eight hundred Jews not executed by Jeckeln's staff company (see n. 59 above).
63. Based on a survey of the testimony of about twenty-five policemen, which appears in ZSL, 1A Js 1495/165.
64. Robert Franz's SS Personnel File, NA-BDC, A-3343, SSO-219.
65. Andrej Angrick, Martina Voigt, Silke Ammerschubert, and Peter Klein, " 'Da hätte man schon ein Tagebuch führen müssen': Das Polizeibatallion 322 und die Judenmorde im Bereich der Heeresgruppe Mitte während des Sommers und Herbstes 1941," in *Die Normalität des Verbrechens: Bilanz und Perspektiven der Forschung zu den nationalsozialistischen Gewaltverbrechen* (Berlin, 1994), 367, n. 1.
66. This is based on the testimony of various surviving members of both Sonderkom-mando 4a and Police Battalion 45. For the former, see the trial materials for Kuno Callsen, ZSL AR-Z 419/62. For the latter, see n. 62 above.
67. Beurteilung, 4 July 1942, Gerhard Riebel's SS Personnel File, NA-BDC, A-3343, SSO-028B.
68. Riebel's Bericht über Judenaktion am 2./3.10.1941, 3 Oct. 1941, Military Archive, Prague, Pol. Rgt. Mitte; copy in the U.S. Holocaust Memorial Museum, RG 48.004M. R 2. On the killings of Jews in Mogilev in general, see Christian Gerlach, "Failure of Plans for an SS Extermination Camp in Mogilev, Belorussia," *Holocaust and Genocide Studies* 11 (1997): 62. Statistics on the number of Jews executed vary slightly.
69. Müller to Einsatzgruppen A, B, C, and D, 30 Aug. 1941, Center-Moscow, 500-1-25, f. 424; copy in U.S. Holocaust Memorial Museum, RG 11.001M, R 183.
70. Heydrich to all Einsatzgruppen, 15 Aug. 1941, Center-Moscow, 500-1-25; copy in U.S. Holocaust Memorial Museum, RG 11.001M, R 183.
71. Sachs to Daluege, Heydrich, Jüttner, and Schmitt, 5 Sept. 1941, copy in Sachs's SS Personnel File, NA-BDC A-3343, SSO-058B. This is the cover letter; I have not been able to locate Sachs's actual report. Text of Daluege's order in German Police Decodes, 13 Sept. 1941, item 12, NA RG 457, Box 1386. Also Polizei-regiment Mitte: Angabe, die nicht in Funksprüche weitergegeben werden dürfen, 16 Sept. 1941, Military Archive, Prague, Pol. Reg. Mitte; copy in U.S. Holocaust Memorial Museum, RG 48.004M, R 2.
72. For some surviving execution reports sent by courier, see U.S. Holocaust Me-morial Museum, RG 48.004M, R 1/101539, 101567, 101613, 101842. I am grateful to Jürgen Matthäus for this reference.
73. Declaration von dem Bach, World Jewish Congress Collection, Box C203, Bach-Zelewski Statement 1946, p. 44, American Jewish Archives.

## 5. TRANSITIONS AND TRANSPORTS

1. Heydrich to Leiter der Stapo(leit)stellen, Kommandeure der Sicherheitspolizei u.d. SD, Leiter der SD- (Leit) Abschnitte, 3 Sept. 1941, U.S. Holocaust Memorial Museum, RG 15.007M, R 33 (Main Commission Warsaw 362/399).

2. Müller to Einsatzgruppen A, B, C, and D, 30 Aug. 1941, Center-Moscow 500-1-25, f. 424; copy in U.S. Holocaust Memorial Museum, RG 11.001M, R 183.

3. The best detailed study of Nazi "euthanasia" is Henry Friedlander, *The Origins of Nazi Genocide* (Chapel Hill, N.C., 1995). See also the good, broader studies by Michael Burleigh, *Death and Deliverance: "Euthanasia" in Germany, 1900–1945* (New York, 1994); and Robert N. Proctor, *Racial Hygiene: Medicine Under the Nazis* (Cambridge, Mass., 1988). For another recent analysis of the political damage from euthanasia and repercussions for the Final Solution, see Götz Aly, *Endlösung: Völkerverschiebung und der Mord an den europäischen Juden* (Frankfurt am Main, 1995), 312–16. For early killings in annexed Polish territory, see Volker Riess, *Die Anfänge der Vernichtung "lebensunwertiges Lebens" in den Reichsgauen Danzig-Westpreussen und Wartheland 1939/40* (Frankfurt am Main, 1995).

   H. G. Adler, *Der verwaltete Mensch: Studien zur Deportation der Juden aus Deutschland* (Tübingen, 1974), 466–67, also stresses the need for secrecy of mass murder as the motive for deportations of German Jews.

4. Philippe Burrin, *Hitler and the Jews: The Genesis of the Holocaust*, trans. Patsy Southgate (London, 1994), 48–50, 121–23, traces Hitler's thinking to uproot German Jews in the event of all-out war at least back to 1935 but dates Hitler's decision to approve deportations and the Final Solution itself at mid-September 1941. The latter is in my view too late. Contrary evidence is presented here and in Richard Breitman, *The Architect of Genocide: Himmler and the Final Solution* (Hanover, N.H., 1992), 152–56.

5. Notizen aus der Besprechung am 10.10.41 über die Lösung von Judenfragen (Prague); copy in U.S. Holocaust Memorial Museum, RG 48.005, R 3.

6. Himmler to Greiser, 18 Sept. 1941, NA RG 242, T-175/R 54/2568695; Notizen aus der Besprechung am 10.10.41, U.S. Holocaust Memorial Museum, RG 48.005, R 3.

7. These discussions and debates went back at least to March 1941; see Breitman, *Architect of Genocide*, 152. On the Aug.–Sept. 1941 discussions involving Goebbels and others, see Peter Witte, "Two Decisions Concerning the Final Solution of the Jewish Question: Deportations to Lodz and Mass Murder at Chelmno," *Holocaust and Genocide Studies* 9 (1995): 320–25. For the competition for Jewish housing, see also Gerhard Botz, *Wohnungspolitik und Judendeportation in Wien 1938 bis 1945: Zur Funktion des Antisemitismus als Ersatz nationalsozialistischer Sozialpolitik* (Vienna, 1975), and Konrad Kwiet, "Von Ghettoisierung zur Deportation," in *Die Juden in Deutschland, 1933–1945: Leben unter nationalsozialistischer Herrschaft*, ed. Wolfgang Benz (Munich, 1988), 639–43.

8. For earlier references to broad plans, see chapter 2. For more details, see Breitman, *Architect of Genocide*, 152–56.
9. Summary of German Police Activities, 24 Mar.–6 Apr. 1940, p. 6, PRO HW 16/3. For more context, see Breitman, *Architect of Genocide*, 98–101.
10. On Himmler's and Heydrich's dealings with the Reich chancellery, see Heydrich to Lammers, 18 Sept. 1941; Ficker's memorandum of 7 Oct. 1941 regarding those with independent power in Poland; and Ficker's memorandum of 25 Oct. 1941 regarding discussions between Lammers and Himmler that left Himmler without a positive resolution; NA RG 242, RG 238, T-1139/R 16/841ff. Breitman, *Architect of Genocide*, 225–27; Aly, *Endlösung*, 177–203, 250–51, 317–18, 350–51.
11. Himmler's agenda notes, 2 Sept. 1941, Center-Moscow, 1372-5-23, f. 425. Himmler's raising this issue with Krüger and Heydrich's order the next day referring to Germany's enemies sowing dissent, as during World War I, suggests that the decision to deport German Jews soon had already been made.
12. Breitman, *Architect of Genocide*, 199.
13. Himmler to Greiser, 18 Sept. 1941, NA RG 242, T-175/R 54/2568695; Heydrich to Himmler, 8 Oct. 1941; Himmler to Übelhör, 9 and 10 Oct. 1941, NA RG 242, T-175/R 54/2568652, 2568662-65; Himmler to Greiser, 11 Oct. 1941, NA RG 242, T-175/R 54/2568650. There is a detailed account of the interactions in Adler, *Verwaltete Mensch*, 172–74. Witte, "Two Decisions," 330–33, sets the decisions about Lodz into a broader context of decision making about Jewish policy, but I do not agree with his argument that Hitler's decision came suddenly in mid-September. See n. 11 above.
14. See above, chapter 2. I had previously written that Poland was the projected site of the Final Solution since early 1941. Based on new evidence presented by Aly, *Endlösung*, 229–79, I would agree that Heydrich must have considered the U.S.S.R. a significant site as well.
15. On the cooperation of various agencies required, see Adler, *Verwaltete Mensch*, 354–465, and Raul Hilberg, *The Destruction of the European Jews* (New York, 1985), vol. 2, 407–16.
16. On 24 Nov. 1941, Himmler informed the State Secretary in the Reich Interior Ministry that all Jewish matters belonged to him. Himmler's agenda notes, 24 Nov. 1941, Center-Moscow, 1372-5-23, f. 360.
17. Notizen aus der Besprechung am 10.10.41, U.S. Holocaust Memorial Museum, RG 48.005, R 3.
18. Daluege to Heydrich, 1 Oct. 1941, and Heydrich to Daluege, 30 Oct. 1941, NA RG 242, T-175/R 123/2648591-615. Daluege naturally disclaimed any jealousy.
19. Himmler's agenda notes, 3 Sept. 1941, Center-Moscow, 1372-5-23, f. 421.
20. Heydrich recognized Daluege's jurisdiction with regard to personnel matters of the HSSPF; see Heydrich to Daluege, 30 Oct. 1941, NA RG 242, T-175/R 123/2648606.
21. Aktennotiz, 20 Nov. 1941, NA RG 242, T-175/R 119/2644961-64.

NOTES 269

22. Summary of German Police Decodes, 1 Oct.–14 Nov. 1941, p. 2, PRO HW 16/6, part 1.
23. Vermerk: Besprechung in Berlin am 23.10.41 . . . , Reichssicherheitshauptamt Verfahren, Berlin 2963/41g (799).
24. Adler, *Verwaltete Mensch*, 177, 363–64, 450–51. Daluege's Schnellbrief, 24 Oct. 1941, International Military Tribunal, *Trial of the Major War Criminals before the International Military Tribunal*, vol. 33 (Nuremberg, 1947), 535–36.
25. Himmler's itinerary, NA RG 242, T-175/R 112/2637705. On events in Mogilev, see Christian Gerlach, "Failure of Plans for an SS Extermination Camp in Mogilev, Belorussia," *Holocaust and Genocide Studies* 11 (1997): 62–64.
26. Himmler's appointment book, 25 Oct. 1941, Center-Moscow, 1372-5-23, f. 389.
27. Breitman, *Architect of Genocide*, 198–201.
28. Ficker's memorandum, 25 Oct. 1941, NA RG 238, T-1139/R 16/84. A month later Heydrich wrote that it was becoming increasingly obvious that Frank was trying to gain control of the Jewish problem in the General Government himself. Heydrich's memo, Endlösung der Judenfrage, 1 Dec. 1941, reprinted by Yehoshua Büchler and analyzed by Büchler and Breitman, "A Preparatory Document for the Wannsee Conference," *Holocaust and Genocide Studies* 9 (1995): 121–29.
29. On Minsk, see chapter 4. Bach-Zelewski may have tried to raise additional funds through expropriation of properties. Himmler had to warn Bach-Zelewski not to make excessive use of his power, backed by a letter from the State Secretary in the Reich chancellery, to seize property in his region; German Police Decodes, 25 Nov. 1941, item 5, PRO HW 16/32.
30. Declaration von dem Bach, World Jewish Congress Collection, Box C203, Bach-Zelewski Statement 1946, p. 23; "Leben eines SS-Generals," *Aufbau*, 6 Sept. 1946, cited by Gerlach, "Failure of Plans," 63.
31. Gerlach, "Failure of Plans," 63; Himmler's appointments, 25 Oct. 1941, Center-Moscow, 1372-5-23, f. 389.
32. This version originally suggested by Aly, *Endlösung*, 342–44, and developed more fully by Gerlach, "Failure of Plans," 61–64, who discusses the mid-November 1941 purchase of a crematorium for Mogilev and Querner's trip there. But the additional information and documentation about Zyklon presented here is new. Leitender Arzt bei Höheren SS und Polizeiführer Riga an SS Oberabschnitt Nordsee, 13 Nov. 1941, German Police Decodes, item 10, PRO HW 16/32. This second document refers to previous letters (and the order of Zyklon) of 1 and 5 Nov.
33. Leitender Arzt bei Höheren SS und Polizeiführer Riga an SS Oberabschnitt Nordsee, 13 Nov. 1941, and Higher SS- und Polizeiführer Ostland an Dessauer Werke für Zyklon und Chemische Zyklon, Dessau, 13 Nov. 1941, German Police Decodes, items 10 and 52, PRO HW 16/32.
34. Jeckeln to Bach-Zelewski, 11 Oct. 1941: "Eintreffe Riga 28.10.41. Bleibe dort einige Tage. Schlage Treffpunkt bei Prützmann"; German Police Decodes, 11 Oct. 1941, item 9, PRO HW 16/32.

35. See n. 33.

36. See Breitman, *Architect of Genocide*, 203.

37. See German Police Decodes, 12 Dec. 1942, items 52–53, PRO HW 16/22.

38. See Gerlach, "Failure of Plans," 63.

39. Hilberg, *Destruction of the European Jews*, vol. 3, 889.

40. Yitzhak Arad, *Belzec, Sobibor, Treblinka: The Operation Reinhard Death Camps* (Bloomington, Ind., 1987), 11; Hans Safrian, *Die Eichmann Männer* (Vienna, 1993), 144–45.

41. Himmler's direct involvement in transferring Magill requested in Jüttner to SS Personnel Main Office, 14 Oct. 1941, Magill's SS Personnel File, NA-BDC, A-3343, SSO-288A. See Magill's Report on the Pripet action, 27 July–11 Aug. 1941, in *Unsere Ehre heisst Treue: Kriegstagebuch des Kommandostabes Reichsführer SS; Tätigkeitsberichte der 1. und 2. Inf. Brigade, der I. SS-Kav. Brigade und vom Sonderkommandos der SS* (Vienna, 1965), 220. Performance appraisal, 28 Oct. 1941, in Magill's SS Personnel File, NA-BDC, A-3343, SSO-288A.

42. Bach-Zelewski's undated appraisal, Magill's SS Personnel File, NA-BDC, A-3343, SSO-288A.

43. German Police Decodes, 11 Dec. 1941, decode #550, PRO HW 16/32.

44. Baubeschreibung, Kriegsgefangenlager [sic] Auschwitz, Military Archive, Prague, OT, Carton 9. I am grateful to Konrad Kwiet for a copy of this document.

45. Gerlach, "Failure of Plans," 65, suggests that gassing experiments in improvised stationary gas chambers were conducted in Mogilev at this time. It now appears that the experiments were extensive and that they involved the use of Zyklon B. On the disadvantages of gas vans, see Breitman, *Architect of Genocide*, 210, 214.

46. Gerlach, "Failure of Plans," 61.

47. German Police Decodes, 28 Nov. 1941, item 36, PRO HW 16/32; Gerlach, "Failure of Plans," 61.

48. Jean-Claude Pressac, *Die Krematorien von Auschwitz* (Munich and Zurich, 1995), 38–41, 64–65, 75, 120.

49. Gerlach, "Failure of Plans," 61.

50. Testimony of Max Eibner, 19 Apr. 1966, Ermittlungsverfahren gegen Sienko (Osnabrück), Zentrale Stelle Ludwigsburg (ZSL) 202 AR-Z 16/67, vol. 4, pp. 66–73. Eibner, however, attributed executions of Jews carried out by the Byelorussian Schutzmannschaften to orders from the SD. That the German gendarmes sometimes killed and directed killing actions is clear from Jürgen Matthäus, "What About the 'Ordinary Men': The German Order Police and the Holocaust in the Occupied Soviet Union," *Holocaust and Genocide Studies* 10 (1996): 134–50, esp. 138–39.

On the total number of Order Police, see Hilberg, *Destruction of the European Jews*. vol. 1, 369. (But Hilberg's relegation of the Order Police to the "second sweep" of the Holocaust is not correct; many participated in the first sweep.)

51. See Vorläufige Wachtvorschrift für die Wache des Ghettos, 20 Nov. 1941, Latvian

State Archives, Riga, 69-1a-19, pp. 30–31. On Jeckeln's staff, see German Police Decodes, 28 Nov. 1941, item 24, NA RG 457, Box 1386.

52. Prützmann to Himmler, 24 Aug. 1941, and Prützmann to Reich Commissar for the Ostland, 24 Aug. 1941, NA RG 242, T-175/R 113/2638876-78. Report by Jäger, head of Einsatzkommando 3, 1 Dec. 1941, Center-Moscow, 500-1-25; copy in U.S. Holocaust Memorial Museum, RG 11.001M, R 1. More generally on the Holocaust in Kowno, see Avraham Tory, *Surviving the Holocaust: The Kowno Ghetto Diary* (Cambridge, 1990). On additional use of municipal police in Kowno, see fragmentary report, n.d. [early 1942], by Einsatzkommando 3, Latvian State Archives, Riga, 1026-1-3; copy in U.S. Holocaust Memorial Museum, RG 18.002M, R 16.

53. Befehl, 3 Oct. 1941, Military Archive, Prague, N Pol. Rgt. 1; also Prützmann to Himmler, Daluege, Heydrich, KDO RFSS, 6 Oct. 1941, Military Archive, Prague, KDO S 1A, copy in U.S. Holocaust Memorial Museum, RG 48.004M, R 2.

54. Report, 24 Nov. 1941, Belarus Central State Archives, Collection 378, Series 1, Folder 698; copy in U.S. Holocaust Memorial Museum, RG 53.002M, R 2.

55. Reports by Commandant in Byelorussia, 8 and 16 Oct. 1941, Belarus Central State Archives, Collection 378, Series 1, Folder 698; copy in U.S. Holocaust Memorial Museum, RG 53.002M, R 2.

56. A late September Einsatzgruppen report mentions 2,278 Jews from the Minsk ghetto executed within three days, with the participation of the Order Police and the support of the military police; see Ereignismeldung UdSSR #92, 23 Sept. 1941, NA RG 242, T-175/R 233/2722555.

57. Higher SS and Police Leader Ostland to Reichkommisar Ostland, 25 Oct. 1941, including report by Reserve Police Battalion 11, covering 14–21 Oct. 1941, Belarus State Archives, Minsk, copy in U.S. Holocaust Memorial Museum, RG 22.001, Folder 18; fragmentary report, n.d. [early 1942], by Einsatzkommando 3, Latvian State Archives, Riga, 1026-1-3.

58. Heinrich Carl to Wilhelm Kube, 30 Oct. 1941, NA RG 238, PS-1104. For a more detailed account, see Christopher R. Browning, *Ordinary Men: Reserve Police Battalion 101 and the Final Solution in Poland* (New York, 1992), 19–23.

59. Report by Commandant in Byelorussia, 10 Nov. 1941, Belarus Central State Archives, Collection 378, Series 2, Folder 698, copy in U.S. Holocaust Memorial Museum, RG 53.002M, R 2; Commandant in Byelorussia Order no. 20, 6 Nov. 1941, Belarus Central State Archives, Minsk, Collection 378, Series 2, Folder 698, copy in U.S. Holocaust Memorial Museum, RG 53.002M, R 2. Also, more generally, see Himmler's order of 6 Nov. 1941, NA RG 242 T-454/R 100/724-30.

60. Shalom Cholawsky, "The Judenrat in Minsk," in *Patterns of Jewish Leadership in Nazi Europe, 1933–1945: Proceedings of the Third Yad Vashem International Historical Conference* (Jerusalem, 1979), 118, 128; Ereignismeldung UdSSR, 1 Dec. 1941, NA RG 242, T-175/R 234/2723329; Hersh Smolar, *The Minsk Ghetto* (New York, 1989), 41–42.

61. Ereignismeldung UdSSR, 5 Jan. 1942, NA RG 238, NO-3257, cited by Adler, *Verwaltete Mensch*, 184.

62. Testimony of Bernhardt Behrendt, 1968, p. 385, RSHA-Verfahren, Berlin.

63. Cholawsky, "The Judenrat," 128.

64. Protokoll über die Hergang der Hauptabteilungs- und Abteilungsleitersitzung am 29 Jan. 1942, Belarus State Archives, Minsk, R 11, Fond 370, Opis 1, Folder 5; copy in U.S. Holocaust Memorial Museum, RG 53.002M, R 11. More generally on Minsk, see Smolar, *Minsk Ghetto*, 73–75, 98–101.

65. Jeckeln to Einsatzstab, Higher SS and Police Leader, South Russia, 23 Oct. 1941, Degenhardt's SS Personnel File, NA-BDC A-3343, SSO-139. Biographical information on Degenhardt and Jeckeln's evaluation of him are also from this file. Degenhardt's later description of his activity in Degenhardt to SS-Oberabschnitt Mitte, 24 Oct. 1942, Degenhardt's SS Personnel File.

66. Interrogation of Jeckeln, 14–15 Dec. 1945, repr. in Helmut Krausnick and Hans-Heinrich Wilhelm, *Die Truppe des Weltanschauungskrieges: Die Einsatzgruppen der Sicherheitspolizei und SD, 1938–1942* (Stuttgart, 1982), 566–69. Captured by the Soviets, Jeckeln admitted during one interrogation that Himmler had briefed him and given him orders beforehand. Jeckeln spoke as if he had not already been Higher SS and Police Leader South; perhaps the Soviets had not yet discovered this or asked him about it. He also incorrectly put the date of his meeting with Himmler as 10 or 11 Nov. and the site as Gestapo headquarters in Berlin. (He was under some stress; the NKVD interrogation lasted until 2:20 a.m.) Himmler's appointment book, however, reveals a meeting with Jeckeln on the evening of 4 Nov. at his East Prussian headquarters; the Jewish question was one of the topics listed. See Himmler's appointments, 4 Nov. 1941, Center-Moscow, 1372-5-23, f. 350.

67. Vermerk, 27 Oct. 1941, YIVO Institute for Jewish Research, New York, Occ E 3-30. Interrogation of Jeckeln, 14–15 Dec. 1945, repr. in Krausnick and Wilhelm, *Die Truppe des Weltanschauungskrieges*, 567; Breitman, *Architect of Genocide*, 215–17.

68. Andrew Ezergailis, *The Holocaust in Latvia, 1941–1944* (Riga, 1996), 247, suggests this.

69. Ezergailis, *Holocaust in Latvia*, 239–40, states that Jeckeln personally selected the site, but Hemicker testified otherwise. Interrogation of Ernst Hemicker, 25 July 1965 and 9 July 1968, ZSL 207 AR-8 21/68. ZSL Rigaverfahren gegen Maywald, et al., 141 Js 534/60 StA Hamburg 207 AR-Z 7/1959.

70. Gesamtaufstellung der im Bereich des Einsatzkommandos 3 bis zum 1. Dezember 1941 durchgeführten Exekutionen, Center-Moscow, 500-1-25, f. 113; Gerald Fleming, *Hitler and the Final Solution* (Berkeley, Calif., 1984), 89; Ezergailis, *Holocaust in Latvia*, 352–54.

71. Ezergailis, *Holocaust in Latvia*, 244, 247–48.

72. Fleming, *Hitler and the Final Solution*, 76–77, 79–80; Ezergailis, *Holocaust in Latvia*, 253.

73. German Police Decodes, 1 Dec. 1941, item 25, PRO HW 16/32.

74. Ezergailis, *Holocaust in Latvia*, 246, 249−54, has a very detailed description.

75. Ibid., 244−45, 254−55. Some Germans who testified later stressed that Latvians alone did the shooting (see Hemicker's testimony in n. 69 above), but this served to avoid incriminating themselves and their former colleagues. See Staatsanwaltschaft bei dem Landgericht Hamburg, Anklageschrift gegen Viktor Bernhard Arajs, 10 May 1976, ZSL 141 Js 534/60, pp. 3553−56.

76. German Police Decodes, 2 Dec. 1941, items 15 and 26, NA RG 457, Box 1386.

77. Lösener Affidavit, 24 Feb. 1948, NA RG 238, T-1139/R 23/796, NG 1944-A; Fleming, *Hitler and the Final Solution*, 80−89.

78. Interrogation of Friedrich Jeckeln, 21 Dec. 1945, repr. in Krausnick and Wilhelm, *Die Truppe des Weltanschauungskrieges*, 548. On the date of the meeting, see German Police Decodes, 1 Dec. 1941, no. 2 Traffic, PRO HW 16/32.

79. See Ezergailis, *Holocaust in Latvia*, 256−61.

80. Hauptmann Salitter, Bericht über die Evakuierung von Juden nach Riga, 26 Dec. 1941; repr. in Adler, *Verwaltete Mensch*, 461−65.

81. Reichskommissar für das Ostland an Höhere SS-und-Polizeiführer Ostland, 3 Dec. 1941, YIVO, Occ 3−33; Memo [by illegible], Riga, 11 Dec. 1941, RSHA-Verfahren, 1Js 1/65, vol. 72, Ostland; Ezergailis, *Holocaust in Latvia*, 356−59. Ezergailis uses the Latvian name Jumpravmuiza, instead of Jungfernhof.

82. Kube to Lohse, 16 Dec. 1941, YIVO Occ 3−36.

83. See Breitman, *Architect of Genocide*, 218.

84. Testimony of Walter Münch, 8 Oct. 1970, Hauptverhandlung, Landes-Gericht für Strafsachen Wien, Strafsache gegen Josef Wendl, 2G Vr 1100/65/Hv 27/70.

85. SS Befehl, 12 Dec. 1941, Latvian State Archives, Riga, P 83-1-80.

86. Himmler's agenda notes, 18 Dec. 1941, Center-Moscow, 1372-5-23, f. 334. In the first published analysis of this meeting and this document, Christian Gerlach, "Die Wannsee-Konferenz, das Schicksal der deutschen Juden und Hitlers politische Grundsatzentscheidung, alle Juden Europas zu ermorden," *Werkstatt Geschichte* 18 (Nov. 1997): 7−44, argues that Hitler made the fundamental decision to murder all the Jews of Europe at this time; earlier killings and deportations were selective. Different scholars, of course, can read a sequence of events and evidence in different ways, and I have presented my own version here. I might also point out that Himmler's notes of many earlier meetings with Hitler did not survive, nor did Himmler's appointments and agenda lists for late June, July, and early August 1941.

## 6. BRITISH RESTRAINT

1. These conclusions emerge inescapably from David Kahn, *Hitler's Spies: German Military Intelligence in World War II* (New York, 1978), esp. 527−29.

2. Robin Denniston, *Churchill's Secret War: Diplomatic Decrypts, the Foreign Office, and Turkey, 1942−44* (New York, 1997), 22 (quote) and 8.

3. Barbara Tuchman, *The Zimmermann Telegram* (New York, 1965); David Kahn, *The Codebreakers: The Story of Secret Writing* (New York, 1967), 282–97.

4. Denniston, *Churchill's Secret War*, 22–24.

5. Christopher Andrew, *Her Majesty's Secret Service: The Making of the British Intelligence Community* (New York, 1987), 450–51; Denniston, *Churchill's Secret War*, 30, 175, n. 47. For the most detail, see Wladyslaw Kozaczuk, *Enigma: How the German Machine Cipher Was Broken, and How It Was Read by the Allies in World War II*, trans. Christopher Kasparek (Lanham, Md., 1984).

6. Andrew, *Her Majesty's Secret Service*, 448–49; Martin Gilbert, *Winston S. Churchill*, vol. 6, *Finest Hour, 1939–1941* (London, 1983), 609–13.

7. See chapter 4 above for a simplified description.

8. History of the German Police Section, 1939–1945 (hereafter, Police Section), PRO HW 3/155. I am grateful to John P. Fox for providing me with a copy of this document.

9. Ibid. Of the 153 days in the first half of 1940 that the cryptographers worked, they succeeded on all but 26 days. See GCCS Report for 1940, dated 31 Jan. 1941, PRO HW 14/11, item 93. I am grateful to John P. Fox for providing me with a copy of this document.

10. Police Section, PRO HW 3/155. F. H. Hinsley et al., *British Intelligence in the Second World War: Its Influence on Strategy and Operations*, vol. 2 (Cambridge, 1981), 670.

11. Police Section, PRO HW 3/155.

12. Ibid. Summaries for 1940 in PRO HW 16/1. There are some surviving transcripts from the early period, winter 1939–40, in PRO HW 16/28 and HW 16/29.

13. Police Section, PRO HW 3/155; GC and CS Report for 1940, PRO HW 14/11, item 93.

14. On the analysts, see Police Summaries, 20 Feb. 1941, PRO HW 16/1. See the undated translation (Dec. 1939) of selective material from Nov. 1939 in PRO HW 16/1; information from German Police Decodes V and VI, 25 Dec. 1939 and 14 Jan. 1940, PRO HW 16/1; and Note on the German SS and Police, with an Appendix of Identifications and Locations, 2 Mar. 1940, PRO HW 16/1.

15. Information from German Police Decodes VII, 28 Jan. 1940, PRO HW 16/1. Christopher R. Browning, *The Path to Genocide: Essays on Launching the Final Solution* (Cambridge, 1992), 10–15.

16. For a sample, see above, chapter 5. For more detail, see Richard Breitman, *The Architect of Genocide: Himmler and the Final Solution* (Hanover, N.H., 1992), 80–82, 92–104, 118–44. For an alternate version, see Browning, *Path to Genocide*, 3–19.

17. Note on the German SS and Police, 2 Mar. 1940, p. 2, PRO HW 16/1.

18. Summary of German Police Decodes 275–323, 21 Aug. 1941, p. 1, PRO HW 16/6, part 1. Police Section, PRO HW 3/155.

19. Summary of German Police Decodes 275–323, 21 Aug. 1941, p. 3, PRO HW 16/6, part 1. Many other examples in PRO HW 16/6.

20. Hinsley's (*British Intelligence*, vol. 2, 671) total of seven reports from the central sector and seventeen reports from the southern sector is incomplete.

21. Summary of German Police Decodes 275–323, 21 Aug. 1941, p. 2, PRO HW 16/6, part 1.

22. Ibid., p. 4.

23. Hinsley, *British Intelligence*, vol. 2, 670; "Files Clear Churchill of Pearl Harbor Cover-up," *The Times* (London), 26 Nov. 1993; David Cesarani, "Secret Churchill Papers Released," *The Journal of Holocaust Education* 4, no. 2 (1995): 225–26.

24. See Gilbert, *Finest Hour*, 1174; Gilbert, *The Holocaust: The Jewish Tragedy* (London, 1986), 186, and "The Most Horrible Crime: Churchill's Prophetic, Passionate and Persistent Response to the Holocaust," *Times Literary Supplement*, 7 June 1996. Quote from *TLS* article.

25. See, for example, Raul Hilberg, *The Destruction of the European Jews* (New York, 1985), vol. 1, 298, 341. Gert Robel, "Sowjetunion," in *Dimensionen des Völkermordes: Die Zahl der jüdischen Opfer des Nationalsozialismus*, ed. Wolfgang Benz (Munich, 1991), 543, has a minimum total of nearly 520,000 killed in the Soviet territories by the Einsatzgruppen and their subdivisions through mid-April 1942.

26. Gilbert, *Holocaust*, 186, and *The Second World War* (London, 1989), 226; John Keegan, "What the Allies Knew," *New York Times*, 25 Nov. 1996, Op-Ed page.

27. The decodes of 4 and 7 Aug. 1941, apparently the latest ones before Churchill's speech of 24 Aug., contained only execution reports from Bach-Zelewski, none from Jeckeln (NA RG 457, Box 1386). See also Cesarani, "Secret Churchill Papers Released," 225–26. Very few messages from Jeckeln were decoded until late August.

28. See above, p. 67.

29. Summary of German Police Decodes 275–323 (3 July–14 Aug. 1941), PRO HW 16/6, part 1; Reports reaching Churchill, PRO HW 1/35 (C 7456). I am grateful to John P. Fox for a copy of this document. Also, Cesarani, "Secret Churchill Papers Released," 225–26.

30. Cesarani, "Secret Churchill Papers Released," 226.

31. Detlef Brandes, *Grossbritannien und seine osteuropäischen Allierten, 1939–1943* (Munich, 1988), 201–2, n. 45. I am grateful to Livia Rothkirchen for this reference. The original message from René (Thümmel) to his Czech underground contact Pavel, 26 July 1941, is in NA RG 242, T-77/R 1050/6526109. The Germans captured these messages in 1943, by which time Thümmel was already jailed. He was executed in 1945.

32. On Thümmel and Czech intelligence, see Frantisek Moravec, *Master of Spies* (London, 1975), quote from 175. Also, Callum MacDonald, *The Killing of SS Obergruppenführer Reinhard Heydrich* (New York, 1989), 54–60, 71, 74–75, 78, 84, 91–93, 113, 125, 145–48; Wesley K. Wark, *The Ultimate Enemy: British Intelligence and Nazi Germany, 1933–1939* (Ithaca, N.Y., 1985), 103; and Nigel West, *MI6: British Secret Intelligence Service Operations, 1909–1945* (New York, 1983), 93. Some

evidence suggests, however, that Thümmel was a double agent, though the British did not recognize this at the time.

33. MacDonald, *Killing*, 78–79.
34. Hinsley, *British Intelligence*, vol. 1, 58.
35. Summary of German Police Decodes 324–343 (3 July–14 Aug. 1941), pp. 1 and 4, PRO HW 16/6, part 1.
36. Ibid., p. 4.
37. Cesarani, "Secret Churchill Papers," 226.
38. Summary of German Police Decodes 344–386 (1–30 Sept. 1941), p. 1, PRO HW 16/6, part 1.
39. Police Section, PRO HW 3/155.
40. Noel Annan, *Changing Enemies: The Defeat and Regeneration of Germany* (London, 1995), 31.
41. Quoted by Patrick Howarth, *Intelligence Chief Extraordinary: The Life of the Ninth Duke of Portland* (London, 1986), 156.
42. Hinsley, *British Intelligence*, vol. 2, 67–68.
43. Summary of German Police Decodes 344–386, 1–30 Sept. 1941, p. 2, PRO HW 16/6, part 1.
44. Ibid., pp. 5–6.
45. On the earlier request by General Heinrich von Stulpnagel, see Hilberg, *Destruction of the European Jews*, vol. 1, 302 and 302, n. 51. General Friderici's approval in German Police Decodes, 30 Oct. 1941, item 6; Jeckeln's approval, German Police Decodes, 30 Oct. 1941, item 37; 19 Nov. 1941, item 32, PRO HW 16/32. British awareness in Summary of German Police Decodes 344–386, 1–30 Sept. 1941, p. 6, PRO HW 16/6, part 1.
46. German Police Decodes, 3 Oct. 1941, items 22 and 23; 4 Oct. 1941, item 20; both PRO HW 16/32.
47. German Police Decodes, 17 Nov. 1941, item 35; 18 Nov. 1941, item 2; both PRO HW 16/32.
48. See Walter Laqueur, *The Terrible Secret: Suppression of the Truth About Hitler's "Final Solution"* (Boston, 1980), 20. One SS soldier or policeman apparently talked to the American military attaché in Berlin. See chapter 8, n. 7.
49. Laqueur, *Terrible Secret*, 68.
50. *Jewish Chronicle*, 24 Oct. and 7 Nov. 1941, cited by Bernard Wasserstein, *Britain and the Jews of Europe, 1939–1945* (Oxford, 1979), 167.
51. Dariusz Stola, "Early News of the Holocaust from Poland," *Holocaust and Genocide Studies* 11 (1997): 4.
52. Laqueur, *Terrible Secret*, 67 and 244, n. 3.
53. Andrew Sharf, *The British Press and Jews under Nazi Rule* (London, 1964), 90–91.
54. See Walter Laqueur and Richard Breitman, *Breaking the Silence: The German Who Exposed the Final Solution* (1986; Hanover, N.H., 1994), 133–38. See also Breitman's videotaped interview with Riegner, 28 Apr. and 11 May 1992, Oral History Collection, U.S. Holocaust Memorial Museum, RG 50.030, nos. 189 and 190.

55. Walter Laqueur's interview with Gerhart Riegner, 30 May 1984; Martin Gilbert, *Auschwitz and the Allies* (New York, 1981), 29.

56. John P. Fox, "The Jewish Factor in British War Crimes Policy in 1942," *English Historical Review* 92 (1977): 87; Richard Bolchover, *British Jewry and the Holocaust* (Cambridge, 1993), 66.

57. Lichtheim to Weizmann, 7 Nov. 1941; repr. in *Archives of the Holocaust: An International Collection of Selected Documents*, vol. 8, *American Jewish Archives, Cincinnati: The Papers of the World Jewish Congress, 1939–1945*, ed. Abraham J. Peck (New York, 1990), 171 (document 45).

58. Postal and Telegraph Censorship Report on Jewry, no. 3, part 1, p. 3, PRO HO 213/953. I am grateful to John P. Fox for a copy of this document. It is possible that the SIS supplied this information and that the "German document" was a disguise. But that would only raise more questions. Where is the decode or intelligence report containing this information? And why didn't the British government alert Polish Jews to the danger in January 1942 through the BBC?

59. Distribution lists appear both on the original German-language decodes and on the British summaries of them. They shift somewhat over time, but I have listed the most frequent recipients.

60. Cited by Wasserstein, *Britain and the Jews*, 164–65.

61. Ibid., 167.

62. Quoted by Tony Kushner, "British Perceptions During the Second World War," in *The Final Solution: Origins and Implementation*, ed. David Cesarani (London, 1994), 251.

63. Charles Cruickshank, *The Fourth Arm: Psychological Warfare, 1938–1945* (London, 1977), 28–33.

64. Ibid., 47–48, 74–76.

65. PRO Foreign Office Papers 371/30900, C 7610, minute by A. David, as quoted by Gilbert, *Auschwitz and the Allies*, 53.

66. Michael Balfour, *Propaganda in War, 1939–1945: Organisations, Policies, and Publics in Britain and Germany* (London, 1979), 299–300.

67. Asa Briggs, *The BBC: The First Fifty Years* (Oxford, 1985), 205–6; Balfour, *Propaganda in War*, 80–102; Cruikshank, *The Fourth Arm*, 101–2.

68. Jean Seaton, "Reporting Atrocities: The BBC and the Holocaust," in *The Media in British Politics*, ed. Jean Seaton and Ben Pimlott (Aldershot, 1987), 164.

69. Jeremy D. Harris, "Broadcasting the Massacres: An Analysis of the BBC's Contemporary Coverage of the Holocaust," *Yad Vashem Studies* 30 (1996): 82–83.

70. Thomas Mann, *Listen, Germany: Twenty-Five Radio Messages to the German People over BBC* (New York, 1943), 50–51, 69–70, 98.

71. BBC Bi-Monthly Survey of European Audiences, Enemy Countries, Germany, Italy, 11 May 1942, p. 2, copy in NA RG 208, Entry 367, Box 255, Folder E 9.2.

72. Ibid., pp. 7–8.

73. Laqueur, *Terrible Secret*, 8–9; Balfour, *Propaganda in War*, 300. Seaton, "Reporting

Atrocities," 158–61, also makes the point that other efforts in the period between the wars to call for political or military action stressed atrocities, for example, in Spain and Ethiopa.

74. Kushner, "British Perceptions," 249–50.

75. Wasserstein, *Britain and the Jews*, 164–66.

76. See Kushner, "British Perceptions," 251, and more generally, his *The Holocaust and the Liberal Imagination: A Social and Cultural History* (Oxford, 1994), 127. Wasserstein, *Britain and the Jews*, 163.

77. Gerhard L. Weinberg, *A World at Arms: A Global History of World War II* (New York, 1994), 348, 350–51. More generally, Ronald W. Zweig, *Britain and Palestine During the Second World War* (Woodbridge, 1986).

78. Richard Breitman, "The Allied War Effort and the Jews, 1942–43," *Journal of Contemporary History* (1985): 135–57.

79. Gilbert, "The Most Horrible Crime," is opposed by Michael J. Cohen, *Churchill and the Jews* (London, 1985). The latter makes some valid points, but within the British political context Churchill still comes off as sympathetic to Jewish aspirations in Palestine.

80. "President Flays Hostage Killings," *New York Times*, 26 Oct. 1941, 1. John P. Fox, "British Intelligence Documents on *Einsatzgruppen* Operations, 1941–42: Their Historical Significance and Current Status in British and American Archives," 15–16 (unpublished paper presented at a conference at Berlin-Strausberg, Ursprünge and Anfänge von Nachrichtendienst-Organisationen, 2–4 May 1997), also quotes Churchill's statement, emphasizing the passage about events in Soviet territory.

81. "President Flays Hostage Killings," *New York Times*, 26 Oct. 1941.

82. Gilbert, *The Holocaust*, 231.

83. Fox, "The Jewish Factor," 86–87.

84. Prime Minister's Draft reply, Foreign Office papers 371/30916 (C 6108), as cited and summarized by Gilbert, *Auschwitz and the Allies*, 50.

85. Aide-mémoire given by the British ambassador to the United States to Secretary of State Hull, 18 July 1940, NA RG 59, Central Decimal File 840.48/3995.

86. Annan, *Changing Enemies*, 13.

87. William Millward, "Life in and out of Hut 3," in *The Codebreakers*, ed. F. H. Hinsley and Alan Stripp (Oxford, 1993), 21, 28; Bradley F. Smith, "Anglo-Soviet Intelligence and the Cold War," in *British Intelligence, Strategy and the Cold War*, ed. Richard J. Aldrich (London, 1992), 55–57.

88. Summary of German Police Decodes 344–386 (1–30 Sept. 1941), p. 1; Summary of German Police Decodes 384–459 (November 1941), p. 1; both in PRO HW 16/6, part 1. Quote from former.

## 7. AUSCHWITZ PARTIALLY DECODED

1. Summary of German Police Decodes 530–575, 16 Dec. 1941–15 Jan. 1942, pp. 1–4; Summary of German Police Decodes 576–648, 16 Jan. 1942–15 Feb. 1942, p. 4; both in PRO HW 16/6, part 1.

2. Summary of German Police Decodes 640–695, 16 Feb.–15 March 1942, p. 6, PRO HW 16/6, part 1.

3. For example, in Operation Karlsbad, 546 were killed in battle and another 471 "finished off"; in Operation Hornung, at least 1,124 were given "special treatment"; German Police Decodes, 25 Oct. 1942, item 18, and 19 Feb. 1943, item 13, PRO HW 16/36 and 16/37, respectively. Also Summary of German Police Decodes 576–648, p. 6, 16 Jan.–15 Feb. 1942, PRO HW 16/6, part 1.

4. German Police Decodes, 10 Mar. 1942, item 20, PRO HW 16/46.

5. Grawitz to Himmler, 4 Mar. 1942, NA RG 238, NO-600, quoted also in Raul Hilberg, *The Destruction of the European Jews* (New York, 1985), vol. 1, 328. See various related letters from Dr. Grawitz to Himmler in early 1942, Bach-Zelewski's SS Personnel File, NA-BDC, A-3343, SSO-023.

6. Summary of German Police Decodes 384–459, 1 Oct.–14 Nov. 1941, p. 2, and Summary of German Police Decodes 640–695, 16 Feb.–15 Mar. 1942, p. 2; both in PRO HW 16/6, part 1.

7. On the gas vans, drawing on a report by Einsatzgruppe B, see Christian Gerlach, "Failure of Plans for an SS Extermination Camp in Mogilev, Belorussia," *Holocaust and Genocide Studies* 11 (1997): 68.

8. German Police Decodes, 10 Mar. 1942, item 6, PRO HW 16/46.

9. Hilberg, *Destruction of the European Jews*, vol. 1, 368–90.

10. Himmler to Bach-Zelewski's office, 19 Mar. 1942, German Police Decodes, PRIT signals, 1–300, PRO HW 16/54; Gerald Fleming, *Hitler and the Final Solution* (Berkeley, Calif., 1984), 135–39.

11. German Police Decodes, 24 July 1942, PRIT signals 301–579, PRO HW 16/55.

12. On the handling of Soviet prisoners of war, see Christian Streit, *Keine Kameraden: Die Wehrmacht und die Soujetischen Kriegsgefangenen, 1941–1945* (Stuttgart, 1978). For Nazi policy on Jewish labor, see Ulrich Herbert, "Labor and Extermination: Economic Interest and the Primacy of Weltanschauung in National Socialism," *Past and Present* 138 (Feb. 1993): 166–67. On the conscription of foreign labor generally, see Ulrich Herbert, *Hitler's Foreign Workers: Enforced Foreign Labor in Germany under the Third Reich* (Cambridge, 1997).

13. Christopher R. Browning, "A Final Hitler Decision for the 'Final Solution'? The Riegner Telegram Reconsidered," *Holocaust and Genocide Studies* 10 (1996): 5–6.

14. Summary of German Police Decodes 530–575, 16 Dec. 1941–15 Jan. 1942, p. 11; Summary of German Police Decodes 640–695, 16 Feb.–15 Mar. 1942, p. 9; both in PRO HW 16/6, part 1. Jewish labor was also used for the huge

Durchgangstrasse IV project in the south, but that was apparently not tied to an order from Hitler.

15. See Hilberg, *Destruction of the European Jews*, vol. 2, 524–25. On the use of Jewish labor generally in Germany, see Wolf Gruner, *Der geschlossene Arbeitseinsatz deutscher Juden: Zur Zwangsarbeit als Element der Verfolgung 1938–1943* (Berlin, 1997).

16. German Police Decodes, 7 Oct. 1942, items 1–4, PRO HW 16/21.

17. Gerlach, "Failure of Plans," 61–69.

18. Shalom Cholawski, "Maly Trostinets," in *Encyclopedia of the Holocaust*, vol. 3, ed. Israel Gutman (New York, 1990), 940–41. Also, Paul Kohl, *Ich wundere mich, dass ich noch lebe: Sowjetische Augenzeugen berichten* (Gütersloh, 1990), 91–96.

19. See Yitzhak Arad, *Belzec, Sobibor, Treblinka: The Operation Reinhard Death Camps* (Bloomington, Ind., 1987), esp. 23.

20. For a brief treatment, see Richard Breitman, *The Architect of Genocide: Himmler and the Final Solution* (Hanover, N.H., 1992), 225–28, 235.

21. See F. H. Hinsley et al., *British Intelligence in the Second World War: Its Influence on Strategy and Operations*, vol. 2 (Cambridge, 1981), 669.

22. The addressee(s) is/are missing in the decode. The sender was Liebehenschel of the WVHA.

23. German Police Decodes, no. 3 Traffic, 11 June 1942, item 8, PRO HW 16/19.

24. German Police Decodes, 24 Aug. 1942, items 55–56 and 64–65, PRO HW 16/19.

25. German Police Decodes, 24 Aug. 1942, items 47–48, PRO HW 16/19; German Police Decodes, 22 Oct. 1942, items 35–36, PRO HW 16/21.

26. Grothmann to Globocnik, 7 Sept. 1942, and Grothmann to Jüttner, 8 Sept. 1942, NA RG 242, T-175/R 113/2638863 and 2638749.

27. See Peter Hayes, *Industry and Ideology: I. G. Farben in the Nazi Era* (Cambridge, 1987), 347–67. Also Benjamin B. Ferencz, *Less Than Slaves: Jewish Forced Labor and the Quest for Compensation* (Cambridge, Mass., 1979), 26–28.

28. German Police Decodes, 5 June 1942, items 5–6, PRO HW 16/19.

29. German Police Decodes, 17 June 1942, item 16, PRO HW 16/19.

30. Yehoshoa R. Büchler, "First in the Vale of Affliction: Slovakian Jewish Women in Auschwitz, 1942," *Holocaust and Genocide Studies* 10 (1996): 307.

31. German Police Decodes, 18 Nov. 1942, item 2, PRO HW 16/22. Primo Levi, *Survival at Auschwitz*, trans. Stuart Woolf (1958; New York, 1996).

32. German Police Decodes, 4 June 1942, item 10, PRO HW 16/19. On Kammler's role in SS construction projects, see Michael Thad Allen, "The Banality of Evil Reconsidered: SS Mid-Level Managers of Extermination Through Work," *Central European History* 30 (1997): 287–92.

33. Jean-Claude Pressac, *Die Krematorien von Auschwitz* (Munich and Zurich, 1995), has the most detailed treatment of construction at the extermination camp but is unreliable on policy decisions as well as some dates. Pressac and Robert-Jan van

Pelt, "The Machinery of Mass Murder at Auschwitz," in *Anatomy of the Auschwitz Death Camp*, ed. Yisrael Gutman and Michael Berenbaum (Bloomington, Ind., 1994), 183–245.

34. Höss was summoned to a private meeting with Kammler and to a general meeting with all camp commanders led by Oswald Pohl on 25 June 1942, German Police Decodes, 18 June 1942, items 17–18, and 24 June 1942, item 32, PRO HW 16/19.

35. Browning, "A Final Hitler Decision," 5–6.

36. Breitman, *Architect of Genocide*, 236–38.

37. German Police Decodes, 20 Nov. 1942, items 38–39, PRO HW 16/22.

38. German Police Decodes, 14 Jan. 1943, items 13–16, PRO HW 16/23.

39. The data from the first months were decoded only in May 1942. By June, the decodes were almost contemporaneous with the radio reports. See the markings at the top of the data sheets in PRO HW 16/10. Auschwitz was designated as F. The British noted the death totals in hand on some of the data sheets and also highlighted some of the death totals in a summary of 26 Sept. 1942, PRO HW 16/6, part 2.

40. The tables of numbers are in PRO HW 16/10.

41. See ref. nr. 2325, 17 Aug. 1940, PRO HW 14/6, which mentions that Colonel Tiltman recently broke the railway ciphers. On the MEW, see Walter Laqueur, *The Terrible Secret: Suppression of the Truth About Hitler's "Final Solution"* (Boston, 1980), 85–86; Hinsley, *British Intelligence*, vol. 1, 357–58.

42. German Police Decodes, 16 July 1942, items 40–41, PRO HW 16/20; German Police Decodes, 7 Oct. 1942, items 1–4, PRO HW 16/21.

43. Laqueur, *Terrible Secret*, 86, suggests that some intelligence files were destroyed.

44. Laqueur, *Terrible Secret*, 238; Chciuk-Celt to Laqueur, 8 Oct. 1979; Chciuk-Celt to Breitman, 24 Feb. 1995.

45. David Engel, *In the Shadow of Auschwitz: The Polish Government-in-Exile and the Jews, 1939–1942* (Chapel Hill, N.C., 1987), 201.

46. Cable from N. [Korbonski], 23 Mar. 1943, for the Polish radio station SWIT, cited by David Engel, *Facing a Holocaust: The Polish Government-in-Exile and the Jews, 1943–1945* (Chapel Hill, N.C., 1993), 231, n. 122.

47. Nazi Black Record, NA RG 165, Box 3138, Poland 6950, from *Poland Fights*, no. 35, 5 Apr. 1943.

48. The courier is tentatively identified as Jerzy Salski by Engel, *Facing a Holocaust*, 209, n. 109. But neither the Polish Underground Movement Study Trust nor Tadeusz Chciuk-Celt, himself an underground courier, was able to provide an identification. I am grateful to both for their assistance.

    The courier said at the outset that he stayed from November 1941 until early December 1942, but his detailed comments about his itinerary contradict his dating. Censorship Report, 5 May 1943, NA RG 226, Entry 191, Box 3, untitled folder.

49. A portion of the document is also quoted by Martin Gilbert, *Auschwitz and the Allies* (New York, 1981), 130.

50. Schwarzbart to Representation of Polish Jews, World Jewish Congress, 27 Apr. 1943, Schwarzbart Papers, M2 535, Yad Vashem. I am grateful to Shlomo Aronson for sending me a copy of this cover letter. For the full document, see Censorship Report, 5 May 1943, NA RG 226, Entry 191, Box 3, untitled folder.

51. Gilbert, *Auschwitz and the Allies*, 130.

52. 18 May 1943, NA RG 218, Joint Chiefs of Staff CCS 334, Polish Liaison (Washington), Folder 3.0.

53. Cover note from Josef Zaranski, counsellor of the Polish embassy, to Randall [British Foreign Office], 18 May 1943, with memo, Extermination of the Jews of Poland, PRO FO 371/34550 (5628/34/55).

54. Gerhard L. Weinberg, *A World at Arms: A Global History of World War II* (New York, 1994), 107 and 964, n. 232.

55. Roger Allen Minute, 27 Aug. 1943, and V. Cavendish-Bentinck Minute, 27 Aug. 1943, PRO FO 371/34551. I am grateful to Stephen Tyas for a copy of this document.

56. Engel, *In the Shadow of Auschwitz*, 184, 304–5, n. 195; Richard Breitman and Alan M. Kraut, *American Refugee Policy and European Jewry, 1933–1945* (Bloomington, Ind., 1987), 152 (on the use of corpses for fat).

57. PRO FO 371/34551.

58. Military Attaché (London) Report 907, 17 Mar. 1944, NA RG 165, Box 3138, Poland 6950. Also F. W. Belin to William L. Langer, 10 April 1944, NA RG 226, Entry 16, 66059. Engel, *Facing a Holocaust*, 287, n. 121, mentions a 15 Sept. 1943 cable from Wanda about Birkenau.

59. Gilbert, *Auschwitz and the Allies*, esp. 339–40.

60. Gilbert discusses Vrba and Wetzler and the repercussions of their report in *Auschwitz and the Allies*, 192–206, 231–61. For Vrba's account, see Rudolf Vrba and Alan Bestic, *I Cannot Forgive* (New York, 1964). See also the recent, though tendentious, updating by Vrba, "Die missachtete Warnung: Betrachtungen über den Auschwitz-Bericht, 1944," *Vierteljahrshefte für Zeitgeschichte* 44 (1996): 1–24.

61. Gilbert, *Auschwitz and the Allies*, 340.

## 8. AMERICAN ASSESSMENTS

1. David S. Wyman, *The Abandonment of the Jews: America and the Holocaust, 1941–1945* (New York, 1984), 20. On the Yiddish press and the Jewish Telegraphic Agency, see Haskel Lookstein, *Were We Our Brothers' Keepers?* (New York, 1985), esp. 25–26.

2. Deborah E. Lipstadt, *Beyond Belief: The American Press and the Coming of the Holocaust, 1933–1945* (New York, 1986), 150–51.

3. Ibid., 155–56.

4. Morris to Secretary of State, 30 Sept. 1941, NA RG 59, CDF 862.4016/2204; Morris to Secretary of State, 14 Oct. 1941, NA RG 59, CDF 862.4016/2205; Morris to Secretary of State, 16 Nov. 1941, NA RG 59, CDF 862.4016/2212; all in LM 193, R 58.

5. Morris to Secretary of State, 18 Oct. 1941, NA RG 59, CDF 862.4016/2206, LM 193, R 58.

6. Morris to Secretary of State, 20 Oct. 1941, NA RG 59, CDF 862.4016/2207, LM 193, R 58; Morris to Secretary of State, 16 Nov. 1941, RG 59, CDF 862.4016/2212, LM 193, R 58.

7. Military Attaché, Berlin, 10 Nov. 1941, copy in NA RG 165, Entry 77, Box 1079, Germany 3500 Jews.

8. Morris to Secretary of State, 16 Nov. 1941, NA RG 59, CDF 862.4016/2212, LM 193, R 58.

9. Summarized in Morris to Secretary of State, 16 Nov. 1941, NA RG 59, CDF 862.4016/2212.

10. See above, chapter 5.

11. John V.H. Dippel, *Two Against Hitler: Stealing the Nazis' Best-Kept Secrets* (New York, 1992), 68–69.

12. Study of War Propaganda, 6 Mar. 1942, p. 20, NA RG 165, Entry 77, Box 1074, Military Intelligence Division, Regional File, Germany 2910–2950.

13. David Bankier, *The Germans and the Final Solution: Public Opinion under Nazism* (Oxford, 1992), 4–9.

14. Study of War Propaganda, Sub-Annex 3, pp. 2, 7.

15. Study of War Propaganda, Sub-Annex 4, p. 10.

16. Study of War Propaganda, Sub-Annex 8, pp. 6, 15. For the diplomat's account, see Morris to Secretary of State, 30 Sept. 1941, NA RG 59, CDF 862.4016/2204, LM 193, R 58.

17. Study of War Propaganda, Sub-Annex 11, unpaginated.

18. Study of War Propaganda, Sub-Annex 12, p. 8.

19. Study of War Propaganda, Sub-Annex 13, p. 10.

20. Study of War Propaganda, pp. 14, 21.

21. Study of War Propaganda, Sub-Annex 7, p. 2.

22. Despatch of 16 Mar. 1942, British Censorship Copy in NA RG 165, Entry 77, Box 1079, Germany 3500 Jews; Wyman, *Abandonment of the Jews*, 20.

23. Lipstadt, *Beyond Belief*, 159–60.

24. Louis P. Lochner, *What About Germany?* (New York, 1942), 238–57. But in a Sept. 1942 radio interview, Lochner told a story he had heard from a rabbi: of eight hundred Jews taken out of Berlin and sent to a concentration camp, five hundred were dead within two weeks. See Joyce Fine, "American Radio Coverage of the Holocaust," *Simon Wiesenthal Center Annual* 5 (1988): 158.

25. *New York Journal American*, 1 June 1942, p. 3, quoted by Lipstadt, *Beyond Belief*, 160.

26. Dariusz Stola, "Early News of the Holocaust from Poland," *Holocaust and Genocide Studies* 11 (1997): 6. For the text of the Bund's report, see Yehuda Bauer, "When Did They Know?" *Midstream*, April 1968.

27. Stola, "Early News of the Holocaust," 6; Martin Gilbert, *Auschwitz and the Allies* (New York, 1981), 43.

28. Stola, "Early News of the Holocaust," 7; Gilbert, *Auschwitz and the Allies*, 43–44; Lipstadt, *Beyond Belief*, 163–64.

29. Quoted by Stola, "Early News of the Holocaust," 8.

30. Lipstadt, *Beyond Belief*, 162–65, contrasts the British and American reactions. See also, Wyman, *Abandonment of the Jews*, 22–23.

31. Fine, "American Radio Coverage," 157.

32. Among the factors supporting this identification: Mayer was then in Lisbon on his way to Switzerland; the same person wrote two follow-up reports on the subject listed as coming from the German frontier; and the report was apparently written by a practiced journalist. There are some other technical clues in the documents.

33. Confidential, 28 June 1942, NA RG 226, Entry 16, 26896.

34. The second report by the same author (Mayer?) came from Lisbon in September 1942 but dealt with the refugee problem there. The third report, dated 7 Nov. 1942, was the follow-up to the report of 28 June (see n. 33 above). For the third report, see NA RG 165, Entry 77, Box 1079, Germany 3500 Jews.

35. Michael Marrus and Robert Paxton, *Vichy France and the Jews* (New York, 1983), 220–79. Wyman, *Abandonment of the Jews*, 30–40, makes the point that the condition of Jews in France and the deportations from France were better reported than any other aspect of the Holocaust. The most detailed study of the deportations from France is Serge Klarsfeld, *Vichy-Auschwitz: Die Zusammenarbeit der deutschen und französischen Behörden bei der "Endlösung der Judenfrage" in Frankreich* (Nördlingen, 1989).

36. Tuck to Secretary of State, 26 Aug. 1942, 11 Sept. 1942, *Foreign Relations of the United States: Diplomatic Papers, 1942* (hereafter, *FRUS*), vol. 2 (Washington, D.C., 1962), 710–13; Breckinridge Long Diary, 12 Sept. 1942, Box 5, Library of Congress. The plan to take Jewish children into the United States failed for other reasons. For the general context, see Richard Breitman and Alan M. Kraut, *American Refugee Policy and European Jewry, 1933–1945* (Bloomington, Ind., 1987), 162–64.

37. Dulles to Donovan, 22 May 1942; Donovan to Wilson, 27 May 1942, NA RG 226, Entry 144, Box 8, Folder 63; Dulles to McDonald, 24 Sept. 1942, James G. McDonald Papers, General Correspondence: Dulles Folder G 113, Columbia University School of International Affairs, New York.

38. On the background and formation of the Office of War Information and OFF, see Clayton R. Laurie, *The Propaganda Warriors: America's Crusade Against Nazi Germany* (Lawrence, Kans., 1996), 64. Also, on the Office of War Information generally, see Allan M. Winkler, *The Politics of Propaganda: The Office of War Information, 1942–1945* (New Haven, Conn., 1978).

39. Bingham to MacLeish, 19 June 1942, summarizing discussions on 30 Apr. and 8 May, NA RG 208, Entry 3, Box 12, War Crimes 1942–44.

40. Ibid.

41. Huse to MacLeish and Bingham, 2 July 1942, NA RG 208, Entry 1, Box 2, Meetings-1-Interdepartmental, June–July 1942.

42. Sweetser to Davis regarding Atrocities Statement by Berle, 29 July 1942, NA RG 208, Entry 4, Box 12, War Crimes, Atrocities, Various Agencies, 1942–44.

43. "Nazi Punishment Seen by Roosevelt," *New York Times*, 22 July 1942.

44. Ibid.

45. Charles Cruickshank, *The Fourth Arm: Psychological Warfare, 1938–1945* (London, 1977), 38. Minutes of the Joint Committee on Information Policy, 1 Sept. 1942, NA RG 208, Entry 1, Box 5, Policies and Procedures-3, Joint Committee on Information Policy, 1942–43.

46. Minutes of 2 Sept. 1942, NA RG 208, Entry 1, Box 2, Meetings-4, Committee on War Information Policy, July–Dec. 1942.

47. Edgar Ansel Mowrer, *Triumph and Turmoil: A Personal History of Our Times* (New York, 1968), 331–34.

48. OWI Overseas Branch, Confidential Central Directive, week of 10–16 Oct. 1942, p. 3, NA RG 208, Entry 359, Box 818, Folder Record Central Directives 1942.

49. Jewish Telegraphic Agency Memorandum, 7 Dec. 1942, American Jewish Committee Archives (now at YIVO), RG 1, EXO-29, JTA Overseas News Agency Folder 1940–43.

50. Breitman and Kraut, *American Refugee Policy*, 171–72; Fine, "American Radio Coverage," 157–58.


## 9.  BREAKTHROUGH IN THE WEST

1. Walter Laqueur and Richard Breitman, *Breaking the Silence: The German Who Exposed the Final Solution* (1986; Hanover, N.H., 1994); E. Thomas Wood and Stanislaw M. Jankowski, *Karski: How One Man Tried to Stop the Holocaust* (New York, 1994).

2. Laqueur and Breitman, *Breaking the Silence*, 115–24.

3. Martin Gilbert, *Auschwitz and the Allies* (New York, 1981), 56, and Monty N. Penkower, *The Jews Were Expendable: Free World Diplomacy and the Holocaust* (Urbana, Ill., 1983), 59–62, both draw on loose recollections by Haim Pazner that Arthur Sommer provided the first information about the Final Solution, which Pazner himself had a role in transmitting to the West. It is clear that Sommer, another anti-Nazi German and an economist with access to good information, passed on information during visits to Switzerland, but no one has yet uncovered evidence in the archives that it reached the West, let alone that it preceded Schulte's. See Laqueur and Breitman, *Breaking the Silence*, 3–4. In a lecture in Jerusalem on 14 May 1991 and in the *Jerusalem Post* on 21 June 1991, Gilbert continued to credit Pazner with helping to pass the first report of the Final Solution to the West.

Riegner, who met Schulte later during the war and promised to keep his identity secret, maintained his promise for four decades. Schulte's identity as the mysterious German industrialist became known in 1983, and Walter Laqueur and I published the relevant documents in 1986. After other scholars continued to dispute the fact that he was Riegner's source, Riegner was moved to write, in a 12 July 1991 letter to the *Jerusalem Post*: "As serious historical research . . . has now established beyond any doubt, the source was a German industrialist, Eduard Schulte, whose role in the discovery of the 'Final Solution' was recognized by Yad Vashem, which honored him as 'righteous among nations.' " Riegner has stated repeatedly that Pazner had nothing to do with the transmission of this information.

In *Jews for Sale: Nazi Jewish Negotiations, 1933–1945* (New Haven, Conn., 1994), 79 and 269, n. 49, Yehuda Bauer charges that Riegner's telegram based on Schulte's information is usually and wrongly considered the first definitive evidence of the Final Solution to reach the West. The problem for Bauer is that Schulte did not report the beginning of the Final Solution and that the Riegner telegram contained a disclaimer that the information could not be confirmed.

4. Christopher R. Browning, "A Final Hitler Decision for the 'Final Solution'? The Riegner Telegram Reconsidered," *Holocaust and Genocide Studies* 10 (1996): 5–8, quote from 8.

5. Laqueur and Breitman, *Breaking the Silence*, 124–48.

6. Ibid., 149.

7. Richard Breitman and Alan M. Kraut, *American Refugee Policy and European Jewry, 1933–1945* (Bloomington, Ind., 1987), 149–50; Saul S. Friedman, *No Haven for the Oppressed: United States Policy Toward Jewish Refugees, 1938–1945* (Detroit, 1977), 131.

8. Norton (Berne) to Foreign Office containing message from Riegner to Silverman, 10 Aug. 1942, and Robert's Minute dated 15 Aug. 1942, PRO FO 371/30917 (C 7853/61/18), cited and quoted by Bernard Wasserstein, *Britain and the Jews of Europe, 1939–1945* (Oxford, 1979), 168. See also, John P. Fox, "The Jewish Factor in British War Crimes Policy in 1942," *English Historical Review* 92 (1977), 92–94.

9. See chapter 7 above.

10. David Engel, *In the Shadow of Auschwitz: The Polish Government-in-Exile and the Jews, 1939–1942* (Chapel Hill, N.C., 1987), 180–82, 299, n. 127. For more details on the Bund's report, see chapter 8 above.

11. Jeremy D. Harris, "Broadcasting the Massacres: An Analysis of the BBC's Contemporary Coverage of the Holocaust," *Yad Vashem Studies* 25 (1996): 72.

12. Ibid., 66, 73–74.

13. In addition, see chapter 8 above. On the British press, see Andrew Scharf, *The British Press and Jews under Nazi Rule* (London, 1964), 91.

14. The lobbying efforts and British government responses were summarized in A. J.

Drexell Biddle, Jr., to Secretary of State, 13 Aug. 1942, NA RG 59, CDF 740.00116 E. W. 1939/527.

15. Engel, *In the Shadow of Auschwitz*, 182 and 299, n. 133.

16. Biddle to Secretary of State, 13 Aug. 1942, NA RG 59, CDF 740.00116 E. W. 1939/527; F. K. Roberts Minute, 6 Aug. 1942, PRO FO 371/30917/60 (C7794/61/18), cited by Wasserstein, *Britain and the Jews*, 306.

17. D. Allen Minute, 10 Sept. 1942, quoted by Wasserstein, *Britain and the Jews*, 169.

18. *The Complete Presidential Press Conferences of FDR* (New York, 1979), vols. 19–20, no. 842.

19. Breitman and Kraut, *American Refugee Policy*, 152; David S. Wyman, *Abandonment of the Jews: America and the Holocaust, 1941–1945* (New York, 1984), 45; Penkower, *Jews Were Expendable*, 67–68; Henry L. Feingold, *The Politics of Rescue: The Roosevelt Administration and the Holocaust* (New Brunswick, N.J., 1970), 169–70.

20. See, for example, Joseph Friedenson and David Kranzler, *Heroine of Rescue: The Incredible Story of Recha Sternbuch Who Saved Thousands from the Holocaust* (Brooklyn, 1984), 87: "What did Wise do after receiving the Riegner cable? Almost nothing He did not contact President Roosevelt; he did not call a press conference to alert the public; and he did not mobilize anyone for action. He referred its contents to the State Department and nothing more."

21. Wise to Frankfurter, 4 Sept. 1942, repr. in *Stephen S. Wise: Servant of the People; Selected Letters*, ed. Carl Hermann Voss (Philadelphia, 1969), 248–49.

22. Breitman and Kraut, *American Refugee Policy*, 152–53; Penkower, *Jews Were Expendable*, 68–69.

23. Wise to Frankfurter, 16 Sept. 1942, repr. in *Stephen S. Wise*, 250–51. More than a year later, Morgenthau recalled this meeting in Minutes of Meeting on Argentina, Jewish Evacuation, 31 Dec. 1943, Morgenthau Diaries, vol. 688, part 2, Franklin D. Roosevelt Library, Hyde Park, N.Y.

24. Wise to Frankfurter, 16 Sept. 1942, repr. in *Stephen S. Wise*, 250–51.

25. Wise to Perlzweig, 17 Sept. 1942, Stephen S. Wise Papers, Box 92, American Jewish Historical Society, Waltham, Mass.

26. Cox to Ciechanowski, 14 Sept. 1942, and Ciechanowski to Cox, 16 Sept. 1942, Oscar Cox Papers, Box 6, Franklin D. Roosevelt Library, Hyde Park, N.Y.

27. Breitman and Kraut, *American Refugee Policy*, 153–57; Wyman, *Abandonment of the Jews*, 47–51. Wyman, however, maintains that Welles showed little energy.

28. William J. vanden Heuvel, "The Holocaust Was No Secret," *New York Times Magazine*, 22 Dec. 1996. Compare the parallel but less extreme formulation by John Keegan, *The Second World War* (New York, 1989), 289: "For the removal and transportation of Europe's Jews was a fact known to every inhabitant of the continent between 1942 and 1945."

29. Wasserstein, *Britain and the Jews*, 169.

30. Cavendish-Bentinck to Cadogan, 8 Oct. 1942, and "C" to de Grey, 14 Oct.

1942, PRO HW 14/54. I am grateful to John P. Fox for providing me with a copy of this document.

31. See epilogue below.

32. Breitman and Kraut, *American Refugee Policy*, 153–54. Also, Wise to Frankfurter, 9 Oct. 1942, Stephen S. Wise Papers, Box 109, Correspondence-Zionism, American Jewish Historical Society.

33. Breitman and Kraut, *American Refugee Policy*, 157; Wyman, *Abandonment of the Jews*, 51, 61. For a detailed discussion of the press coverage, see Deborah E. Lipstadt, *Beyond Belief: The American Press and the Coming of the Holocaust, 1933–1945* (New York, 1986), 180–83.

34. Wood and Jankowski, *Karski*, 135–43; Engel, *In the Shadow of Auschwitz*, 198. Engel gives 25 Nov. as the date when the Polish government-in-exile broke its official silence about the deportations from Warsaw.

35. Law's Memorandum of 26 Nov. 1942, PRO FO 371/30923 (C 11923/61/18). I am grateful to John P. Fox for a copy of this document.

36. Winant to Secretary of State, 7 Dec. 1942, NA RG 59, CDF 740.00116 E. W. 1939/660; Wasserstein, *Britain and the Jews*, 170–71.

37. David Engel, "Jan Karski's Mission to the West, 1942–44," *Holocaust and Genocide Studies* 5, no. 4 (1990): esp. 363–65, incorrectly maintains both that there is no contemporary written account of what Karski reported about Nazi persecution of Jews and that Karski failed to report promptly to Jewish officials his version of what he saw in Warsaw and near Belzec. Engel has, however, exposed some inaccuracies in accounts later reconstructed by Karski.

38. Wood and Jankowski, *Karski*, 143, 147, 287, n. 143.

39. Weekly Political Intelligence Summary no. 165, 2 Dec. 1942, copy in NA RG 59, Microfilm M-982/R 146.

40. The full telegram is reprinted in Wood and Jankowski, *Karski*, 150.

41. This account was sent by Zygielbojm through the diplomatic pouch to the Polish embassy in Washington, which passed it on to the Jewish Labor Committee. A copy reached the Office of Strategic Services, NA RG 200, Box 11, Folder 107. Wood and Jankowski, *Karski*, 288, n. 150, suggest the embellishment and alterations.

42. NA RG 200, Box 11, Folder 107.

43. Wood and Jankowski, *Karski*, 117–19, 142–47.

44. Biddle to Secretary of State, 18 Dec. 1942, with Raczyński to Biddle, 9 Dec. 1942, NA RG 59, CDF 740.00116 E. W. 1939/712; Raczyński to Eden, 9 Dec. 1942, PRO FO 371/30924 (C 12313/61/18). I am grateful to John P. Fox for a copy of the latter document. See also, Engel, *In the Shadow of Auschwitz*, 200.

45. Fox, "Jewish Factor," 99–101; Breitman and Kraut, *American Refugee Policy*, 157–59; Arthur D. Morse, *While Six Million Died: A Chronicle of American Apathy* (New York, 1967), 33.

46. Jean Seaton, "Reporting Atrocities: The BBC and the Holocaust," in *The Media in British Politics*, ed. Jean Seaton and Ben Pimlott (Aldershot, 1987), 167.

47. Wyman, *Abandonment of the Jews*, 71; Wood and Jankowski, *Karski*, 152; Lipstadt, *Beyond Belief*, 184.

48. "Rabbi Wise phoned from New York that Sumner Welles had told him the President wished to see him . . ." (Watson Memo for the Files, 30 Nov. 1942, OF 76-C, Franklin D. Roosevelt Library, Hyde Park, N.Y.). Breitman and Kraut, *American Refugee Policy*, 157–58; Wyman, *Abandonment of the Jews*, 71–72.

49. Engel, *In the Shadow of Auschwitz*, 200. Winant to Secretary of State, 7 Dec. 1942, NA RG 59, CDF 740.00116 E. W. 1939/692; Sikorski to Welles, 12 Dec. 1942, NA RG 59, CDF 740.00116 E. W. 1939/739, referring to their meeting of 4 Dec. 1942.

50. Winant to Secretary of State, 7 Dec. 1942, NA RG 59, CDF 740.00116 E. W. 1939/660 and 692; Raczyński to Biddle, 9 Dec. 1942, included with Biddle to Secretary of State, 18 Dec. 1942, NA RG 59, CDF 740.00116 E. W. 1939/712; Engel, *In the Shadow of Auschwitz*, 200.

51. Winant to Secretary of State, 7 Dec. 1942, NA RG 59, CDF 740.00116 E. W. 1939/692; Wood and Jankowski, *Karski*, 152.

52. Winant to Secretary of State, 8 Dec. 1942, NA RG 59, CDF 740.00116 E. W. 1939/664.

53. The most detailed account from Held's report is in the Jewish Labor Committee Archives, summarized and partly quoted by Penkower, *Jews Were Expendable*, 85–86. See also, *Bulletin of the World Jewish Congress* (Jan. 1943): 10, which has the last quote.

54. See chapter 6.

55. "Retribution," in *A New Dictionary of Quotations on Historical Principles from Ancient and Modern Sources* (New York, 1957), 1030.

56. See chapter 14.

57. James de Rothschild-Colonel Harvie Watt, 16 Dec. 1942, Prem 4/51/8, and Martin-V. G. Lawford, 18 Dec. 1942, PRO FO 371/32682, W17520, as quoted by Michael J. Cohen, *Churchill and the Jews* (London, 1985), 269.

58. Wasserstein, *Britain and the Jews*, 172.

59. Ibid., 172–73.

60. *Parliamentary Debates (Hansard's)*, House of Commons, 17 Dec. 1942, 2082–2087, quoted almost entirely by Wasserstein, *Britain and the Jews*, 173.

61. JR (Randall) Minute, 14 Jan. 1943, in PRO FO 371/34361 (C 255/18/62).

62. *The Parliamentary Debates, House of Lords*, Fifth Series, vol. 125 (London, 1943), 17 Dec. 1942, cols. 609–10.

## 10. REACTIONS TO PUBLICITY

1. Robert Gellately, *The Gestapo and German Society: Enforcing Racial Policy, 1933–1945* (Oxford, 1991), 140–41; BBC European Audience Estimates, Germany, 4–5, cumulative three-year survey, dated 28 June 1943, copy in NA RG 208,

Entry 367, Box 255, E 9.2, BBC European Intelligence Series 4: BBC Surveys (hereafter, Cumulative BBC Survey).

2.  Cumulative BBC Survey, 1.

3.  Cumulative BBC Survey, 5–6.

4.  BBC Surveys of European Audiences, Germany, 22 May 1943, p. 3, copy in NA RG 208, Entry 367, Box 255, E 9.2: European Intelligence Surveys European Audiences, Germany (hereafter, BBC Survey, 22 May 1943).

5.  Cumulative BBC Survey, 3; Hoare to Eden, regarding Feb. 1943 conversation with German diplomat by secret source, PRO FO 371/34427 (C 1632/55/18); Report from Istanbul, on travelers from Berlin 8 Feb. 1943, PRO FO 371/34428 (C 2584/55/G18); Press Reading Bureau to Political Intelligence Dept., 27 Mar. 1943, with account of conditions in Germany from German journalist who had left Berlin for Sweden on 11 Feb. 1943, PRO FO 371/34429 (C 3769/55/18).

6.  Cumulative BBC Survey, 4. Roughly 1.5 percent of the German population was thought to be capable of listening to the English broadcasts. On the Poles, see Eden's memo for the War Cabinet based on conversation with Jan Karski, 4 Feb. 1943, FO 371/34550 (C 1943/34/e).

7.  Political Warfare Executive, Central Directive, week beginning 10 Dec. 1942, copy in NA RG 208, Entry 359, Box 831, PWE Central Directives 1942. Also cited by Bernard Wasserstein, *Britain and the Jews of Europe, 1939–1945* (Oxford, 1979), 174.

8.  Political Warfare Executive, Central Directive, week beginning 17 Dec. 1942, copy in NA RG 208, Entry 359, Box 831, Folder: PWE—Central Directives 1942.

9.  David Bankier, *The Germans and the Final Solution: Public Opinion under Nazism* (Oxford, 1992), 113.

10. See epilogue.

11. Wasserstein, *Britain and the Jews*, 176–77; P. W. Scarlett to F. K. Roberts, 3 Mar. 1943, Publicity and Propaganda for Polish Atrocities, PRO FO 371/34550 (C 2471/34/G).

12. See chapter 8 above. The central directives issued by the OWI Overseas Branch for the week of 17 Dec. 1942 contained no mention of the Allied Declaration on Nazi extermination policy. See NA RG 208, Entry 359, Box 818, Record Central Directives 1942.

13. Edward J. Bliss, *In Search of Light: The Broadcasts of Edward R. Murrow, 1938–1961* (New York, 1967), 91, cited by Joyce Fine, "American Radio Coverage of the Holocaust," *Simon Wiesenthal Center Annual* 5 (1988): 158.

14. On the Voice of America, see Holly Cowan Shulman, *The Voice of America: Propaganda and Democracy, 1941–1945* (Madison, Wis., 1990), 26–27, 42–74.

15. Special Guidance: Atrocity and Terror Stories, 8 Jan. 1943, NA RG 208, Entry 363, Box 828, Record Special Guidances, Sept. 1942–Dec. 1943.

16. Political Warfare Executive, Central Directive, week beginning 24 Dec. 1942, copy in NA RG 208, Entry 359, Box 831, PWE—Central Directives 1942.

17. Political Warfare Executive, Central Directive, week beginning 7 Jan. 1943, copy in NA RG 208, Entry 359, Box 831, PWE—Central Directives 1942.

18. Yisrael Gutman and Shmuel Krakowski, *Unequal Victims: Poles and Jews During World War II* (New York, 1986).

19. They knew more about the mass shootings than about the extermination camps, and rumor and imagination supplied some details. On this issue, see particularly, Walter Laqueur, *The Terrible Secret: Suppression of the Truth About Hitler's "Final Solution"* (Boston, 1980), and Bankier, *The Germans and the Final Solution*, 104–12.

20. Press Reading Bureau to Political Intelligence Dept., 27 Mar. 1943, PRO FO 371/34429 (C 3769/55/18).

21. Hoare to Eden, with attached report from Secret Source, PRO FO 371/34427 (C 1632/55/18 [Feb. 1943?]); Consul General in Tangier to Mr. Roberts, 10 Mar. 1943, PRO FO 371/34428 (C 2937/55/18).

22. Ridley Prentice, Lisbon, to Political Intelligence Dept., 12 Mar. 1943, PRO FO 371/34428 (C 3243/55/18). For samples of somewhat earlier negative German reactions to deportations of German Jews, see Sarah Gordon, *Hitler, Germans, and the "Jewish Question"* (Princeton, N.J., 1984), 192–95.

23. See Gellately, *The Gestapo and German Society*, esp. 129–58.

24. BBC Survey, 22 May 1943, pp. 6–7, 9–10.

25. A copy, based on notes made at the scene, was passed by the Poles to the British, who received it in May 1943. See PRO FO 371/34454 (C 5964/233/18). I am grateful to Stephen Tyas for a copy of this document.

26. PRO FO 371/34454 (C 5964/233/18).

27. The following is drawn from Nathan Stoltzfus, *Resistance of the Heart: Intermarriage and the Rosenstrasse Protest in Nazi Germany* (New York, 1996), 192–257. Unless otherwise noted, I have used this book as my source on the Rosenstrasse protest.

28. Stoltzfus, *Resistance*, 171–72. On the problems of mixed marriages in other countries as well as Germany, see Raul Hilberg, *Perpetrators, Victims, Bystanders* (New York, 1992), 131–38.

29. Raul Hilberg, *The Destruction of the European Jews* (New York, 1985), vol. 2, 430.

30. Bankier, *The Germans and the Final Solution*, 133–37; also BBC Survey, 22 May 1943, pp. 9–10.

31. Ian Kershaw, *Popular Opinion and Political Dissent in the Third Reich: Bavaria, 1933–1945* (Oxford, 1983), 365–66; Marlis Steinert, *Hitler's War and the Germans: Public Mood and Attitude During the Second World War*, trans. Thomas E.J. de Witt (Athens, Ohio, 1977), 143.

32. Kershaw, *Popular Opinion*, 367.

33. Bankier, *Germans and the Final Solution*, 145.

34. Karl Schleunes, *The Twisted Road to Auschwitz: Nazi Policy Toward German Jews, 1933–1939* (Urbana, Ill., 1969), 53–61, 261–62; Kershaw, *Popular Opinion*, esp. 275–76, 377; Bankier, *Germans and the Final Solution*, esp. 154–55. For a very different view of the significance of Hitler's anti-Semitic rhetoric, see Hans

Mommsen, *From Weimar to Auschwitz*, trans. Philip O'Connor (Chapel Hill, N.C., 1991), 224–53.

35. The most famous instance was in Hitler's 30 Jan. 1939 speech to the Reichstag, in which he threatened that, if Jews forced Germany into a war, the result would be the annihilation of the Jews of Europe.

36. Allegedly drawn from a book by Theodore Kaufmann, *Germany Must Die*. See Wolfgang Benz, "Judenvernichtung aus Notwehr? Die Legenden um Theodore N. Kaufmann," *Vierteljahrshefte für Zeitgeschichte* 29 (1981): 615–30; Bankier, *Germans and the Final Solution*, 148; Steinert, *Hitler's War*, 137–38.

37. BBC Surveys of European Audiences: Germany, 11 May 1942, p. 12, copy in NA RG 208, Entry 367, Box 255, E 9.2.

38. See Richard Breitman, *The Architect of Genocide: Himmler and the Final Solution* (Hanover, N.H., 1992), 50–51.

39. See Hitler's threats of extermination in Daniel J. Goldhagen, *Hitler's Willing Executioners: Ordinary Germans and the Holocaust* (New York, 1996), 147–48, 161–63, 504–5, n. 124.

40. Quoted by Steinert, *Hitler's War*, 141–42.

41. Retinger to Strang, 25 Feb. 1943, with accompanying memo from Zygielbojm, PRO FO 371/34362 (C 2247/18/62).

42. In his letter to Müller, Himmler misdated Wise's statement as Sept. 1942, a time when Wise had not yet started to speak publicly about the Final Solution. The copy of whatever document Himmler received about Wise does not survive, only Himmler's letter to Müller does.

43. Himmler to Müller, 30 Nov. 1942, NA RG 242, T-175/R 58/2521486.

44. Leni Yahil, *The Holocaust: The Fate of European Jewry, 1932–1945*, trans. Ina Friedman and Haya Galai (New York, 1990), 449–50; Blobel's affidavit, NA RG 238, Nuremberg Document NO-3947.

45. Personal Staff RFSS to Reich Security Main Office, 6 Dec. 1942, NA RG 242, T-175/R 20/2524929.

46. "Reutermeldung aus London über Ausrottung der Juden wird übers." "Erklärung der Präsidenten des Weltjuden Kongr. Lady Reading wird übersandt." Himmler's Log of Secret Correspondence (summaries only), Himmler to SD, 6 and 10 Dec. 1942, NA RG 242, T-580/R 45A.

47. PWE Central Directive for week beginning 31 Dec. 1942, PRO FO 898/289, cited by Wasserstein, *Britain and the Jews*, 175.

48. *The Goebbels Diaries*, ed. Louis B. Lochner, quoted by Wasserstein, *Britain and the Jews*, 175.

49. Berger to Himmler, 11 Dec. 1942, NA RG 238, Nuremberg Document NO-1117.

50. Himmler to Bormann, 18 Dec. 1942, Akten der Parteikanzlei, Microfiche 102/01039. In this document, Himmler offered a draft of demands for Hitler to raise with French Premier Laval.

51. Himmler to Ribbentrop, 29 Jan. 1943, NA RG 242, T-175/R 68/2584430.

52. Himmler to Ganzenmüller, 20 Jan. 1943, NA RG 242, T-175/R 76/2594493-94.

53. "Bandenverdächtige Männer, Frauen u. Kinder in Lager Lublin u. Auschwitz verbringen," Himmler to Higher SS and Police Leaders et al., 6 Jan. 1943, Himmler's Log of Secret Correspondence (summaries only), NA RG 242, T-580, R 45A.

54. Richard Breitman, "Himmler and Bergen-Belsen," in *Belsen in History and Memory*, ed. Jo Reilly, David Cesarani, Tony Kushner, and Colin Richmond (London, 1997), 73.

55. Himmler to Ribbentrop, [illegible] Jan. 1943, NA RG 242, T-175/R 65/25806-42-43.

56. The Earl of Avon (Sir Anthony Eden), *The Eden Memoirs: The Reckoning* (London, 1965), 358, quoted by Wasserstein, *Britain and the Jews*, 174.

57. Eden to Cabinet Committee on Refugees, 10 Mar. 1944, PRO CAB 95/15/138, cited by Wasserstein, *Britain and the Jews*, 182.

58. Foreign Office to Embassy, Washington, D.C., 23 Mar. 1943, PRO FO 371/36655 (W 4236/49/48).

59. Minute of 22 Dec. 1942, PRO FO 371/32682 (W17521), quoted by Michael J. Cohen, *Churchill and the Jews* (London, 1985), 268. Richard Law had reached much the same view on 16 Dec. See Wasserstein, *Britain and the Jews*, 178.

60. See particularly, Matthews to Secretary of State, 20 Feb. 1943, summarizing a conversation with Richard Law, NA RG 59, Lot File 52D 408, Box 3, Bermuda Conference Background. There are discussions of some lobbying efforts in Wasserstein, *Britain and the Jews*, 176–83, and Tony Kushner, *The Holocaust and the Liberal Imagination: A Social and Cultural History* (Oxford, 1994), 173–80. Additional documentation of efforts to influence British government policy may be found in PRO FO 371/36648, 36649, and 36650.

61. Minutes and related documents in PRO FO 371/36648. See also PRO CAB 95/15, cited and summarized by Wasserstein, *Britain and the Jews*, 183.

62. Minutes of committee meeting, 31 Dec. 1942, PRO FO 371/36648. Also quoted and commented on by Wasserstein, *Britain and the Jews*, 115–16.

63. Minutes of Chiefs of Staff Committee, 31 Dec. 1942, PRO CAB 121/001, A/Policy/Air/1, vol. 1. I am grateful to John P. Fox for a copy of this document.

64. Wasserstein, *Britain and the Jews*, 306–7.

65. D. Allen Minute, 14 Jan. 1943, and A. Walker Minute, 21 Jan. 1943, PRO FO 371/34361 (C 555/18/62).

66. PRO FO 371/36648, quoted by Wasserstein, *Britain and the Jews*, 179.

67. Nunn (Home Office) to Walker (Foreign Office), 5 Jan. 1943, and Walker to Nunn, 6 Jan. 1943, PRO FO 371/36648.

68. Rathbone to N. Malcolm, 17 Feb. 1943, and Sir H. Emerson to Foreign Office, 24 Feb. 1943, with attached analysis by Rathbone, 12 Feb. 1943, titled, "The Nazi Massacres of Jews and Poles, What Rescue Measures Are Practically Possible?" PRO FO 371/36653 (W3321/49/49).

69. Richard Law Memorandum of Conversation with Alexander Easterman, 7 Jan. 1943, PRO FO 371/36648.

70. See chapter 6 above.

71. Reading to Churchill, 16 Jan. 1943, and Draft of Churchill to Reading, attached to Lawford to Brown, 26 Jan. 1943, PRO FO 371/36650 (W 1409/40/48).

72. Copy of the British statement in Parliament in NA RG 59, CDF 840.48 Refugees/3633.

73. Foreign Office to Stockholm, 6 Jan. 1943, PRO FO 371/34361.

74. See chapter 9 above, and Richard Breitman and Alan M. Kraut, *American Refugee Policy and European Jewry, 1933–1945* (Bloomington, Ind., 1987), 156–57.

75. See chapter 9 above. For more details, see Breitman and Kraut, *American Refugee Policy*, 149–50.

76. British Embassy, Washington, D.C., to Eastern Department, Foreign Office, 30 Dec. 1942, PRO FO 371/34361; Reams to American Embassy, London, 10 Dec. 1942, NA RG 59 CDF 740.00116 E. W. 1939/674A; quote from Memorandum [Reams to Travers], 15 Dec. 1942, NA RG 59, Lot File 52D 408, Box 3, Bermuda Conference Background. On the State Department's continuing disclaimers, well after the Allied Declaration of 17 Dec. 1942, see, for example, E. Wilder Spaulding to Murphy, 18 Jan. 1943, NA RG 59 CDF 740.00116 E. W. 1939/685.

77. Durbrow Memorandum, undated but stamped received 25 Jan. 1943, NA RG 59 CDF 8600/4016/644 1/2.

78. British Embassy, Washington, D.C., to Eastern Department, Foreign Office, 30 Dec. 1942, PRO FO 371/34361.

79. Hull to American Legation, Bern, 10 Feb. 1943, NA RG 59, CDF 740.00116 E. W. 1939/753 Confidential File. See also David S. Wyman, *The Abandonment of the Jews: America and the Holocaust, 1941–1945* (New York, 1984), 81.

80. See Flexner Memorandum for Governor Lehman, 17 Feb. 1943, NA RG 169, Box 36, Refugees-Jewish, OFRRO Subject File.

81. This is a summary of a more detailed account in Breitman and Kraut, *American Refugee Policy*, 183–84, which cites the original sources.

82. Squire to Harrison, 10 Mar. 1943, with attached Riegner to Wise, NA RG 84, American Legation, Bern, Confidential File 1943, 840.1 Jews.

83. Norton (Berne) to Foreign Office, 28 May 1943, and related documents in PRO FO 371/34362 (C 6109/18/62).

## 11. COMPETITION AND COLLABORATION

1. Copy of the aide-mémoire of 20 Jan. 1943 in *Foreign Relations of the United States*, vol. 1, 1943, pp. 134–37. See also Bernard Wasserstein, *Britain and the Jews of Europe, 1939–1945* (Oxford, 1979), 184–85.

2. Halifax to Foreign Office, 26 Jan. 1943, PRO FO 371/36650 (W 1649/49/48).

3. Richard Breitman and Alan M. Kraut, *American Refugee Policy and European Jewry,*

*1933–1945* (Bloomington, Ind., 1987), 175; David S. Wyman, *Abandonment of the Jews: America and the Holocaust, 1941–1945* (New York, 1984), 106; Halifax to Foreign Office, 6 Mar. 1943, regarding conversation between Campbell and Welles, 5 Mar. 1943, PRO FO 371/36654.

4. A. Walker Minute, 28 Jan. 1943, PRO FO 371/36650 (W 1649/49/48).

5. Summarized in Callman to Secretary of State, 23 Feb. 1943, NA RG 59, Lot File 52D 408, Box 3, Bermuda Conference Background.

6. On Eden in cabinet on 22 Feb. 1943, see Wasserstein, *Britain and the Jews*, 187.

7. The exchange with Eden in Parliament and the *Manchester Guardian* article are summarized in Callman to Secretary of State, 26 Feb. 1943, NA RG 59, Lot File 52D 408, Box 3, Bermuda Conference Background.

8. Breckinridge Long's draft with Long to Welles, Long Papers, Box 212, Library of Congress. Final text in *Foreign Relations of the United States: Diplomatic Papers, 1943 (FRUS)*, vol. 1, 140–44. Wyman, *Abandonment of the Jews*, 106–7, followed the British view that the Americans had not properly notified London in advance of publication. But during his conversation with British Minister Campbell, Welles declared that Washington had given its response to the Foreign Office first. Welles memo, 4 Mar. 1943, Sumner Welles Papers, Box 164, Folder 8, Franklin D. Roosevelt Library, Hyde Park, N.Y.

9. Welles Memo, 4 Mar. 1943, Welles Papers, Box 164, Franklin D. Roosevelt Library, Hyde Park, N.Y.

10. Halifax to Foreign Office, 5 Mar. 1943, and Foreign Office minutes by Randall and Butler, 8 Mar. 1943, PRO FO 371/36654.

11. For a detailed discussion of the background to the Bermuda Conference, see Wyman, *Abandonment of the Jews*, 107–13, and Wasserstein, *Britain and the Jews*, 188–91.

12. Brodetsky and Stein to Undersecretary of State for Foreign Affairs, 25 Feb. 1943, and draft for Law to Brodetsky and Stein, 15 Mar. 1943, PRO FO 371/36654 (W 3468/49/48).

13. Foreign Office to British Embassy, Washington, D.C., 19 Mar. 1943, PRO FO 371/36655 (W 4236/49/48).

14. Randall memo of conversation with Secretary of Swiss legation, 18 Mar. 1943, PRO FO 371/36655 (W 4607/49/48). For a broad study of Swiss response to Jewish refugees, see Jacques Picard, *Die Schweiz und die Juden, 1933–1945: Schweizerischer Antisemitismus, jüdische Abwehr, und internationale Migrations- und Flüchtlingspolitik* (Zurich, 1997).

15. Foreign Office to British Embassy, Washington, D.C., and British Embassy to Foreign Office, 17 March 1943, PRO FO 371/36655 (WH383/49/48).

16. See chapter 9 above.

17. E. Thomas Wood and Stanislaw M. Jankowski, *Karski: How One Man Tried to Stop the Holocaust* (New York, 1994), 167–69.

18. Eden Memorandum, 17 Feb. 1943, for Distribution to War Cabinet, PRO FO 371/34550 (C 1943/34/e).

19. Quote from Law to Halifax for Eden, 18 Mar. 1943, PRO FO 371/36655 (WH383/49/48).

20. Hull's Memorandum of Conversation, 22 Mar. 1943, *FRUS 1943*, vol. 3, 28–32.

21. *Parliamentary Debates*, Fifth Series, vol. 126, House of Lords, 23 Mar. 1943, 856–57.

22. Strang's note, PRO FO 371/36658 (W 5684/49/48), cited by Wasserstein, *Britain and the Jews*, 189. Welles to Proskauer and Wise, 25 March 1943, and related documents in American Jewish Committee Archives, Joseph M. Proskauer Collection, RG 1, EXO-16, Emergency Committee 1943, YIVO Institute for Jewish Research. Also, Welles to Wise, 26 March 1943, Welles Papers, Box 93, Folder 12, Franklin D. Roosevelt Library, Hyde Park, N.Y.

23. Angora Chancery to Refugee Department, Foreign Office, 3 Mar. 1943, PRO FO 371/36655 (W 4325/49/48).

24. Monty N. Penkower, *The Jews Were Expendable: Free World Diplomacy and the Holocaust* (Urbana, Ill., 1983), 106–7, summarizes the meeting based on the original sources but misdates it at the end of February.

25. According to Proskauer to Wise, 29 Mar. 1943, Welles was instrumental in keeping the Bulgarian situation under discussion (American Jewish Committee Archives, Proskauer Collection, RG 1, EXO-16, Emergency Committee 1943).

26. Breitman and Kraut, *American Refugee Policy*, 177; Wasserstein, *Britain and the Jews*, 188 and 188, n. 18. According to Harry Hopkins's summary, Eden pledged the admission of about sixty thousand more Jews to Palestine, which would have far exceeded the limit of the official White Paper. If Eden in fact said sixty thousand, he obviously did not expect that many Jews to emerge.

27. Oliver Harvey Diary, 25 Apr. 1943, quoted by Wasserstein, *Britain and the Jews*, 34.

28. Meeting of the Joint Emergency Committee on European Jewish Affairs, 10 Apr. 1943, American Jewish Committee Archives, Proskauer Collection, RG 1, EXO-16, Emergency Committee 1943. See also Wyman, *Abandonment of the Jews*, 112.

29. Wise to Welles, 31 Mar. 1943, and Welles to Wise, 5 Apr. 1943, NA RG 59 CDF 840.48 Refugees/3734.

30. Johnson to Secretary of State, 13 and 17 Apr. 1943, NA RG 59 CDF 840.48 Refugees/3748 Confidential File and 3755 Confidential File.

31. Steven Koblik, *The Stones Cry Out: Sweden's Response to the Persecution of the Jews, 1933–1945* (New York, 1988), 62–63; Johnson to Secretary of State, 13, 17, and 20 Apr. 1943, NA RG 59 CDF 840.48 Refugees/3748, 3755, and 3761 Confidential File.

32. Henry L. Feingold, *The Politics of Rescue: The Roosevelt Administration and the Holocaust* (New Brunswick, N.J., 1970), 192–97; Wyman, *Abandonment of the Jews*, 108–11.

33. Halifax to Foreign Office, from Secretary of State for Foreign Affairs for Prime

Minister, 27 Mar. 1943, Avon [Anthony Eden] Papers, PRO Microfilm FO 954, R 2, Con/43/1.

34. Copies of the minutes in RG 59, Lot File 52D 408, Box 3, Bermuda Conference Minutes. Detailed summaries of the course of the conference in Wyman, *Abandonment of the Jews*, 112–19, 341–43; Wasserstein, *Britain and the Jews*, 190–201; Feingold, *Politics of Rescue*, 197–207.

35. Law to Eden, 21 Apr. 1943, Avon Papers, PRO Microfilm FO 954, R 2, Con/43/2.

36. See Wyman, *Abandonment of the Jews*, 116–19; Wasserstein, *Britain and the Jews*, 205–21.

37. Archbishop of Canterbury to Eden, 7 May 1943, and Eden to Archbishop of Canterbury, 21 May 1943, PRO FO 371/36661 (W 7131/49/48).

38. Mallet (Stockholm) to Eden, 24 May 1943, PRO FO 371/36662 (W 8253/49/48); Welles to Long, 21 May 1943, and Long to Brandt, 21 May 1943, NA RG 59 CDF 840.48 Refugees/3799 and 3805 1/2; also Mallet to Foreign Office, 7 June 1943, PRO FO 371/36662 (W 8553/49/48).

39. Many of the basic German Foreign Office documents about this proposal were published in translation by John Mendelsohn, *The Holocaust: Selected Documents in Eighteen Volumes*, vol. 7, *Jewish Emigration, the SS St. Louis Affair and Other Cases* (New York, 1982), 170–213. The quote is from 173.

40. NA RG 242, T-120/R 4202/E 422450-51.

41. Koblik, *Stones Cry Out*, 62–63. On the protracted diplomatic exchanges, see n. 39 above.

42. Memo of Conversation, 24 June 1943, Welles Papers, Box 164, Folder 10, Franklin D. Roosevelt Library, Hyde Park, N.Y.

43. For a capsule assessment of Berle, see Irwin F. Gellman, *Secret Affairs: Franklin Roosevelt, Cordell Hull, and Sumner Welles* (Baltimore, 1995), 141–42.

44. Daily bulletin of the Jewish Telegraphic Agency, copy obtained by the British Foreign Office. The comment came from A. Walker. See PRO FO 371/36661 (W 7186/49/48).

45. Bradley F. Smith, *The Ultra-Magic Deals: And the Most Secret Special Relationship* (Novato, Calif., 1993), 150. On Friedman, see David Kahn, *The Codebreakers: The Story of Secret Writing* (New York, 1967), 369–93.

46. Smith, *The Ultra-Magic Deals*, 150, 161.

47. David Reynolds, *The Creation of the Anglo-American Alliance, 1937–1941: A Study in Competitive Cooperation* (Chapel Hill, N.C., 1981); Gerhard L. Weinberg, *A World at Arms: A Global History of World War II* (New York, 1994), esp. 84–89, 152–59.

48. Smith, *Ultra-Magic Deals*, 1–42, does a nice job integrating the intelligence background to World War II into the broader setting of British-American relations.

49. Ibid., 35, 43–51.

50. Ibid., 55–56.

51. Ibid., 58–63.

52. Ibid., 81–89.

53. Unsigned letter to Major G. Stevens, British embassy, Washington, D.C., 4 Nov. 1942, PRO HW 14/57. I am grateful to John P. Fox for a copy of this document.

54. Smith, *Ultra-Magic Deals*, 140.

55. Ibid., 151–52; Telford Taylor, "Anglo-American Signals Intelligence Cooperation," in *Codebreakers: The Inside Story of Bletchley Park*, ed. F. H. Hinsley and Alan Stripp (Oxford, 1993), 71.

56. Smith, *Ultra-Magic Deals*, 152–54; Taylor, "Anglo-American Signals," 72.

57. Interview with Arthur Levinson, 19 May 1997.

58. Walter Eytan, "The Z Watch in Hut 4, Part II," in *Codebreakers,* 58–60.

59. F. H. Hinsley et al., *British Intelligence in the Second World War: Its Influence on Strategy and Operations*, vol. 2, (Cambridge, 1981), 669. See also, Walter Laqueur, *The Terrible Secret: Suppression of the Truth About Hitler's "Final Solution"* (Boston, 1980), 85, who cites unnamed sources who assured him that messages to and from the RSHA were read and that they provided information about the mass murder of the Jews.

60. Summary of interrogation of Barth, approximately mid-Nov. 1943, in PRO HW 16/1, pp. 47–49.

61. See NA RG 238, Microfilm Series M-1019/R 5/240ff.

62. German Police Decodes, no. 1 Traffic, 15 Oct. 1943, PRO HW 16/38.

63. Smith, *Ultra-Magic Deals*, 154–55.

64. This may be seen on the distribution lists on the decodes in PRO HW 16/39. The first distribution to Taylor that I found came in early 1944. See German Police in 1943 [Feb. 1944] in HW 16/61.

65. Telford Taylor, *The Anatomy of the Nuremberg Trials: A Personal Memoir* (New York, 1992), 26.

## 12. THE TREASURY DEPARTMENT'S OFFENSIVE

1. For the most detailed accounts, see Richard Breitman and Alan M. Kraut, *American Refugee Policy and European Jewry, 1933–1945* (Bloomington, Ind., 1987), 182–221; David S. Wyman, *The Abandonment of the Jews: America and the Holocaust, 1941–1945* (New York, 1984), 178–330; Monty N. Penkower, *The Jews Were Expendable: Free World Diplomacy and the Holocaust* (Urbana, Ill., 1983), 122–82; Henry L. Feingold, *The Politics of Rescue: The Roosevelt Administration and the Holocaust* (New Brunswick, N.J., 1970), 248–94.

2. See David Kranzler, *Thy Brother's Blood: The Orthodox Jewish Response to the Holocaust* (New York, 1984), chapter 3. On disunity within the American Jewish community, see, among others, Feingold, *Politics of Rescue*, 218–22.

3. Tony Kushner, "The Meaning of Auschwitz: Anglo-American Responses to the Hungarian Jewish Tragedy," in *Genocide and Rescue: The Holocaust in Hungary*, ed. David Cesarani (Oxford, 1997), 160–62.

4. This was roughly the comparison that Richard Law made in a letter to Eden, circulated to the British cabinet. See Bernard Wasserstein, *Britain and the Jews of Europe, 1939–1945* (Oxford, 1979), 201–2. Clarence Pickett of the American Friends Service Committee also thought, in June 1943, that public pressure and passage of a resolution in Congress would not be sufficient to get President Roosevelt to reconsider American policy with regard to relief to suffering peoples in occupied Europe. Pickett Journal, 15 June 1943, Pickett Papers, American Friends Service Committee Archives, Philadelphia. On earlier American decisions and discussions on relief, see Feingold, *Politics of Rescue*, 186–89.

5. Welles to Roosevelt, 2 Mar. 1943, Welles Papers, Box 152, Folder 3, Franklin D. Roosevelt Library, Hyde Park, N.Y.

6. Pickett Journal, 15 June 1943, Pickett Papers, American Friends Service Committee Archives, Philadelphia.

7. See chapter 6 above. Also Tuvia Ben-Moshe, *Churchill: Strategy and History* (Boulder, Colo., 1992), 317–20; Alex Danchev, "Great Britain: The Indirect Strategy," in *Allies at War: The Soviet, American, and British Experience, 1939–1945*, ed. David Reynolds, Warren F. Kimball, and A. O. Chubarian (New York, 1994), 11–17.

8. Martin Gilbert, *Road to Victory: Winston S. Churchill, 1941–1945* (London, 1986), 402–14; quote from 409. Gilbert, however, does not mention any discussion of the kind related by Sayre.

9. Report by Stettinius, 22 May 1944, on visit to London, 7–29 Apr. 1944, *Foreign Relations of the United States: Diplomatic Papers, 1944 (FRUS)*, vol. 3, p. 7; quoted by Wasserstein, *Britain and the Jews*, 326.

10. See chapter 11 above.

11. Berne (Norton) to Foreign Office, 8 July 1943, PRO FO 371/36663 (W 9994/49/48).

12. Jonathan Steinberg, *All or Nothing: The Axis and the Holocaust* (London, 1990); Susan Zucotti, *The Italians and the Holocaust: Persecution, Rescue, Survival* (New York, 1987). Nicola Carraciolo, *Uncertain Refuge: Italy and the Jews During the Holocaust*, trans. Florette Rechnitz Koffler and Richard Koffler (Urbana, Ill., 1995).

13. This plan suggested by Riegner was conveyed by Rabbi Wise to Sumner Welles in May 1943. It received serious consideration only in July. See particularly Meltzer's Memorandum, Proposed Arrangement for Relief and Evacuation of Refugees in Rumania and France, 30 July 1943, NA RG 59 CDF 840.48 Refugees/4211. Penkower, *Jews Were Expendable*, 128–30, has a detailed account of the whole course of events.

14. The most detailed account, based on Karski's recollections, is in E. Thomas Wood and Stanislaw M. Jankowski, *Karski: How One Man Tried to Stop the Holocaust* (New York, 1994, 197–201.

15. Breitman and Kraut, *American Refugee Policy*, 246. Handwritten notation about Roosevelt on Meltzer's Memorandum, Proposed Arrangement for Relief and Evacuation of Refugees in Rumania and France, 30 July 1943, NA RG 59 CDF 840.48 Refugees/4211. On Pehle and Karski, see Wood and Jankowski, *Karski*,

201. On Roosevelt's letter to Wise, see Wyman, *Abandonment of the Jews*, 180.

16. Travers to Emmons, 27 Aug. 1943, NA RG 59 CDF 740.00116 E. W. 1939/
816.

17. Visa Division [Robert C. Alexander] Draft Letter to van Paassen, 18 Sept. 1943,
and related documents in NA RG 59 CDF 840.48 Refugees/4679.

18. Feis to Hull, 4 Aug. 1943, marked Urgent, NA RG 59 CDF 862.4016/2269;
Morgenthau to Hull, 5 Aug. 1943, NA RG 59 CDF 840.48 Refugees/4212; Hull
to American Legation, Bern, 6 Aug. 1943, NA RG 59 CDF 862.4016/2269;
Breitman and Kraut, *American Refugee Policy*, 186; Penkower, *Jews Were Expendable*,
131–32; Wyman, *Abandonment of the Jews*, 180–81.

19. On Welles, see the fascinating account in Irwin F. Gellman, *Secret Affairs: Franklin
Roosevelt, Cordell Hull, and Sumner Welles* (Baltimore, 1995), 302–17; also Benjamin Welles, *Sumner Welles: FDR's Global Strategist* (New York, 1997), 341–54.

20. Reams to Stettinius, 8 Oct. 1943, NA RG 59 CDF 840.48 Refugees/4683 1/5.

21. Berle to Hull, 16 Sept. 1943, NA RG 59 CDF 840.48 Refugees/4502; Long
Memorandum, 26 Oct. 1943, NA RG 59 CDF 862.4016/2292.

22. See Breitman and Kraut, *American Refugee Policy*, 186–87; Wyman, *Abandonment
of the Jews*, 181–82; Penkower, *Jews Were Expendable*, 131–32.

23. Dieter Pohl, *Von der Judenpolitik zum Judenmord: Der Distrikt Lublin des General-
gouvernements, 1939–1944* (Frankfurt am Main, 1993).

24. Johnson to Secretary of State, 30 Sept. 1943, NA RG 59 CDF 840.48 Refugees/
4522.

25. On Denmark, see Leni Yahil, *The Rescue of Danish Jewry* (Philadelphia, 1969); and
the recent opposed articles by Gunnar S. Paulsson, "The Bridge Over the Øresund:
Historiography on the Expulsion of the Jews from Nazi-Occupied Denmark," and
Hans Kirchhof, "Denmark: A Light in the Darkness of the Holocaust; A Reply
to Gunnar S. Paulsson," in *Journal of Contemporary History* 30 (1995): 431–79. On
Sweden, see Steven Koblik, *The Stones Cry Out: Sweden's Response to the Persecution
of the Jews* (New York, 1988), and the recent dissertation by Paul A. Levine, "From
Indifference to Activism: Swedish Diplomacy and the Holocaust, 1938–1944"
(Uppsala, 1996).

26. Johnson to Secretary of State, 9 Oct. 1943, regarding conversation with Boheman,
NA RG 59 CDF 840.48 Refugees/4557.

27. Winant to Secretary of State, 13 Oct. 1943, NA RG 59 CDF 840.48 Refugees/
4565.

28. Wyman, *Abandonment of the Jews*, 186–87, 193–95; Breitman and Kraut, *American
Refugee Policy*, 188.

29. Stettinius to Long, 11 Nov. 1943, Stettinius Papers, Box 215, Asst. Sec. Long,
Oct. 1943, University of Virginia; Meeting of the Undersecretary with the Assistant Secretaries, Political Advisers, and the Geographic Division Heads, 11 Nov.
1943, Stettinius Papers, Box 732, Meetings with Asst. Secs., Oct. 1943; Stettinius
to Hayden [Raynor], 21 Nov. 1943, Stettinius Papers, Box 727, Refugees.

30. Hull to American Embassy, for Biddle, 10 Dec. 1943, RG 59, Lot File 52D 408, Box 2, IGC-WRB.

31. Wyman, *Abandonment of the Jews*, 197–98; Breitman and Kraut, *American Refugee Policy*, 183–84.

32. Winant to Secretary of State, 15 Dec. 1943, NA RG 59 CDF 840.51 Frozen Credits/12144, quoted by Wasserstein, *Britain and the Jews*, 247.

33. Minutes of Meetings on Jewish Evacuation, 17, 18, and 19 Dec. 1943, Henry Morgenthau, Jr., Diaries, vol. 688, part 2, Franklin D. Roosevelt Library, Hyde Park, N.Y.

34. Minutes of Meeting on Jewish Evacuation, 20 Dec. 1943, Morgenthau Diaries, vol. 688, part 2.

35. See chapter 10 above.

36. Minutes of Meeting on Argentina, Jewish Evacuation, 31 Dec. 1943, Morgenthau Diaries, vol. 688, part 2, Breitman and Kraut, *American Refugee Policy*, 188–89.

37. Breitman and Kraut, *American Refugee Policy*, 190.

38. Ibid., 191.

39. Wasserstein, *Britain and the Jews*, 248–49.

40. Ibid., 249. On later use of blocked accounts, see particularly Yehuda Bauer, *American Jewry and the Holocaust: The American Jewish Joint Distribution Committee* (Detroit, 1981), 422–34, and *Jews for Sale: Nazi-Jewish Negotiations, 1933–1945* (New Haven, Conn., 1994), 220–38.

41. War Refugee Board to American Embassy, London, 9 Feb. 1944, copy in Stettinius Papers, Box 745, War Refugee Board, University of Virginia. More generally, on the subject of the American military's reaction to the founding of the War Refugee Board and the non-involvement of the armed forces, see Wyman, *Abandonment of the Jews*, 292–93.

42. Raynor to Pehle, 5 Feb. 1944, with attached British Memorandum, 25 Jan. 1944, War Refugee Board Records, Box 30, Franklin D. Roosevelt Library, Hyde Park, N.Y.

43. See Eden to Cabinet Committee on Refugees, 7 Feb. 1944, quoted by Wasserstein, *Britain and the Jews*, 323.

44. Breitman and Kraut, *American Refugee Policy*, 193–95.

45. Ibid., 196.

46. Copy in NA RG 208, Entry 359, Box 116, Refugees—Policy.

47. Summary Report of the Activities of the War Refugee Board with Respect to the Jews in Hungary, 9 Oct. 1944 (hereafter Summary—WRB—Hungary), 8, War Refugee Board Records, Box 34, Hungary I, Franklin D. Roosevelt Library, Hyde Park, N.Y.

48. London to Office of War Information, 24 Mar. 1944, NA RG 208, Entry 359, Box 116, Refugees—Policy.

49. Steinhardt to Secretary of State, 29 Mar. 1944, copy in NA RG 208, Entry 359, Box 116, Refugees—Policy; Wyman, *Abandonment of the Jews*, 237–38.

50. OWI—Thomason to Control Desk, N.Y., and Sherwood, Backer, London, 25 Apr. 1944, NA RG 208, Entry 359, Box 116, Refugees—Policy.

51. Breitman and Kraut, *American Refugee Policy*, 211; Wyman, *Abandonment of the Jews*, 236.

52. Yehuda Bauer, "Conclusion: The Holocaust in Hungary; Was Rescue Possible?" in *Genocide and Rescue*, 196–97, 206–7. Shlomo Aronson, "The Quadruple Trap: The Holocaust in Hungary," in *Genocide and Rescue*, 93–122, makes extensive use of the trap metaphor, applying it in a broader sense.

53. Randolph L. Braham, *The Politics of Genocide: The Holocaust in Hungary*, rev. and enl. ed. (New York, 1994), vol. 2, offers the most thorough account.

54. Interrogation of Andor Gross [Grosz], 22 June 1944, PRO FO 371/42811. The most revealing interrogation and analysis of Brand was by the American envoy Ira Hirschmann—see Memorandum to Ambassador Steinhardt, 22 June 1944, regarding interview with Joel Brand, copy in NA RG 107, ASW 400.38.

55. Braham, *Politics of Genocide*, vol. 2, 936, 943–44; Richard Breitman and Shlomo Aronson, "The End of the Final Solution? Nazi Attempts to Ransom Jews in 1944," *Central European History* 25 (1992): 189–90.

56. The most detailed treatment is in Bauer, *Jews for Sale*, 172–95. See also Braham, *Politics of Genocide*, vol. 2, 1078–88.

57. Walter Laqueur, *The Terrible Secret: Suppression of the Truth About Hitler's Final Solution* (Boston, 1980), 85 n. F. H. Hinsley et al., *British Intelligence in the Second World War: Its Influence on Strategy and Operations*, vol. 2 (Cambridge, 1981), 669, states that the British never broke the most secret code of the SD. What about others?

58. Summary, 13 Apr. 1944, p. 4, covering information received 1 Mar. 4–9 Apr. 1944, PRO HW 16/6, part 2.

59. See Bauer, *Jews for Sale*, 174–90, for the most detailed treatment.

60. Summary—WRB—Hungary, 9 Oct. 1944, p. 9a-13, War Refugee Board Records, Box 34, Hungary I, Franklin D. Roosevelt Library, Hyde Park, N.Y.; Wyman, *Abandonment of the Jews*, 237–38.

61. Ribbentrop to Veesenmayer, 10 July 1944, and Wagner's Report for Ribbentrop Concerning the Results and Status of the Anti-Jewish Measures in Hungary, 31 Oct. 1944, repr. (in German) in *The Destruction of Hungarian Jewry: A Documentary Account*, ed. Randolph L. Braham (New York, 1963), 522–24, 700. Also Richard Breitman, "Nazi Jewish Policy in 1944," in *Genocide and Rescue*, 78.

62. Braham, *Politics of Genocide*, vol. 2, 872–81.

63. Summary—WRB—Hungary, 9 Oct. 1944, pp. 17–25, War Refugee Board Records, Box 34, Hungary I, Franklin D. Roosevelt Library, Hyde Park, N.Y.; Wyman, *Abandonment of the Jews*, 239–40.

64. Breitman and Kraut, *American Refugee Policy*, 210; Summary—WRB—Hungary, 9 Oct. 1944, p. 9, War Refugee Board Records, Box 34, Hungary I, Franklin D. Roosevelt Library, Hyde Park, N.Y.

65. Breitman and Aronson, "The End of the Final Solution?" 193–202.
66. David S. Wyman, "Why Auschwitz Was Never Bombed," *Commentary* 65 (May 1978): 37–46; Wyman, *Abandonment of the Jews*, 292–98. Reanalyzed with some new evidence but with very different perspectives by James H. Kitchens III, "The Bombing of Auschwitz Revisited," *The Journal of Military History* (1994): 233–66; Richard Levy, "The Bombing of Auschwitz Revisited: A Critical Analysis," *Holocaust and Genocide Studies* 10 (1996): 267–98; and Stuart G. Erdheim, "Could the Allies Have Bombed Auschwitz-Birkenau?" *Holocaust and Genocide Studies* 11 (1997): 129–70. St. Martin's Press will publish a collection of articles on the subject in a volume to be edited by Michael Neufeld. In my view, Kitchens and Levy do establish some of the difficulties of bombing such a target, even though I disagree with many other portions of their argument.
67. See chapter 10 above.
68. See the details in Wasserstein, *Britain and the Jews*, 307–8.
69. See chapter 7 above.
70. Wyman, *Abandonment of the Jews*, 298.
71. Breitman and Kraut, *American Refugee Policy*, 219–20; Wyman, *Abandonment of the Jews*, 300.
72. See p. 201 above.
73. I am drawing here on the literature in n. 66 above but agreeing with Wyman and Erdheim about the actual motives at the time for rejection.
74. Winston S. Churchill, *The Second World War*, vol. 6, *Triumph and Tragedy* (Boston, 1953), 693. Also Prime Minister's Personal Minute, M. 844/4: PRO, FO 371/42809, WR27, quoted by Martin Gilbert, *Road to Victory: Winston S. Churchill, 1941–1945* (London, 1986), 847; Michael J. Cohen, *Churchill and the Jews* (London, 1985), 298.
75. Raul Hilberg, *The Destruction of the European Jews* (New York, 1985), vol. 3, 1139.
76. See Gilbert, *Road to Victory*, 846, and his *Auschwitz and the Allies* (New York, 1981), 270.
77. See Wasserstein, *Britain and the Jews*, 308–20; Gilbert, *Auschwitz and the Allies*, 262–311; Cohen, *Churchill and the Jews*, 296–304.
78. Summary of German Police Decodes, 1–31 Aug. 1944, pp. 7–8, PRO, HW 16/6.
79. Hans Safrian, *Die Eichmann Männer* (Vienna, 1993), 305; Braham, *Politics of Genocide*, vol. 2, 893.
80. This conclusion is supported by Safrian, *Eichmann Männer*, 306.
81. Wasserstein, *Britain and the Jews*, 316–18.
82. Cohen, *Churchill and the Jews*, 299.
83. Gilbert, *Auschwitz and the Allies*, 212–322.
84. Ibid., 340.
85. Ibid., 340–41.
86. Cohen, *Churchill and the Jews*, 303–6. I will address Churchill's behavior further in the conclusion.

87. Levy, "Bombing of Auschwitz Revisited," 276, 280–82.
88. Ibid., 276.


13. THE MILLS OF THE GODS

1. John P. Fox, "The Jewish Factor in British War Crimes Policy in 1942," *English Historical Review* 92 (1977): 89.
2. Ibid., 89, 95–97; Bernard Wasserstein, *Britain and the Jews of Europe, 1939–1945* (Oxford, 1979), 169.
3. Cavendish-Bentinck to Cadogan, 8 Oct. 1942, and "C" to de Grey, 14 Oct. 1942, PRO HW 14/54, 4/18/1; unsigned notes, 16 and 19 Oct. 1942, PRO HW 14/55; Unsigned, undated cover note mentioning Major Evans, PRO HW 16/44.
4. Copy in NA RG 457, Box 1386, German Police and SS Messages. Also in PRO HW 16/45.
5. Arieh J. Kochavi, "The British Foreign Office versus the United Nations War Crimes Commission during the Second World War," *Holocaust and Genocide Studies* 8 (1994): 30, 44.
6. On the subject generally, see Bradley F. Smith, *The American Road to Nuremberg: The Documentary Record, 1944–1945* (Stanford, Calif., 1982). There is considerable earlier material in OSS and OWI records. Quote from OSS Planning Group, Proposed Convention for Extradition of Axis War Criminals, 16 Jan. 1943, NA RG 226, Entry 144, Box 8, Folder 63. I am grateful to Christof Mauch for a copy of this document.
7. MacLeish Memorandum, 21 Jan. 1943, NA RG 208, Entry 1, Box 5, Policies and Procedures—3, Joint Committee on Information Policy, 1943; Foreign Office (Eden) to British Embassy, Washington, 14 Jan. 1943, PRO FO 371/34363.
8. Siepmann to MacLeish, 21 Jan. 1943, NA RG 208, Entry 1, Box 5, Policies and Procedures—3, Joint Committee on Information Policy, 1942–43.
9. Kochavi, "British Foreign Office," 44; Telford Taylor, *The Anatomy of the Nuremberg Trials* (New York, 1992), 29.
10. Kochavi, "British Foreign Office," 33–34. But Simon had not committed Britain to prosecuting crimes against Jews, and the Foreign Office resisted the idea. See Fox, "The Jewish Factor," 96–98.
11. Arieh J. Kochavi, "Britain and the War Criminals Question at the Conclusion of the Second World War: The Military Dimension," *The British Journal of Holocaust Education* 2 (1993): 138–39.
12. MI 14 is on the distribution list for all the police and SS decodes in 1943 and 1944 in PRO, HW 16.
13. The German Police in 1943, ms. in PRO HW 16/61, GML and Ciro/Pearl 141–91. It is, however, true that the British in 1943 were decoding a lower percentage of messages from the Soviet territories. This had partly to do with the

refusal of Soviet intelligence to cooperate with the British (in supplying intercepts) as they had in 1942. See epilogue.

14. See, for example, German Police Decodes, No. 1A Traffic, 21, 23, 26, 30 June 1944, items 6, 2, 4, 9, and 7, respectively, PRO HW 16/41.

15. Declaration reprinted in Smith, *American Road to Nuremberg*, 13–14. On the subject of the Moscow Declaration, see Arieh J. Kochavi, "The Moscow Declaration, the Kharkov Trial, and the Question of a Policy on Major War Criminals," *History* 76 (1991): 401–17.

16. See quotation on p. 209 above.

17. Quoted by Kochavi, "Britain and the War Criminals," 138.

18. MI 14 apparently produced a bound volume composed of information from the decodes about SS and police men. The data were organized by rank and then alphabetically by individual. For the lower ranks, the volume often lists specific mentions in particular decodes, sometimes with summary of content. No. 140, 30 Apr. 1944–1 Jan. 1945, (Pearl/Zip and Ciro/Pearl), PRO HW 16/60.

19. Noel Annan, *Changing Enemies: The Defeat and Regeneration of Germany* (London, 1995), 3.

20. Melland's Lecture at Peal House, 19 Oct. 1943, text in PRO, WO 208/2924. Quotes from pp. 1, 36.

21. Melland's Lecture for First Army Group, 2 Feb. 1944, esp. p. 4. Text in PRO WO 208/2924.

22. Handwritten notes attached to Melland's lecture notes in PRO WO 208/2924; SHAEF G-2, Evaluation and Dissemination Section, *The German Police*, Apr. 1945, copy in the Library of the U.S. Holocaust Memorial Museum.

23. SHAEF, *The German Police*, 21–22.

24. Ibid., 52–54.

25. On British hopes for SHAEF jurisdiction, see Kochavi, "Britain and the War Criminals," 134–37. Quote from SHAEF, G-2, E.D.S. Report #30, SS in the Orpo, 16 June 1945, NA RG 319, IRR, XE 020820.

26. Black List of German Police, SS and Miscellaneous Party and Paramilitary Personalities, prepared by M.I. 4/14, Sept 1945, PRO, WO 208/4350.

27. See chapter 4 above.

28. German Police Decodes, 16 June 1942, PRIT signals 301–579, PRO HW 16/55.

29. Note on the Operations of the War Crimes Interrogation Unit, created 1 Jan. 1946, PRO WO 208/4294.

30. GC and CS, Air and Military History, vol. 13, The German Police, copy in NA RG 457, Box 91. This history was declassified in 1996.

31. Air and Military History, vol. 13, 235–37.

32. BAOR Revised Admin Inst. no. 94, 22 Sept. 1945, regarding automatic arrest; Legal Division, Adv. H.Q. Control Commission for Germany (British Element), to Control Office for Germany and Austria, 31 Dec. 1945; PRO WO 32/12208.

33. Directive #24, 12 Jan. 1946, repr. in *Entnazifizierung: Politische Säuberung und Re-habilitierung in den vier Besatzungszonen, 1945–1949*, ed. Clemens Vollnhals (Munich, 1991), 107–18.

34. Coldstream to Attorney General regarding conversation with General Betts, 21 Oct. 1945; Report of Heyman Working Party, 24 April 1946, regarding Disposal of War Criminals, Nazis, Militarists, and Potentially Dangerous Criminals; all in PRO WO 32/12208. Taylor, *Anatomy of the Nuremberg Trials*, 282.

35. See Lutz Niethammer, *Die Mitläuferfabrik: Die Entnazifizierung am Beispiel Bayern* (Berlin, 1982). There is a short side-by-side comparison of American and British efforts at denazification in Tom Bower, *The Pledge Betrayed: America and Britain and the Denazification of Post-War Germany* (New York, 1982), 144–72; also, *Entnazifizierung*, ed. Vollnhals, 9–34.

36. Justus Fürstenau, *Entnazifizierung: Ein Kapitel deutscher Nachkriegspolitik* (Neuwied, 1969), 43–45, lists 64,500 arrested through 1946 in the British zone and 34,000 of them released in the same period. Bower, *Pledge Betrayed*, 207–12.

37. See one case study in Andrej Angrick, Martina Voigt, Silke Ammerschubert, and Peter Klein, " 'Da hätte man schon ein Tagebuch führen müssen': Das Polizei-bataillon 322 und die Judenmorde im Bereich der Heeresgruppe Mitte während des Sommers und Herbstes 1941," in *Die Normalität des Verbrechens: Bilanz und Perspektiven der Forschung zu den nationalsozialistischen Gewaltverbrechen* (Berlin, 1994), 350–66.

38. See chapter 10 above.

39. Callum MacDonald, *The Killing of SS Obergruppenführer Reinhard Heydrich* (New York, 1989), 186–87.

40. G-2 Summary of Interrogation of Daluege, 12 June 1945, and Daluege's hand-written statement; Ecer (Czech) Interrogation of Daluege, 21 July 1945; NA RG 319, IRR File Daluege XE 002394, Box 544.

41. SHAEF Political Office British to G-2, CI, 21 June 1945, NA RG 319, IRR File Daluege, Box 544.

42. There is a War Office file on Daluege, but it contains no sensitive information. See PRO, WO 208/4448.

43. Helmut Krausnick and Hans-Heinrich Wilhelm, *Die Truppe des Weltanschauungs-krieges: Die Einsatzgruppen der Sicherheitspolizei und SD, 1938–1942* (Stuttgart, 1982), 566–70, 641; Yitzhak Arad, "Friedrich Jeckeln," *Encyclopedia of the Holocaust*, vol. 1, ed. Israel Gutman (New York, 1990), 741.

44. Bach-Zelewski did discuss Himmler's visit to Minsk in mid-August 1941 and the executions carried out in his presence but blamed Einsatzgruppen officials, rather than himself. He also managed somehow to avoid a formal interrogation on this subject: his discussion of it came only in a newspaper interview. See "Leben eines SS-Generals," 6 Sept. 1946, *Aufbau*, and the more detailed version in Declaration von dem Bach, World Jewish Congress Collection, Box C203, Bach-Zelewski Statement 1946.

45. Biographical entry on Bach-Zelewski in *Encyclopedia of the Holocaust*, vol. 1, ed. Gutman, 136.

46. For 7 Aug. 1941, see chapter 4 above. On the intelligence summary of Bach-Zelewski's career, see German Police, Addresses-Names-Personalities, 1941–1945, PRO HW 16/62.

47. Taylor, *Anatomy*, 243.

48. Ibid., IMT, *Trial*, vol. 4, 475–85.

49. Taylor, *Anatomy*, 244.

50. *New York Times*, 21 Mar. 1972, p. 44.

51. Raul Hilberg, *The Destruction of the European Jews* (New York, 1985), vol. 3, 1086–87.

52. Letter from Bundesarchiv Koblenz to Zentrale Stelle Ludwigsburg, 18 Nov. 1966, ZstL 202 AR-27/66. I am grateful to Konrad Kwiet for this reference.

## CONCLUSION

1. See Hitler's September 1935 comments along these lines, reported by Walter Gross, in Philippe Burrin, *Hitler and the Jews: The Genesis of the Holocaust*, trans. Patsy Southgate (London, 1994), 48–50. Also Hermann Graml, *Antisemitism in the Third Reich*, trans. Tim Kirk (Oxford, 1992), esp. 92–93.

2. Richard Breitman, *The Architect of Genocide: Himmler and the Final Solution* (Hanover, N.H., 1992).

3. Burrin, *Hitler and the Jews*, 49; Breitman, *Architect of Genocide*, 50–52, 64.

4. Ruth Bettina Birn, *Die Höheren SS- und Polizeiführer: Himmlers Vertreter im Dritten Reich* (Düsseldorf, 1986).

5. Götz Aly, *Endlösung: Völkerverschiebung und der Mord an den europäischen Juden* (Frankfurt am Main, 1995), 342–44; Christian Gerlach, "Failure of Plans for an SS Extermination Camp in Mogilev, Belorussia," *Holocaust and Genocide Studies* 11 (1997).

6. See above, chapters 2 and 5.

7. See above, chapter 2, p. 35. Heydrich's 31 July 1941 draft for Göring used both the phrases "Final Solution of the Jewish question" and "total solution of the Jewish question." For the text, see *Documents of Destruction: Germany and Jewry, 1933–45* (London, 1972), 88–89.

8. Maurice Ashley, *Churchill as Historian* (New York, 1968), 18.

9. Gerhard L. Weinberg, *Germany, Hitler, and World War II: Essays in Modern German and World History* (Cambridge, 1995), 292–94. Similarly, Tuvia Ben-Moshe, *Churchill: Strategy and History* (Boulder, Colo., 1992), 328–30; Robin Denniston, *Churchill's Secret War: Diplomatic Decrypts, the Foreign Office, and Turkey, 1942–44* (New York, 1997), 186, n. 1.

10. David Dutton, *Anthony Eden: A Life and Reputation* (London, 1997), treats a series of themes and events in Eden's career; it does not attempt complete coverage.

11. See ibid., esp. 1–24.

12. Ibid., 35–109, quote from 109.

13. Ibid., 142–45.

14. Cavendish-Bentinck Minute, 27 Aug. 1943, in PRO, FO 371/34551.

15. See introduction.

16. Patrick Howarth, *Intelligence Chief Extraordinary: The Life of the Ninth Duke of Portland* (London, 1986); Walter Laqueur, *The Terrible Secret: Suppression of the Truth About Hitler's "Final Solution"* (Boston, 1980), 83 and 245, n. 18.

17. Barry M. Katz, "The Holocaust and American Intelligence," in *The Jewish Legacy and the German Conscience: Essays in Memory of Rabbi Joseph Asher*, ed. Moses Rischin and Raphael Asher (Berkeley, 1991), 297–307; Meredith Hindley, "Negotiating the Boundary of Unconditional Surrender: The War Refugee Board in Sweden and Nazi Proposals to Ransom Jews, 1944–1945," *Holocaust and Genocide Studies* 10 (1996): 52–77; Meredith Hindley, "The Strategy of Rescue and Relief: The Use of OSS Intelligence by the War Refugee Board in Sweden, 1944–45," *Intelligence and National Security* 12 (1997): 145–65. See the forthcoming article by Shlomo Aronson, "The Office of Strategic Services and the Holocaust at Nuremberg," in *Holocaust and Genocide Studies* 12 (1998).

18. Neumann's classic work *Behemoth* (1944) contains fundamentally inaccurate notions as to what was behind Nazi anti-Semitism. On Dwork and Duker, and with some additional comments on Neumann, see Aronson, "The Office."

19. Hindley, "The Strategy of Rescue and Relief," 145, 160–61.

20. Dulles for the Minister, 18 May 1944, NA RG 226, Entry 190C, Box 6, Folder 33.

21. See chapter 12 above.

22. Noel Annan, *Changing Enemies: The Defeat and Regeneration of Germany* (London, 1995).

23. William Rubinstein, *The Myth of Rescue: Why the Democrats Could Not Have Saved More Jews from the Nazis* (London, 1997).

24. Addresses by Fertig Perlzweig and Leon Kubowitzki, 23 June 1944, American Jewish Congress Records, Box 3, Administrative Committee 1944, American Jewish Historical Society, Waltham, Mass. See also, chapter 8 above.

25. For OWI's clash with the War Refugee Board over the Vrba-Wetzlar report about Auschwitz, see Richard Breitman and Alan M. Kraut, *American Refugee Policy and European Jewry, 1933–1945* (Bloomington, Ind., 1987), 201–2. Quote from OWI to London, 4 Dec. 1944, NA RG 208, Entry 359, Box 117, War Crimes— Miscellaneous.

26. See Breitman and Kraut, *American Refugee Policy*, 160–63.

# EPILOGUE

1. F. H. Hinsley et al., *British Intelligence in the Second World War: Its Influence on Strategy and Operations*, vol. 2 (Cambridge, 1981), 671; GC and CS, Air and Mil-

itary History, vol. 13, The German Police, 235–37, copy in NA RG 457, Box 91.

2. See David Bankier, *The Germans and the Final Solution: Public Opinion under Nazism* (Oxford, 1992), 113.
3. D. L. Hewitt, Government Communications Headquarters, to Dr. J. P. Fox, 15 Mar. 1994.
4. Dr. John P. Fox to the editor, *The Times* (London), 16 Nov. 1996.
5. Lord Lester to Dr. John Fox, 18 Nov. 1996.
6. John Keegan, "What the Allies Knew," *New York Times*, 25 Nov. 1996, Op-Ed page.
7. Bradley F. Smith, "Anglo-Soviet Intelligence Cooperation and Roads to the Cold War," in *British Intelligence, Strategy and the Cold War, 1945–1951*, ed. Richard J. Aldrich (London, 1992), 52–54.
8. Smith, "Anglo-Soviet Intelligence," 58, 62, n. 22–23.
9. Nicholls to Crankshaw, 20 Mar. 1942, PRO HW 14/31, item 210. I am grateful to John P. Fox for a copy of this document.
10. British Military Mission, Moscow to War Office, Nicholls MI 8 from Crankshaw, 15 Apr. 1942, PRO HW 14/34, item 172. I am grateful to John P. Fox for a copy of this document.
11. Crankshaw to Commander Travis, 28 Sept. 1942, PRO, HW 14/53, item 333; Crankshaw to Chairman Y Committee, 13 Nov. 1942, PRO HW 14/58, item 275. I am grateful to John P. Fox for a copy of these documents.
12. See chapter 10 above.
13. Edward Crankshaw, *Russia and the Russians* (New York, 1948), and *Cracks in the Kremlin Wall* (New York, 1951).
14. Edward Crankshaw, *Gestapo: Instrument of Tyranny* (New York, 1956), 53.
15. GPD and Notes for Russia, 1943–44, and Memo to Mr. C. Barclay, n.d. [1944], PRO HW 16/16.
16. See Noel Annan, *Changing Enemies: The Defeat and Regeneration of Germany* (London, 1995), 3.
17. Safer to Breitman, 25 Nov. 1996.
18. *Parliamentary Debates, House of Lords*, Fifth Series, vol. 576, col. WA6, 26 Nov. 1996.
19. "Nazi Messages Reveal Secret of Jews' Slaughter," *The Times* (London), 19 May 1997; "Jews Massacred in Holocaust Test-Run," *Independent*, 20 May 1997.
20. PRO Guide, Government Code and Cypher School: German Police Section: Decrypts of German Police Communications During Second World War, 1939–1945, Mar. 1997, 1.
21. Information from David Marwell.
22. British intelligence commented on 1 Oct. 1942 that it was able to read Swiss ciphers to a large extent. See PRO HW 14/54.
23. Document on Himmler, PRO, WO 208/4431 (Pf. 71281/B.2b/JC). File on Kaltenbrunner, PRO WO 208/4478.
24. Anthony Eden, *The Reckoning: The Memoirs of Anthony Eden* (Boston, 1965).

# INDEX

Abwehr (German military intelligence), 84, 95
Adam, Uwe Dietrich, 252*n1*
Adler-Rudel, Saloman, 183
Agudas Israel, 142, 143
Air Ministry, British, 101, 210
Albert, Archduke of Hungary, 166
Allen, Denis, 141–42, 145, 213
Allen, Michael Thad, 280*n32*
Allen, Roger, 119
Allied Control Council, 219
Alsace-Lorraine, German police battalions in, 33
Aly, Götz, 267*n3*, 268*n14*, 269*n32*
American Friends Service Committee, 130, 193, 299*n4*
American Historical Association (AHA), 235
American Jewish Committee, 133, 151–52, 182
American Jewish Congress, 23, 132, 139, 144
American Jewish Joint Distribution Committee, 23, 127, 207
Andrew, Christopher, 89
Anglican Church, 176
Anglo-Jewish Association, 107

anti-Semitism; American, 23, 193; analysis of impact of, 21–23; in Austria, 52; of Eicke, 31; German tradition of, 6, 23, 159–60, 163, 225–26; in Hitler's worldview, 13, 14; propaganda of, 30, 49, 126; of Stalinist regime, 11; widespread in Europe, 105
*Apocalypse, The* (newspaper), 100
Arajs, Viktor, 83
Armenians, Turkish massacre of, 154
Army, U.S., 188; Signal Corps, 189; Special Branch, 187
Aronson, Shlomo, 302*n52*
Ashley, Maurice, 228
Associated Press, 123, 126, 145
Association of Swiss Jewish Communities, 139
Atherton, Ray, 198
Auschwitz, 32, 61, 215, 221, 231; cover-up of killings at, 165; deportations to, 72, 112, 114–16, 162, 167, 194, 204, 218; gas chambers at, 72, 76, 77, 116–18, 120–21; information available to Allies on, 113–21, 138, 140, 281*n39*; proposed bombing raids on, 207–11
*Auschwitz and the Allies* (Gilbert), 120–21

Austria, deportation of Jews from, 72, 100, 101
Austria-Hungary, 52

Babi Yar massacre, 65, 66, 123, 247n4
Bach-Zelewski, Erich von dem, 39–40, 46, 47, 49, 61, 73, 110, 226, 227, 256n55, n56, 257n57, 263–64n38, 269n29; and auxiliary police battalions, 53; at Berlin briefing by Daluege, 43; communications between Germany and, 57, 58, 60, 67, 94, 275n27; gas chambers and crematoria requested by, 62, 75–77, 112; illness of, 111; mass killings carried out by, 48, 50, 55, 59–60, 66, 74–75, 92, 238, 260n32, 306n44; in planning of Soviet campaign, 40, 41; and war-crimes investigations, 218, 222
Badoglio, Pietro, 194
Balfour Declaration, 101
Bankier, David, 248n11
Barth, Robert, 190–91
Bartov, Omer, 260n38
Bauer, Yehuda, 286n3
Bechtolsheim, Gustav von, 79
Beer Hall Putsch, 13, 28
Belgium, 97, 106, 215; deportation of Jews from, 120, 121; Jewish refugees from, 186, 193; in World War I, 8
Belzec extermination camp, 112, 113, 147–51, 165, 221
Beneš, Edvard, 95
Berditschev ghetto, 65
Bergen-Belsen concentration camp, 167, 207, 219
Berger, Gottlob, 166
Bergson, Peter, 192, 198
Berle, Adolf, 186, 187, 197
Bermuda Conference, 181–87, 194, 201, 228
Birkenau, 72, 77, 114, 116, 117, 120, 121, 165, 204, 207–11, 215

Blair, Tony, 244
Blitzkrieg, 97
Blobel, Paul, 165
B'nai B'rith, 132, 152
Board of Deputies of British Jews, 107, 179
Bock, Fedor von, 60
Boheman, Erik, 183, 185
Bohemia-Moravia, deportation of Jews from, 120
Böhme, Hans Joachim, 43
Bolsheviks, 14, 34–36, 45, 48, 52, 60, 94, 162, 219, 238
"Boniface" documents, 89
Bormann, Martin, 54, 55, 164, 261n3
Botz, Gerhard, 267n7
Bower, Tom, 306n35
Bracken, Brendan, 141
Bradfisch, Otto, 61
Braham, Randolph, 205, 206
Brand, Joel, 205, 210, 302n54
Brauchitsch, Walther von, 34, 35
Brazil, 189
British Broadcasting Corporation (BBC), 102–4, 125, 128, 140, 150, 155–57, 159, 160, 163, 164, 175, 203, 233, 277n58
British Intelligence in the Second World War (Hinsley), 238
Browning, Christopher, 5–7, 138, 248n4
Bulgaria, 171, 175, 182, 186
Bund, 128, 129, 140, 149–50
Burckhardt, Carl, 173
Burrin, Philippe, 267n4
Butler, Harold, 134
Byelorussia, 44, 46, 49–52, 60, 73, 74, 78–81, 85, 270n50

Cadogan, Alexander, 144
Campbell, Ronald, 178, 295n8
Canada, 11
Canaris, Wilhelm, 84

Catholic Center Party, German, 104
Catholics, 14
Cavendish-Bentinck, Victor, 9, 101, 119, 144, 212, 230–31
Central Intelligence Agency (CIA), 246
Chamberlain, Neville, 230
Chciuk-Celt, Tadeusz, 116, 281n48
Chelmno extermination camp, 4, 86, 112, 165, 221, 227
Chicago Daily News, 132
Chiefs of Staff Committee, British, 169, 188
Childers, Thomas, 250n23
China, 132; Japanese atrocities in, 131
Churchill, Winston, 105–6, 138, 141, 152–53, 171–72, 188, 215, 227–30, 278n80; and code-breaking operations, 42, 88–89, 93–94; and Hungarian Jews, 206, 209; and information on atrocities from governments-in-exile, 95; and proposed bombing of Auschwitz, 209–11; and reprisal bombings, 169–70; refugee policy of, 185; relief activities opposed by, 193; speech denouncing Nazi atrocities by, 92–93, 97, 106, 109, 275n27; and war-crimes trials, 107, 133, 212, 214; Zionism supported by, 105, 278n79
Cohen, Ben, 214
Cohen, Michael J., 210, 211, 278n79
Cold War, 243
Columbia Broadcasting System (CBS), 129, 157, 243
Command Staff RFSS, 57, 60
Communists, 20, 29, 190, 218, 230; executions of, 4, 44, 60, 66, 79, 80, 223; German, 18–19, 22; Spanish, 115; see also Bolsheviks
concentration camps, 20, 31, 112, 113, 126, 157, 195; see also names of specific camps
Conference Group for European History, Archives Committee of, 235–36

Congress, U.S., 176, 193, 198, 199, 299n4
Conservative Party, British, 107
Council of Polish Jews in Britain, 141
Cox, Oscar, 143, 198, 199
Cranborne, Viscount, 180–81
Crankshaw, Edward, 90–91, 242–43
crematoria, 70, 77–78, 112, 138, 165, 226, 269n32; at Auschwitz, 114, 116–17, 120, 140, 207, 208
Criminal Police, German, 28, 253n12
Croatia, 190, 191
Curtis Brown Ltd., 24
Curzon, Lord, 89
Czechoslovakia, 65, 70, 103, 107, 112, 222; deportation of Jews from, 116; government in exile of, 95, Military Archive, 239; Order Police in, 217, 218; reprisals in, 132, 221
Czerniakow, Adam, 147

Dachau concentration camp, 219
Daily Telegraph, The, of London, 128
Daluege, Kurt, 4, 27–34, 45, 110, 226, 243, 252n1, n2, 258n2, 261n8, 263n31; and auxiliary police battalions, 52–53; background of, 27–28; Berlin briefing of subordinates by, 43–44; Bialystok speech on destruction of enemies by, 47–48; communications between Soviet-based forces and, 56, 58–60, 68, 96–98, 215, 262n13; competition between Heydrich and, 31, 73, 258n4; and deportation of German Jews, 74; and Hitler's rise to power, 28; and mass killings, 65, 67, 257n57; in planning of Soviet campaign, 36–40; in Polish campaign, 31–34; relations between army commanders and, 54, 261n1; war-crimes investigation of, 218, 221–22
David, A., 103
Death's Head regiments, 31–32

Degenhardt, Herbert, 81, 98
denazification, 218, 220, 223
Denmark, 97; evacuation of Jews from, 197–98
Denniston, Alastair, 189
deportations of Jews, 91, 113, 127, 138–39, 151, 153, 190, 227; to Auschwitz, 72, 112, 114–16, 162, 167, 194, 204, 218; from Austria, 100, 101; from France, 86, 130–31, 167; from Germany, 71–75, 78, 80–86, 99, 100, 101, 103, 108, 123–24, 127, 138, 162, 226–27; from Hungary, 63–64, 123, 203–7, 209–10; from Netherlands, 103–4, 112; from Rumania, 113; from Warsaw ghetto, 143, 147–51
Dill, John, 97
Donovan, William J., 131
Double Playfair coding system, 58, 59, 97, 109
Double Transposition coding system, 58, 89, 97, 109
Drechsler, Otto-Heinrich, 83
DuBois, Josiah, 198–200
Dugdale, Edgar, 24, 25
Duker, Abraham, 231
Dulles, Allen, 131, 231
Dunn, James, 196
Durbrow, Elbridge, 174
Dutton, David, 229–30, 307n10
Dwork, Charles Irving, 231

Easterman, Alexander, 143, 145–46, 171
Economic Warfare, British Ministry of, 101, 102, 115, 197, 199
Eden, Anthony, 146, 153, 157, 200, 203, 209, 229–30, 246; and Allied Declaration of December 17, 1942, 168; and information on atrocities from governments-in-exile, 95, 151; refugee policy of, 172, 178, 180–82, 185, 206, 296n26; relief policy of,

141, 193–94, 243–44; reprisal raids opposed by, 170; and war-crimes trials, 213–15
Egypt, 105, 182
Eher Verlag, 24
Eibner, Max, 78, 270n50
Eichmann, Adolf, 3, 4, 31, 72, 74, 112, 113, 204–5, 210, 217, 218
Eicke, Theodor, 31–32
Einsatzgruppen, 4, 41, 43–44, 80, 96, 257n57, 306n44; auxiliary police organized by, 52, 260n40; communications between Germany and, 56–59, 68; gas vans provided to, 85; independence of, 40, 257n59; mass killings carried out by, 47, 64, 66–67, 73, 165, 190–91, 247–48n4, 271n56, 275n25; in planning of Soviet campaign, 36–38, 258n61; in Poland, 31; relations between army and, 54; war-crimes charges against, 220, 221, 223
Einsatzkommandos, 4, 32, 43–44, 46, 50–51, 56, 61, 62, 78–80, 82, 217, 258n61, 262n9
Eisenhower, Dwight D., 143
Eisenstadt, Stuart, 246
El Alamein, Battle of, 161
Elting, Howard, Jr., 139
Emergency Committee to Save the Jewish People of Europe, 192, 196, 198
Engel, David, 288n34, n37
Enigma coding system, 58, 68, 89, 113, 187–91, 215, 241, 244
Erdheim, Stuart G., 303n73
Estonia, 44, 52
Eternal Jew, The (film), 49
"euthanasia" program, 69–70, 72, 160
extermination camps, 75, 112, 113, 138; see also names of specific camps
Eytan, Walter, 190
Ezergailis, Andrew, 272n69

Fangman, Helmut, 254n20

Fascists, 131, 134

Federal Bureau of Investigation, 187

Fegelein, Hermann, 61

Feiner, Leon, 149

Feis, Herbert, 196

Fieseler Storch planes, 57

Final Solution, 6, 7, 10, 33, 137, 161, 168, 183, 190, 198, 205, 225, 231, 233, 267n4, 285–86n3, 292n42; Allied Declaration denouncing, 151, 166, 175–76, 192, 202, 229; American and British skepticism about, 131, 144, 150, 173; communications policy on, 67; evolution of, 110–12, 227; German reaction to foreign publicity about, 163, 164; Heydrich and, 4, 35, 86; involvement of German allies in, 171; military setbacks and, 167; Order Police functions in, 78, 226; Polish underground report on, 147, 180; propaganda to prepare German people for, 49, 260n27; and proposed bombing of gas chambers, 207–8; Riegner's telegram about, 172; technology of, see gas chambers; threats against collaborators in, 211; war-crimes charges against perpetrators of, 222

Finland, 171

Fisher, P. C., 125

Fleisher, J. M., 125–26

Foreign Office, British, 175, 193, 202, 295n8; and Allied Declaration of December 17, 1942, 154, 157, 168, 229; Central Department, 107; Churchill and, 152–53, 230; and decodes, 101, 213; and Hungarian Jews, 209–10; and Polish underground information sources, 118–19, 129; Political Intelligence Department, 147; and refugee policy, 170–72, 177, 180, 181, 187, 199; refusal to publicize Nazi atrocities, 102–3; and Riegner's report,

100, 140, 141, 144–46; skepticism about Final Solution in, 150, 231; and war-crimes trials, 144, 214, 222, 304n10

Foreign Service, U.S., 23

Fox, John P., 240–41, 244

France, 14, 194–95; code breaking by, 89–90; codes of, 189; cross-Channel invasion of, 193, 201; deportation of Jews from, 86, 116, 120, 121, 130, 167, 215, 284; German invasion of, 90; German police battalions in, 33; hostage executions in, 106; Jewish refugees from, 186, 194, 197, 201, 233; occupation of, 97; Vichy, 11, 130, 170; in World War I, 8, 160

Frank, Hans, 13, 71, 75, 249n4, 269n28

Frank, Karl Hermann, 222

Frankfurter, Felix, 8, 142

Franz, Hermann, 33

Franz, Robert, 66

Free Corps, 27, 38

Freedom of Information Act (FOIA), 236–37, 246

French North Africa, 161

Friderici, Erich, 98–99

Friedenson, Joseph, 287n20

Friedman, William, 187

Fritzsche, Peter, 250n23

Ganzenmüller, Albert, 167

gas chambers, 4, 67, 75–77, 81, 84, 104, 112, 119–20, 138, 140, 165, 226–27, 270n45; at Auschwitz-Birkenau, 72, 116–18, 120–21; at Belzec, 149; in "euthanasia" program, 69–70, 72; Himmler's plans for, 61–62; proposed bombing of, 207–11; at Sobibor, 129

gas vans, 77, 84–86, 99, 130, 217

Gerlach, Christian, 269n32, 273n86

German Army, 30, 31, 71, 73, 110, 111; in Soviet campaign, 34–38, 54, 55,

German Army (cont.)
60, 98–99; war-crimes testimony on, 222
German National People's Party, 19
German Police, The (American-British handbook), 217
Gestapo, 29, 30, 43, 156, 159, 253n12, 255n33, 272n66; and American reporters, 125–27; at Auschwitz, 118; breaking of codes of, 190; in Czechoslovakia, 95; Daluege in, 28; deportation of German Jews by, 72, 74, 127, 162; war-crimes charges against, 216, 219
Gestapo: Instrument of Tyranny (Crankshaw), 243
ghettos, 69, 111, 129; Allied policy on relief for, 107–8, 141; in Poland, 71, 72, 123, 141 (see also Warsaw ghetto); in Soviet territories, 49–50, 62, 65, 66, 74–75, 78–84
Gilbert, Martin, 93, 118, 120–21, 210, 211, 285n3, 299n8
Gillette, Guy, 198
Globocnik, Odilo, 72, 73, 75, 113, 114
Goebbels, Joseph, 49, 70, 104, 124, 155, 160–62, 164, 166, 221
Goldhagen, Daniel Jonah, 5–6
Goldmann, Nahum, 181
Gordon, Sarah, 291n22
Göring, Hermann, 21, 22, 28, 35, 54, 71, 223
Government Code and Cypher School, British, 219
Government Communications Headquarters, British, 240–41
governments-in-exile, 107, 199; see also specific countries
Graml, Hermann, 250n24
Grawitz, Ernst, 111
Greece, 97; deportation of Jews from, 120, 121; Order Police in, 217
Greiser, Arthur, 70

Grigg, Joseph, 127, 128
Grossman, Vasily, 265n60
Grosz, Andor, 205
Guggenheim, Paul, 139
Gyorgy, Andreas, 205
Gypsies, 4, 72, 115, 120, 211, 223

Halder, Franz, 37
Halifax, Lord, 181, 182, 186
Harrison, Leland, 139, 142, 145, 174
Harvest Festival operation, 197
Held, Adolph, 152
Hemicker, Ernst, 272n69
Herbert, Ulrich, 279n12
Heydrich, Reinhard, 4, 27–33, 53, 78, 85, 227, 243, 258n61, 268n14, 269n28; assassination of, 112, 132, 218, 221; and deportation of German Jews, 71, 73, 74, 81, 83, 268n11; Jeckeln and, 39; message to Daluege's June 1941 Berlin briefing from, 43–44, 258n4; and operations in conquered Soviet territories, 54–56, 67, 68, 262n19; in planning of Soviet campaign, 34–37, 40; public opinion as concern of, 69, 70, 162
Higher SS and Police Leaders, 5, 31, 37–40, 43–45, 47, 72–76, 80, 91, 226, 256n48, 257n57, n59, 262n19
Hilberg, Raul, 209, 247n4, 270n50, 291n28
Himmler, Heinrich, 4, 26, 63, 94, 185–86, 216, 246, 250n15, 256n55, 257n57, n59, 260n40, 261n1, n4, 268n16, 269n29, 272n66, 273n86, 292n50; anti-Semitic rhetoric of, 163; authority in East of, 54–55; auxiliary police forces created by, 52–53; camp record-keeping requirements of, 115; communications between subordinates in Soviet territories and, 56–61, 98, 238; Communists and Jews equated by, 19–20; Daluege and, 27–28, 31,

263n31; and deportation of Jews from Germany, 70–74, 81, 83, 85, 86, 227, 268n11; execution sites visited by, 67, 75; and gas chambers, 62, 75–77, 84, 111–13, 138; Heydrich and, 30, 31, 243; and Hungarian Jews, 205, 207; Mann on, 103; *Mein Kampf* as influence on, 7, 15–17, 20, 225; in Minsk, 61, 263n38, 306n44; motivation of police battalions for mass killing by, 47–49; Order Police expanded by, 34; and planning of Soviet campaign, 34–41, 45; and Poland, 32; and proposed bombing raids on Auschwitz, 208; Prützmann and, 38–39; on sanctity of orders, 51; suicide of, 221; and Warsaw ghetto, 129, 147, 150, 151; and Western publicity about Final Solution, 164–68, 292n42

Hindenburg, Paul von, 18, 19, 21

Hinsley, F. H., 92, 205, 238–39

Hirschmann, Ira, 203, 205, 302n54

Hitler, Adolf, 3, 7, 13–17, 20, 31, 128–30, 151, 161, 166, 167, 182, 184, 194, 205, 225, 267n4, 273n86, 292n50; American Jewish protests against, 132–33; British propaganda on, 102; Canaris and, 84; Daluege and, 28, 29, 252n2; depopulation of conquered countries planned by, 135; East Prussian headquarters of, 57, 62; Eden's view of, 230, 244; evacuation of Jews from Germany ordered by, 74; on German defeat in World War I, 160; Heydrich and, 73; Horthy and, 204, 206; International Red Cross negotiations with, 173; invasion of Britain planned by, 97; and invasion of Soviet Union, 34, 36, 37, 40, 54–55, 93; January 1939 speech on annihilation of Jews, 49, 161–62, 124, 292n35; and Jews as forced laborers, 111–12; loyalty of majority of Ger-

mans to, 159; orders extermination of Jews, 86–87, 152; Political Warfare Executive central directive on, 156; in pre–World War I Austria-Hungary, 52; and proposed bombing raids on Auschwitz, 207–8; public opinion as concern of, 69, 70; rise to power of, 5, 17–19, 100; Rumbold's assessment of, 21–26; Schulte's revelations about, 138; SS and, 32; suicide of, 221; timing of commands of, 41; underestimation of enemy by, 88

*Hitler's Willing Executioners* (Goldhagen), 5

Hohenthal, W. D., 125

Holland, *see* Netherlands

Home Office, British, 169, 170

Hooft, Willem Visser't, 175

Hopkins, Harry, 182, 296n26

Horthy, Miklós, 166, 204, 206, 211

Höss, Rudolf, 32, 112, 114, 254n24, 281n34

Houghton Mifflin (publisher), 24, 25

House of Commons, British, 139, 153, 166, 178, 186

House of Lords, British, 144, 154, 178, 180–81, 244

House of Representatives, U.S., 198

Howe, Quincy, 129

Hull, Cordell, 181, 182, 196–97, 199–201, 215, 229

Hungary, 127, 166–67, 215; deportation of Jews from, 63–64, 123, 171, 202–7, 209–11, 231–32

Hurst and Blackett (publisher), 24

Hyman, Joseph, 23

I. G. Farben corporation, 114

Information, British Ministry of, 101, 102, 141

Intergovernmental Committee on Refugees, 178, 196, 198, 202

Interior Ministry, German, 84

International Military Tribunal, 191, 219, 257n56
International Red Cross, 173, 206
Italy, 89; Allied-occupied, 190; codes of, 189; deportation of Jews from, 121, 167, 171, 194; Order Police in, 217

Jacobsen, S. Bertrand, 127
Japan, 89, 134; breaking of code used by, 188; war crimes perpetrated by, 131, 203
Jeckeln, Friedrich, 39–41, 73, 76, 227, 256n55, 265n53, 272n69, 275n27; at Berlin briefing by Daluege, 43; communications between Germany and, 57, 58, 67, 83, 84, 86, 94, 262n19; and construction of gas chambers, 84; Degenhardt and, 81, 98; mass killings carried out by, 59–60, 62–65, 76, 99, 265n59, 266n62; war-crimes charges against, 218, 222, 226, 272n66
Jewish Agency for Palestine, 100, 175, 181, 183
Jewish Chronicle, The, 100, 106, 133, 152
Jewish Labor Committee, 132, 152, 288n41
Jewish Rescue Committee, 205, 207
Jewish Telegraphic Agency (JTA), 100, 122, 127
Jodl, Alfred, 36
Johnson, Herschel, 183
Joint (American-British) Committee on Information Policy, 214
Joint Emergency Committee for European Jewish Affairs, 182
Joint Intelligence Committee, British, 9, 97, 101, 119, 213, 245
Jud Süss (film), 49
Justice Department, U.S., 143, 198; Office of Special Investigations (OSI), 245
Jüttner, Hans, 36

Kallmeyer, Herbert, 76
Kaltenbrunner, Ernst, 246
Kammler, Hans, 114, 280n32, 281n34
Karski, Jan, 8, 145–50, 180, 195, 229, 288n37
Katyn Forest massacre, 119, 162
Katzmann, Fritz, 73
Keegan, John, 241, 243–44, 287n28
Keitel, Wilhelm, 35
Kershaw, Ian, 248n11
KGB, 84
Kitchens, James H., III, 303n66
Klarsfeld, Serge, 284n35
Knoblauch, Kurt, 40
Korbonski, Stefan, 117
Korsemann, Gerret, 43, 55, 57, 58, 226, 258n2
Kowno ghetto, 78–79
Kranzler, David, 287n20
Krüger, Friedrich-Wilhelm, 72, 75, 268n11
Kubowitski, Leon, 232
Kushner, Tony, 193
Kwiet, Konrad, 45, 239, 267n7

Labour Party, British, 139, 244
La Guardia, Fiorello, 150
Landespolizei, 28
Laqueur, Walter, 8, 205, 286n3, 298n59, 302n57
Latvia, 44, 52, 57, 59, 81, 83–85, 127, 273n75
Laurie, Clayton R., 284n38
Laval, Pierre, 130, 292n50
Law, Richard, 145–46, 157, 171, 180, 183–85, 209, 293n59
Lechthaler, Franz, 79–80
Lester, Lord, 241, 244
Levi, Primo, 114
Levinson, Arthur, 189, 263n23
Levy, Richard, 211, 303n66
Libya, 161
Lichtheim, Richard, 100, 101

Lithuania, 43, 44, 52, 78–82, 110, 127
Lloyd George, David, 89
Lochner, Louis P., 123, 126, 127, 283n24
Lodz ghetto, 72
Logau, Friedrich von, 152
Lohse, Hinrich, 81, 83
Long, Breckinridge, 183, 196, 197, 199, 200
Long, Leo, 243
Longfellow, Henry Wadsworth, 152
Lucas (cryptanalyst), 90
Lutz, Charles, 206
Luxembourg, deportation of Jews from, 72
Luxford, Ansel, 198–200

McClelland, Roswell, 207
McCloy, John J., 132, 208–9
McCormack, Alfred, 187
Macfarlane, Noel Mason, 241
MacLeish, Archibald, 131, 132, 134
Magic decodes, 188, 191
Magill, Franz, 77
Maidanek extermination camp, 112, 167, 221
Maisky, Ivan, 151
Mallmann, Klaus-Michael, 248n4
Maly Trostinets extermination camp, 112
Manchester Guardian, 178
Mann, Thomas, 103
Marshall, George C., 144
Martin, John Miller, 152
Marwell, David, 245
Marxists, 15, 17, 22
Matthäus, Jürgen, 248n4, 270n50
Mauthausen concentration camp, 104
Mayer, Gerald M., 129, 284n32, n33
Mein Kampf (Hitler), 7, 13–17, 20, 22, 24–25, 225
Melland, Brian, 216, 217, 243
Mellet, Lowell, 132
Meltzer, Bernard, 200

Mendelsohn, John, 297n39
Menzies, Graham Stewart, 92, 95, 188–89, 212, 232
Messersmith, George S., 20–21, 23, 26
Mexico, 88
Miller, Irving, 200
Minsk ghetto, 49–50, 62, 79–81
Mogilev ghetto, 66, 75
Molotov, Vyacheslav, 215
Mommsen, Hans, 291–92n34
Monowitz camp, 114
Monsky, Henry, 152
Montua, Max, 46–48, 50, 75
Moravec, Frantisek, 95
Morgenthau, Henry, Jr., 143, 196–200, 202, 206, 208
Morrison, Herbert, 168–69
Moscow Conference, 215
"Most Secret Sources," 89, 101
Mowrer, Edgar Ansel, 132, 134
Müller, Heinrich, 29, 43, 56, 72, 164–65, 255n33, 258n61, 292n42
Mulligan, Timothy Patrick, 261n3
Murrow, Edward R., 157
Muslims, 105
Mussolini, Benito, 194, 230

Nagel, Gottlieb, 45
National Archives, U.S., 235, 237
National Broadcasting Company (NBC), 125, 129, 150
National Security Agency (NSA), U.S., 189, 236, 237, 244–46; Historical Cryptographic Collection, 239
Navy, U.S., 188
Nebe, Arthur, 47, 61, 62, 73
Netherlands, 97, 106, 183, 215; deportation of Jews from, 103–4, 116, 120, 121, 218; German police battalions in, 33
Neumann, Franz, 231, 308n18
New York Herald Tribune, 123, 145
New York Journal American, 123

*New York Times, The,* 106, 123, 127, 150, 204, 223, 241; *Magazine,* 143–44

Nicholls, Col., 242

NKVD (Soviet Secret Police), 80, 272*n66*

Norton, Clifford, 194

Norway, 97, 106, 183, 193, 215; German police battalions in, 33, 217

Nuremberg war-crimes trials, 191, 219–23

October Revolution, 79

Oechsner, Frederick, 126, 127

Office of Facts and Figures, U.S., 131

Office of Governmental Reports, U.S., 132

Office of Strategic Services (OSS), U.S., 120, 131, 139, 231–32, 246; Research and Analysis Branch, 231

Office of War Information (OWI), U.S., 129, 131, 132, 134–35, 157, 203, 204, 231–33, 290*n12*

Ogorreck, Ralf, 258*n7*

Operation Barbarossa, 34–35, 37, 39

Operation Reinhard, 112, 113, 148

Oppenheimer, Joseph Süss, 49

Oranienburg concentration camp, 77

Order Police (Ordnungspolizei), 4–7, 9, 28–30, 43, 226, 238–39, 257*n57,* *n59,* 270*n50*; British decoding of messages of, 89–92, 109, 113, 191, 241, 242; in planning of Soviet campaign, 34, 37–38, 40, 41; in Poland, 31–33; Reserve Battalions, 53; in Soviet territory, 45–52, 55–66, 78–80, 82, 83, 94, 95, 110, 190, 247–48*n4,* *271n56*; war-crimes charges against, 215, 217–21

*Ordinary Men* (Browning), 5, 248*n4*

Ordnungspolizei, *see* Order Police

Palestine, 172, 182, 184–86, 202, 205, 278*n79,* 296*n26*; Arab influence on

British policy in, 105, 122, 171, 181; Balfour declaration on, 101; Hungarian Jews and, 206; Jews from, in British armed forces, 133

Papen, Franz von, 18

Parliament, British, 141–42, 168, 169, 171, 172, 176–78, 184; *see also* House of Commons; House of Lords

Paul, Randolph, 198

Pazner, Haim, 285–86*n3*

Peck, Abraham, 263–64*n38*

Pehle, John, 195, 198–202

Pell, Robert, 202

Penkower, Monty N., 285*n3,* 296*n24,* 299*n13*

Perlzweig, Maurice, 181

Phillips, E. D., 219, 238

Pickett, Clarence, 193, 299*n4*

Playfair coding system, 58, 59

Pohl, Oswald, 62, 73, 114, 281*n34*

Pokrovsky, Col., 223

Poland, 71, 97, 127, 138, 164, 215, 231, 268*n14*; BBC broadcasts in, 156; code breaking by, 89; deportation of Jews to, 90, 130, 153; Directorate of Civilian Resistance, 116; extermination camps in, 75, 112; ghettos in, 74 (*see also* Warsaw ghetto); government-in-exile of, 100, 116, 118–19, 128–29, 140, 153–54, 207; Jewish refugees from, 182, 183, 185; Katyn Forest massacre in, 119, 162; laborers shipped to Germany from, 111; mass killings in, 5, 31–34, 100–2, 106, 140, 158, 174; Order Police in, 51, 217; proposed British reprisal bombings of, 169; reports from underground in, 128, 129, 137, 145–51, 180, 195, 230; report to Parliament of atrocities in, 141–42; SS in, 125; transports of Jews in, 116; *see also* Auschwitz

*Poland Fights,* 117

Polish National Council, 118, 128, 140, 141, 148, 157, 164
Political Police, Bavarian, 29
Political Warfare Executive (PWE), British, 102–3, 155–58, 166, 230, 233
Political Warfare Mission, British, 203
Portal, Charles, 169
Portugal, 89, 181, 182; codes of, 189
Pressac, Jean-Claude, 280n33
Propaganda Ministry, German, 49, 126, 160
Proskauer, Joseph M., 182, 296n25
Protestants, 14
Prützmann, Hans-Adolf, 38–41, 43, 56–59, 61, 73, 74, 76, 78, 99, 226, 227, 256n48, n55
Public Record Office, British, 244, 245
Purple code, 188
Puttkamer, Alfred von, 60

Querner, Rudolf, 75, 76, 269n32

Raczyński, Edward, 128–29, 151
Randall, Alec, 180
Rasch, Otto, 73
Rathbone, Eleanor, 171
Reading, Lady, 166, 171
Reams, Robert Borden, 173, 183, 197
refugees, Jewish, 64, 233; Britain and, 168–72, 194, 199–202; coordinated Allied policy on, 177–87, 194, 201; Swedish acceptance of, 183, 186, 197–98; United States and, 192–93, 195–202
Reich, Das (newspaper), 124
Reich Security Main Office (RSHA), 4, 31, 56, 58, 83, 114, 138, 161, 166, 210, 217, 246, 258n61, 298n59
Reichstag, 18–19, 28, 49, 128, 292n35
Reichswehr, 38
Reifner, Udo, 254n20
Reinecke, Hermann, 37
"Report to the Secretary on the Acqui-

escence of This Government in the Murder of the Jews" (DuBois), 200
Reuters news service, 166
Ribbentrop, Joachim von, 167, 186
Riebel, Gerhard, Lt., 66
Riegner, Gerhart, 100, 139–46, 152, 153, 172–75, 194–95, 200, 286n3, 287n20, 299n13
Riess, Volker, 267n3
Riga ghetto, 78, 81–85
Robel, Gert, 275n25
Roberts, Frank, 107, 140
Rogers, Will, 198
Röhm, Ernst, 223
Roosevelt, Franklin Delano, 131–33, 138, 144, 186, 227–30, 287n20; and Allied Declaration denouncing Nazi killing of Jews, 153; on American edition of Mein Kampf, 25; and Bermuda conference, 182, 185; execution of hostages by Germans denounced by, 106, 107; Jewish leaders meet with, 150–52, 195; Karski and, 195; and Riegner's report, 142; and rescue and relief efforts, 193, 197–204, 206, 299n4; war-crimes trials advocated by, 212
Roques, Karl von, 60
Rosenberg, Alfred, 35, 54, 55, 81
Rosenberg, Israel, 152
Rothschild, James de, 152, 153, 166
Royal Air Force (RAF), 107, 132, 141, 145, 157, 169, 209
Rubinstein, William, 232
Rumania, 170, 175, 194–95, 197, 199, 201, 207, 232; deportation of Jews from, 113, 123
Rumbold, Horace, 21–26
Ruthenia, 46; White, 50, 55, 62

SA (Sturmabteilung), 15, 16, 20, 27, 258n2
Sachs, Ernst, 59, 67

Safer, Morley, 243–44
Sagalowitz, Benjamin, 139
St. James's Declaration, 107
Salski, Jerzy, 281n48
Samuel, Herbert, 154
Sarvar camp, 210
Saturday Evening Post, The, 131–32
Sayre, Francis, 193, 299n8
Schellenberg, Walter, 227,
    255n33
Schenckendorf, Max von, 46
Schlake, Robert, 58
Schleicher, Kurt von, 18
Schmelt organization, 112
Schulte, Eduard, 138–39, 285–86n3
Schutzmannschaften (auxiliary police),
    52–53, 79, 270n50
Schutzstaffel, see SS
Schwarzbart, Ignacy, 118, 128,
    148
SD (Sicherheitsdienst), 46, 69, 78, 79,
    82, 83, 166, 253n12, 270n50; break-
    ing of codes of, 190, 302n57; in Hun-
    gary, 205; police officials as members
    of, 31; public opinion reports of, 7,
    162; war-crimes charges against, 216,
    219
Secret Intelligence Service (SIS), British,
    92, 96–97, 137–38, 153, 188–89,
    218, 277n58
Security Police, German, 28–31, 37,
    40, 57, 69, 78, 79, 91, 210, 221,
    257n57
Senate, U.S., 198
Serbia, 191
Shaw, George Bernard, 102
Shertok, Moshe, 181
Sherwood, Robert, 135
Sicherheitsdienst, see SD
Sikorski, Wladislaw, 140, 151, 169
Silverman, Sidney, 139–42, 145–46,
    153
Simon, John, 144, 212, 304n10

Sinclair, Archibald, 209
Slovakia, deportation of Jews from, 114,
    115, 120, 170
Smith, Bradley F., 188, 297n48
Sobibor extermination camp, 112–14,
    129, 147, 148, 150, 151, 165, 191,
    221
Social Democrats: German, 8, 19, 22;
    Swedish, 100
Sommer, Arthur, 285n3
Sonderkommandos, 66, 165, 258n61
Soviet Union, 10–11, 24, 132, 159,
    202, 205, 227, 241–43, 268n14; and
    Allied denunciation of Final Solution,
    151; breaking of code of, 89; Chur-
    chill's speech on, 92–93; civil ad-
    ministration for occupied territories in,
    54–55; communications system be-
    tween Germany and, 56–59; counter-
    offensive in, 161, 167; crematorium
    constructed in, 77–78; deportation of
    German Jews to, 80–82, 84, 86, 108,
    124, 127; destruction of evidence of
    genocide in, 165; German invasion of,
    4, 34–40, 43–44, 90, 105, 109, 110,
    122; Hungary and, 206; Katyn Forest
    massacre by, 119, 162; mass killings of
    Jews in, 35, 46–52, 55–56, 59–69,
    78–80, 82–85, 93–97, 102, 111,
    130, 190–91, 218, 226, 238, 240,
    244, 247n4, 265n60, 275n26; Poland
    and, 71; prisoners of war from, at
    Auschwitz, 116–18; proposed depor-
    tation of Jews to, 72–73; repatriation
    of Volhynian Germans from, 91; and
    war-crimes trials, 107, 214, 215, 220,
    222
Spain, 159, 167–68; codes of, 89; and
    Hungarian Jews, 206; refugees in, 181,
    182, 201
SS (Schutzstaffel), 4, 6, 7, 15, 16, 27, 29,
    30, 32, 35–37, 46, 75, 79, 163, 168,
    207, 225, 237, 239, 253n12, 305n18;

Berlin hospital run by, 111; British decoding of messages of, 3, 9, 119, 144, 146, 147, 154, 191, 212; Budget and Construction Office, 73, 77; concentration camps controlled by, 20; and deportation of German Jews, 72–74; Economic-Administrative Office (WVHA), 62, 74, 112–15; and gas chambers and crematoria, 75–78; in Hungary, 166; in Italy, 194; in Poland, 33, 34, 91, 125, 138, 197; propaganda films screened for, 49; in Soviet territory, 44, 54–64, 66, 67, 69, 83, 85, 86, 93, 96, 98, 110, 127, 190, 238; war-crimes charges against, 218–23; see also Higher SS and Police Leaders; Waffen-SS

Stadler, Glen, 126, 127

Stahlecker, Franz Walter, 44, 261n1

Stalin, Joseph, 13, 61, 119

Stalingrad, battle of, 161, 167

Stanley, Oliver, 168–69

State Department, U.S., 145, 153, 176, 193, 229, 231, 287n20; European Division, 143, 173–75, 196, 198; Foreign Funds Control Division, 196, 200; Near Eastern Division, 196; refugee policy of, 177–79, 182, 183, 185; skepticism about Final Solution in, 139–40, 142, 144, 150; Special War Problems Division, 173; and Treasury Department rescue efforts, 192, 195–202; Visa Division, 173, 174, 195; and war-crimes trials, 132; Wise's dispute with, 172–75

Steinhardt, Laurence, 203

Steinhorn, Norbert, 254n20

Steinkopf, Alvin, 126

Stennes, Walter, 27

Sternbuch, Recha, 142

Sternbuch, Yitzchok, 142

Stettinius, Edward R., 194, 197, 198

Stoltzfus, Nathan, 291n27

Strang, William, 181, 182

Strasser, Gregor, 15

Streckenbach, Bruno, 258n61

Streit, Christian, 279n12

Sturmabteilung, see SA

Sudeten-Germans, 65

Supreme Headquarters Allied Expeditionary Force (SHAEF), Counter-Intelligence Division, 217–18

Sweden, 100, 159, 172, 181, 183, 185, 186; codes of, 189; evacuation of Danish Jews to, 197–98; and Hungarian Jews, 206

Switzerland, 130, 167–68, 172, 174, 185, 246; American investigation of Nazi policy toward Jews centered in, 143, 152; and Hungarian Jews, 206–7; Jewish organizations in, 139; OSS outpost in, 131, 231; refugees in, 180, 181, 194, 201

Taylor, Myron, 145, 202

Taylor, Telford, 187, 189, 191, 221–23, 298n64

Temple, William, Archbishop of Canterbury, 151, 166, 168, 178, 181, 185

Tesch, Bruno, 76

Tesch and Stabenow, 75–77

Theresienstadt concentration camp, 70, 83

Thümmel, Paul, 95, 275n31, 276n32

Tillich, Paul, 135

Tiltman, Brigadier John, 89

Times, The (London), 25, 100, 128, 151, 241

Topf Company, 77

transports, see deportations of Jews

Treasury Department, U.S., 192, 195–201, 229, 233

Treblinka extermination camp, 112, 113, 119, 147, 148, 150, 151, 165, 221

Tuck, S. Pinkney, 130

Turkey, 170, 182, 203, 205; massacre of Armenians by, 154; in World War I, 88–89, 105
Turner, Henry Ashby, Jr., 250n25

Ukraine, 76, 81, 222; auxiliary police units formed by Nazis in, 46, 52; deportation of Jews to, 127; investigation of war crimes in, 191, 218, 244; mass killings of Jews in, 60–66, 84, 95, 100, 111, 123, 247n4
Ultra decodes, 89, 101, 109, 188, 189, 191, 241, 242
Uniformed Police, German, 4
Union of Orthodox Rabbis of the United States, 152
United Nations, 177, 179; War Crimes Commission, 144, 212, 214, 218
United Press, 125–27
United States Holocaust Memorial Museum, 239
U.S.S.R., see Soviet Union

Vansittart, Robert, 140
Vatican, 145
Versailles, Treaty of, 30
Voice of America (VOA), 157
Volhynian Germans, 91
Völkischer Beobachter (newspaper), 19, 24
Vrba, Rudolf, 121, 208

Waffen-SS, 31, 37, 40, 58, 62, 66, 77, 92, 110, 190, 238, 257n57; Leibstandarte Adolf Hitler division, 162
Wagner, Eduard, 36
Wallenberg, Raoul, 206
Wanda (Polish informant), 120
Wannsee Conference, 86, 97, 101
War Cabinet, British, 178, 180, 213, 215; Committee on the Reception and Accommodation of Jewish Refugees, 168, 202
war-crimes trials, 107, 141, 219–23; Dulles's proposal for, 131; gathering of evidence for, 212–14, 218; Moscow Declaration and, 215
War Department, U.S., 132, 188, 201, 208–9
War Office, British, 147, 217, 246; War Crimes Interrogation Unit, 218
War Refugee Board, U.S., 192, 200–4, 206–9, 211, 231–33
Warsaw ghetto, 72, 129, 142; deportations from, 143, 147–51, 288n34; uprising in, 117
Wasserstein, Bernard, 210, 295n11
Weimar Republic, 16, 18, 21, 22, 39, 52, 250
Weinberg, Gerhard, 14, 51, 228, 235–36
Weizmann, Chaim, 25, 100–1
Welles, Sumner, 177–79, 185, 186, 193, 197, 229, 295n8; Wise and, 142, 143, 145, 150–51, 172–73, 175, 182, 183, 296n25, 299n13
Wertheim, Maurice, 151–52
Westermann, Edward B., 248n4
Wetzler, Alfred, 121, 208
Winant, John G., 146, 151
Winkelmann, Otto, 205
Wirth, Joseph, 104
Wise, Stephen S., 23, 164, 292n42; Roosevelt and, 151, 152, 195; transmission of Riegner's information to, 139, 141–43, 174–75, 200, 287n20; and Treasury Department rescue and relief efforts, 197, 198; Welles and, 142, 143, 145, 150–51, 172–73, 175, 182, 183, 296n25, 299n13
Witte, Peter, 267n7, 268n13

Wolff, Karl, 36, 40, 61–62
World Council of Churches, 175
World Jewish Congress, 100, 118, 143, 148, 166; American media and, 129; British Foreign Office and, 145–46, 171; German source of information to, 137, 139; and refugee policy, 181, 194, 199–202; Rescue Department, 232
World War I, 8, 15, 16, 23, 25, 27, 30, 35, 39, 46, 58, 59, 69, 70, 228, 268n11; Allied propaganda in, 104, 119, 126; British code breaking during, 88–89, 243; Jewish veterans of, 83; Turkish massacre of Armenians during, 154

Wyman, David S., 284n35, 295n8, n11, 301n41, 303n73

Yad Vashem, 286n3
Yugoslavia, 97, 106, 207; Order Police in, 217

Zenner, Carl, 73, 261n4
Zimmermann telegram, 88
Zionism, 100–1, 105, 128, 150; see also Palestine
Zygielbojm, Szmul, 128, 140, 148, 164, 288n41
Zyklon B gas, 75–77, 84, 85, 226, 269n32, 270n45